W9-BDH-308

$2·50 C

CODE

CODE

and other laws

of cyberspace

LAWRENCE LESSIG

BASIC
BOOKS

A MEMBER OF THE PERSEUS BOOKS GROUP

Copyright © 1999 by Lawrence Lessig

Published by Basic Books,
A Member of the Perseus Books Group

All rights reserved. Printed in the United States of America. No part of
this book may be reproduced in any manner whatsoever without written
permission except in the case of brief quotations embodied in critical
articles and reviews. For information, address Basic Books, 10 E. 53rd
Street, New York, NY 10022-5299.

Book design by Victoria Kuskowski

A CIP catalog record for this book is available
from the Library of Congress

ISBN 0-465-03912-X

99 00 01 02 / 10 9 8 7 6 5 4 3 2

FOR CHARLIE NESSON, WHOSE EVERY IDEA

SEEMS CRAZY—FOR ABOUT A YEAR.

CONTENTS

PREFACE

In the spring of 1996, at an annual conference organized under the name "Computers, Freedom, and Privacy" (CFP), two science-fiction writers told stories about cyberspace's future. Vernor Vinge spoke about "ubiquitous law enforcement," made possible by "fine-grained distributed systems"; through computer chips linked by the Net to every part of social life, a portion dedicated to the government's use. This architecture was already being built—it was the Internet—and technologists were already describing its extensions. As this network of control became woven into every part of social life, it would be just a matter of time, Vinge said, before the government claimed its fair share of control. Each new generation of code would increase this power of government. The future would be a world of perfect regulation, and the architecture of distributed computing—the Internet and its attachments— would make that perfection possible.

Tom Maddox followed Vinge. His vision was very similar, though the source of control, different. The government's power would not come just from chips. The real source of power, Maddox argued, was an alliance between government and commerce. Commerce, like government, fares better in a better regulated world. Property is more secure, data are more easily captured, and disruption is less of a risk. The future would be a pact between these two forces of social order.

Code and *commerce.*

When these two authors spoke, the future they described was not yet present. Cyberspace was increasingly everywhere, but it was hard to imagine it tamed to serve the ends of government. And commerce was certainly interested, though credit card companies were still warning customers to stay far away from the Net. The Net was an exploding social space of something. But it was hard to see it as an exploding space of social control.

I didn't see either speech. I listened to them through my computer, three years after they spoke. Their words had been recorded; they now sit archived on a server at MIT.[1] It takes a second to tune in and launch a replay of their speeches about a perfectly ordered network of control. The very act of listening to these lectures given several years before—served on a reliable and indexed platform that no doubt recorded the fact that I had listened, across high-speed, commercial Internet lines that feed my apartment both the Net and ABC News—confirmed something of their account. One can hear in the audience's reaction a recognition both that these authors were talking fiction—they were science-fiction writers, after all—and that the fiction they spoke terrified.

Three years later it is no longer fiction. It is not hard to understand how the Net could become the perfect space of regulation or how commerce would play a role in that regulation. The current battle over MP3—a technology for compressing audio files for simple distribution across the Net—is a perfect example. Last year MP3 was quite the rage: CDs were copied and e-mailed, and web sites were built with thousands of songs archived and ready for anyone to take. "Free music" joined the list of free stuff that the Internet would serve.

But this year the story has changed. The recording industry is pushing a standard that would make it easier to control the distribution of these files; Congress has passed a statute that makes it a felony to produce software that evades this control; and one company that produces Sony Walkman–like machines to play MP3 files has already announced plans to enable its machine to comply with these standards of control. Control will be *coded*, by *commerce*, with the backing of the government.

Vinge and Maddox were first-generation theorists of cyberspace. They could tell their stories about perfect control because they lived in a world that couldn't be controlled. They could connect with their audience because it wanted to resist the future they described. Envisioning this impossible world was sport.

Now the impossible has been made real. Much of the control in Vinge's and Maddox's stories that struck many of their listeners as Orwellian now seems quite reasonable. It is possible to imagine the system of perfect regulation that Vinge described, and many even like what they see. It is inevitable that an increasingly large part of the Internet will be fed by commerce, and most don't see anything wrong with that either. Indeed, we live in a time (again) when it is commonplace to say: let business take care of things. Let business self-regulate the Net. Net commerce is the new hero.

This book continues Vinge's and Maddox's stories. I share their view of the Net's future; much of this book is about the expanding architecture of regulation that the Internet will become. But I don't share the complacency of the self-congratulatory cheers echoing in the background of that 1996 recording. It was obvious in 1996 who "the enemy" was; nothing is obvious now.

The future is Vinge's and Maddox's accounts together, not either alone. If we were only in for the dystopia described by Vinge, we would have an obvious and powerful response: Orwell gave us the tools, and Stalin gave us the resolve, to resist the totalitarian state. A spying and invasive Net controlled by Washington is not our future. *1984* is in our past.

And if we were only in for the future that Maddox described, many of our citizens would believe this utopia, not science fiction. A world where "the market" runs free and the evil we call government, defeated, would, for them, be a world of perfect freedom.

But neither story alone describes what the Internet will be. Not Vinge alone, not Maddox alone, but Vinge and Maddox together: a future of control in large part exercised by technologies of commerce, backed by the rule of law.

The challenge of our generation is to reconcile these two forces. How do we protect liberty when the architectures of control are managed as much by the government as by the private sector? How do we assure privacy when the ether perpetually spies? How do we guarantee free thought when the push is to propertize every idea? How do we guarantee self-determination when the architectures of control are perpetually determined elsewhere? How, in other words, do we build a world of liberty when the threats are as Vinge and Maddox together described them?

The answer is not in the knee-jerk antigovernment rhetoric of our past. Reality is harder than fiction; governments are necessary to protect liberty, even if also sufficient to destroy it. But neither does the answer lie in a return to Roosevelt's New Deal. Statism has failed. Liberty is not to be found in some new D.C. alphabet soup (WPA, FCC, FDA . . .) of bureaucracy.

A second generation takes the ideals of the first and works them out against a different background. It knows the old debates; it has mapped the dead-end arguments of the preceding thirty years. The objective of a second generation is to ask questions that avoid dead-ends and move beyond them.

There is great work out there from both generations. Esther Dyson, John Perry Barlow and Todd Lapin still inspire, and still move on (Dyson is now the temporary chair of an organization some think will become the government of the Internet; Barlow now spends time at Harvard). And in the second generation, the work of Andrew Shapiro, David Shenk, and Steven Johnson is becoming well known and is compelling.

My aim is this second generation. As fits my profession (I'm a lawyer), my contribution is more long-winded, more obscure, more technical, and more obtuse than the best of either generation. But as fits my profession, I'll offer it anyway. In the debates that rage right now, what I have to say will not please anyone very much. And as I peck these last words before e-mailing the manuscript off to the publisher, I can already hear the reactions: "Can't you tell the difference between the power of the sheriff and the power of Walt Disney?" "Do you really think we need a government agency regulating software code?" And from the other side: "How can you argue for an architecture of cyberspace (open source software) that disables government's ability to do good?"

But I am also a teacher. If my writing produces angry reactions, then it might also effect a more balanced reflection. These are hard times to get it right, but the easy answers to yesterday's debate won't get it right.

I have learned an extraordinary amount from the teachers and critics who have helped me write this book. Hal Abelson, Bruce Ackerman, James Boyle, Jack Goldsmith, and Richard Posner gave patient and excellent advice on earlier drafts. I am grateful for their patience and extremely fortunate to have had their advice. Larry Vale and Sarah Whiting guided my reading in the field of architecture, though no doubt I was not as patient a student as I should have been. Sonya Mead helped me put into pictures what it would take a lawyer ten thousand words to say.

An army of students did most of the battle on earlier drafts of this book. Carolyn Bane, Rachel Barber, Enoch Chang, Ben Edelman, Timothy Ehrlich, Dawn Farber,

Melanie Glickson, Bethany Glover, Nerlyn Gonzalez, Shannon Johnson, Karen King, Alex Macgillivray, Marcus Maher, David Melaugh, Teresa Ou, Laura Pirri, and Wendy Seltzer provided extensive, if respectful, criticism. And my assistants, Lee Hopkins and Catherine Cho, were crucial in keeping this army in line (and at bay).

Three students in particular have influenced my argument, though none are fairly called "students." Harold Reeves takes the lead in chapter 8. Tim Wu forced me to rethink much of part 1. And Andrew Shapiro showed me the hopefulness in a future that I have described in very dark terms.

I am especially indebted to Catherine Marguerite Manley, whose extraordinary talent, both as a writer and a researcher, made it possible to finish this work long before it otherwise could have been finished. Thanks also to Tawen Chang and James Stahir for their careful review of the notes, and work to keep them honest.

This is a not a field where one learns by living in libraries. I have learned everything I know from the conversations I have had, or watched, with an extraordinary community of academics and activists, who have been struggling over the last five years both to understand what cyberspace is and to make it better. This community includes the scholars and writers I discuss in the text, especially the lawyers Yochai Benkler, James Boyle, Mark Lemley, David Post, and Pam Samuelson. I've also benefited greatly from conversations with nonlawyers, especially Hal Abelson, John Perry Barlow, Joseph Reagle, Paul Resnick, and Danny Weitzner. But perhaps more importantly, I've benefited from discussions with the activists, in particular the Center for Democracy and Technology, the Electronic Frontier Foundation, and the American Civil Liberties Union. They have made the issues real, and they have done much to defend at least some of the values that I think important.

This book would not have been written, however, but for a story by Julian Dibbell, a conference organized by Henry J. Perritt, and many arguments with David Johnson. I am grateful to all three for what they have taught.

I began this project as a fellow at Harvard's Program on Ethics and the Professions. I am grateful to Dennis Thompson for his skeptical encouragement that year. The Berkman Center for Internet and Society at Harvard Law School has made much of my research possible. I am grateful in particular to Lillian and Myles Berkman for that support, and especially to the center's executive director and my sometime coteacher, Jonathan Zittrain, for his support and, more important, friendship. I've dedicated this book to the director of the Berkman Center, Charlie Nesson, who has given me the space and support to do this work and a certain inspiration to push it differently.

But more significant than any of that support has been the patience, and love, of the person to whom I've dedicated my life, Bettina Neuefeind. Her love will seem crazy, and wonderful, for much more than a year.

CODE

PART ONE

regulability

ONE

code is law

A DECADE AGO, IN THE SPRING OF 1989, COMMUNISM IN EUROPE DIED—COLLAPSED, AS a tent would fall if its main post were removed. No war or revolution brought communism to its end. Exhaustion did. Born in its place across Central and Eastern Europe was a new political regime, the beginnings of a new political society.

For constitutionalists (as I am), this was a heady time. I had just graduated from law school in 1989, and in 1991 I began teaching at the University of Chicago. Chicago had a center devoted to the study of the emerging democracies in Central and Eastern Europe. I was a part of that center. Over the next five years I spent more hours on airplanes, and more mornings drinking bad coffee, than I care to remember.

Eastern and Central Europe were filled with Americans telling former Communists how they should govern. The advice was endless and silly. Some of these visitors literally sold constitutions to the emerging constitutional republics; the balance had innumerable half-baked ideas about how the new nations should be governed. These Americans came from a nation where constitutionalism had worked, yet apparently had no clue why.

The center's mission, however, was not to advise. We knew too little to guide. Our aim was to watch and gather data about the transitions and how they progressed. We wanted to understand the change, not direct it.

What we saw was striking, if understandable. Those first moments after communism's collapse were filled with antigovernmental passion—with a surge of anger directed against the state and against state regulation. Leave us alone, the people seemed to say. Let the market and nongovernmental organizations—a new society—take government's place. After generations of communism, this reaction was completely understandable. What compromise could there be with the instrument of your repression?

A certain American rhetoric supported much in this reaction. A rhetoric of libertarianism. Just let the market reign and keep the government out of the way, and freedom and prosperity would inevitably grow. Things would take care of themselves. There was no need, and could be no place, for extensive regulation by the state.

But things didn't take care of themselves. Markets didn't flourish. Governments were crippled, and crippled governments are no elixir of freedom. Power didn't disappear—it simply shifted from the state to mafiosi, themselves often created by the state. The need for traditional state functions—police, courts, schools, health care—didn't magically go away. Private interests didn't emerge to fill the need. Instead, needs were unmet. Security evaporated. A modern if plodding anarchy replaced the bland communism of the previous three generations: neon lights flashed advertisements for Nike; pensioners were swindled out of their life savings by fraudulent stock deals; bankers were murdered in broad daylight on Moscow streets. One system of control had been replaced by another, but neither system was what Western libertarians would call freedom.

At just about the time when this post-communist euphoria was waning—in the mid-1990s—there emerged in the West another "new society," to many just as exciting as the new societies promised in post-communist Europe. This was cyberspace. First in universities and centers of research, and then within society generally, cyberspace became the new target of libertarian utopianism. Here freedom from the state would reign. If not in Moscow or Tblisi, then here in cyberspace would we find the ideal libertarian society.

The catalyst for this change was likewise unplanned. Born in a research project in the Defense Department, cyberspace too arose from the displacement of a certain architecture of control. The tolled, single-purpose network of telephones was displaced by the untolled and multipurpose network of packet-switched data. And thus the old one-to-many architectures of publishing (television, radio, newspapers, books) were supplemented by a world where everyone could be a publisher. People could communicate and associate in ways that they had never done before. The space promised a kind of society that real space could never allow—freedom without anarchy, control without government, consensus without power. In the words of a manifesto that will define our generation: "We reject: kings, presidents and voting. We believe in: rough consensus and running code."[1]

As in post-Communist Europe, first thoughts about cyberspace tied freedom to the disappearance of the state. But here the bond was even stronger than in post-Communist Europe. The claim now was that government *could not* regulate cyberspace, that cyberspace was essentially, and unavoidably, free. Governments could threaten, but behavior could not be controlled; laws could be passed, but they would be meaningless. There was no choice about which government to install—none could reign. Cyberspace would be a society of a very different sort. There would be definition and direction, but built from the bottom up, and never through the direction of a state. The society of this space would be a fully self-ordering entity, cleansed of governors and free from political hacks.

I taught in Central Europe during the summers of the early 1990s; I witnessed the transformation in attitudes about communism that I described at the start of this chapter. And so I felt a bit of déjà vu when in the spring of 1995, I began to teach the law of cyberspace, and saw in my students these very same post-communist thoughts about freedom and government. Even at Yale—not known for libertarian passions—the students seemed drunk with what James Boyle would later call the "libertarian gotcha":[2] no government could survive without the Internet's riches, yet no government could control what went on there. Real-space governments would become as pathetic as the last Communist regimes. It was the withering of the state that Marx had promised, jolted out of existence by trillions of gigabytes flashing across the ether of cyberspace. Cyberspace, the story went, could *only* be free. Freedom was its nature.

But why was never made clear. That *cyberspace* was a place that governments could not control was an idea that I never quite got. The word itself speaks not of freedom but of control. Its etymology reaches beyond a novel by William Gibson (*Neuromancer*, published in 1984) to the world of "cybernetics," the study of control at a distance.[3] Cybernetics had a vision of perfect regulation. Its very motivation was finding a better way to direct. Thus, it was doubly odd to see this celebration of non-control over architectures born from the very ideal of control.

As I said, I am a constitutionalist. I teach and write about constitutional law. I believe that these first thoughts about government and cyberspace are just as misguided as the first thoughts about government after communism. Liberty in cyberspace will not come from the absence of the state. Liberty there, as anywhere, will come from a state of a certain kind.[4] We build a world where freedom can flourish not by removing from society any self-conscious control; we build a world where freedom can flourish by setting it in a place where a particular kind of self-conscious control survives. We build liberty, that is, as our founders did, by setting society upon a certain *constitution*.

But by "constitution" I don't mean a legal text. Unlike my countrymen in Eastern Europe, I am not trying to sell a document that our framers wrote in 1787. Rather, as the British understand when they speak of their constitution, I mean an *architecture*—not just a legal text but a way of life—that structures and constrains social and legal power, to the end of protecting fundamental *values*—principles and ideals that reach beyond the compromises of ordinary politics.

Constitutions in this sense are built, they are not found. Foundations get laid, they don't magically appear. Just as the founders of our nation learned from the anarchy that followed the revolution (remember: our first constitution, the Articles of Confederation, was a miserable failure of do-nothingness), so too are we beginning to see in cyberspace that this building, or laying, is not the work of an invisible hand. There is no reason to believe that the grounding for liberty in cyberspace will simply emerge. In fact, as I will argue, quite the opposite is the case. As our framers learned, and as the Russians saw, we have every reason to believe that cyberspace, left to itself, will not fulfill the promise of freedom. Left to itself, cyberspace will become a perfect tool of control.[5]

Control. Not necessarily control by government, and not necessarily control to some evil, fascist end. But the argument of this book is that the invisible hand of cyberspace is building an architecture that is quite the opposite of what it was at cyberspace's birth. The invisible hand, through commerce, is constructing an architecture that perfects control—an architecture that makes possible highly efficient regulation. As Vernor Vinge warned in 1996, a distributed architecture of regulatory control; as Tom Maddox added, an axis between commerce and the state.[6]

This book is about that change, and about how we might prevent it. When we see the path that cyberspace is on—an evolution I describe in part 1—we see that much of the "liberty" present at cyberspace's founding will vanish in its future. Values that we now consider fundamental will not necessarily remain. Freedoms that were foundational will slowly disappear.

If the original cyberspace is to survive, and if values that we knew in that world are to remain, we must understand how this change happens, and what we can do in response. That is the aim of part 2. Cyberspace presents something new for those who think about regulation and freedom. It demands a new understanding of how regulation works and of what regulates life there. It compels us to look beyond the traditional lawyer's scope—beyond laws, regulations, and norms. It requires an account of a newly salient regulator.

That regulator is the obscurity in the book's title—*Code.* In real space we recognize how laws regulate—through constitutions, statutes, and other legal codes. In cyberspace we must understand how code regulates—how the software and hardware that make cyberspace what it is *regulate* cyberspace as it is. As William Mitchell puts it, this code is cyberspace's "law."[7] *Code is law.*

This code presents the greatest threat to liberal or libertarian ideals, as well as their greatest promise. We can build, or architect, or code cyberspace to protect values that we believe are fundamental, or we can build, or architect, or code cyberspace to allow those values to disappear. There is no middle ground. There is no choice that does not include some kind of *building.* Code is never found; it is only ever made, and only ever made by us. As Mark Stefik puts it, "Different versions of [cyberspace] support different kinds of dreams. We choose, wisely or not."[8]

My argument is not for some top-down form of control; my claim is not that regulators must occupy Microsoft. A constitution envisions an environment; as Justice Holmes said, it "call[s] into life a being the development of which [can not be] foreseen."[9] Thus, to speak of a constitution is not to describe a one-hundred-day plan. It is instead to identify the values that a space should guarantee. It is not to describe a "government"; it is not even to select (as if a single choice must be made) between bottom-up or top-down control. In speaking of a constitution in cyberspace we are simply asking: What values are protected there? What values will we build into the space to encourage certain forms of life?

The "values" here are of two sorts—substantive and structural. In the American tradition, we worried about the second first. The framers of the Constitution of 1787 (enacted without a Bill of Rights) were focused on structures of government. Their aim was to ensure that a particular government (the federal government) did not become too powerful. And so they built into its design checks on the power of the federal government and limits on its reach over the states.

Opponents of that Constitution insisted that more checks were needed, that the Constitution needed to impose substantive limits on government's power as well as structural limits. And thus the Bill of Rights was born. Ratified in 1791, the Bill of Rights promised that the federal government will not remove certain protections—of speech, privacy, and due process. And it guaranteed that the commitment to these substantive values will remain despite the passing fancy of normal government. These values were to be entrenched, or embedded, in our constitutional design; they can be changed, but only by changing the Constitution's design.

These two kinds of protection go together in our constitutional tradition. One would have been meaningless without the other. An unchecked structure could easily have overturned the substantive protections expressed in the Bill of Rights, and without substantive protections, even a balanced and reflective government could have violated values that our framers thought fundamental.

We face the same questions in constituting cyberspace, but we have approached them from an opposite direction. Already we are struggling with substance: Will cyberspace promise privacy or access? Will it preserve a space for free speech? Will it facilitate free and open trade? These are choices of substantive value, and they are the subject of much of this book.

But structure matters as well. What checks on arbitrary regulatory power can we build into the design of the space? What "checks and balances" are possible? How do we separate powers? How do we ensure that one regulator, or one government, doesn't become too powerful?

Theorists of cyberspace have been talking about these questions since its birth.[10] But as a culture, we are just beginning to get it. We are just beginning to see why the architecture of the space matters—in particular, why the *ownership* of that architecture matters. If the code of cyberspace is owned (in a sense that I describe in this book), it can be controlled; if it is not owned, control is much more difficult. The lack of ownership, the absence of property, the inability to direct how ideas will be used—in a word, the presence of a commons—is key to limiting, or checking, certain forms of governmental control.

One part of this question of ownership is at the core of the current debate between open and closed source software. In a way that the American founders would have instinctively understood, "free software" or "open source software"—or "open code," to (cowardly) avoid taking sides in a debate I describe later—is itself a check on arbitrary power. A structural guarantee of constitutionalized liberty, it functions as a type of separation of powers in the American constitutional tradition. It stands alongside substantive protections, like freedom of speech or of the press, but its stand is more fundamental. As I argue by the end of this book, the first intuition of our founders was right: structure builds substance. Guarantee the structural (a space in cyberspace for open code), and (much of) the substance will take care of itself.

In part 3, I bring these questions back down to the ground. I consider four areas of controversy—intellectual property, privacy, free speech, and sovereignty—and identify values within each that are now at risk. The interaction between law and code helps constitute these values. My aim is to show how we might respond to the risk, using the tools from part 2.

That's the hopeful part. My final part is not. I end by asking whether we—meaning Americans—are up to the challenge that these choices present. Given our present tradition in constitutional law and our present faith in representative government, are we able to respond collectively to the changes I will have described?

My strong sense is that we are not. We are at a stage in our history when we urgently need to make fundamental choices about values, but we trust no institution of government to make such choices. Courts cannot do it, because as a legal culture we don't want courts choosing among contested matters of values, and Congress should not do it because, as a political culture, we so deeply question the products of ordinary government.

Change is possible. I don't doubt that revolutions remain in our future; the open code movement is just such a revolution. But I fear that it is too easy for the government to dislodge these revolutions, and that too much will be at stake for it to allow the revolutionaries to succeed. Our government has already criminalized the core ethic of this movement, transforming the meaning of *hacker* into something quite alien to its original sense. This, I argue, is only the start.

Things could be different. They are different elsewhere. But I don't see how they could be different for us just now. This no doubt is a simple confession of the limits of my own imagination. I would be grateful to be proven wrong. I would be grateful to watch as we relearn—as the citizens of the former Communist republics are learning—how to escape our disabling ideas about the possibilities for governance.

I begin in the first chapter with four stories about cyberspace, which will set out four themes to guide the balance of the book. These themes describe what is different here. Even if despair about governance is the same, at least these things are different.

TWO

four puzzles from cyberspace

MOST PEOPLE THINK THAT TO UNDERSTAND *LAW*, YOU NEED TO UNDERSTAND A SET OF *rules*. That's a mistake, as Stanley Fish taught us.[1] The law is best understood through stories—stories that teach what is later summarized in a catalog of rules.

So it is with stories that I begin. Each (there are four) captures a theme that recurs throughout the book. Each is meant both to orient and to disorient—that is, to show ways in which cyberspace is both like and unlike real space. At the end of this chapter, I come clean about the themes and provide a map. For now, just focus on the stories.

BORDERS

It was a very ordinary dispute, this argument between Martha Jones and her neighbors.[2] It was the sort of dispute that people have had since the start of neighborhoods. It didn't begin, this particular dispute, in anger. It began with a misunderstanding. In this world, misunderstandings like this are far too common. Martha thought about that as she wondered whether she should stay. There were other places she could go. Leaving would mean abandoning what she had built, but frustrations like this were beginning to get to her. Maybe, she thought, it was time to move on.

The argument was about borders—about where her land stopped. It seemed like a simple idea, one you would have thought the powers-that-be would have worked out many years before. But here they were, her neighbor Dank and she, *still* fighting about borders. Or rather, about something fuzzy at the borders—about something of Martha's that spilled over into the land of others. This was the fight, and it all related to what Martha did.

Martha grew flowers. Not just any flowers, but flowers with an odd sort of power. They were beautiful flowers, and their scent entranced. But however beautiful, these flowers were also poisonous. For this was Martha's weird idea: to make flowers of extraordinary beauty which, if touched, would kill. Strange no doubt, no one said that Martha wasn't strange. She was unusual, as was this neighborhood. But sadly, disputes like this were not.

The start of the argument was predictable enough. Martha's neighbor, Dank, had a dog. Dank's dog died. And of course, the dog died because it had eaten a petal from one of Martha's flowers. A beautiful petal, and now a dead dog. Dank had his own ideas about these flowers, and about this neighbor, and he expressed those ideas—perhaps with a bit too much anger, or perhaps with anger appropriate to the situation.

"There is no reason to grow deadly flowers," Dank yelled across the fence. "There's no reason to get so upset about a few dead dogs," Martha replied. "A dog can always be replaced. And anyway, why have a dog that suffers when dying? Get yourself a pain-free dog, and my petals will cause no harm."

I came into the argument at about this time. I was walking by, in the way one walks in this space. (Some would say I was teleporting, but we needn't complicate the story with jargon. Let's just say I was walking.) I saw the two neighbors getting increasingly angry with each other. I had heard about the disputed flowers—about how some petals carried their poison. It seemed to me a simple problem to solve, but I guess it's simple only if you understand how problems like this get made.

Dank and Martha were angry because in a sense they were stuck. Both had built a life in the neighborhood, invested many hours there, and come to understand its limits. This is a common condition: we all build our lives in places with limits. We all are disappointed at times. What was different about Dank and Martha?

One difference was the nature of the space, or context, where their argument was happening. This was not "real space" but a kind of virtual space. It was "Avatar space," and Avatar space is quite different from the space we call real.[3]

Real space is the place where you are just now: your office, your den, maybe a pool. It's a world defined by both laws that are man-made and others that are not. "Limited liability" for corporations is a man-made law. It means that the directors of a corporation (usually) cannot be held personally liable for the sins of the company. Limited life for humans is not a man-made law: we all will die. In real space our lives are subject to both sorts of law, though in principle we could change one sort.

But there are other sorts of laws in real space as well. You bought this book, I trust, or you borrowed it from someone who did. If you stole it, you are a thief, whether you are caught or not. Social norms define our language; our language would define you as a thief, and not just because you took something. There are plenty of ways to take something but not be thought of as a thief. If you and a group of friends come across a pile of money blowing in the wind, taking a few dollars will not make you a thief; indeed, not taking a few dollars might make you a chump. But stealing this book from the bookstore (even when there are so many left for others) marks you as a thief. Social norms make it so, and we live life subject to these norms.

Some of these norms can be changed collectively, even if not individually. I can choose to burn my draft card, but I cannot choose whether doing so will make me a hero or a traitor. I can refuse an invitation to lunch, but I cannot choose whether doing so will make me rude. I have choices in real life, but escaping the consequences entailed by these laws is not one of my choices. These laws constrain us in ways that are so familiar as to be all but invisible.

Avatar space is different. It is, first of all, a virtual space—like a cartoon on a television screen. But unlike a cartoon, avatar space enables you to control the characters on the screen in real time. At least, you control *your* character—one among many characters controlled by many others in this space. One builds the world one will inhabit here. As a child, you grew up learning the physics that governed the world of Roadrunner and Wile E. Coyote (violent but forgiving); your children will grow up *making* the world of Roadrunner and Wile E. Coyote (still violent, but maybe not so forgiving). They will define the space and then live out the story. Their choices will make the laws of that space real.

This is not to say that Avatar space is unreal. There is real life in Avatar space, constituted by how people interact. The space is where people interact—much as they interact in real space no doubt, but with some important differences. In Avatar space the interaction is in a virtual medium. In 1990s speak, the interaction is *in* cyberspace. People "jack" into these virtual spaces. They do things there.

The things people do there are highly varied. Some simply get together and gab: they appear (in a form they select, with qualities they choose and biographies they have written) in a virtual room and type messages to each other. Or they walk around (again, the ambiguity is not a slight one) and talk to people. My friend Rick does this as a cat—a male cat, he insists. As a male cat, Rick parades around this space and talks to anyone who's interested. He aims to flush out the cat-loving sorts. The rest, he reports, he punishes.

Others do much more in Avatar space than gab. Some, for example, homestead. Depending on the world and its laws, citizens are given plots of undeveloped land, which they hold as long as they develop them. People spend extraordinary amounts of time building a life on these plots. (Isn't it extraordinary the way these people waste time? While you and I spend up to seventy hours a week working for firms we don't own and building futures we're not sure we'll enjoy, these people are designing and building things and making a life, even if only a virtual one. Scandalous.) They build houses—by designing and then constructing them—have family or friends move in, and pursue hobbies or raise pets. They may grow trees or odd plants—like Martha's.

Avatar space grew out of "MUD" or "MOO" space.[4] MUDs and MOOs are virtual worlds as well, but they are text-based virtual worlds. There are no pictures or cartoons on a MUD or MOO screen, just text, reporting what someone says and does. You can construct objects in these spaces and have them do things, but the objects act only through the mediation of text. (Their actions are generally quite simple, but even simple can be quite funny. One year, in a MUD that was part of my cyberlaw class, someone built a character named JPosner. If you poked JPosner, he muttered, "Poking is inefficient." Another character was FEasterbrook. Stand in a room with FEasterbrook and use the word "fair," and FEasterbrook would repeat what you said, substituting the word "efficient." "It's not fair" became "You mean, it's not efficient.")

Although it was easy for people who liked texts or who wrote them to understand the attraction of these text-based realities, and to see how they could constitute a reality, it was not so easy for the many people who didn't have that fondness for texts. But there is no such limitation in Avatar space. It is the movie version of a cyberspace novel. You build things here, and they survive your leaving. You can build a house, and people walking down the street see it. You can let them come in, and in coming into your house, they see things about you. Or they can see how you construct your world. If the particular Avatar space permits it, they can see how you've changed the laws of the real world. In real space, for instance, people slip on wet floors, but in the space you've built that law may not exist.

Here we get back to Martha and Dank. In their exchange—when Martha blamed Dank for having a dog that died with pain—they revealed what is amazing about this space. Martha's remarks ("Why do you have a dog that suffers when dying? Get yourself a pain-free dog, and my petals will cause no harm") may have struck you as odd. You may have thought, "How weird that someone would think that the fault lay not in the poison petals but in a dog that died with pain." But in this space Dank *did* have a choice about how his dog would die. Maybe not a choice about whether "poison" would "kill" a dog, but a choice about whether the dog would suffer when it died. He also had a choice about whether a copy of the dog could be made, so that if it died it could "come back to life." In Avatar space these possibilities are not given by God. Or rather, if they are defined by God, then *we* are God. The possibilities in Avatar space are determined by the *code*—the software, or architecture, that makes the Avatar space what it is. "What happens when" is a statement of logic; it asserts a relationship that is manifested in code. In real space we don't make much of the code. In Avatar space we do.

So, when Martha said what she said about the dog, Dank made what seemed to me an obvious response. "Why do your flowers have to stay poisonous once they leave your land? Why not make the petals poisonous only when on your land? When they leave your land—when, for example, they are blown onto my land—why not make them harmless?"

It was an idea, but it didn't really help. For Martha made her living selling these poisonous plants. Others too liked the idea of this art tied to death. So it was not a solution to make poisonous plants that were poisonous only on Martha's property, unless Martha was also interested in collecting a lot of very weird people on her land.

But the idea did suggest another. "Okay," said Dank, "why not make the petals poisonous only when in the possession of someone who has purchased them? If they are stolen, or if they blow away, then let the petals lose their poison. But when kept by the owner of the plant, let the petals keep their poison. Isn't that a solution to the problem that both of us face?"

The idea was ingenious. Not only did it help Dank; it helped Martha as well. For the code, as it existed, did allow theft. (People want reality in that virtual space; there will be time enough for heaven later.) But if Martha could modify the code slightly so that theft removed a plant's value, that change would protect the profit in her plants as well as Dank's dogs. Here was a solution that made both neighbors better off—what economists call a *pareto superior* move.[5] And it was a solution that was as possible as any other. All it required was a change of code.

Think for a second about what's involved here. "Theft" entails (at minimum) a change in possession. But in Avatar space "possession" is just a relation defined by the software that defines the space. That same code must also define the properties that possession yields. It must distinguish, for example, between having a cake and eating it. In both cases you "possess" the cake, but in the second case what you possess must change over time. With each "bite," you possess less.

So why not the same solution to Martha and Dank's problem? Why not define ownership to include the quality of poisonousness, and possession without ownership to be possession without poison? Rather than resolve the dispute between Martha and Dank by making one of them change his or her behavior, why not change the laws of nature to eliminate the conflict altogether?

We're a short way into this relatively short book, and what I'm about to say may make it a very short book indeed (for you at least). This book is all about the question raised by this simple story, and about the simplicity in this apparently simple answer. This is not a book about Avatar space; the story about Martha and Dank is the first and last example that will include Avatars. But it is a book about cyberspace. My claim is that cyberspace will raise precisely the questions that Martha and Dank confronted, as well as the questions that their solution raised. What does it mean to live in a world where problems can be programmed away? And when, in that world, *should* we program problems away?

It is not Avatar space that makes these questions interesting problems for law; the very same problems will arise outside of Avatar space, and outside MUDs and MOOs. The problems of these spaces are problems of cyberspace generally, and as more of our life becomes wired, these questions will become more pressing.

But I have learned enough in this business to know that I can't convince you of this with an argument. (I've spent the last five years talking about this subject; at least I know what doesn't work.) If you see the point, good for you. If you don't, I must *show* you. So my method for readers of the second sort must be more indirect. Proof, for them, will come in a string of stories, which aim to introduce and disorient. That, again, is the purpose of this chapter. Out of confusion, something useful will emerge.

Let me describe a few other places, and the oddities that inhabit them.

GOVERNORS

A state—call it "Boral"—doesn't like gambling, even though some citizens like to gamble. But the state is the boss; the people have voted; the law is as it is. Gambling in the state of Boral is illegal.

Then comes the Internet. With the Net wired into their phones, some citizens of Boral decide that Internet gambling is the next "killer app." Someone sets up servers that provide access to online gambling. The state doesn't like this business; the businessmen are just illegal gamblers. Shut down your servers, the attorney general warns, or we will lock you up.

Wise even if dishonest, the gamblers agree to shut down their servers in the state of Boral. But they don't exit the gambling business. Instead, they rent space on a server in an "offshore haven." This offshore web server hums away, once again making gambling available on the Net.

And just as available to people in Boral. For here's the important point: given the architecture of the Internet (at least as it was), it doesn't matter where in real space the server is set up. Access doesn't depend on geography. Nor, depending on how clever the gambling sorts are, does access require that the user know anything about who owns or runs the real server. The user's access can be passed through anonymizing sites that make it practically impossible in the end to know what went where.

The Boral attorney general faces a difficult problem. She may have moved the gamblers out of her state, but she hasn't succeeded in reducing gambling on the Net. She once would have had a group of people she could punish, but now she has made them essentially free from punishment. The world for this attorney general has changed. By going online, the gamblers moved into a world where behavior, so the argument goes, is no longer regulable.

Regulable. I am told there is no such word, though lawyers apparently do not know that fact. By "regulable" I mean simply that a certain behavior is capable of regulation. The term is comparative, not absolute—in some place, at some time, a certain behavior will be more regulable than at another place and in another time. My claim about Boral is simply that the Net makes gambling less regulable there than it was before the Net.

JAKE'S COMMUNITIES

If you had met Jake at a party in Ann Arbor (were Jake at a party in Ann Arbor), you would have forgotten him.[6] If you didn't forget him, you might have thought, here's another quiet, dweeby University of Michigan undergraduate, terrified of the world, or at least of people in the world.

You wouldn't have figured Jake for an author—and quite a famous short-story author, within his circle at least. Jake was a character in his own stories, yet who he was in his stories was quite different from who he was in "real" life. If, that is, after reading his stories you still thought this distinction between "real life" and "not real life" made much sense.

Jake wrote stories about violence—about sex as well, but mainly about violence. They seethed with hatred, especially of women.

In real space Jake had quite successfully hidden this propensity. He was one of a million boys: unremarkable, indistinguishable, harmless. Yet however inoffensive in real space, his harmfulness in cyberspace was increasingly well known. His stories were published in USENET, in a group called alt.sex.stories.

USENET is a part of most spaces on the Net. It isn't a network, except in the sense that the personal ads of a national newspaper are a network. It is a protocol—a set of rules named the net news transfer protocol (NNTP)—for exchanging messages intended for public viewing. These messages are organized into "newsgroups," and the newsgroups are organized into subjects. Most of the subjects are quite technical. Many are related to hobbies. Some are related to sex. Some messages in the sex newsgroups come with attached files that can be converted to pictures. But some, like Jake's, are simply stories.

There are thousands of newsgroups, each carrying hundreds of messages. Anyone with access to a USENET server can get access to the messages (or at least to the ones his administrator wants him to read), and anyone with access can post a message or respond to one already posted. Imagine a public bulletin board on which people post questions or comments. Anyone can read the board and add his or her own thoughts. Now imagine fifteen thousand boards, each with hundreds of "threads" (strings of arguments, each tied to the next). That, in any one place, is USENET. Now imagine these fifteen thousand boards, with hundreds of threads each, on millions of computers across the world. Post a message in one group, and it is added to that group's board everywhere. That, for the world, is USENET.

Jake, as I said, posted to a group called alt.sex.stories. "Alt" in that name refers to the hierarchy that the group sits within. There were seven primary hierarchies.[7] Alt was created in reaction to the initial seven: groups are added to the seven through a formal voting process among participants in the groups, but groups are added to alt based solely on whether administrators choose to carry them. Usually, administrators will carry them if they are popular.

Among these groups that are carried only on demand, alt.sex.stories is quite popular. As with any writing space, if stories are "good" by the standards of the space—if they are stories that users of the space demand—they are followed and their authors become well known. Lots of trash is sputtered out on USENET, but if a writer is known to write valuable stuff, his or her trash will be sifted out.

Jake's stuff was valuable in this sense. His stories, about kidnapping, torturing, raping and killing women, were as graphic and repulsive as any such story could be—which is why Jake was so famous among like-minded sorts. He was a supplier to these people, a constant and consistent fix. They needed these accounts of innocent women being violated. Jake supplied them for free.

One night in Moscow, a sixteen-year-old girl read a story by Jake. She showed it to her father, who showed it in turn to Richard DuVal, a Michigan alum. DuVal was shocked at the story, and angry that it bore the tag "umich.edu" on the account. He called his alma mater and complained. They took the complaint seriously.[8]

The university contacted the police; the police contacted Jake with handcuffs and a jail cell. A slew of doctors examined Baker. Some concluded that he was a threat. The government agreed with them, especially after it seized his computer and discovered e-mails between Jake and a Canadian fan who was planning to execute in real space one of the stories published in cyberspace. At least, that's what the e-mails said. No one could tell for certain what the two men intended. Jake said it was all pure fiction, and indeed, there was no evidence that the words had ever described something that was not purely fictional.

Federal charges were brought against Jake, for the transmission of a threat. Jake said that his stories were only words, protected by the First Amendment to the U.S. Constitution. A month and a half later a court agreed, and the charges were dropped.[9]

I don't care so much just now about whether Jake Baker's words should have been protected by the Constitution.[10] My concern is Jake Baker himself, a person *normed* into apparent harmlessness by real-space society but set free in cyberspace to become the author of this violence. People said Jake was brave, but he wasn't "brave" in real space. He didn't express his hatred in classes, among friends, or in the school newspaper. He slithered away to cyberspace, and only there did his deviancy flourish. He could do that because of something about him, and because of something about cyberspace.

Jake was in effect an author and publisher in one. He wrote stories, and as quickly as he finished them he published them—to some thirty million computers across the world within a few days. His potential audience was larger than twice that for the top fifteen best-selling novels combined, and though he made nothing from his work, the demand for it was high. Jake had discovered a way to mainline his depravity into the veins of a public for whom this stuff was otherwise quite difficult to find. (Even *Hustler* wouldn't publish the likes of this.)

Of course, there were other ways Jake could have published. He could have offered his work to *Hustler,* or worse. But no real-world publication would have given Jake a comparable audience. Jake's readership was potentially millions, stretching across country and continent, across culture and taste.

This reach was made possible by the power in the network: anyone anywhere could publish to everyone, everywhere. The network allowed publication without filtering, editing, or responsibility. One could write what one wanted, sign it or not, post it to machines across the world, and within hours the words would be everywhere. The network removed the most important constraint on speech in real space—the separation of publisher from author. There is vanity publishing in real space, but only the rich can use it to reach a broad audience. For the rest of us, real space affords only the access that the publishers want to give us.

But the most significant feature of this story about Jake is how cyberspace permitted him to escape the constraints of real space. Cyberspace is not, of course, a place; you don't go anywhere when you are there. But it is also quite true that the world Jake lived in when writing was a space quite different from the space he lived in here. He was free there of real-life constraints. He was free of the norms and understandings that had successfully formed him into a member of a college community. Maybe he wasn't perfectly at home; maybe he wasn't the happiest. But the world of the University of Michigan had succeeded in steering him away from the life of a psychopath—except when it gave him access to the Net. On the Net he was someone else.

WORMS THAT SNIFF

A "worm" is a bit of computer code that is spit out on the Net and works its way into the systems of vulnerable computers. It is not a "virus" because it doesn't attach itself to other programs and interfere with their operation. It is just a bit of extra code that does what the code writer says. The code could be harmless, simply sitting on someone's machine. Or it could be harmful, corrupting files or doing other damage that its author commands.

Imagine a worm designed to do good (at least in the minds of some). Imagine that the code writer is the FBI and that the FBI is looking for a particular document belonging to the National Security Agency (NSA). Suppose that this document is classified and illegal to possess without the proper clearance. Imagine that the worm propagates itself on the Net, finding its way onto hard disks wherever it can; once on a computer's hard disk, it scans the entire disk. If it finds the NSA document, it sends a message back to the FBI saying as much. If it doesn't, it erases itself. Finally, assume that it can do all this without "interfering"[11] with the operation of the machine. No one would know it was there; it would report back nothing except that the NSA document was on the hard disk.[12]

Is the worm unconstitutional? This is a hard question that at first seems to have an easy answer. The worm is engaging in a government-initiated search of citizens' disks. There is no reasonable suspicion (as the law ordinarily requires) that the disk holds the document for which the government is searching. It is instead a generalized, suspicionless search of private spaces by the government.

From the standpoint of the Constitution—the Fourth Amendment in particular—you don't get any worse than that. The Fourth Amendment was written against the background of just this sort of abuse. Kings George II and George III would give officers a "general warrant" authorizing them to search through private homes looking for evidence of a crime.[13] No suspicion was needed before the officer ransacked your house, but because he had a warrant, you were not able to sue the officer for trespass. The aim of the amendment was to require at least suspicion, so that the burden of the search fell on a reasonably chosen class.[14]

But is the worm really the same as the King's general search? There is one important difference: unlike the victims of the general searches that the framers of our Constitution were concerned about, the computer user never knows that his or her disk is being searched by the worm. With the general search, the police were breaking into a house and rummaging through private stuff. With the worm, it is a bit of computer code that does the breaking, and (I've assumed) it can see only one thing. The code can't read private letters; it doesn't break down doors; it doesn't interfere with ordinary life. And the innocent have nothing to fear.

The worm is silent in a way that King George's troops were not. It searches perfectly and invisibly, discovering only the guilty. It does not burden the innocent; it does not trouble the ordinary citizen; it captures only what is outside the protection of the law.

This difference complicates the constitutional question. The worm's behavior is like a generalized search in that it is a search without suspicion, but it is unlike the paradigm case of a generalized search in that it creates no disruption of ordinary life and finds only contraband. In this way, the worm is like a dog sniff—which at least at airports is constitutionally permissible without probable cause[15]—but better. Unlike the dog sniff, the worm doesn't even let the computer user know when there is a search (and hence the user suffers no anxiety).

Is the worm, then, constitutional? That depends on your conception of what the Fourth Amendment protects. On one view, the amendment protects against suspicionless governmental invasions, whether those invasions are burdensome or not. On a second view, the amendment protects against invasions that are burdensome, allowing only those for which there is adequate suspicion that guilt will be uncovered. The paradigm case cited by the framers does not distinguish between these two very different protections. It is *we*, instead, who must choose.

Let's take the example one step further. Imagine that the worm does not simply search every machine it encounters but can be put on a machine only with judicial authorization—say, a warrant. Now the suspicionless-search part of the problem has been removed. But imagine a second part: the government requires that networks be constructed so that a worm, with judicial authorization, could be placed on a machine. Machines in this regime must be worm-ready, even though worms will be deployed only with judicial warrant.

Is there any constitutional problem with this? I explore this question in much greater detail in chapter 11, but for now, notice its salient feature. In both cases, we are describing a regime that allows the government to collect data about us in a highly efficient manner, that is, inexpensively for both the government and the innocent. This efficiency is made possible by technology, which permits searches that before would have been far too burdensome and far too invasive. In both cases, then, the question comes to this: When the ability to search without burden increases, does the government's power to search increase as well? Or more darkly, as James Boyle puts it: "Is freedom inversely related to the efficiency of the available means of surveillance? If so, we have much to fear."[16]

This question, of course, is not limited to the government. One of the defining features of modern life is the emergence of technologies that make data collection and processing extraordinarily efficient. Most of what we do—hence, most of what we are—is recorded outside our homes. When you make telephone calls, data are recorded about whom you called, when, how long you spoke, and how frequently you made such calls.[17] When you use your credit cards, data are recorded about when, where, and from whom you made purchases. When you take a flight, your itinerary is recorded and, probably by the time this book reaches print, profiled by the government to determine whether you are likely to be a terrorist.[18] No doubt Hollywood's image—of a world where one person sitting behind a terminal tracks the life of another—is wrong. But not terribly wrong. It's not that systems so easily track a single individual. But it is easy to imagine an agency sorting through all the data the system collects to identify those individuals most likely to be committing crimes. The intrusiveness is slight, and the payoff great.

Both private and public monitoring, then, have the same salient feature: monitoring, or searching, can increase without increasing the burden on the individual searched. How should we think about this change? How should the protection the framers gave us be applied?

THEMES

Four stories, four themes, each a window onto one aspect of cyberspace that will be central in all that follows. My aim in the balance of this book is to work through the issues raised by these four themes. So then let me end this chapter with a map of the four, laid out in the order of the book. That order begins with story number two.

Regulability

Regulability means the capacity of a government to regulate behavior within its proper reach. In the context of the Internet, that means the ability of the government to regulate the behavior of its citizens (and perhaps others as well) on the Net. My second story, about gambling in Boral, was thus about regulability, or more specifically, about the changes in regulability that cyberspace brings. Before the Internet, it was relatively easy for the attorney general of Boral to control gambling within her jurisdiction; after the Internet, when the servers moved outside of Boral, regulation became much more difficult.

For the regulator, this story captures the problem that cyberspace presents generally. The architecture of cyberspace makes regulating behavior difficult, because those whose behavior you're trying to control could be located in any place (meaning outside of your place) on the Net. Who someone is, where he is, and whether law can be exercised over him there—all these are questions that government must answer if it is to impose its will. But these questions are made impossibly difficult by the architecture of the space—at least as it was.

The balance of part 1 is about this question of regulability. I ask whether "unregulability" is necessary. Can we imagine a more regulable cyberspace? And is this the cyberspace we are coming to know?

Regulation by Code

The story about Avatar space is a clue to answering the question about regulability. If in Avatar space we can change the laws of nature—making possible what before was impossible, or making impossible what before was possible—why can't we change regulability in cyberspace? Why can't we imagine a cyberspace where behavior can be controlled?

For this, importantly, is just what Avatar space was. Avatar space is "regulated," though the regulation is special. In Avatar space regulation came through *code*. The rules in Avatar space are imposed, not through sanctions, and not by the state, but by the very architecture of the particular space. A law is defined, not through a statute, but through the code that governs the space.

This is the second theme of this book: there is regulation of behavior in cyberspace, but that regulation is imposed primarily through code. What distinguishes different parts of cyberspace are the differences in the regulations effected through code. In some places life is fairly free, in other places controlled, and the difference between them is simply a difference in the architectures of control—that is, a difference in code.

If we combine the first two themes, we come to a central argument of the book: the *regulability* described by the first theme depends on the *code* described in the second. Some architectures of cyberspace are more regulable than others; some architectures enable better control than others. Thus, whether a part of cyberspace—or cyberspace generally—can be regulated turns on the nature of its code. Its architecture will affect whether behavior can be controlled. To follow Mitch Kapor, its architecture is its politics.[19]

And from this an important point follows: if some architectures are more regulable than others—if some give government more control than others—then governments should favor some architectures more than others, if regulability is the government's aim.

This fact is a threat to those who worry about governmental power; it is a reality for those who would do something about governmental power. Some designs enable government more than others; some designs enable government differently; some designs should be chosen over others.

It is here that questions of open source software matter. Among the designs that enable or disable government's power to regulate, open code will hold an important place. It will check, as I argue more extensively later, the top-down power of government while enabling an extremely effective scope for bottom-up control.

To restate theme two: the code is a regulator, and the government has a greater interest in the code that regulates better than others.

Competing Sovereigns

But regulation by whom? Boral was just one state. Its problems were not the problems of its neighbors. And the rules we live by while in Boral, or while in a particular Avatar space, need not be the rules that we live by generally.

This was the issue raised most importantly by Jake Baker. His story raises the question of competing authority. Jake lived in Ann Arbor, Michigan. His life there was subject to the norms of Ann Arbor, and he apparently adapted to these norms reasonably well. The authority of that space governed Jake, and as far as anyone knew, it appeared to govern him exclusively.

But in cyberspace Jake's norms changed. When Jake went to cyberspace, his behavior changed. He was governed there by a set of norms different from the norms that governed him in Ann Arbor.

The problem was that when he went to cyberspace, he never left Ann Arbor. "Going" in cyberspace functions differently from "going" in real space. When you "go" somewhere in real space, you leave; when you "go" to cyberspace, you don't leave anywhere. You are never *just* in cyberspace; you never just *go* there. You are always both in real space and in cyberspace at the same time.

And so too with Jake. While sitting in a dorm at the University of Michigan, he was able to teleport himself—in the only normatively significant sense—to a different world where the norms of civility and decency that governed outside his dorm room did not obtain. Cyberspace gave Jake the chance to escape Ann Arbor norms and to live according to the norms of another place. It created a *competing authority* for Jake and gave him the chance to select between these competing authorities merely by switching his computer on or off.

Again, my point is not that no similar possibility exists in real space—it plainly does. There is no doubt a Jake living in Hackensack, New Jersey (a suburban town with suburban values), who drives every night into lower Manhattan and lives for a few hours according to the "rules" of lower Manhattan. Those rules are not the rules of Hackensack; that life is different. Like Ann Arbor Jake, the Hackensack Jake lives under competing authorities. But between the lives of these two Jakes, there is a difference in degree that ripens into a difference in kind. The Ann Arbor Jake raises a more significant problem for Ann Arbor than the Hackensack Jake raises for Hackensack. The differences are greater, and the effect more pervasive.

Nor should we think too narrowly about the competing normative communities into which a Jake might move. The valences here are both positive and negative. It is escape when a gay teen in Iowa can leave the norms of Iowa through a gay chat room on America Online;[20] it is escape when a child predator escapes the norms of ordinary society and engages a child in online sex.[21] Both escapes are enabled by the architecture of cyberspace as we now know it.

The difference between these two escapes is our view about the underlying norm. I call the first escape liberating, and the second criminal. There are some who would call both escapes criminal, and some who would call both liberating. The question isn't about name-calling, but about the consequences of living in a world where we can occupy both sorts of space at the same time. Which sovereign should govern?

Latent Ambiguity

The worm tells a different story still. Though it is a technology for searching, the worm functions differently from searching in the ordinary case. The ordinary or paradigm case is a search that carries costs: the burdens of the search, the insecurities it might create, the exposure it might make possible to invasions beyond a legitimate reach.[22] The worm erases those costs: the burden is gone, the search is (practically) invisible, and the searching technology is programmed to find only what is illegal. This is a search without the ordinary costs of a search, and it raises a question about how such a search should, under the Constitution, be understood.

A fair view of the Constitution's protections could go in either of two ways. It may be that we see the worm's invasion as inconsistent with the dignity that the amendment was written to protect,[23] or it may be that we see the invasion of the worm as so unobtrusive as to be reasonable. The answer could be either, which means that the change reveals a *latent ambiguity* in the original constitutional value. Either answer is possible, so now we must choose one or the other.

You may not buy my story of the worm. You may think it is pure science fiction. By the end of the book, however, I will convince you that there are any number of cases in which a similar ambiguity troubles our constitutional past. In many of them our Constitution yields no answer to the question of how it should be applied, because at least two answers are possible—that is, in light of the choices that the framers actually made.

For Americans, this ambiguity creates a problem. If we lived in an era when courts felt entitled to select the answer that in the context made the most sense, there would be no problem. Latent ambiguities would be answered by choices made by judges—the framers could have gone either way, but we choose to go this way.

But we don't live in such an era, and so we don't have a way for courts to resolve these ambiguities. As a result, we must rely on other institutions. My claim, a dark one, is that we have no such institutions. If our ways don't change, our constitution in cyberspace will be a thinner and thinner regime.

Cyberspace will present us with ambiguities over and over again. It will press this question of how best to go on. We have tools from real space that will help resolve the interpretive questions by pointing us in one direction or another, at least some of the time. But in the end the tools will guide us even less than they do in real space and time. When the gap between their guidance and what we do becomes obvious, we will be forced to do something we're not very good at doing—deciding what we want, and what is right.

My aim is not to lament choice. It is to highlight its nature and effect, as well as an aspect of the transformation that we can expect this transformation in technology to create—one with which we, uniquely, are unable to reckon.

My aim is to use these four themes to understand cyberspace as it is, and cyberspace as I believe it is becoming as it moves from a world of relative freedom to a world of relatively perfect control. These themes will help us to see why and to understand how we might respond to this transformation—how we might reclaim the values that are important in this space, and how we might insist on bringing to it values that are now absent.

THREE

is-ism

The rise of an electronic medium that disregards geographical boundaries throws the law into disarray by creating entirely new phenomena that need to become the subject of clear legal rules but that cannot be governed, satisfactorily, by any current territorially based sovereign.

David Johnson and David Post, "Law and Borders—The Rise of Law in Cyberspace," *Stanford Law Review* 48 (1996): 1367, 1375

Some things never change about governing the Web. Most prominent is its innate ability to resist governance in almost any form.

Tom Steinert-Threlkeld, "Of Governance and Technology," Inter@ctive WeekOnline, October 2, 1998

THERE'S A MEME ABOUT CYBERSPACE THAT MARKS NATIVES FROM ITS FIRST GENERA-tions—an idea that defines first-generation thought about the place. Cyberspace, it is said, cannot be regulated. It "cannot be governed"; its "innate ability" is to resist regulation. That is its nature, its essence, the way things are. Not that cyberspace cannot be broken, or that government cannot shut it down. But *if cyberspace exists,* so first-generation thinking goes, government's power over behavior there is quite limited. In its essence, cyberspace is a space of no control.

Nature. Essence. Innate. The way things are. This kind of rhetoric should raise suspicions in any context. It should especially raise suspicion here. If there is any place where nature has no rule, it is in cyberspace. If there is any place that is constructed, cyberspace is it. Yet the rhetoric of "essence" hides this constructedness. It misleads our intuitions in dangerous ways.

This is the fallacy of "is-ism"—to confuse how something is with how it must be. There is certainly a way that cyberspace *is*. That much is true. But how cyberspace *is* is not how cyberspace has to be. There is no single way that the Net *has* to be; no single architecture defines the nature of the Net. The possible architectures of something that we would call "the Net" are many, and the character of life within those different architectures is diverse.

The next few chapters extend this point. But the argument can be summarized in a single line: whether the Net is *unregulable* depends, and it depends on its *architecture*.[1]

With some architectures, behavior on the Net cannot easily be controlled; with others it can. With some it cannot be controlled through top-down regulation; with others it can. Among the many possible architectures that the Net might have, the aim of this part is to argue that it is evolving in a very particular direction: from an unregulable space to one that is highly regulable. The "nature" of the Net might once have been its unregulability; that "nature" is about to flip.

To see the flip, you must first see a contrast between two different cyber-places. The contrast is a clue about how the Net could be made more regulable.

I don't mean the descriptions that follow to be technical; I don't offer them as complete definitions of types of networks, or types of control. I offer them to illustrate—to sketch enough to see a far more general point.

CYBER-PLACES: HARVARD VERSUS CHICAGO

The Internet was born at universities in the United States. Its first subscribers were researchers, but as a form of life, its birth was its link to the university and university life. It swept students online, pulling them away from a very different life in real space. The Net was a legal intoxicant of college campuses in the mid-1990s. As the *New York Times* columnist J. C. Herz wrote in her first book about cyberspace:

> When I look up, it's four-thirty in the morning. "No way." I look from the clock to my watch. Way. I've been in front of this screen for six hours, and it seems like no time at all. I'm not even remotely tired. Dazed and thirsty, but not tired. In fact, I'm euphoric. I stuff a disheveled heap of textbooks, photocopied articles, hilighters and notes into my backpack and run like a madwoman up the concrete steps, past the security guard, and outside into the predawn mist. . . .
>
> I stop where a wet walkway meets a dry one and stand for a sec. . . . [I] start thinking about this *thing* that buzzes around the entire world, through the phone lines, all day and all night long. It's right under our noses and it's invis-

ible. It's like Narnia, or Magritte, or *Star Trek,* an entire goddamned world. Except it doesn't physically exist. It's just the collective consciousness of however many people are on it.

This really is outstandingly weird.[2]

But not all universities adopted the Net in the same way. The access they granted was not the same; the rules they imposed were different. One example of this difference comes from two places I know quite well, though many other examples could make the same point.

At the University of Chicago, if you wanted access to the Internet, you simply connected your machine to jacks located throughout the university.[3] Any machine with an Ethernet connection could be plugged into these jacks. Once connected, your machine had full access to the Internet—access, that is, that was complete, anonymous, and free.

The reason for this freedom was a decision by an administrator—the Provost, Geoffrey Stone, a former dean of the law school and a prominent free speech scholar. When the university was designing its net, the technicians asked Stone whether anonymous communication should be permitted. Stone, citing the principle that the rules regulating speech at the university should be as protective of free speech as the First Amendment, said yes: people should have the right to communicate at the university anonymously, because the First Amendment to the Constitution guarantees the same right vis-à-vis governments.[4] From that policy decision flowed the architecture of the University of Chicago's net.

At Harvard the rules are different. If you plug your machine into an Ethernet jack at the Harvard Law School, you will not gain access to the Net. You cannot connect your machine to the net at Harvard unless the machine is registered—licensed, approved, verified. Only members of the university community can register their machines. Once registered, all interactions with the network are monitored and identified to a particular machine; the user agreement carries a warning about this practice. Anonymous speech on this net is not permitted—it is against the rules. Access can be controlled based on who you are, and interactions can be traced based on what you did.

This design also arose from the decision of an administrator, one less focused than Geoffrey Stone on the protections of the First Amendment. Controlling access was the ideal at Harvard; facilitating access was the ideal at Chicago. Harvard chose technologies that make control possible, while Chicago chose technologies that facilitate access.

These two networks differ in at least two important ways. First and most obviously, they differ in the values they embrace.[5] This difference is by design. At the University of Chicago, First Amendment values determined network design. Different values determined Harvard's design.

But the two networks differ in a second way as well. Because access is controlled at Harvard and identity is known, actions can be traced back to their root in the network. In the Chicago network the identity and actions of users cannot be known. Monitoring, tracking, or following behavior at Chicago is harder than it is at Harvard. Behavior in the Harvard network is more controllable than behavior in the University of Chicago network.

The networks thus differ in the extent to which they make behavior within each network *regulable*. This difference is simply a matter of *code*—a difference in the software. Regulability is not determined by the essential nature of these networks. It is determined instead by their architecture.

These two networks are just two points on a spectrum of possible network design. At one extreme we might place the Internet—a network defined by a suite of protocols that are open and nonproprietary and that require no personal identification to be accessed and used. (I describe this architecture more extensively in chapter 4.) At the other extreme are traditional closed, proprietary networks, which grant access only to those with express authorization; control, therefore, is tight. In between are networks that mix elements of both the Harvard network and networks that are Internet-open and generally accessible but that build on top of this open protocol architectures that enable some degree of control. These mixed networks add control to the Internet; they layer elements of control on top.

It is the middle kind of network that I focus on here. The network at the University of Chicago is the model of the Internet in, say, 1995—let's call it Net95. The second is the model of any number of closed networks that both predate the Internet and still exist today—for example, the ATM network, which makes it possible to get cash at 2:00 A.M. in Bogotá. The third—the middle type, the Harvard architecture—adds something to Net95. It layers on top of the Internet suite code that enables more control.[6] The code of this network is not inconsistent with the underlying protocols of the Internet. It is still based, in the language of the engineers, in "TCP/IP," the name for the suite of protocols that define the Internet (see chapter 4). But it adds to this suite a set of protocols that facilitate further control. The Harvard network is the Internet-plus, where the "plus" adds the means of control. (Though here the control lies only in knowing who a user is, not in knowing what content he or she is trafficking.)

All three designs are communication networks that are "like" the Internet. They raise a question: When we say that the Internet is "unregulable," which network are we describing? And if we pick an unregulable network, just *why* is it unregulable? What features about its design make it so? And could those features be different?

My point in aligning the three should be obvious. If some networks are more regulable than others, this is simply a function of the network's design. The design of an unregulable network could be changed; it could be transformed into a regulable network. The key is to identify the features of the unregulable space and to imagine them changed to make the space more regulable.

Consider three features of Net95's design that make it hard for a regulator to control behavior there. From the perspective of the regulator, these features are "imperfections"—they limit the data that the Net collects, either about the user or about the material he or she is using.

The first imperfection is information about users—in a word, *credentials*. Net95 has no way to verify who someone is, or more important, to verify features or attributes of the "someone" using the Net. Indeed, there is no way to verify that it is a "someone" at all. In the words of the famous *New Yorker* cartoon of two dogs sitting in front of a PC, "On the Internet, nobody knows you're a dog."[7] You can use the Net anonymously. You could build a (ro)bot to use the Net. No one need know your name, and there is no easy way to verify your age, your sex, or where you live. The Net knows only as much as you choose to tell, and it cannot even verify that information.

The second imperfection is information about the data—the *labels* or, as Nicholas Negroponte put it, the "headers."[8] Just as we have no system for obtaining verifiable information about the attributes of users, we have no system for obtaining verifiable information about the data on the Net. Data are out there—search engines report them to us—but there is no consistent or uniform way to know what they are. Pictures of flesh come across a screen, but the system cannot tell whether the pictures are medical photos or pornography. Data about bodily functions come across the wire, but the system cannot tell whether the data are from medical records or a novel. Nothing puts the bits into context, at least not in a way that a machine can use. Net95 had no requirement that data be labeled. "Packets" of data are labeled, in the sense of having an address. But beyond that, the packets could contain anything at all.

The final imperfection ties the first two together: because there is no simple way either to know who someone is or to classify data, there is no simple way to make access to data depend on who the user is and on the data he or she wants access to. In a word, there is no simple way to *zone* cyberspace.[9] In real space we have all sorts of zonings. Children cannot enter bars, men cannot enter women's bathrooms, the badly dressed cannot enter a trendy club. In countless ways we make access to spaces depend on who someone is. But in the cyberspace of Net95, because we cannot know the credentials of the user or the nature of the data, we cannot easily condition access on the credentials or the data.

These imperfections make regulating the Net difficult. But from the perspective of the anarchist, the libertarian, or the lover of the Net as it was, they are not imperfections at all. They are features. They do not disable something important from the Net as it was; they enable something important about the Net as it was—liberty. They are virtues of a space where control is limited, and they help constitute that space. The constitution of Net95 is unregulability; these features of its code make it so.

But Harvard shows the regulator how the "bugs" in Net95 might be eliminated. The Net *could* know the credentials of the user and the nature of the data and still be "the Net." The choice is not only between the Internet and a closed proprietary network. Harvard suggests a middle way. Control could be layered onto the platform of the Internet. *Architectures of control* could be layered on top of the Net to "correct" or eliminate "imperfections" of control. Architectures of credentials and architectures that label could, in other words, facilitate architectures of control.[10]

That is the first, and very small, claim of this early chapter in a story about emerging control: architectures of control are possible; they could be added to the Internet that we know.

But nothing yet shows how. What would get us from the relatively unregulable libertarian Net to a highly regulable Net of control?

This is the question for the balance of part 1. I move in two steps. In chapter 4, my claim is that *even without the government's help*, we will see the Net move to an architecture of control. In chapter 5, I sketch how government might help. The trends promise a highly regulable Net—not the libertarian's utopia, not the Net your father (or more likely your daughter or son) knew, but a Net whose essence is the character of control.

A Net, in other words, that flips the Internet as it was.

FOUR

architectures of control

MY AIM IN THE LAST CHAPTER WAS TO CRACK ONE MEME ABOUT THE NATURE OF THE Net—that the Net has a nature, and that its nature is liberty. I argued instead that the nature of the Net is set in part by its architectures, and that the possible architectures of cyberspace are many. The values that these architectures embed are different, and one type of difference is *regulability*—a difference in the ability to control behavior within a particular cyberspace. Some architectures make behavior more regulable; other architectures make behavior less regulable. These architectures are displacing architectures of liberty.

This chapter suggests how and why. In a nutshell: the why is commerce, and the how is through architectures that enable identification to enable commerce. As the Net is being remade to fit the demands of commerce, architectures are being added to make it serve commerce more efficiently. Regulability will be a by-product of these changes. Or put differently, the changes that make commerce possible are also changes that will make regulation easy.

I don't pick out commerce to pick on commerce. My argument is not that commerce is the enemy, nor that there is any necessary connection between commerce and regulability.[1] There is no doubt that commerce will flourish in the future of the Internet, and no doubt that is a good thing. The presence of commerce in the Net's future, however, does not mean that the Net of the future will be the same as the Net of the past. Commerce will change the Net, and my aim in this chapter is to help us understand how.

IDENTITY AND AUTHENTICATION: REAL SPACE

By "identity" I mean something more than just who you are. I mean all the facts about you that are true as well. Your identity, in this sense, includes your name, your sex, where you live, what your education is, your driver's license number, your social security number, your purchases on Amazon.com, whether you're a lawyer—and so on.

"Authentication" is the process by which aspects of your identity become known. Some become known when you reveal them; others become known whether you choose to reveal them or not. Perfect authentication would mean that others know for certain all the facts about you; happiness comes from others knowing a good deal less.

In real space much about your identity is revealed whether you want it revealed or not. Many of the facts about you, that is, are *automatically asserted* and *self-authenticating*. This is a fact about real-space life. If I walk into a bank, the teller will know a lot about me even if I don't say a thing: he will know I'm a puffy, middle-aged white guy with glasses and blondish hair; he will know I'm not big and not strong, though I am somewhat tall. He will know all this whether I want to tell him or not. I could, in principle, try to hide some of these facts—I could put on a mask, walk on stilts, and try to enter the bank incognito. But if I did, I would be more likely to get tackled by a security guard than to hide any feature about myself. Hiding usually does not hide itself very well; usually we reveal that we are hiding.

Other facts about me, however, are not automatically asserted or automatically self-authenticating. Some facts you can learn only if I tell you ("I broke my leg when I was six"); some you cannot authenticate without resorting to some other source—*credentials*. The police officer wants a driver's license, not your word that you are authorized to drive. A law school wants a copy of your college transcript, not a letter from you telling them that you graduated at the top of your class. A bank wants the deed on your house, not just a promise that you will repay the mortgage. In all these cases, facts about you must be *authenticated* by a document, and hence by an institution that stands behind the document.

Real-space life thus carries with it this mix of authenticating and authenticated credentials. Social life is a constant negotiation between these different credentials. In a small town, in a quieter time, documents as credentials were not terribly necessary. You were known by your face, and your face carried with it a reference (held in the common knowledge of the community) about your character. As life becomes more anonymous, social institutions must construct credentials to authenticate facts about you that in an earlier time, or in a smaller social world, would have been authenticated by the knowledge of the community about who you are.

The point may be obvious: the regulability of real-space life depends on these credentials. The fact that witnesses can identify who committed a crime, either because they know the person or because of self-authenticating features such as "he was a white male, six feet tall," enhances the ability of the state to regulate against that crime. If criminals were invisible or witnesses had no memory, crime would increase. The fact that fingerprints are hard to change and can now be traced to convicted felons increases the likelihood that felons will be caught again. Relying on a more changeable physical characteristic would reduce the ability of the police to track repeat offenders. The fact that cars have license plates and are registered by their owners increases the likelihood that a hit-and-run driver will be caught. Without licenses, and without systems registering owners, it would be extremely difficult to track car-related crime. In all these cases, and in many more, features of real-space life make regulating real-space life possible.

The state, as one regulator, thus depends on these features being as they are. Often the state will intervene, either to ensure that these credentials remain usable as credentials[2] or to substitute new credentials when an earlier credential becomes useless. The state punishes counterfeiters of state documents as a way of increasing the reliability of state documents. The state issues other credentials (driver's licenses) to increase the reliability of its verification.

This, then, is the nature of real-space regulation: much about who we are is revealed, and we have built institutions that can credential what cannot authentically be revealed. Both social life and state regulation depend on this mix. And both react as elements within this mix change.

IDENTITY AND AUTHENTICATION:
CYBERSPACE

Identity and authentication in cyberspace are different. The Internet is built on a simple suite of protocols—the basic TCP/IP suite. The TCP/IP suite includes protocols for exchanging packets of data between two machines "on" the Net.[3] (I explore this idea in greater detail in chapter 8. For now, think of the packets as small packages of information wrapped in an envelope with an address stamped on the outside.) To exchange these packets, the system needs at least two bits of data—the address of the machine from which the data are being sent, and the address of the machine to which the data are being sent. These are called Internet protocol (IP) addresses. They look like this: 128.34.35.204. Simplified brutally, a packet of data is carried "to" and "from" these addresses as it works its way across the Internet.

These protocols, however, reveal nothing about the user of the Internet, and very little about the data being exchanged. Although the IP address is sufficient to move the data from one machine to another, it has no necessary connection to any physical unit in the world. IP addresses are virtual addresses; the virtual can change. Nor do the IP protocols tell us much about the data being sent. In particular, they do not tell us who sent the data, from where the data were sent, to where (geographically) the data are going, for what purpose the data are going there, or what kind of data they are. None of this is known by the system, or knowable by us simply by looking at the data. From the perspective of the network, this other information is unnecessary surplus. Like a daydreaming postal worker, the network simply moves the data and leaves interpretation of the data to the applications at either end.

This minimalism in design is intentional. It reflects both a political decision about disabling control and a technological decision about the optimal network design. The designers were not interested in advancing social control; they were concerned with network efficiency. Thus, this design pushes complexity out of the basic Internet protocols, leaving it to the applications, or ends, to incorporate any sophistication that a particular service may require.[4]

When this basic protocol is translated into Internet access—when, for instance, you are browsing a web page—this minimal identification means that the server delivering the web page knows nothing about you *from the Internet protocol itself.* (We will consider later how it does learn things about you from other applications that sit on top of the Internet protocol.) The web server simply knows that you are located on the Internet at an IP address, and that you are coming onto the Net with a TCP/IP-compliant protocol.

It is as if you were in a carnival funhouse, with the lights dimmed to darkness and voices coming from around you, but from people you do not know and from places you cannot identify. The system knows that there are entities out there interacting with it, but it knows nothing about who those entities are. Whereas in real space—and here is the important point—anonymity has to be created, in cyberspace anonymity is the given.

IDENTITY AND AUTHENTICATION: REGULABILITY

This difference between the architectures of identity in real space and in cyberspace has profound consequences for the regulability of behavior in cyberspace. If regulation hangs upon identity—that is, on knowing at least something about the person being regulated—then in cyberspace, under TCP/IP's design, there is very little that the regulator would necessarily know. Unlike real space, cyberspace reveals no self-authenticating facts about identity. In real space you reveal your sex, your age, how you look, what language you speak, whether you can see, whether you can hear, how intelligent you are. In cyberspace you reveal only an address, and one that has no necessary relationship to anything else about you.

The absence of self-authenticating facts in cyberspace reduces its regulability. If a state, for example, wants to regulate obscenity or control children's access to "indecent" speech, the Internet architecture provides no help. Both data and people are unidentified in this world, and while it is often possible to make good guesses, it is also easy to make good guesses impossible. With the Internet architecture of Net95, it is easy to hide who you are. Perhaps more important, it is difficult to assert facts about your identity in a credible way. On the Internet it is both easy to hide that you are a dog and hard to prove that you are not.

All this is true under one architecture of the Internet. Claims about the difference between real space and cyberspace depend on this difference in design. The lesson of the last chapter, however, was that architectures could be different. We could imagine different architectures that would better help us identify who individuals are and authenticate other facts about them.

In the balance of this chapter, I want to introduce one such architecture. I will consider questions—about its use or justification, its possible threats to privacy or anonymity, or the likelihood of its becoming a dominant architecture—in later chapters. My aim here is to convince you that there are such architectures and to sketch the regulability that such an architecture would permit.

ARCHITECTURES OF IDENTIFICATION

How then could we layer architectures of identity onto the existing identity-ignorant architectures of TCP/IP?[5]

Consider three common techniques used today to identify someone on the Internet. There are others, and the description of these three will not be complete. But a sketch of these three reveals two features of a "pass-technology" that will be central to the architectures of identification that the Net is now building.

The first technique is a password. You have an account on a system; the account has your account name and password; when you access the system, you must provide both bits of information. The combination is what verifies that you are authorized to use the system.

There are any number of examples of identification of this sort. America Online (AOL) is a well-known one. You must type in a password associated with a particular "screen name" before you can enter AOL. Lexis—a provider of online legal resources—is a second, though Lexis requires only a single password (not an account name as well) to enter. Uses of the database are then charged to that password.

A password system has well-known advantages and disadvantages. The main advantage is its security—at least as long as the user keeps his or her password secret. The disadvantage is cost and the inconvenience of continually using passwords to move from one space to another.[6] If every site on the Net required some sort of password, then surfing would be as tedious as crossing Manhattan during Friday rush hour.

A second, and much cruder system avoids this inconvenience. This system uses verification through a "cookie"—a small entry made by your browser to a "cookie file" on your hard disk that allows a site to know who you are.[7] When you first purchase a book from Amazon.com and establish an account, for example, Amazon.com's server places an entry in your cookie file. When you return to that site, your browser sends the cookie along with the request for the site; the server can then set your preferences according to your account. Amazon.com can recommend books for you to buy, given the pattern of purchases you have made before.

The main advantage in this system is its seamless verification. Unless you have your browser set to notify you of cookie exchanges, you can surf through sites that deposit and consume cookies with little interruption.

The disadvantage is the danger that your cookie file could be manipulated or even copied to other systems.[8] It could also provide a key with which providers can learn about you. If a common cookie identifies you across a number of sites (because these sites have subscribed, for example, to a common tracking system), then, in principle, if you have revealed information about yourself in one of those places, the other places could know it as well.

Cookies are less secure than passwords, though of course they are doing something very different. This difference does not mean they are useless. The security we need is a function of the risk we are protecting against. Certainly, the NSA should not use cookies as the system for granting access to databanks of national secrets. But there is no reason why a portal site like Yahoo should not use cookies to figure out who you are and to give you the news that you have previously selected. You have little incentive to lie about this; Yahoo! has little reason to care if you do. With so little at stake, an unobtrusive if insecure system is perfectly adequate.

A third technology would marry the benefits of the first two. This is the technology of digital signatures, which enables *digital certificates,* a kind of passport on the Internet. They would authenticate any type of information about a machine and, if unlocked by a pass-phrase or biometric device, about you—your name, your citizenship, your age, whether you are a lawyer. While the details of the architecture are many, suffice it for now to define them as encrypted digital objects that can be used to authenticate facts about someone.

Digital certificates would reside on your computer (under at least some designs); a server would automatically (and invisibly) check the certificate as you entered the site. If you held the right certificate, you would be let in, and as you were let in, the server would then "know" the certified facts about you. It would "know," that is, that you were a man, or that you came from Canada, or that you were over the age of twenty-five. And it could do or know all this without ever asking you anything at all. Certificates could become the kind of self-authenticating credential that we know in real space, but unlike in real space, there would be no limit to the facts the certificate could certify.

Digital certificates would make possible a secure system of identification that could operate as seamlessly as cookies but with much more data certified. They rely, however, on technologies of cryptography. To see how, we must take a detour into the workings of cryptography, and then consider again how this technology could be molded to the form of identification.

CRYPTOGRAPHY: CONFIDENTIALITY
VERSUS AUTHENTICATION

Here is something that will sound very extreme but is at most, I think, a slight exaggeration: encryption technologies are the most important technological breakthrough in the last one thousand years. No other technological discovery—from nuclear weapons (I hope) to the Internet—will have a more significant impact on social and political life. Cryptography will change everything.

I say this not because I have the space in this book, or ability in any case, to prove this claim to you. I say this to emphasize. It's not important that you understand the underlying technologies, though it would be great if more people did. What is important is that you get a hint of the purposes to which these technologies can be turned, and the consequences of their power.

Cryptography is Janus-faced: it has an ambiguous relationship to freedom on the Internet. As Stewart Baker and Paul Hurst put it, cryptography "surely is the best of technologies and the worst of technologies. It will stop crimes and it will create new crimes. It will undermine dictatorships, and it will drive them to new excesses. It will make us all anonymous, and it will track our every transaction."[9]

Cryptography can be all these things, both good and bad, because encryption can serve two fundamentally different ends. In its "confidentiality" function it can be "used to keep communications secret." In its "identification" function it can be "used to provide forgery-proof digital identities."[10] It thus enables freedom from regulation (as it enhances confidentiality), but it can also enable regulation (as it enhances identification).[11]

Its traditional use is secrets. Encrypt a message, and only those with the proper key can open and read it. This type of encryption has been around as long as language itself. But until the mid-1970s it suffered from an important weakness: the same key that was used to encrypt a message was also used to decrypt it. So if you lost that key, all the messages hidden with that key were also rendered vulnerable. If a large number of messages were encrypted with the same key, losing the key compromised the whole archive of secrets protected by the key. This risk was significant. You always had to "transport" the key needed to unlock the message, and inherent in that transport was the risk that the key would be lost.

In the mid-1970s, however, a breakthrough in encryption technique was announced by two computer scientists, Whitfield Diffie and Martin Hellman.[12] Rather than relying on a single key, the Diffie-Hellman system used two keys—one public, the other private. What is encrypted with one can be decrypted only with the other. Even with one key there is no way to infer the other.

This discovery was the clue to an architecture that could build an extraordinary range of confidence into any network, whether or not the physical network itself was secure. Even if the wires are tapped, this type of encryption still achieves its magic. We can get a hint of how in a series of cases whose accumulating impact makes the potential clear.

A. If I want to send a message to you that I know only you will be able to read, I can take your public key and use it to encrypt that message. Then I can send that message to you knowing that only the holder of the private key (presumably you) will be able to read it. *But you cannot be sure it is I who sent you the message.* Because anyone can encrypt a message using your public key and then send it to you, you have no way to be certain that I was the one who sent it. Therefore, consider the next example.

B. Before I send the message I have encrypted with your public key, I can encrypt it with my private key. Then when you receive the message from me, you can first decrypt it with my public key, and then decrypt it again with your private key. After the first decryption, you can be sure that I (or the holder of my private key) was the one who sent you the message; after the second decryption, you can be sure that only you (or other holders of your private key) actually read the content of the message. But how do you know that what I say is the public key of Larry Lessig is actually the public key of Larry Lessig? How can you be sure, that is, that the public key you are using is actually the public key it purports to be? Here is where the next example comes in.

C. If there is a trustworthy third party (say, my bank, or the Federal Reserve Board, or the ACLU) with a public key (a fact I am able to verify because of the prominence of the institution), and that third party verifies that the public key of Larry Lessig is actually the public key of Larry Lessig, then along with my message sent to you, encrypted first in your public key and second in my private key, would be a certificate, issued by that institution, itself encrypted with the institution's private key. When you receive the message, you can use the institution's public key to decrypt the certificate; take from the certificate my public key (which you now are fairly confident is my public key); decrypt the message I sent you with the key held in the certificate (after which you are fairly confident comes from me); and then decrypt the message encrypted with your public key (which you can be fairly confident no one else has read). If we did all that, you would know that I am who I say I am and that the message was sent by me; I would know that only you read the message; and you would know that no one else read the message along the way.

I could add any number of complications (for example, how can I be certain that you are who you say you are? Clue: the same way you can be certain that I am who I say I am), and I have hidden a number of important simplifications. For example, it turns out that it is simpler not to encrypt the whole message with a dual key system but rather to encrypt only a symmetric key[13] using a dual key system.[14] My aim, however, is simply to outline the basic elements of this architecture: a system of dual or asymmetric encryption, and a system of trusted third parties that can certify facts about you. The world I am describing would have both of these elements automatically and seamlessly executed.

The encryption I've been describing is called "public key" encryption—again, because it has two keys, one public, one private, unlike traditional single key encryption. As the last step of this encryption process makes clear, the system depends on an infrastructure—not an infrastructure of special wires or protected pathways, but an infrastructure of trust, which can provide not perfect confidence but *enough* confidence through the multiplication of assertions about authenticity to make it certain *enough* that the fact certified by a particular signature is true.

An infrastructure that supports a public key system is called "PKI" (public key infrastructure).[15] The first point to see is the potential that a well-established PKI creates. With a robust PKI, the possibilities for identification become extraordinary. Individuals could carry certificates that authenticate any number of facts about themselves—who they are; personal attributes (age, citizenship, sex, marital status, sexual orientation, HIV status); professional credentials (college degrees, bar certification, and so on). These certificates could reside on their personal computers, and when they attempted to enter an Internet site, that site would check the certificate and let them pass if they held the proper certificate. It would deny access if they did not. A world with a robust PKI would enable an unlimited range of cheap authentication, and hence an unlimited range of zoning—of conditioning access to Internet sites based on the credentials held by the user.

But only *if.* Whether such architectures will come to exist is a different question. Systems close to these are already being developed, though none operate as generally as I've just described. The dominant model of certificates today is identification—certificates that verify that you are who you say you are. As described by Verisign, the current leader issuing digital certificates:

> Think of Digital IDs as the electronic equivalent of driver licenses or passports that reside in your Internet browser and e-mail software. They contain information that uniquely identifies you, and allow you to: Digitally sign a message so your recipient knows that a message really came from you. Encrypt a message so your intended recipient can decrypt and read its contents and attachments.
>
> By digitally signing and encrypting your e-mail you can ensure that your confidential messages and attachments are protected from tampering, impersonation and eavesdropping.[16]

But verifying a user's identity is only the first part of the architecture I am describing; any model limited to identity will have limited appeal. Businesses do not really care that I am able to certify that I am Larry Lessig, and that Larry Lessig works for Harvard. What they want to know is whether I have the authority to purchase fifty thousand computers for Harvard if they receive from me an order for fifty thousand computers. Or whether a certain loan officer is authorized to commit to a certain size loan. Or they want to know whether a representative is actually authorized to make a specific commitment.

In short, what is desired is a more flexible system of certification—a system, that is, that allows people to certify any sort of fact or statement that they would want to make. So, for example, if I am authorized to purchase computer equipment for Harvard Law School, Harvard Law School would give me a certificate that authenticates that fact; someone would in turn certify that the certificate I hold from Harvard Law School is in fact a certificate from Harvard Law School; and when MicroWarehouse receives an e-mail with an order for fifty thousand computers, it would automatically work through the system of certifications to confirm the order.

This more flexible system is the kernel of an architecture of identity that would render cyberspace regulable. The architecture would allow you to certify any fact or statement about yourself to which you could get a third party to attest.[17] In principle, you could hold a credential for every aspect of your "identity"—every fact about yourself that you wanted to authenticate—from your age all the way down to the grade you got in spelling in the second grade. (As Michael Froomkin suggests, Lily Tomlin's joke, "It will be a mark on your permanent record that will follow you for the rest of your life," is no longer a joke.)[18] Depending on how much you trust the third party, that certification would allow you (as the skeptical user) to believe the person making the assertions.

But again, why would we expect this system to develop? What benefit would it produce, and who stands to gain from this benefit? I've laid responsibility at the foot of Internet commerce. What needs of Internet commerce would push us to a certificate-rich architecture?

THE CONTROLS FOR COMMERCE

The Internet was built for research, not commerce. (Indeed, until 1991 the National Science Foundation forbade its use for commerce.)[19] Its protocols were open and unsecured; it was not designed to hide. Data transmitted over this net could easily be intercepted and stolen; confidential data could not easily be protected.

Early users did not seem to mind this drawback. If secrecy was important, they were quite capable of encrypting a message. And for most communication, security was not important. In this world the ethic was openness, and openness was affordable.

But commerce is not so laid-back. At first, vendors were quite anxious about on-line transactions; credit card companies initially did not want their numbers used in cyberspace—at least, not until cyberspace changed. From the start commerce has pushed for changes in the architectures of the Net to enable more secure and safer commerce.

Of course, there is nothing new about this or about commerce on the wires. As Jane Winn puts it, electronic commerce is "arguably as old as the telegraph."[20] The 1970s saw a vast increase in closed architecture systems that used the wires (either proprietary or not) to exchange data to facilitate commerce. The significance of the recent birth of e-commerce is that it takes place on an open, unsecured network.[21] The challenge for commerce on the early Net was to develop architectures that, while sharing in the network advantages of the Internet,[22] would restore some of the security that commerce requires.

A kind of "open-system" security was needed, and the most successful early example was Netscape's secure socket layer (SSL) protocol.[23] Beginning with Netscape Enterprise Server 2.0, secure servers could exchange encrypted transactional information with Internet browser clients. For example, you could send your credit card number across the Net, and neither you nor Visa would have to worry that it would be intercepted and republished.

The great advantage of SSL was its simplicity and economy, benefits it gained by mixing the best of two different encryption key techniques, symmetric and asymmetric encryption algorithms. The advantage of symmetric encryption is efficiency—it is easier for the computer to decrypt using a symmetric key. The disadvantage is security—you have to pass the symmetric key around, and sometimes it gets lost. The advantage of asymmetric, or public key, encryption is security—you do not have to pass around a private key and risk the loss of the key. The disadvantage is efficiency—it takes a lot of computing power to decrypt an asymmetrically encrypted message.

SSL mixes these two techniques by encrypting the symmetric key asymmetrically. Once encrypted, the symmetric key is safe to use on an insecure network. But because a key is relatively small, it is not a terrible computational burden to decrypt it on the other side. By using asymmetric encryption to protect the key, there is no danger that the key will be revealed in transmission, but by using a symmetric key to encrypt all other data exchanged, the computational burden on both sides is reduced.

The trouble with SSL, however, is that it is trustworthy only if you can trust the merchant on the other side. Your information is not likely to leak in the transmission from client to server. But if the owner of the server is not to be trusted, then the risk you should worry about is not a leaky pipeline.

Other protocols have been proposed to deal with the problem of the untrustworthy merchant, the most prominent of which is the secure electronic transaction (SET) protocol.[24] SET is a standard adopted by a consortium of credit card companies for exchanging credit card data to facilitate greater security, using a protocol that still simply sits on top of the basic Internet protocol.[25] With SET, you can be confident that your credit card number will not be overheard and that the merchant cannot misuse your number.

These two protocols are just the first steps in constructing an architecture of security for e-commerce. (Though SET may be a misstep: developed by committee, it is a standard that has proven too complicated to implement effectively.)[26] They are significant improvements, but they do not represent the real change to come. For e-commerce to develop fully, the Net will need a far more general architecture of trust—an architecture that makes possible secure and private transactions.

The elements of any such architecture are summarized well by Gail L. Grant.[27] This architecture would have to provide (1) authentication, to ensure the identity of the person you are dealing with; (2) authorization, to ensure that the person is sanctioned for a particular function; (3) privacy, to ensure that others cannot see what exchanges there are; (4) integrity, to ensure that the transmission is not altered en route; and (5) nonrepudiation, to ensure that the sender of a message cannot deny that he sent it.

In real space we achieve each of these elements through familiar real-space architectures of trust. So familiar have these become that we are likely not only to forget the efforts originally made to erect some of them, but also to ignore the features of real space that make these architectures possible. It is usually obvious if an envelope has been opened. If a signature has been changed, we can usually tell. People we know self-authenticate, since we recognize them when they come into a store. If we do not know them, we can check a driver's license or the validity of their credit card. (Possessing a valid credit card is another kind of self-authentication, though obviously an imperfect one.) We check authorization with structures such as purchase orders or letters of introduction. We protect privacy by using secure envelopes, and we protect integrity by checking for evidence of tampering on a letter that has been received. We use systems of certified exchange (certified mail, guaranteed delivery) to avoid the problem of repudiation of receipt or sending.

These architectures in real space become invisible to us, but they are obviously constructs, and just as obviously they are expensive to construct. (This is the difficulty Russia faces now.) If e-commerce is to develop, we must erect equivalent architectures in cyberspace. Commerce will have to develop ways to provide vendors with sufficient security in online transactions while minimizing the burden of that security.

Again, the core of any such architecture will be tools of encryption and PKI. The core would permit the authentication of a digital certificate that verifies facts about you—your identity, citizenship, sex, age, or the authority you hold. And while we could erect an architecture of certification today—there are private certificate servers that we could use to issue certificates covering any conceivable fact—the system would not support e-commerce until these certificates were part of a general public key infrastructure that permitted secure and trustworthy communication with anyone on the Net. An architecture that contained all these elements would provide e-commerce with a security greater than the best security in real space. My view is that online commerce will not fully develop until such an architecture is established.

There are many plans for deploying this architecture.[28] Some imagine the government as the certifying authority; others imagine trusted third parties (like banks) in that role. Any number of paths are possible.[29] The key to all of these, however, is not that a government requires people to hold such IDs.[30] The key instead is *incentives:* systems that build the incentives for individuals voluntarily to hold IDs. When architectures accommodate users who come with an ID installed and make life difficult for users who refuse to bear an ID, certification will spread quickly.

Cookies have spread in just this way. Because many people are concerned with the privacy implications of cookies, browsers have enabled users to choose whether to accept them. With one click, you can disable the deposit of cookies and so prevent the owner of a web site from selling information about you.

But this privacy comes at a cost. Users who choose this option are either unable to use areas of the Net where cookies are required or forced constantly to choose whether a cookie will be deposited. Most find the hassle too great and simply accept cookies on their machine.

We will see a similar development with digital IDs. Life will be easier for those who carry ID than for those who do not. Servers will make exchanges cheaper, or simpler, if data can be authenticated. Just as it is easier to accept cookies automatically, so too will it be easier to authenticate facts about yourself. Life in an authenticating world will be simpler for those who authenticate.

If the system spreads with incentives, then we can see why commerce is so good at spreading the system. Commerce has an incentive itself to increase the authentication and certification of transactions in cyberspace. And it is in a good position to give incentives to consumers. Incentives are commerce's best tool of regulation, and commerce is fairly good at deploying them.

Nonetheless, there is room for skepticism. No doubt there will be significant hurdles for the community to overcome as competitors fix on standards that provide a sufficiently robust yet flexible exchange. No doubt there are lots of reasons to wonder whether this infrastructure of security can develop on its own. In my view, we can see enough to be confident that it is already developing: technologies that build encryption into the background of an application are becoming common; networks are rapidly integrating digital signatures; and a host of companies (called "certificate authorities") now provide digital certificates.[31]

You do not have to believe in the invisible hand to be convinced that this infrastructure of trust is coming. Even if you doubt that private interests alone could achieve this coordination, another factor suggests that the character of the Net is about to flip. If commerce alone cannot succeed in establishing these architectures, government is in a strong position to bring about just the changes that commerce needs.

The government can help commerce. How it does so is the subject of the chapter that follows.

F I V E

regulating code

I'VE ARGUED THAT AS THE NET CHANGES TO ENABLE COMMERCE, ONE BY-PRODUCT OF
this change will be to enable regulation. But let's say you don't buy it. Let's say that
you don't believe that the invisible hand acting alone will erect the infrastructure of
trust (and in turn regulation) that I said commerce needed. Let's say you think the
coordination needed is too great and that market incentives will create more confusion than guidance. If you are right, if commerce on its own does not flip the Net,
will the Net remain unregulable?

The answer is no. Commerce does not act alone, and it is not morally opposed to
partnerships with government. If commerce needs help constructing this architecture of trust, or (more likely) if the government begins to understand the value of an
architecture of trust for its own regulatory objective, then government will help
push the code along.

But how? So far I have left standing the assumption that it is impossible for the
government to regulate the Net, that there is something in the nature of the Net that
makes such regulation unworkable. So how is it possible for government to help? If
the Net is unregulable, how could government regulate it to make the Net more regulable?

REGULATING ARCHITECTURE

To see how, we must distinguish between two claims. One is that, *given the architecture of the Net as it is,* it is difficult for government to regulate behavior on the
Net. The other is that, given the architecture of the Net, it is difficult for the government to *regulate the architecture of the Net.* The first claim, I believe, is true.
The second is not. Even if it is hard to regulate behavior given the Net as it is, it is
not hard for the government to take steps to alter, or supplement, the architecture

of the Net. And it is those steps in turn that could make behavior on the Net more regulable.

This is a regulatory two-step: the Net cannot be regulated now, but if the government regulates the architecture of the Net, it could be regulated in the future. And when government regulation of the architecture of the Net is tied to the changes that commerce is already introducing, I argue, the government will need to do very little to make behavior on the Net highly regulable.

This strategy of regulation is nothing new. From the beginning of the modern state, government has been regulating to make its regulations work better. My point is only to apply this commonplace to cyberspace. I want you to see how this old strategy works here.

I begin the chapter with some examples of regulation working, or not working, in spaces close to cyberspace. Once you see the pattern, you will see how the pattern might be applied elsewhere.

Telephones

The architecture of the telephone network[1] has undergone a radical shift as it has moved from a circuit-switched to a packet-switched network. There is a certain irony in this change: digital networks were the original design of the Internet. When the first architects of what would become the Internet went to AT&T in the early 1960s for help in building this digital network, AT&T told them that a packet-switched network could not work.[2] Indeed, AT&T at first refused to give the designers any help at all, so convinced were they that the design was a waste of time. But however convinced they were, eventually they changed their minds. Now we have a telephone system that is increasingly like the Internet.

Digital telephone networks work in the same way as the Net. Packets of information are spewed across the system. As with the Internet, nothing ensures that they will travel in the same way, or along the same path. They take the most efficient path, which depends on the demand at any one time.

But this creates the problem that the Communications Assistance for Law Enforcement Act of 1994 (CALEA) was designed to solve.[3] As telephone networks have moved from analog to digital, and as switching technologies have moved from central switching to distributed, this change (in the code regulating networks) has had an important consequence for law enforcement. Because there is no longer a predictable path through which a telephone call will pass, it is no longer an easy matter to tap a phone. Whereas tapping telephones was once relatively simple, it is now quite difficult.

This is the case at least with *one version* of the architecture of a digitally switched telephone network. Other versions would be less difficult to tap. The question that regulators faced was which version the telephone network should adopt. And the difference between versions is just a choice of code. Some codes cost more than others, and some codes protect privacy better than others. So the choice among codes becomes a choice among values. Congress asked whether this choice should be solely private (made by telephone engineers) or partially public (influenced by Congress). It chose the latter.

Of course, regulating the network code is not the only means of regulation that Congress had. Congress could have compensated for any loss in crime prevention resulting from the change in the network code by changing the punishments. If a change in network architecture made it more difficult to catch criminals, Congress could simply increase the threatened punishment or devote more resources to investigation.

This is just what happened, Seventh Circuit Court of Appeals Chief Judge Richard Posner argues, when the Warren Court constitutionalized criminal procedure. To compensate for the increased difficulty in convicting a criminal, Congress radically increased criminal punishments.[4] Professor William Stuntz has made a similar point.[5] The Constitution, in this story, acted as an exogenous constraint to which Congress could adjust. If the protections of the Constitution increased, then Congress could compensate by increasing punishments.

When the constraint is imposed by code, however, Congress has a more direct way to respond: it can legislate to change the code. Congress can require that telephone companies adopt a code architecture that makes the network wiretap-accessible.

This is just what CALEA did. No doubt CALEA's ultimate aim in requiring this architecture is to reduce crime, but it pursues this aim indirectly, by modifying the code to constrain individuals who might want to engage in crime. Because the government can once again tap when it has authority to tap, digital networks are no longer as helpful for criminals. Hence, the payoff from crime is reduced.

This is law regulating code. Its indirect effect is to improve law enforcement, but it does so by modifying code-based constraints on law enforcement. It selects an architecture that distributes the burdens of code in a collectively valued way.[6]

Regulation like this works because telephone companies are few. It is relatively easy for the government to verify that the telephone company is complying with its rules; it would be hard to establish a rogue telephone company (outside the context of Internet telephony at least). Thus, indirect regulation depends on there being a useful target for regulation. But if there is such a target, and that target can control the code of the network, then the government can regulate the code.

Telephones: Part 2

Four years after Congress enacted CALEA, the FBI petitioned the Federal Communications Commission (FCC) to enhance even further government's power to regulate. Among the amendments the FBI proposed was a regulation designed to require disclosure of the locations of individuals using cellular phones.[7]

The idea was this. Cellular phone systems, to ensure seamless switching between transmitters, collect information about the location of a user when she is using a cellular phone. Beyond billing, the phone companies do not need this information for any other purpose. But the FBI has interests beyond those of the phone service. The FBI would like that data made available to it whenever it has a "legitimate law enforcement reason" for requesting it. The amendment to CALEA would require the cellular company to provide this information, which is a way of indirectly requiring that it write its code to make the information retrievable.[8]

The original motivation for this requirement was simple enough. Emergency service providers needed a simple way to determine where an emergency cellular phone call was coming from. But of course, if that were the only purpose of the change, the system could be designed to report location information only when an emergency call is made. Instead, the push is to require the collection of this information whenever a call is made.

If it succeeds, then the FBI succeeds by getting Congress to legislate a different code for cellular phones. If Congress regulates the code, tracking individuals becomes easier, and thus the regulability of those tracked increases.

T a p e s

A compact disc (CD) recording is a digital recording. Like any digital recording, it can, in principle, be copied perfectly. But before the advent of digital tapes, and then computers, there was no medium onto which a digital CD could be perfectly copied. To copy it onto an audiotape was to make an analog recording of the digital file. Quality would be lost in the copy.

This imperfection in copying ability was a type of protection for CD producers. Real-space code, as it were, constrained the ability of copyright thieves to copy CDs onto tape and sell them as pirated editions. The inferiority of such tapes kept most of the public in the legitimate CD market.

Digital audio technology (DAT) threatened to change this balance. DAT was the application of digital technology to tape: a digital recording on a CD could be digitally, and hence perfectly, copied onto a tape. You could buy one CD and make many copies of it onto DAT tape, each copy having the same fidelity as the first. The code governing the copying of audio recordings thus changed, eliminating the old code's implicit protections.

Congress could have responded to this change in any number of ways. It could have used law to regulate behavior directly, by increasing the penalty for illegal copying. It could have funded a public ad campaign against illegal copying or funded programs in schools to discourage students from buying pirated editions of popular recordings. Or Congress could have taxed blank tapes and then transferred the revenue to owners of copyrighted material.

Instead, Congress chose to regulate the code of digital reproduction.[9] It required producers of digital recording devices to install in their systems a chip that implements a code-based system to monitor the copies of any copy made on that machine.[10] The chip would allow a limited number of personal copies. On copies of copies, the quality of the recording would be degraded. Congress in essence required that the code of digital copying be modified to restore the imperfections that were "natural" in the earlier code.

This again is Congress regulating code as a means of regulating behavior—mandating that multiple copies be imperfect as a way to minimize illegal copying. Like the telephone regulation, this regulation succeeds because there are relatively few manufacturers of DAT technology. Again, given a limited target, the government's regulation can be effective.

Televisions

A fourth example is much closer to cyberspace. The Telecommunications Act of 1996 required the television industry to develop and implement the "V-chip."[11] The V-chip would facilitate the automatic blocking of television broadcasts, based on criteria of content that have not yet been completely determined. The crudest proposals involve something like the Motion Picture Association's movie rating system; the more sophisticated envision selections based on a much richer set of factors.

The legislation was passed in response to the perception that violence on television had increased dramatically, and that this increase was harmful to kids. People were concerned that TV violence would affect behavior. Studies had suggested as much; less reflective evidence had confirmed it. Congress sought to discourage the violence by providing a way to filter it out.[12]

Given the state of First Amendment law, it would have been difficult for Congress to restrict violence on TV directly. (Though the regulation of broadcasting has been subject to special First Amendment rules,[13] and the life of these doctrines now seems limited.)[14] Even if applied only to children's television, such regulation would raise difficult constitutional questions—difficult enough, that is, to motivate Congress to seek a different way.

Thus Congress chose code. It required television manufacturers and media producers to develop a technology to rate what is broadcast on television so that parents could block what they do not want their children to see. It requires that televisions be built with a code that facilitates discrimination by consumers of television broadcasting. And it does this to advance a social aim of the government: to empower parents. By giving parents more power to discriminate, Congress indirectly discourages an ill (exposure to violence) that it is constitutionally unable to regulate directly.[15]

Encryption

The examples so far have involved regulations directed against code writers. But sometimes the government tries to act indirectly by using the market to regulate the code. An example is the government's failed attempt to secure Clipper as the standard for encryption technology.[16]

I have already sketched the Janus-faced nature of encryption: the same technology enables both confidentiality and identification. The government is concerned with the confidentiality part. Encryption allows individuals to make their conversations or data exchanges untranslatable except by someone with a key. How untranslatable is a matter of debate,[17] but we can put that debate aside for the moment: it is too untranslatable for the government's liking. So the government sought to control the use of encryption technology by getting the Clipper chip accepted as a standard for encryption.

The mechanics of the Clipper chip are not easily summarized, but its aim is to permit encryption that keeps open a back door for the government.[18] A conversation could be encrypted so that others could not understand it but the government would have the ability (in most cases with a court order) to decrypt the conversation using a special key.

The Clinton administration first thought that the best way to ensure the creation of this technology was through direct regulation—by banning all other encryption technology. This strategy proved controversial, so the government then fixed on a different technique.[19] It subsidized the development and deployment of the Clipper chip.

The thinking was obvious: if the government could get industry to use Clipper by making Clipper the cheapest technology, then it could indirectly regulate the use of encryption. The market would do the regulation for the government.[20]

The subsidy plan failed. Skepticism about the quality of the code itself, and about the secrecy with which it had been developed, as well as strong opposition to any governmentally directed encryption regime (especially a U.S.-sponsored regime), led most to reject the technology. This forced the government to take another path.

That alternative is for our purposes the more interesting. In the government's most recent proposals, the authors of encryption code would be regulated directly—with a requirement that they build into their code a back door through which the government could gain access.[21] While the proposals have been various, they all aim at ensuring that the government has a way to crack whatever encryption code a user selects.

Compared with other strategies—banning the use of encryption or flooding the market with an alternative encryption standard—this mode presents a number of advantages.

First, unlike banning the use of encryption, this mode of regulation does not directly interfere with the rights of use by individuals. It therefore is not vulnerable to a strong, if yet unproven constitutional claim that an individual has a right "to speak through encryption."[22] It aims only to change the mix of encryption technologies available, not to control directly any particular use by an individual. State regulation of the writing of encryption code is just like state regulation of the design of automobiles: individual use is not regulated. Second, unlike the technique of subsidizing one market solution, this solution allows the market to compete to provide the best encryption system, given this regulatory constraint. Finally, unlike both other solutions, this solution involves the regulation of only a relatively small number of actors, since manufacturers of encryption technology are far fewer in number than users or buyers of encryption systems.

Like the other examples in this section, then, this solution is an example of the government regulating code directly so as to better regulate behavior indirectly. As in other examples, the government uses the architecture of the code to reach a particular substantive end. Here the end, as with digital telephony, is to ensure that the government's ability to search certain conversations is not blocked by emerging technology.

Circumvention

My final example is the most recent. As I discuss in some detail in chapter 10, many businesses are developing systems for protecting intellectual property in cyberspace. The problem is the same as with digital audio technology. Copies in cyberspace are digital and free; digital copies are perfect; free copies are cheap. The fear is that cyberspace will become the place where copyright can be defeated. Using MP3 technologies, for example, a CD recording can be compressed to a file the size of the Word file containing this book and in seconds e-mailed to one hundred friends around the world.

The systems being developed in response will make it hard to copy without permission. How hard, and how they will work, are questions we can postpone for now. Suffice it to say that the systems are designed to give holders of intellectual property more power over the distribution of that property.

These protections are built into the systems through code. But code can also be used to circumvent such protections. (Remember the copy protection systems for software common in the early 1980s, and the cracking software used to defeat them.) Using circumvention software, then, users could defeat the protection that code creates.

Congress responded to this threat.[23] In the 1998 Digital Millennium Copyright Act, Congress made it a felony to write and sell software that circumvents copyright management schemes.[24] In the judgment of Congress, regulating users alone would be difficult but regulating the code that users use would not be as difficult.

CERTIFICATION AND REGULABILITY

All six of these examples describe a behavior that the government wants to regulate, but which it cannot (easily) regulate directly. So government regulates behavior indirectly by regulating architectures, which in turn influence or constrain behavior differently. This indirect regulation, at times quite effective, suggests a way of thinking about the example that started us down this road—certification.

At the start of this chapter we asked: What steps could government take, not to regulate a particular behavior, but to increase the regulability of behavior in cyberspace generally? My claim was that this goal could be achieved by increasing the capacity of sites on the Net to identify whom they are dealing with—to know either who the user is or what credentials, or features, he or she possesses.

Regulability then depends in part on identification—not perfect identification (the police do not need to know my name to tell me to slow my car down), but enough for the government to know what regulations the user is subject to, and when he has violated them.

How can the government facilitate this identification—assuming, of course, that commerce has not by itself created a sufficient demand for credentials?

It seems clear from the six examples above that the best target of such regulation will not be the individual. If the government required all individuals to carry a digital ID, there would no doubt be a revolution. Americans are antsy enough about a national identity card.[25] They are not likely to be interested in an Internet identity card.

But it does not follow that government cannot create incentives for people to adopt identification technologies, even without directly mandating them. There is no requirement that all citizens have a driver's license, but you would find it very hard to get around without one, even if you do not drive. The government does not require that you keep state-issued identification on your person, but if you want to fly to another city, you must show at least one form of such identification. The lesson is simple: make the incentive to carry ID so strong that no government requirement is necessary.

In the same way, the government could create incentives to enable digital IDs, not by regulating individuals directly but by regulating intermediaries. Intermediaries are fewer, their interests are usually commercial, and they are ordinarily pliant targets of regulation.

Consider some of the means that the government could employ to achieve this end:

- Sites on the Net have the ability to condition access based on whether someone carries the proper credential. The government has the power to require sites to impose a condition that users carry the proper credentials. For example, the state could require that gambling sites check the age and residency of anyone trying to use the site. Many sites could be required to check the citizenship of potential users, or any number of other credentials. As more and more sites complied with this requirement, individuals would have a greater and greater incentive to carry the proper credentials. The more credentials they carried, the easier it would be to impose regulations on them.[26]
- The government could give a $50 tax break to anyone who filed his or her income tax signed by a properly certified authority; it could certify these authorities based on whether they coded certificates in the way the government

wanted, and whether they permitted the certificates to be used for purposes beyond the government's limited use.

- The government could impose a 10 percent Internet sales tax and then exempt anyone who purchased goods with a certificate that authenticated their state of residence; the state would then be able to collect whatever local tax applied when it was informed of the purchase.[27]
- The government could charge users for government publications unless they gained access to the site with a properly authenticated certificate.
- As in other Western democracies, the government could mandate voting[28]— and then establish Internet voting; voters would come to the virtual polls with a digital identity that certified them as registered.

All these alternatives would use the same strategy of indirect regulation that marked the original six examples. The state would regulate intermediate providers, enabling those providers to regulate users, who would find their access conditioned on providing credentials, which make it easier for the state to regulate. The state would be using the market to regulate individuals, and to make the Net itself more regulable.

We can extend this model of regulation to the regulation of code itself. The government could require Internet service providers (ISPs), for example, to employ software that facilitates traceability by conditioning access on the user's providing some minimal level of identification. Call this a "traceability regulation." Many ISPs would resist it, but the government could then require that major commercial institutions (including credit institutions) be prohibited from dealing with any ISP not certified to be in compliance with the traceability regulation. Some major institutions, in turn, might resist this requirement, but not many. For major institutions in a competitive market, the threat of governmental prosecution far outweighs any incentive to violate the law. These two steps would create a great incentive for local ISPs to facilitate traceability.

Such a rule, of course, raises serious constitutional questions. I consider some of them in the chapters that follow. My aim here is simply to sketch the techniques that could enable an effective ID requirement in cyberspace. The point is that within an integrated commercial and noncommercial network the government's power over commercial entities leverages into a power over noncommercial entities. Bringing commerce to the Net was the first, essential, and perhaps sufficient step in making the Net regulable. More active intervention by the government will make it even more so.

So far, however, governments have not been good at encouraging an architecture of identification. Not only have they been slow, but through clumsy legislation they have inhibited its growth.[29] In my view, however, these errors are short-term. We cannot count on the government making errors forever, especially when so much hangs on the construction of an effective PKI architecture.

A crucial assumption is built into all these examples. I've assumed that there are entities responsible for the code that individuals use, and that these entities can be effectively regulated. And as the open code software movement grows, it is important to ask whether this assumption is really true. The government can regulate the telephone companies (they are few in number, well known, and loaded with tangible assets), but how can it regulate code writers? In particular, how can the government regulate code writers who are committed to resisting precisely such regulation?

This is the topic of the last chapter in part 2—the effect of the open code movement on government's power to regulate. But we can make a few points here.

In a world where the code writers were the sort of people who governed the Internet Engineering Task Force[30] of a few years ago, government's power to regulate code would be slight. The underpaid heroes who built the Net have ideological reasons to resist government's mandate. They are not likely to yield to its threats. And unlike some commercial interests, they do not have millions riding on a single architecture winning out in the end. Thus, they would provide an important check on the government's power over the architectures of cyberspace.

But as code writing becomes commercial—as it becomes the product of a smaller number of large companies—the government's ability to regulate it increases. The more money there is at stake, the less inclined businesses (and their backers) are to bear the costs of promoting an ideology.

The best example is the history of encryption. From the very start of the debate over the government's control of encryption, techies have argued that such regulations are silly. Code can always be exported; bits know no borders. So the idea that a law of Congress would control the flow of code was, these people argued, absurd.

The fact is, however, that the regulations had a substantial effect. Not on the techies—who could easily get encryption technologies from any number of places on the Net—but on the businesses writing software that would incorporate such technology. Netscape or IBM was not about to build and sell software in violation of U.S. regulations. The United States has a fairly powerful threat against these two companies. As the techies predicted, regulation did not control the flow of bits. But it did quite substantially inhibit the development of software that would use these bits.[31]

The effect has been profound. Companies that were once bastions of unregulability are now becoming producers of technologies that facilitate regulation. For example, Network Associates, inheritor of the encryption program PGP, was originally a strong opponent of regulation of encryption; now it offers products that facilitate corporate control of encryption and recovery of keys.[32] Key recovery facilitates a corporate back door, which in many contexts is far less restricted than a governmental back door.

Cisco is a second example.[33] In 1998 Cisco announced a router product that would enable an ISP to encrypt Internet traffic at the link level—between gateways, that is.[34] But this router would also have a switch that would disable the encryption of the router data and facilitate the collection of unencrypted Internet traffic. This switch could be flipped at the government's command; in other words, the data would be encrypted only so long as the government allowed it to be.

The point in both cases is that the government is a player in the market for software. It affects the market both by creating rules and by purchasing product. Either way, it influences the supply of commercial software providers who exist to provide what the market demands.

Veterans of the early days of the Net might ask these suppliers, "How could you?"

"It's just business," is the obvious reply.

EAST COAST AND WEST COAST CODE

Throughout this section, I've been speaking of two sorts of code. One is the "code" that Congress enacts (as in the tax code or "the U.S. Code"). Congress passes an endless array of statutes that say *in words* how to behave. Some statutes direct people; others direct companies; some direct bureaucrats. The technique is as old as government itself: using commands to control. In our country, it is a primarily East Coast (Washington, D.C.) activity. Call it "East Coast Code."

The other is the code that code writers "enact"—the instructions imbedded in the software and hardware that make cyberspace work. This is *code* in its modern sense. It regulates in the ways I've begun to describe. The code of Net95, for example, regulated to disable centralized control; code that encrypts regulates to protect privacy. In our country (MIT excepted), this kind of code writing is increasingly a West Coast (Silicon Valley, Redmond) activity. We can call it "West Coast Code."

West Coast and East Coast Code can get along perfectly fine not paying much attention to the other. Each, that is, can regulate within its own domain. But the story of this chapter is "East meets West": what happens when East Coast Code recognizes how West Coast Code is regulating, and when East Coast Code sees how it might interact with West Coast Code to induce it to regulate differently.

This interaction has changed. The power of East Coast Code over West Coast Code has increased. When software was the product of hackers and individuals located outside of any institution of effective control (for example, the University of Illinois or MIT), East Coast Code could do little to control West Coast Code.[35] But as code has become the product of companies, the power of East Coast Code has increased. When commerce writes code, then code can be controlled, because commercial entities can be controlled. Thus, the power of East over West increases as West Coast Code becomes increasingly commercial.

There is a long history of power moving west. It tells of the clash of ways between the old and the new. The pattern is familiar. The East reaches out to control the West; the West, partially, resists.

We are seeing in cyberspace a shift that history has seen many times before. But we are not yet done with the East's control of the West. There is one final step to take before the power of the state to make cyberspace regulable is completely clear.

This final step links this chapter's argument with the last chapter's account of identification.

REGULATING THE ID-ENABLED WORLD

In my story so far, I've described a certain kind of cooperation between East Coast code and West Coast Code. I've argued that commerce alone has an interest in creating an architecture of identification, and I've laid out just how the government might influence the architecture of the Net to create the requirement of some sort of identification, or traceability. The final step in this argument is to make explicit what has been implicit throughout—that an ID-enabled world facilitates regulation.

How will the internal passports of digital ID enable regulation? The proof comes in two steps. In the first, I lay out how an ID-enabled world would enable regulation for a particular problem of regulation—in this case, gambling. In the second, I show how this technique generalizes. Although not every government may want to solve the problem of gambling, every government does have some problem that it wants to solve. The ID-enabled world can help each government solve its own regulatory problem. Thus, governments share an interest in an ID-enabled world, even if they do not share an interest in the particular regulations such a world makes possible.

Let's return to the problem of Internet gambling and consider it both with and without digital IDs. My claim is that a certificate-rich Internet solves the problem of regulability. Once you see this point with respect to this single example, you will see the point more generally.

Gambling is one of the stock examples given by cyberlibertarians to show why behavior in cyberspace is unregulable. Take the case of Minnesota, which has a strong state policy against gambling.[36] Its legislature has banned its citizens from gambling, and its attorney general has vigorously enforced this legislative judgment—both by shutting down gambling sites in the state and by threatening legal action against sites outside of the state if they let citizens from Minnesota gamble.

This threat, cyberlibertarians argue, will have no effect on gambling on the Internet, nor on the gambling behavior of Minnesota citizens.[37] The proof is fairly straightforward. Imagine a gambling server located in Minnesota. When Minnesota makes gambling illegal, that server can move outside of Minnesota. From the standpoint of citizens in Minnesota, the change has (almost) no effect. It is just as easy to access a server located in Minneapolis as one located in Chicago. So the gambling site can easily move yet keep all its Minnesota customers.

Suppose that Minnesota then threatens to prosecute the owner of the Chicago server. It is relatively easy for the attorney general to persuade the courts of Illinois to prosecute the illegal server in Chicago (assuming it could be shown that the behavior of the server was in fact illegal). So the server simply moves from Chicago to Cayman, making it one step more difficult for Minnesota to prosecute but still no more difficult for citizens of Minnesota to get access. No matter what Minnesota does, it seems the Net helps its citizens beat the government. The Net, oblivious to geography, makes it practically impossible for geographically limited governments to enforce their rules over actors on the Net.

Now, however, imagine a world where everyone holds a digital ID, and not necessarily a governmentally issued ID; any ID will do. As you pass onto a site, the site checks your ID. If you do not hold the proper ID for that type of site—if you are under eighteen and it is an adult site, or if you are from Minnesota and it is a gambling site—the site does not let you pass. But if you hold a proper ID, the site does let you pass. This process occurs invisibly, or machine to machine. All the user knows is that she has gotten in, or if she has not, then why.[38]

In this story, then, the interests of Minnesota are respected. Its citizens are not allowed to gamble. But Minnesota's desires do not determine the gambling practices of people from outside the state. Only citizens of Minnesota are disabled by this regulation; other citizens can gamble.

This is regulation at the level of one state, for one problem. But why would other states cooperate with Minnesota? Why would any other jurisdiction want to carry out Minnesota's regulation?

The answer is that they would not if this were the only regulation at stake. Minnesota wants to protect its citizens from gambling, but New York may want to protect its citizens against the misuse of private data. The European Union may share New York's objective; Utah may share Minnesota's.

Each state has its own stake in controlling certain behaviors, and these behaviors are different. But the key is this: the same architecture that enables Minnesota to achieve its regulatory end can also help other states achieve their regulatory ends. And this can initiate a kind of quid pro quo between jurisdictions.

The pact would look like this. Each state would promise to enforce on servers within its jurisdiction the regulations of other states for citizens from those other states, in exchange for having its own regulations enforced in other jurisdictions. New York would require that servers within New York keep Minnesotans away from New York gambling servers, in exchange for Minnesota keeping New York citizens away from privacy-exploiting servers. Utah would keep EU citizens away from privacy-exploiting servers, in exchange for Europe keeping Utah citizens away from European gambling sites. Each state would enforce a set of regulations for the other states, in exchange for the other states enforcing its own set of regulations.

This structure, in effect, is precisely the structure that is already in place for regulating interstate gambling. According to federal law, interstate Internet gambling is not permitted unless the user is calling from a gambling-permissive state into another gambling-permissive state.[39] If the user calls from a gambling-restrictive state or into a gambling-restrictive state, he or she has committed a federal offense.

The same structure could be used to support local regulation of Internet behavior. With a simple way to verify citizenship, a simple way to verify that servers are discriminating on the basis of citizenship, and a federal commitment to support such local discrimination, we could easily imagine an architecture that enables local regulation of Internet behavior.

And if all this could occur within the United States, it could occur between nations generally. There is the same interest internationally in enforcing local laws as there is nationally—indeed, the interest is most likely even higher. An ID, or certificate-rich, Internet would facilitate international zoning and enable this structure of international control.

Stop. Don't turn away. I know at least some of the thousands of reasons you have for rejecting the structure I've just described. Some of those reasons are normative—you hate the world I am describing. Or you hate the idea that cyberspace would become like this world. *I do too.* I am not promoting an idea, I am arguing that this is the world we are moving to. Those who want to resist this world, or at least its worst features, had better understand the evolution. There are critical architectural decisions that need to be made, and we must begin to make those decisions now.

Others might not be so opposed to the emerging ID-enabled world I am describing but may simply believe that it is unlikely to come about. They believe that the desire of governments to facilitate such discrimination is not terribly strong, and in any case, the technology to enable it would be too difficult to erect.

These two points, of course, operate together. Some governments, regardless of the cost, are willing to adopt technologies to block access. (China is an example.) But other countries would not go to such great lengths to control access. If the cost were too high, they would simply leave the regulation aside and move on to other, more important activities (Taiwan).

This trade-off—between cost and the willingness to regulate—is one we have seen before. It is a theme that recurs in many contexts. Cost for the government is liberty for us. The higher the cost of a regulation, the less likely it will be pursued as a regulation. Liberty depends on the regulation remaining expensive.

When it becomes easy or cheap to regulate, however, this contingent liberty is at risk. We can expect more regulation. In these cases, if we want to preserve liberty, we need to develop affirmative arguments for it. We will need these affirmative arguments to prevent identity-based regulation of the Net. As I explain in the balance of this book, there is both a surprisingly great desire for nations to embrace regimes that facilitate jurisdiction-specific regulation and a significant reason why the costs of regulation are likely to fall. We should expect, then, that there will be more such regulation. Soon.

The proof that this capacity for regulation will emerge is the subject of the next chapters. To end this chapter, we need only answer one question. Assuming that these architectures for identification will emerge, what follows about the regulability of cyberspace?

The answer, I trust, is obvious: putting to one side the question of identifying content (which I consider in detail in chapter 12), an architecture for selective certification would dramatically increase the power of local governments to impose requirements on their citizens. Sites would be required to condition admission on the certificates held by users, and the Internet would shift from being an essentially unregulable space locally to a highly regulable space. Rules imposed by local jurisdictions could be made effective through their recognition by other jurisdictions. Servers, for example, would recognize that access is conditioned on the rules imposed by jurisdictions.

The effect, in short, would be to *zone* cyberspace based on the qualifications carried by individual users. It would enable a degree of control of cyberspace that few have ever imagined. Cyberspace would go from being an unregulable space to, depending on the depth of the certificates in the space, the most regulable space imaginable.

One final line of resistance: even if these architectures emerge, and even if they become common, there is nothing to show that they will become universal, and nothing to show that at any one time they could not be evaded. Individuals can always work around these technologies of identity. No control that they could effect would ever be perfect.

True. The control of a certificate-rich Internet would never be complete. But there is a fallacy lurking in the argument: just because perfect control is not possible does not mean that effective control is not possible. Locks can be picked, but that does not mean locks are useless. And in the context of the Internet, even partial control would have powerful effects.

A fundamental principle of bovinity is operating here, and elsewhere. Tiny controls, consistently enforced, are enough to direct very large animals. The controls of a certificate-rich Internet are tiny, I agree. But we are large animals. I think it is as likely that the majority of people would resist these small but efficient regulators of the Net as it is that cows would resist wire fences. This is who we are, and this is why these regulations work.

One final twist to this bovine account. So far I've been discussing a relatively cumbersome technology for identification—certificates. These are cumbersome because to tie the certificate to a person (as opposed to a machine), we still need some sort of link—through, for example, a pass-phrase. These phrases can be a hassle; if they change, they can be easy to forget.

There is an easier way. Already computer manufacturers are exploring biometric devices that would make it simple to tie a person to a machine. Compaq, for example, is considering a thumbprint reader: when you sit at your keyboard, it would verify that you are who you say you are. Who needs a password when you have a thumb?[40]

So what will happen when these technologies become cheap and easy? When you can choose between remembering a pass-phrase, typing it every time you want access to your computer, and simply using your thumb to authenticate who you are? Or if not your thumb, then your retina, or whatever body part turns out to be cheapest to certify? When it is easiest simply to give identity up, will anyone resist giving it up?

For if this is selling your soul, then trust that there are truly wonderful benefits to be had. Imagine a world where all your documents exist on the Internet in a "virtual private network," accessible by you from any machine on the Net and perfectly secured by a biometric key.[41] You could sit at any machine, call up your documents, do your work, answer your e-mail, and move on—everything perfectly secure and safe, locked up by a key certified by the markings in your eye.

This is the easiest and most efficient architecture to imagine. And it comes at (what some think) is a very low price—authentication. Just say who you are, plug into an architecture that certifies facts about you, give your identity away, and all this could be yours.

There was an awful movie released in 1996 called *Independence Day*. The story is about an invasion by aliens. When the aliens first appear, many earthlings are eager to welcome them. For these idealists, there is no reason to assume hostility, and so a general joy spreads among the hopeful across the globe in reaction to what before had seemed just a dream: really cool alien life.

Soon after the aliens appear, however, and well into the celebration, the mood changes. Quite suddenly, Earth leaders realize that the intentions of these aliens are not friendly. Indeed, their intentions are quite hostile. Within a very short time of this realization, Earth is captured. (Only Jeff Goldblum realizes what's going on beforehand, but he always gets it first.)

My story here is similar (though I hope not as awful). We have been as welcoming and joyous about the Net as the earthlings were about the aliens in *Independence Day;* we have accepted its growth in our lives without questioning its final effect. But at some point, we too will come to see a potential threat. We will see that cyberspace does not guarantee its own freedom but instead carries an extraordinary potential for control. And then we will ask: How should we respond?

I have spent many pages making a point that some may find obvious. But I have found that, for some reason, the people for whom this point should be most important do not get it. Too many take this freedom as nature. Too many believe liberty will take care of itself. Too many miss how different architectures embed different values, and that only by selecting these different architectures—these different codes—can we establish and promote our values.

Now it should be apparent why I began this book with an account of the rediscovery of the role for self-government, or control, that has marked recent history in post-Communist Europe. Market forces encourage architectures of identity to facilitate online commerce. Government needs to do very little—indeed, nothing at all—to induce just this sort of development. The market forces are too powerful; the potential here is too great. If anything is certain, it is that an architecture of identity will develop on the Net—and thereby fundamentally transform its regulability.

But isn't it clear that government should do something to make this architecture consistent with important public values? If commerce is going to define the emerging architectures of cyberspace, isn't the role of government to ensure that those public values that are not in commerce's interest are also built into the architecture?

Architecture is a kind of law: it determines what people can and cannot do. When commercial interests determine the architecture, they create a kind of privatized law. I am not against private enterprise; my strong presumption in most cases is to let the market produce. But isn't it absolutely clear that there must be limits to this presumption? That public values are not exhausted by the sum of what IBM might desire? That what is good for America Online is not necessarily good for America?

Ordinarily, when we describe competing collections of values, and the choices we make among them, we call these choices "political." They are choices about how the world will be ordered and about which values will be given precedence.

Choices among values, choices about regulation, about control, choices about the definition of spaces of freedom—all this is the stuff of politics. Code codifies values, and yet, oddly, most people speak as if code were just a question of engineering. Or as if code is best left to the market. Or best left unaddressed by government.

But these attitudes must be mistaken. Politics is that process by which we collectively decide how we should live. That is not to say a space where we collectivize—a collective can choose a libertarian form of government. The point is not the substance of the choice. The point about politics is process. Politics is the process by which we *reason* about how things ought to be.

A decade ago, in a powerful trilogy drawing together a movement in legal theory, Roberto Unger preached that "it's all politics."[42] That we should not accept the idea that any part of what defines the world as it is, is removed from politics. That everything should be considered "up for grabs," everything subject to reform.

Many understood Unger to be arguing that we should in fact put everything up for grabs all the time, that nothing should be certain or fixed, that everything should be in flux, constantly changing. But that is not what Unger meant.

His meaning was instead just this: That we interrogate the necessities of any particular social order; that we ask whether they are in fact necessities; that we demand that those necessities justify the powers that they order. As Bruce Ackerman puts it, we must ask of every exercise of power: Why?[43] Perhaps not exactly at the moment when the power is exercised, but sometime.

"Power," in this account, is just another word for constraints that humans can do something about. Meteors crashing to earth are not "power" within the domain of "it's all politics." Where the meteor hits is not politics, though the consequences may well be. Where it hits, however, is nothing we can do anything about.

But the architecture of cyberspace *is* power in this sense; how it is could be different. Politics is about how we decide. Politics is how that power is exercised, and by whom.

If code is law, then, as William Mitchell writes, "control of code is power": "For citizens of cyberspace, . . . code . . . is becoming a crucial focus of political contest. Who shall write that software that increasingly structures our daily lives?"[44]

As the world is now, code writers are increasingly lawmakers. They determine what the defaults of the Internet will be; whether privacy will be protected; the degree to which anonymity will be allowed; the extent to which access will be guaranteed. They are the ones who set its nature. Their decisions, now made in the interstices of how the Net is coded, define what the Net is.

How the code regulates, who the code writers are, and who controls the code writers—these are questions that any practice of justice must focus in the age of cyberspace. The answers reveal how cyberspace is regulated. My claim in this part of the book is that cyberspace is regulated, and that the regulation is changing. Its regulation is its code, and its code is changing.

We are entering an age when the power of regulation will be relocated to a structure whose properties and possibilities are fundamentally different. As I said about Russia at the start of this book, one form of power may be destroyed, but another is taking its place.

Our aim must be to understand this power and to ask whether it is properly exercised. As David Brin asks, "If we admire the Net, should not a burden of proof fall on those who would change the basic assumptions that brought it about in the first place?"[45]

These "basic assumptions" were grounded in liberty and openness. An invisible hand now threatens both. We need to understand how.

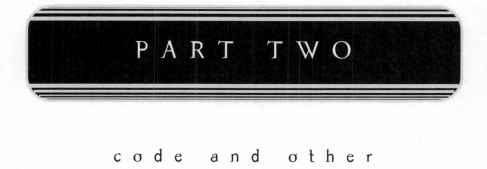

PART TWO

code and other regulators

Part 1 set up the problem: cyberspace will not take care of itself. Its nature is not given. Its nature is its code, and its code is changing from a place that disabled control to a place that will enable an extraordinary kind of control. Commerce is making that happen; government will help. Before this happens, we should decide whether this is the way we want things to be.

In part 2 we will prepare for that choice. I begin by describing a more complex sense of the life that code makes possible. That's chapter 6. What makes these places *feel* as they do? What architectures make possible the life within each? And how might that life change as the structures that constitute them—their architectures—change?

Chapter 7 is about the techniques for that change. Building on the pattern I described in chapter 5, I offer a general model of regulation that is applicable to cyberspace as well as real space. My aim is to convey a sense of the power that government has here, and a stronger sense of why that power will increase—not decrease—over time.

I then describe an important limitation to this power—in terms from the introduction, a structural constraint on government's power. This is the limit implicit in the open code movement. As I argue in chapter 8, the power that government obtains through the techniques I sketched in chapter 5, open code takes away. There is thus a competition about regulability, mediated by the ownership of the code.

The aim in the end is to see what is at stake, what is possible, and what limits there are on what is possible. The argument is not against regulation; the argument is against a particularly narrow, and useless, conception of regulation. Once we have a better view of how regulation works, we will see more clearly how we might choose the space cyberspace should be.

S I X

c y b e r s p a c e s

CYBERSPACE IS NOT A PLACE. IT IS MANY PLACES. THE CHARACTER OF THESE MANY places is not identical. They instead differ in ways that are fundamental. These differences come in part from differences in the people who populate these places. But demographics alone won't explain the variance. Something more is going on.

Here is a test. Read the following passage, and ask yourself whether the description rings true for you:

> I believe virtual communities promise to restore to Americans at the end of the twentieth century what many of us feel was lost in the decades at the beginning of the century—a stable sense of community, of place. Ask those who've been members of such a virtual community, and they'll tell you that what happens there is more than an exchange of electronic impulses in the wires. It's not just virtual barn raising. . . . It's also the comfort from others that a man like Phil Catalfo of the WELL can experience when he's up late at night caring for a child suffering from leukemia, and he logs on to the WELL and pours out his anguish and fears. People really do care for each other and fall in love over the Net, just as they do in geographic communities. And that "virtual" connectedness is a real sign of hope in a nation that's increasingly anxious about the fragmentation of public life and the polarization of interest groups and the alienation of urban existence.[1]

There are two sorts of reactions to talk like this. To those who have been in this place for some time, such talk is extremely familiar. These people have been on nets from the start. They moved to the Internet from more isolated communities—from a local BBS (bulletin board service), or as Mike Godwin (the author of the passage) likes to put it, from a "tony" address like "The WELL." For them the Net is a space for conversation, connections, and exchange, a wildly promising location for making life in real space different.

But if you are a recent immigrant to this "space" (the old-timers call you "new-bies"), you are likely to be impatient with talk like this. When people talk about "community," about special ways to connect, or about the amazing power of this space to alter lives, you are likely to ask, "What is this idea of cyberspace as a place?" For newbies, those who have simply e-mailed or surfed the World Wide Web, the "community" of the Net is an odd sort of mysticism. How can anyone think of these pages full of advertisements and spinning Mickey Mouse icons as a community, or even as a space? To the sober newbie, this just sounds like hype high on java.[2]

Newbies are the silent majority of today's Net.[3] However much we romanticize the old days when the Net was a place for conversation and exchange, this is not its function for most of its users now. Certainly, the world is into "chat," but even ignoring the large portion of that space devoted to sex, chat is not the stuff the WELL was made of. Most people do not understand what chat or a MOO really is—maybe they have heard talk about them, but they do not understand what they are about. They do not understand what life in the community of the WELL, or a MOO, is really like.

In its feel, cyberspace has changed.[4] How it looks, what you can do there, how you are connected there—all this has changed. Why it has changed is a complicated question—a complete answer to which I can't provide. Cyberspace has changed in part because the people—who they are, what their interests are—have changed, and in part because the capabilities provided by the space have changed.

But part of the change has to do with the space itself. Communities, exchange, and conversation all flourish in a certain type of space; they are extinguished in a different type of space.[5] My hope is to illuminate the differences between these two environments.

The next sections describe different cyber-places. The aim is an intuition about how to think through the differences that we observe. This intuition, in turn, will help us see something about where cyberspace is moving.

THE VALUES OF A SPACE

Spaces have values.[6] They express these values through the practices or lives that they enable or disable. Differently constituted spaces enable and disable differently. This is the first idea that we must make plain. Here is an example.

At the start of the Internet, communication was through text. Media such as USENET newsgroups, Internet Relay Chat, and e-mail all confined exchange to text—to words on a screen, typed by a person (or so one thought).

The reason for this limitation is fairly obvious: the bandwidth of early Net life was very thin. In an environment where most users connected at 1,200 baud, if they were lucky, graphics and streaming video would have taken an unbearably long time to download, if they downloaded at all. What was needed was an efficient mode of communication—and text is one of the most efficient.[7]

Most think of this fact about the early Net as a limitation. Technically, it was. But this technical description does not exhaust its normative description as an architecture that made possible a certain kind of life. From this perspective, limitations can be features; they can enable as well as disable. And this particular limitation enabled classes of people who were disabled in real-space life.

Think about three such classes—the blind, the deaf, and the "ugly."* In real space these people face an extraordinary array of constraints on their ability to communicate. The blind person in real space is constantly confronted with architectures that presume he can see; he bears an extraordinary cost in retrofitting real-space architectures so that this presumption is not totally exclusionary. The deaf person in real space confronts architectures that presume she can hear; she too bears an extraordinary cost in retrofitting these architectures. The "ugly" person in real space (think of a bar or a social club) confronts architectures of social norms that make his appearance a barrier to a certain sort of intimacy. He endures extraordinary suffering in conforming to these architectures.

In real space these three groups are confronted with architectures that disable them relative to "the rest of us." But in cyberspace, in its first iteration, they did not.

The blind could easily implement speech programs that read the (by definition machine-readable) text and could respond by typing. Other people on the Net would have no way of knowing that the person typing the message was blind, unless he claimed to be. The blind were equal to the seeing.

The same with the deaf. There was no need to hear anything in this early Internet. For the first time many of the deaf could have conversations, or exchanges, in which the most salient feature was *not* that the person was deaf. The deaf were equal to the hearing.

And the same with the "ugly." Because your appearance was not transmitted with every exchange, the unattractive could have an intimate conversation with others that was not automatically defined by what they looked like. They could flirt or play or be sexual without their bodies (in an extremely underappreciated sense) getting in the way. This first version of the Net made these people equal to "the beautiful." In a virtual chat room, stunning eyes, a captivating smile or impressive biceps don't do it. Wit, engagement, and articulateness do.

The architecture of this original cyberspace gave these groups something that they did not have in real space. More generally, it changed the mix of benefits and burdens that people faced—the literate were enabled and the attractive disabled relative to real space. Architectures produced these enablings and disablings.

---

*It is an important fact about us that it is awkward even to use such a word—"ugly"—as if it describes objective features of humans. I acknowledge the complexity here, and the importance of the escape from humiliation that some parts of society give and other parts of society do not. But we cannot assume away the burdens that the unattractive suffer relative to the less unattractive. My claim is not that these are at the level of starvation, or death; my claim is not about their significance. My only aim is to link what I believe is a disadvantage to features of a space.

I've told this story as if it matters only to those who in real space are "disabled." But of course, "disabled" is relative.[8] It is more accurate to say that the space changes the meaning of the enabled. A friend—a strikingly beautiful and powerful woman, married, and successful—described for me why she spends hours in political chat spaces, arguing with others about all sorts of political topics:

> You don't understand what it's like to be me. You have lived your whole life in a world where your words are taken for their meaning; where what you say is heard for what it says. I've never had a space, before this space, where my words were taken for what they meant. Always, before, they were words of "this babe," or "wife," or "mother." I could never speak as I. But here, I am as I speak.

Clearly, the space is enabling her, even though one would not have said that in real space she was "disabled."[9]

Over time, as bandwidth has expanded, this architecture has changed. So has the mix of benefits and burdens changed. When graphics entered the Net through the World Wide Web, the blind became "blind" again. As sound files or speech in Avatar spaces have been created, the deaf have become "deaf" again. And as chat rooms have started segregating into spaces where videocams capture real images of the people chatting, and spaces where there is just text, the video-unappealing are again unappealing.[10] As the architectures change, definitions of who is "disabled" change as well.

My point is not to argue that the Net should not change—though of course, if it can change in ways that minimize the disabling effect of sound and graphics, then it no doubt should.[11] However important, my point is not really about the "disabled" at all. I use this example simply to highlight a link—between these structures of code and the world this code enables. Codes constitute cyberspaces; spaces enable and disable individuals and groups. The selections about code are therefore in part a selection about who, what, and, most important, what *ways of life* will be enabled and disabled.

CYBER-PLACES

We can build on this point by looking at a number of "communities" that are constituted differently and that constitute different forms of life, and by considering what makes these differences possible.

America Online

America Online (AOL) is an online service provider—the largest in the world with some twelve million subscribers in 1998.[12] With twice the population of Massachusetts (at least), AOL describes itself as a "community." A large community perhaps, but a community nonetheless.

This community has a constitution—not in the sense of a written document (though there is that as well), but in the sense of a way of life that defines life for those who live there. Its founding vision was that community would make this place sing. So from its start, AOL's emphasis has been on enabling people to interact, through chat, bulletin boards, and e-mail. Earlier providers, obsessed with providing content or advertising, limited or ignored the possibilities for interaction and exchange, but AOL saw interaction as the stuff that makes cyberspace different. It built itself on building a community, establishing itself as a place where people could say what they wanted.[13]

This interaction is governed by the rules of the place. Some of these rules are formal, others customary. Among the formal are express terms to which every member subscribes upon joining AOL. These terms regulate a wide range of behaviors in this space, including the behavior of AOL members anywhere on the Internet.[14]

Increasingly, these rules have become controversial. AOL policies have been called "Big Brother" practices. Arguments that get heated produce exchanges that are rude. But rudeness, or offensiveness, is not permitted in AOL's community. When these exchanges are expunged, claims of "censorship" arise.[15]

My aim here, however, is not to criticize these rules of "netiquette." AOL also has other rules that regulate AOL members—rules expressed not in contracts but rather through the very architectures of the space. These rules constitute the most important part of AOL's constitution, yet they are probably the part considered last when we think about what regulates behavior in this cyber-place.

So consider some examples:

As a member of AOL you can be any one of five people. This is just one amazing feature of the space. When you start an account on AOL, you have the right to establish up to five identities, through five different "screen names" that in effect establish five different accounts. Some users, of course, use the five screen names to give other family members access to AOL. But not everyone uses an AOL account like this. Think about the single woman, signing up for her first AOL account. AOL gives her up to five identities that she can define as she wishes—five different personae she can use in cyberspace.

What does that mean? A screen name is just a label for identifying who you are when you are on the system. It need not (indeed, often cannot) be your own name. If your screen name is "StrayCat," then people can reach you by sending e-mail to "straycat@aol.com." If you are online, people can try to talk to you by paging StrayCat on the AOL system; a dialogue would then appear on your screen asking whether you want to talk to the person who paged you. If you enter a chat room, the list of residents there will add you as "StrayCat."

But who is StrayCat? Here is a second dimension of control. StrayCat is who StrayCat says she is. She can choose to define herself as no one at all. If she chooses to place a description of herself in the members' directory, that description can be as complete or incomplete as she wishes. It can be true or false, explicit or vague, inviting or not. A member stumbling across StrayCat, then, in a chat room set up for stamp collectors could get her profile and read that StrayCat lives in Cleveland and is single and female. What happens next is anyone's guess.

Yet this need only be one of StrayCat's five identities. Let's say there is a different persona that StrayCat likes to have when she wanders through chat rooms. She can then select another screen name and define it in the directory as she wishes. Perhaps when StrayCat is having a serious discussion in a newsgroup or political list she prefers to speak as herself. She could then select a screen name close to her own name and define it according to who she really is. At other times StrayCat may like to pretend to be a man—engaging in virtual cross-dressing, and all that might bring with it. One of her screen names could then be a man's. And so on. The point is the multiplicity that AOL allows, and the freedom this multiplicity permits.

No one except StrayCat needs to know which screen names are hers. She is not required to publish the full list of her identities, and no one can find out who she is (unless she breaks the rules). (After revealing to the U.S. Navy the name of one of its members so that the Navy could prosecute the person for being a homosexual, AOL adopted a very strict privacy policy that promises never to allow a similar transgression to happen again.)[16]

So in AOL you are given a fantastic power of pseudonymity that the "code writers" of real space simply do not give. You could, of course, try in real space to live the same range of multiple lives, and to the extent that these lives are not incompatible or inconsistent, you could quite often get away with it. For instance, you could be a Cubs fan during the summer and an opera buff during the winter. But unless you take extraordinary steps to hide your identity, in real space you are always tied back to you. You cannot simply define a different character; you must make it, and more important (and difficult), you must sustain its separation from your original identity.

That is a first feature of the constitution of AOL—a feature constituted by its code. A second is tied to speech—what you can say, and where.

Within the limits of decency, and so long as you are in the proper place, you can say what you want on AOL. But beyond these limits, speech on AOL is constrained in a more interesting way. Not the constraint of rules. My point instead is about the range of permissible speech governed by the character of the potential audience. There are places in AOL where people can gather; there are places where people can go and read messages posted by others. But there is no space where everyone gathers at one time, or even a space that everyone must sooner or later pass through. There is no public space where you could address all members of AOL. There is no town hall or town meeting where people can complain in public and have their complaints heard by others. There is no space large enough for citizens to create a riot. The owners of AOL, however, can speak to all. Steve Case, the "town mayor," writes "chatty" letters to the members.[17] AOL advertises to all its members and can send everyone an e-mail. But only the owners and those they authorize can do so. The rest of the members of AOL can speak to crowds only where they notice a crowd. And never to a crowd greater than twenty-three.

This is another feature of the constitution of the space that AOL is, and it too is a feature defined by code. That only twenty-three people can be in a chat room at once is a choice of the code engineers. While their reasons could be many, the effect is clear. One can't imagine easily exciting members of AOL into public action. One can't imagine easily picketing the latest pricing policy. There are places to go to complain, but you have to take the trouble to go there yourself. There is no place where members can complain en masse.

Real space is different in this respect. Much of free speech law is devoted to preserving spaces where dissent can occur—spaces that can be noticed, and must be confronted, by nondissenting citizens.[18] In real space there are places where people can gather, places where they can leaflet. People have a right to the sidewalks, public streets, and other traditional public forums. They may go there and talk about issues of public import or otherwise say whatever they want. Constitutional law in real space protects the right of the passionate and the weird to get in the face of the rest. But no such design is built into AOL.[19]

This is not to romanticize the power of real-space public forums. We have become such a nonpolitical society that if you actually exercised this constitutionally protected right, people would think you a nut. If you stood on a street corner and attacked the latest tax proposal in Congress, your friends would be likely to worry—and not about the tax proposal. There are exceptions—events can make salient the need for protest—but in the main, though real space has fewer controls through code on who can speak where, it has many more controls through norms on what people can say where. Perhaps in the end real space is much like AOL—the effective space for public speech is limited, and often unimportant. That may well be. But my aim here is to identify the feature and to isolate what is responsible for it. And once again, it turns out to be a feature built into the code.

A third feature of AOL's constitution also comes from its code. This is traceability. While members are within the exclusive AOL content area (in other words, when they're not using AOL as a gateway to the Internet), AOL can (and no doubt does) trace your activities and collect information about them. What files you download, what areas you frequent, who your "buddies" are—all this is available to AOL. These data are extremely valuable; they help AOL structure its space to fit customer demand. But gaining the ability to collect these data required a design decision. This decision too was part of the constitution that is AOL—again, a part constituted by its code. It is a decision that gives some but not others the power to watch.

AOL is not exclusive in this enabling capacity. It shares the power. One wonderful feature of the online space is something called "buddy lists." Add someone to your buddy list, and when he comes online you hear the sound of a creaking door and are notified that he is online. (The "buddy" need not know he is being watched, though he can, if he knows, block the watching.) If that person goes into a chat area and you "locate" him, you will be told in what chat area he is. This power, given to ordinary users, can have complicated consequences. (Imagine sitting at work with your buddy feature turned on, watching your spouse come online, enter a chat area, and—you get the point.) This ability to monitor is built into the space. Individuals can turn it off, at least for a single watcher, but only if they know about it and think to change it.

Consider one final feature of the constitution of AOL, closely linked to the last: commerce. In AOL you can buy things. You can buy things and download them, or buy things and have them sent to your home. When you buy, you buy with a screen name. And when you buy with a screen name, AOL knows (even if no one else does) just who you are. It knows who you are, it knows where you live in real space, and most important, it knows your credit card number and the security it provides.

AOL knows who you are—this is a feature of its design. All your behavior on AOL is watched; all of it is monitored and tracked back to you as a user. AOL promises not to collect data about you individually, but it certainly collects data about you as part of a collective. And with this collective, and the link it provides back to you, AOL is a space that can better, and more efficiently, sell to you.

These four features mark AOL space as different from other places in cyberspace. It is easier for AOL to identify who you are, and harder for individuals to find out who you are; easier for AOL to speak to all its "citizens" as it wishes, and harder for dissidents to organize against AOL's views about how things ought to be; easier for AOL to market, and harder for individuals to hide. AOL is a different normative world; it can create this different world because it is in control of the architecture of that world. Members in that space face, in a sense, a different set of laws of nature; AOL makes those laws.

My aim is not to criticize the creation of this world or to say that it is improper. No doubt AOL makes promises to its members that are designed to allay some of the concern that this control creates, and no doubt if the place became oppressive, the market would provide plenty of alternatives.

Rather my objective is to impart a sense of what makes AOL the way it is. It is not just written rules; it is not just custom; it is not just the supply and demand of a knowing consuming public. What makes AOL is in large part the structure of the space. You enter AOL and you *find* it to be a certain universe. This space is constituted by its code. You can resist this code—you can resist how you find it, just as you can resist cold weather by putting on a sweater. But you are not going to change how it is. You do not have the power to change AOL's code, and there is no place where you could rally AOL members to force AOL to change the code. You live life in AOL subject to its terms; if you do not like them, you go elsewhere.

These features of the AOL space have important implications for how it is regulated. Imagine there is a problem on AOL that AOL wants to stop. It wants to prevent or at least control a certain behavior. What tools does AOL have?

First, it has all the tools that any club, fraternity, or "community" might have. It can announce rules for its members (and AOL certainly does). Or it can try to stigmatize the behavior, to use the norms of the community to help regulate the problem. This AOL does as well. Alternatively, if the problem comes from the overuse of a particular resource, then the managers at AOL can price that resource differently, exacting a tax to reduce its usage, or a different price for those who use it too much.

But AOL has something more at hand. If AOL does not like a certain behavior, then in at least some cases it can regulate that behavior by changing its architecture. If AOL is trying to control indecent language, it can write routines that monitor language usage; if there is improper mixing between adults and kids, AOL can track who is talking to whom; if there is a virus problem caused by people uploading infected files, it can run the files automatically through virus checkers; if there is stalking or harassing or threatening behavior, AOL can block the connection between any two individuals.

In short, AOL can deal with certain types of problems by changing its code. Because the universe that AOL members know (while in AOL) is defined by this code, AOL can use the code to regulate its members.

Think a bit about the power I am describing—and again, I am not complaining or criticizing or questioning this power, only describing it. As you move through this space that AOL defines—entering a chat area, posting a message to a bulletin board, entering a discussion space, sending instant-messages to another person, watching or following other people, uploading or downloading files from sites, turning to certain channels and reading certain articles, or obsessively paging through a space looking for pictures of a certain actor or actress—as you do any of these things, AOL is, in an important sense, *there*. It is as if the system gives you a space suit that you use to navigate the space but that simultaneously monitors your every move.

In principle, the potential for control is extraordinary. Imagine AOL slowing the response time for a certain kind of service it wants to discourage, or channeling the surfer through ads that it wants customers to see, or identifying patterns of behavior that its monitors would watch, based on the fear that people with patterns like X are typically dangerous to people of type Y. I do not think AOL engages in activities like these, and I am not even saying that there would be anything wrong if it did. But it is important to note that the potential for control in this "community" is unlimited—not in the sense that AOL could make life miserable (since people would then leave), but in the sense that it has a regulatory tool that others, in both real space and other cyberspaces, do not. Its power is, of course, checked by the market, but it has a tool of control that others in the market, but outside cyberspace, do not have.

In principle, then, AOL must choose. Every time AOL decides that it wants to regulate a certain kind of behavior, it must select from among at least four modalities—rules, norms, prices, or architecture. And when selecting one of these four modalities, selecting architecture as a regulator will often make the most sense.

Counsel Connect

David Johnson began Counsel Connect (CC) in 1992 as an online lawyers' cooperative. The idea was simple: give subscribers access to each other; let them engage in conversations with each other; and through this access and these conversations, value would be created. Lawyers would give and take work; they would contribute ideas as they found ideas in the space. A different kind of law practice would emerge—less insular, less exclusive, more broadly based.

I thought the idea amazing, though many thought it nuts. For a time the system was carried by Lexis; in 1996 it was sold to American Lawyer Media, L.P.; in 1997 it migrated to the Internet and remains there today. It boasts thousands of subscribers, though it is hard to know how many of them contribute to the discussion online. Many no doubt simply watch the discussions of others, perhaps linking three or four discussion groups of their particular interest, plus a few of more general interest.

This is how the more interesting feature of the space is designed: legal topics are divided into discussion groups, with each group led by a discussion leader. The leader is not a moderator; he or she has no power to cancel a post. The leader is there to inspire conversation—to induce others to speak by being encouraging or provocative.

There are today some ninety groups in this space. The poster of a particular message may have it removed, but if the poster does not remove it, it stays—at first in the list of topics being discussed, and later in an archive that can be searched by any member.

Members pay a fee to join and get an account with their real name on it. Postings use members' real names, and anyone wondering who someone is can simply link to a directory. Members of CC must be members of the bar, unless they are journalists. Others have no right to access; the community here is exclusive.

Postings in the space look very much like postings in a USENET newsgroup. A thread can be started by anyone, and replies to a thread are appended to the end. Because messages do not move off the system, you can easily read from the start of a thread to its end. The whole conversation, not just a snippet, is preserved to be read.

These features of CC space were obviously designed. The architects of the space chose to enable certain features and to disable others. We can list here some of the effects of these choices.

First, there is the effect of being required to use your own name. You are more likely to think before speaking and to be careful about being right before saying something definitive. You are constrained by the community, which will judge what you say, and in this community you cannot escape from being linked to what you have said. Responsibility is a consequence of this architecture, but so is a certain inhibition. Does a senior partner at a leading law firm really want to ask a question that will announce his ignorance about a certain area of law? Names cannot be changed to protect the ignorant, so they will often simply not speak.

Second, there is an effect from forcing all discussion into threads. Postings are kept together; a question is asked, and the discussion begins from the question. If you want to contribute to this discussion, you must first read through the other postings before responding. Of course, this is not a technical requirement—you certainly have a choice not to read. But if you do not read through the entire thread, you could well be repeating what another has said and so reveal that you are speaking without listening. Again, the use of real names ties members' behavior to the norms of the community.

Third, there is the effect of reputation: the reputation you build in this space is based on the kind of advice you give. Your reputation survives any particular post and is, of course, affected by any subsequent posts. These posts are archived and searchable. If you say one thing about topic X and then the opposite later on, you are at least open to a question about consistency.

Fourth, there is the effect of tying reputation to a real name in a real community of professionals. Misbehaving here matters elsewhere. CC thus gets the benefit of that community—it gets the benefit, that is, of the norms of a particular community. These norms might support relatively productive community behavior—more productive, that is, than the behavior of a group whose members are fundamentally mixed. They might also support punishing those who deviate from appropriate behavior. Thus, CC gets the benefit of community sanction to control improper behavior, whereas AOL must rely on its own content police to ensure that people stay properly on topic.

We can describe the world of CC that these features constitute in two different ways, just as we can describe the world AOL constitutes in two different ways. One is the life that CC's features make possible—highly dialogic and engaged, but monitored and with consequences. The other is the regulability by the manager of the life that goes on in the CC space. And here we can see a significant difference between this space and AOL.

CC can use the norms of a community to regulate more effectively than AOL can. CC benefits from the norms of the legal community; it knows that any misbehavior will be sanctioned by that community. There is, of course, less "behavior" in this space than in AOL (you do fewer things here), but such as it is, CC behavior is quite significantly regulated by the reputations of members and the consequences of using their real names.

These differences together have an effect on CC's ability to regulate its members. They enable a regulation through modalities other than code. They make behavior in CC more regulable by norms than behavior in AOL is. CC in turn may have less control than AOL does (since the controlling norms are those of the legal community), but it also bears less of the burden of regulating its members' behavior. Limiting the population, making members' behavior public, tying them to their real names—these are the tools of self-regulation in this virtual space.

But CC is like AOL in an important way. Neither is a democracy. Management in both cases controls what will happen in the space—again, not without constraint, for the market is an important constraint. But in neither place do "the people" have the power to control what goes on. Perhaps they do, indirectly, in CC more than AOL, since it is the norms of "the people" that regulate behavior in CC. But these norms cannot be used against CC directly. The decisions of CC and AOL managers may be affected by market forces—individuals can exit, competitors can steal customers away. But voting doesn't direct where either CC or AOL goes.

That's not the case with the next cyber-place. At least, not anymore.

L a m d a M O O

LamdaMOO is a virtual reality. It is a text-based virtual reality. People from across the world (today close to six thousand of them) link to this space and interact in ways that the space permits. The reality is the product of this interaction. Individuals can participate in the construction of this reality—sometimes for upwards of eighty hours a week. For some this interaction is the most sustained human contact of their entire lives. For most it is a kind of interaction unmatched by anything else they know.

In the main, people just talk here. But it is not the talk of an AOL chat room. The talk in a MUD is in the service of construction—of constructing a character and a community. You interact in part by talking, and this talking is tied to a name. This name, and the memories of what it has done, live in the space, and over time people in the space come to know the person by what these memories recall.

The life within these MUDs differ. Elizabeth Reid describes two different "styles"[20]—social-style MUD and an adventure or game-style MUD. Social MUDs are simply online communities where people talk and build characters or elements for the MUD. Adventure MUDs are games, with (virtual) prizes or power to be won through the deployment of skill in capturing resources or defeating an enemy. In either context, the communities survive a particular interaction. They become virtual clubs, though with different purposes. Members build reputations through their behavior in these clubs.

You get a character simply by joining the MOO (though in LamdaMOO the waiting list for a character extends over many months). When you join the space, you define the character you will have. At least, you define certain features of your character. You select a name and a gender (no gender is an option as well) and describe your character. Some descriptions are quite ordinary (Johnny Manhattan is "tall and thin, pale as string cheese, wearing a neighborhood hat").[21] Others, however, are quite extraordinary. (Legba, for instance, is a Haitian trickster spirit of indeterminate gender, brown-skinned and wearing an expensive pearl gray suit, top hat, and dark glasses.)[22]

Julian Dibbell broke the story of this space to the nonvirtual world in an article in the *Village Voice*.[23] The story that was the focus of Dibbell's article involved a character called Mr. Bungle who, it turns out, was actually a group of NYU undergraduates sharing this single identity. Bungle entered a room late one evening and found a group of characters well known in that space. The full story cannot be told any better than Dibbell tells it. For our purposes, the facts will be enough.[24]

Bungle had a special sort of power. By earning special standing in the LamdaMoo community, he had "voodoo" power: he could take over the voices and actions of other characters and make them appear to do things they did not really do. This Bungle did that night to a group of women and at least one person of ambiguous gender. He invoked this power, in this public space, and took over the voices of these people. Once they were in his control, Bungle "raped" these women, violently and sadistically, and made it seem as if they enjoyed the rape.

The "rape" was virtual in the sense that the event happened only on the wires. "No bodies touched," as Dibbell describes it.

> Whatever physical interaction occurred consisted of a mingling of electronic signals sent from sites spread out between New York City and Sidney, Australia.
>
> . . . He commenced his assault entirely unprovoked at, or about 10 P.M. Pacific Standard Time. . . . [H]e began by using his voodoo doll to force one of the room's occupants to sexually service him in a variety of more or less conventional ways. That this victim was exu. . . . He turned his attentions now to Moon-dreamer . . . forcing her into unwanted liaisons with other individuals present in the room. . . . His actions grew progressively violent. . . . He caused Moon-dreamer to violate herself with a piece of kitchen cutlery. He could not be stopped until at last someone summoned Iggy . . . who brought with him a gun of near wizardly powers, a gun that didn't kill but enveloped its targets in a cage impermeable even to a voodoo doll's powers.[25]

Rape is a difficult word to use in any context, but particularly here. Some will object that whatever happened in this virtual space, it has nothing to do with rape. Yet even if "it" was not "rape," all will see a link between rape and what happened to these women there. Bungle used his power over these women for his own (and against their) sexual desire; he sexualized his violence and denied them even the dignity of registering their protest.

For our purposes, whether what happened here was really rape is beside the point. What matters is how the community reacted. The community was outraged by what Bungle had done, and many thought something should be done in response.

They gathered then, this community of members of LamdaMOO, in a virtual room at a set time, to discuss what to do. Some thirty showed up, the largest meeting the community had known. Some thought that Bungle should be expelled— "toaded," as it is described, killed for purposes of the MOO. Others thought that nothing should be done; Bungle was certainly a creep, but the best thing to do to creeps was simply to ignore them. Some called on the Wizards of the space—the creators, the gods—to intervene to deal with this character. The Wizards declined: their job, they replied, was to create the world; the members had to learn to live within it.

There was really no law that governed what Bungle had done. No real-space law reached sexual pranks like this, and neither did any explicit rule of LamdaMOO.[26] This troubled many who wanted to do something. Invoking real-space ideals about fair notice and due process, these people argued that Bungle could not be punished for violating rules that did not exist at the time.

Two extremes eventually emerged. One side urged vigilantism: Bungle was a miscreant, and something should be done about him. But what shouldn't be done, they argued, was for LamdaMOO to respond by creating a world of regulation. LamdaMOO did not need a state; it needed a few good vigilantes. It needed people who would enforce the will of the community without the permanent intrusion of some central force called the state. Bungle should be expelled, killed, or "toaded"— and someone would do it. If only the group resisted the call to organize itself into a state.

The other side promoted just one idea: democracy. With the cooperation of the Wizards, LamdaMOO should establish a way to vote on rules that would govern how people in the space behaved. Any question could be made the subject of a ballot; there was no constitution limiting the scope of what democracy could decide. An issue decided by the ballot would be implemented by the Wizards. From then on, it would be a rule.

Both extremes had their virtues. Both invited certain vices. The anarchy of the first risked chaos. It was easy to imagine the community turning against people with little or no warning; one imagined vigilantes roaming the space, unconstrained by any rules, "toading" people whose crimes happened to strike them as "awful." For those who took this place less seriously than real space, this compromise was tolerable. But what was tolerable for some was intolerable to others—as Bungle had learned.

Democracy seemed natural, yet many resisted it as well. The idea that politics could exist in LamdaMOO seemed to sully the space. The thought that ideas would have to be debated and then voted on was just another burden. Sure, rules would be known and behavior could be regulated, but it all began to seem like work. The work took something from the fun the space was to have been.

In the end, both happened. The debate that evening wound down after almost three hours. No clear resolution had found its way in. But a resolution of sorts did occur. As Dibbell describes it:

It was also at this point, most likely, that TomTraceback reached his decision. TomTraceback was a wizard, a taciturn sort of fellow who'd sat brooding on the sidelines all evening. He hadn't said a lot, but what he had said indicated that he took the crime committed against exu and Moondreamer very seriously, and that he felt no particular compassion toward the character who had committed it. But on the other hand he had made it equally plain that he took the elimination of a fellow player just as seriously, and moreover that he had no desire to return to the days of wizardly intervention. It must have been difficult, therefore, to reconcile the conflicting impulses churning within him at that moment. In fact, it was probably impossible, for . . . as much as he would have liked to make himself an instrument of the MOO's collective will, [he surely realized that under the present order of things] he must in the final analysis either act alone or not act at all.

So TomTraceback acted alone.

He told the lingering few players in the room that he had to go, and then he went. It was a minute or two before 10 P.M. He did it quietly and he did it privately, but all anyone had to do to know he'd done it was to type the @*who* command, which was normally what you typed if you wanted to know a player's present location and the time he last logged in. But if you had run a @*who* on Mr. Bungle not too long after TomTraceback left emmeline's room, the database would have told you something different.

"*Mr_Bungle*," it would have said, "is not the name of any player."

The date, as it happened, was April Fool's Day, but this was no joke: Mr. Bungle was truly dead and truly gone.[27]

When the Wizards saw this, they moved to the other extreme. With no formal decision by the citizens, the Wizards called forth a democracy. Starting May 1, 1993,[28] any matter could be decided by ballot, and any proposition receiving at least twice as many votes for as against would become the law.[29] Many wondered whether this was an advance or not.

There is a lot to think about in this story, even in my savagely abridged version.[30] But I want to focus on the sense of loss that accompanied the Wizards' decision. There is a certain romance tied to the idea of establishing a democracy—Kodak commercials with tearful Berliners as the Wall comes down and all that. The romance is the idea of self-government and of establishing structures that facilitate it. But LamdaMOO's move to self-government, through structures of democracy, was not just an achievement. It was also a defeat. The space had failed. It had failed, we could say, to self-regulate. It had failed to engender values in its population sufficient to avoid just the sort of evil Bungle had perpetrated. The debate marked the passage of the space from one kind of place to another. From a space self-regulated to a space regulated by self.

It might seem odd that there would be a place where the emergence of democracy would so depress people. But this kind of reaction is not uncommon in cyberplaces. Katie Hafner and Matthew Lyon tell a story of the emergence of a "widget" called the FINGER command on UNIX, that would allow users to see when the last time another user had been on the computer, and whether she had read her mail. Some thought (not surprisingly, I should think) that this command was something of an invasion of privacy. Whose business was it when I was last at my machine, and why should they get to know whether I have read my mail?

A programmer at Carnegie Mellon University, Ivor Durham, changed the command to give the user the power to avoid this spying finger. The result? "Durham was flamed without mercy. He was called everything from spineless to socially irresponsible to a petty politician, and worse—but not for protecting privacy. He was criticized for monkeying with the openness of the network."[31]

The values of the UNIX world were different. They were values embedded in the code of UNIX. To change the code was to change the values, and members of the community fought that change.

So too with the changes to LamdaMoo. Before the balloting, LamdaMoo was regulated through norms. These regulations of social structures were sustained by the constant policing of individual citizens. They were the regulations of a community; the rise of democracy marked the fall of this community. Although norms would no doubt survive the establishment of a democracy, their status was forever changed. Before the democracy, a struggle over which norms should prevail could be resolved only by consensus—by certain views prevailing in a decentralized way. Now such a struggle could be resolved by the power of a majority—not through what a majority *did*, but through how they voted.

I've romanticized this bizarre little world far more than I intended. I do not mean to suggest that the world of LamdaMOO before democracy was necessarily better than the one after. I want only to mark a particular change. Like CC, and unlike AOL, LamdaMOO is a place where norms regulate. But unlike CC, LamdaMOO is now a place where members have control over restructuring the norms.

Such control changes things. Norms become different when ballots can overrule them. And code becomes different when ballots can order Wizards to change the world. These changes mark a movement from one kind of normative space to another, from one kind of regulation to another.

In all three of these cyber-places, code is a regulator. But there are important differences among the three. Norms have a relevance in CC and LamdaMOO that they do not in AOL; democracy has a relevance in LamdaMOO that it does not have in CC or AOL. And monitoring has a relevance in AOL that it does not have in LamdaMOO or CC (since neither of the latter two use data about individuals for commercial purposes, either internal or external to the organization). Code constitutes these three communities; as Jennifer Mnookin says of LamdaMoo, "politics [is] implemented through technology."[32] Differences in the code constitute them differently, but some code makes community thicker than others. Where community is thick, norms can regulate.

The final space in this survey is also constituted by code, though in this case the "management" has less ability to change its basic architecture. This code is net code—a protocol of the Internet that is not easily changed by a single user. At least it was not easy for me.

.law.cyber

His name was IBEX, and no one knew who he was. I probably could have figured it out—I had the data to track him down—but after he did what he did, I did not want to know who he was. He was probably a student in the very first class about cyberspace that I taught, and I would have failed him, for I was furious about what he had done. The class was "The Law of Cyberspace"; version one of that class was at Yale.

I say version one because I had the extraordinary opportunity to teach that class at three extraordinary law schools—first at Yale, then at the University of Chicago, and finally at Harvard. These were three very different places, with three very different student bodies, but one part of the course was the same in each place. Every year a "newsgroup" was associated with the class—an electronic bulletin board where students could post messages about questions raised in the course, or about anything at all. These postings began conversations—threads of discussion, one message posted after another, debating or questioning what the earlier message had said.

These newsgroups constituted what philosophers might call "dialogic communities." They were spaces where discussion could occur, but where what was said was preserved for others to read, as in CC. That was the dialogic part. The community was what was made over time as people got to know each other—both in this space and in real space. One year students in the class and students outside the class (who had been watching the .law.cyber discussions develop) had a party; another year the students outside the class were invited to attend one class. But over the three years, at three different schools, it was clear that three communities had been made. Each was born on a particular date, and each lived for at least a couple of months.

My story here comes from Yale. Yale is an odd sort of law school, though odd in a good way. It is small and filled with extremely bright people, many of whom do not really want to be lawyers. It fashions itself as a community, and everyone from the dean on down (not a "Yale" way to describe things) strives continuously to foster and sustain this sense of community among the students. To a large extent, it works—not in the sense that there is perpetual peace, but in the sense that people everywhere are aware of this sense of community. Some embrace it, others resist it, but the resistance, like an embrace, says that something is there. One does not resist the community of people on a Greyhound bus.

One extraordinary feature of the Yale Law School is "the Wall." The Wall is a place where people can post comments about whatever in the world they want to say. A letter can be posted about gay rights at Yale, or a protest about Yale's treatment of unionized workers. Political messages are posted as well as points about law. Each posting makes additional ones possible—either scribbled on the original post or appended underneath the post.

An extraordinary sign for any visitor, the Wall is located right at the center of the law school. In the middle of a fake Gothic structure is a stone space with scores of papers posted in random fashion. Around the posts stand wandering students, reading what others have said. This is Yale's speakers' corner, though the speakers are writers, and the writing is substantive. There is little to be gained on the Wall through rhetoric; to gain respect there, you must say something of substance.

One rule, however, governs this space. All postings must be signed; any posting without a signature is removed. Originally, no doubt, the rule meant that the posting be signed by the person who wrote it. But because this is Yale, where no rule can exist without a thousand questions raised, a custom has emerged whereby an anonymous post can be signed by someone not its author ("Signed but not written by X"). That signature gives the post the pedigree it needs to survive on the Wall.

The reasons for this rule are clear, but so too are its problems. Let's say you want to criticize the dean for a decision he has made. The dean, however sweet, is a powerful person. You might well prefer to post a message without your name attached to it. Or say you are a student with political views that make you an outsider. Posting a message with those views and your signature might draw the scorn of your classmates. Free speech is not speech without consequence, and scorn, or shame, or ostracism, are likely consequences of lots of speech.

Anonymity, then, is a way around this dilemma. With anonymity, you can say what you want without fear. In some cases, for some people, the right to speak anonymously makes sense.

Still, a community might want to resist this right. Just as anonymity might give you the strength to state an unpopular view, it can also shield you if you post an irresponsible view. Or a slanderous view. Or a hurtful view. You might want to question the policies of the dean, or you might want falsely to accuse a fellow student of cheating. Both utterances benefit from anonymity, but the community has good reason to resist utterances like the second.

As far as I know, IBEX never said anything on the Wall. Instead, he spoke in the newsgroup associated with my class. By design, the newsgroup was open to anyone at Yale who wanted to speak. Unlike the Wall, however, the technology allowed users to call themselves whatever they wanted. "IBEX," of course, was a pseudonym. For purposes of the Wall, a pseudonym was just like anonymous speech—you had to use your real name. But in a newsgroup a pseudonymous posting is quite different from an anonymous posting. Over time you can come to know the character of a pseudonym. In the class that year, along with IBEX, we had SpeedRacer, MadMacs, Cliff-Claven, Aliens, blah, and Christopher Robbin. While members of the class might know who these participants were (we all knew who MadMacs was, but only a few of us knew SpeedRacer), each pseudonym had a character whether people knew who they were or not.

The character of IBEX was bad. This much was clear from the start. Before IBEX appeared, life in the space flourished. At first people were timid, but polite. Brave souls would post an idea or a joke. The conversation would continue around the idea or joke for a bit. After a couple of weeks the conversation would become quite intense. Patterns of exchange began. People had questions; others had answers. People stumbled as they spoke, but they were beginning, slowly, to speak.

Some things about how they spoke were immediately noticeable. First, women spoke more in this space than they did in class. Maybe not more in a statistically significant sense, but more.[33] Second, helpers quickly developed, and those who received their help. Soon a class developed online—a real class that identified itself as such and spoke as a class in a way that a teacher dreams of in real space, and in a way I had never known.

Why this happened I could not really say. Una Smith may have been a catalyst. I said that I taught this course three times. Each time (without my intervention at all) there was an Una Smith participating in the newsgroup. At Yale she was a real person, but after Yale I thought of her as a type. She was always a woman from outside the class; she was always extremely knowledgeable about the Net and about USENET; and she always wandered into my (virtual) class and began telling the others how they should behave. When someone violated a norm of the Net, Una would correct them. Often this instruction was not taken terribly well (these were, after all, law students). Soon the class would rally to defend the instructed and to challenge her to defend her rules. And of course, expert that she was, she usually had an answer that did defend the rules she had dictated. This exchange soon became a focus of the class. Una had drawn their anger, and the class gained cohesiveness as a result.

About a month and a half into the course, the group reached an apex of sorts. It became the best it would be. I remember the moment well. Early on a spring afternoon I noticed that someone had posted the first line of a poem. By the end of the day, without any coordination, the class had finished the poem. There had been rhythm to the exchanges; now there was rhyme. Things hummed in the newsgroup, and people were genuinely surprised about this space.

It was then that IBEX appeared. I think it was just after we had discussed anonymity in class, so maybe his later claims to have been serving a pedagogical role were true. But he appeared after one of our classes—appeared, it seemed, just to issue an attack on another member of the class. Not an attack on his ideas, but on him. So vicious and so extensive was this attack that when I read it, I didn't know quite how to understand it. Could it have been real?

Almost immediately, conversation in the group died. It just stopped. No one said anything, as if everyone were afraid that the monster that had entered our space would turn his fury on one of them next. Until, that is, the victim responded, with an answer that evinced the wounds of the attack. IBEX's words had cut. The victim was angry and hurt, and he attacked back.

But his salvo only inspired another round of viciousness, even more vile than the first. With this, other members of the class could not resist joining in. IBEX was attacked by a string of characters in the class as cowardly for hiding behind a pseudonym and as sick for what he had said. None of this had any effect. IBEX came back, again and again, with an ugliness that was as extreme as it was unrelenting.

The space had been changed. Conversation fell off, people drifted away. Some no doubt left because they were disgusted with what had happened; others did not want to be IBEX's next target. There was a brief period of life in the space as people rallied to attack IBEX. But as he came back again and again, each time more vicious than the last, most simply left the space. (One time IBEX came back to protest that he had been wronged; in the week before, he claimed, he had not posted anything, but someone wearing the white sheet of IBEX had posted in IBEX's name, so that he, the real IBEX, had been defamed. The class had little sympathy.)

But it was not just the online class that changed. As we met face to face each week I felt the atmosphere bend. People felt the creature in the room, though no one could believe he was a student at the Yale Law School. This was their classmate, hiding behind a smile, or a joke, in real space, but vicious in cyberspace. And the very idea that this evil was hidden under a smile changed how people felt about smiles.

Some called this the "David Lynch effect," an allusion to the film producer who portrays the rot of society just under freshly painted facades. We felt in that class the rot of our community just under the surface of smiling and functional students. There was a (relatively tame) Jake Baker in our midst. The space had permitted behavior that destroyed community—community that the space itself had created. Community had been created in part through the ability to hide—to hide behind a benign pseudonym; to hide hesitation, or editing, in the writing; to hide your reaction; to hide that you were not paying attention. These anonymities had made the community what it was. But the same anonymity that created the community gave birth to IBEX as well, and thus took the community away.

HOW ARCHITECTURES MATTER AND SPACES DIFFER

I said this at the start, but now it should have some real meaning: cyberspace is not *a* place; it is many places. Its places don't have one nature; the places of cyberspace have many different "natures." These natures are not given, they are made. They are set (in part at least) by the architectures that constitute these different spaces. These architectures are themselves not given; these architectures of code are set by the architects of cyberspace—code writers.

The spaces I have described *here* are different. These differences have been the purpose of my description. My aim has been to remind you of the different character that these places have, and to remind you again of the reasons that these places have these differences.

In some places there is community—that is, a set of norms that are self-enforcing within the group. Features such as visibility (as opposed to anonymity) and nontransience help create those norms; anonymity, transience, and diversity make it harder to create community.

In places where community is not fully self-enforcing, norms are supplemented either by rules imposed through code or by rules recognized through democratic procedures. These supplements may further some normative end, but at times they are in tension with the goal of community building.

If we had to simplify this diversity of spaces by finding one dimension along which we could rank them, that dimension might be their amenability to outside control. "Community" in the sense that I've used the word means a group able to enforce its own norms among its members. In this, the groups I've discussed are universally vulnerable—.law.cyber being the most vulnerable. But as we move from .law.cyber to CC to LamdaMOO to AOL, the ability to enforce a norm on the group from the outside increases. In .law.cyber, people within the space can argue all they want about introducing a new norm or changing an existing one, but a norm becomes a group norm only if the whole group comes to see it as valuable, and so adopts it. No external control is possible.

The possibility of external control is greater in CC, though CC and AOL share a market constraint. In both, management can change the code to bring about a particular end, but if that end is too far removed from what most members think the space is about, they may simply leave. As a result, AOL has more control than CC; because the range of behavior on AOL is wider, the range of possible rules in this space is greater as well.

In LamdaMOO the story is more complicated. Nothing really binds people to a particular MOO. (There are thousands, and most are free.) But because characters in a MOO are earned rather than bought, and because this takes time and characters are not fungible, it becomes increasingly hard for members of a successful MOO to move elsewhere. They have the right to exit, but in the sense that Soviet citizens had the right to exit—namely, with none of the assets they had built in their particular world.

The members of a MOO are in a sense the most vulnerable to changes imposed from the outside. Because the world of the MOO is (like AOL) completely constricted by code (whether collectively or individually), it is here that the control has the potential to be the greatest.

TRADE-OFFS OF CONTROL

Our look at these contrasting spaces should give depth to the idea that architecture matters and highlight the different ways in which the code of a cyberspace might enable or disable certain forms of life. Cyberspaces differ not only in the amount of regulation that each permits; they also differ in the values they embrace and the kind of regulation they permit. Some spaces can be regulated by norms; code can change that. Some places cannot be regulated by norms; sometimes code can change that as well. The regulating norms can be those of real space as well as of cyberspace. And, as we saw in the discussion of Jake Baker, the architecture of cyberspace may permit an escape from the regulations of real space into a space regulated very differently. The choices are rich, but they are *choices*.[34]

If we let the invisible hand work unimpeded, these choices will be made according to the set of interests that are expressed by commerce on the Net. In some cases, certainly, those interests will be constrained by government. But now we must think specifically about how we could structure the choices we will confront and how we could resolve the conflicts of values these spaces will present.

Our choices in each case are two. We can try to make cyberspace the same as real space, investing it with the same values, or we can give cyberspace values and properties that are fundamentally different.

There is no general answer as to which choice we should make. But if we decide we should preserve values from real space, we need a way to think about how. And if we decide we should change values from real space, then change them to what?

The next chapter is about how we might constitute values differently. It is grounded in a broader sense of this idea of "regulation." Using this broader sense, we will see what control might be possible. And in chapter 8, we will see some of the limits on that control.

Both chapters are about how we might exercise choice. This chapter has been about the differences in cyberspaces that these choices make. In part 3, we will consider which differences we should want and which we should avoid. We will, in other words, practice this choice.

S E V E N

what things regulate

JOHN STUART MILL WAS AN ENGLISHMAN, THOUGH ONE OF THE MOST INFLUENTIAL political philosophers in America in the nineteenth century. His writings ranged from important work on logic to a still striking text, *The Subjection of Women*. But his continuing influence comes from a relatively short book titled *On Liberty*. Published in 1859, this powerful argument for individual liberty and diversity of thought represents an important view of liberal and libertarian thinking in the second half of the nineteenth century.

"Libertarian," however, has a specific meaning for us. It associates with arguments against government.[1] Government, in the modern libertarian's view, is the threat to liberty; private action is not. Thus, the good libertarian is focused on reducing government's power. Curb the excesses of government, the libertarian says, and you will have ensured freedom for your society.

Mill's view was not so narrow. He was a defender of liberty and an opponent of forces that suppressed it. But those forces were not confined to government. Liberty, in Mill's view, was threatened as much by norms as by government, as much by stigma and intolerance as by the threat of state punishment. His objective was to argue against these private forces of coercion. His work was a defense against liberty-suppressing norms, because in England at the time these were the real threat to liberty.

Mill's method is important, and it should be our own. It asks, What is the threat to liberty, and how can we resist it? It is not limited to asking, What is the threat to liberty *from government?* It understands that more than government can threaten liberty, and that sometimes this something more can be private rather than state action. Mill was not so concerned with the source. His concern was with liberty.

Threats to liberty change. In England norms may have been the problem in the late nineteenth century; in the United States in the first two decades of the twentieth century it was state suppression of speech.[2] The labor movement was founded on the idea that the market is sometimes a threat to liberty—not just because of low wages, but also because the market form of organization itself disables a certain kind of freedom.[3] In other societies, at other times, the market is the key, not the enemy, to liberty.

Thus, rather than think of an enemy in the abstract, we should understand the particular threat to liberty that exists in a particular time and place. And this is especially true when we think about liberty in cyberspace. For my argument is that cyberspace teaches a new threat to liberty. Not new in the sense that no theorist has conceived of it before. Others have.[4] But new in the sense of newly urgent. We are coming to understand a newly powerful regulator in cyberspace, and we don't yet understand how best to control it.

This regulator is code—or more generally, the "built environment" of social life, its architecture.[5] And if in the middle of the nineteenth century it was norms that threatened liberty, and at the start of the twentieth state power that threatened liberty, and during much of the middle twentieth the market that threatened liberty, my argument is that we understand how in the late twentieth century, and into the twenty-first, it is a different regulator—code—that should be our concern.

But it is not my aim to say that this should be our new single focus. My argument is not that there is a new single enemy different from the old. Instead, I believe we need a more general understanding of how regulation works. One that focuses on more than the single influence of any one force such as government, norms, or the market, and instead integrates these factors into a single account.

This chapter is a step toward that more general understanding.[6] It is an invitation to think beyond the narrow threat of government. The threats to liberty have never come solely from government, and the threats to liberty in cyberspace certainly will not.

A D O T ' S L I F E

There are many ways to think about constitutional law and the limits it may impose on government regulation. I want to think about it from the perspective of someone who is regulated or constrained. That someone regulated is represented by this (pathetic) dot—a creature (you or me) subject to the different constraints that might regulate it. By describing the various constraints that might bear on this individual, I hope to show you something about how these constraints function together.

Here then is the dot.

How is this dot "regulated"?

Let's start with something easy: smoking. If you want to smoke, what constraints do you face? What factors *regulate* your decision to smoke or not?

One constraint is legal. In some places at least, laws regulate smoking—if you are under eighteen, the law says that cigarettes cannot be sold to you. If you are under twenty-six, cigarettes cannot be sold to you unless the seller checks your ID. Laws also regulate where smoking is permitted—not in O'Hare Airport, on an airplane, or in an elevator, for instance. In these two ways at least, laws aim to direct smoking behavior. They operate as a kind of constraint on an individual who wants to smoke.[7]

But laws are not the most significant constraints on smoking. Smokers in the United States certainly feel their freedom regulated, even if only rarely by the law. There are no smoking police, and smoking courts are still quite rare. Rather, smokers in America are regulated by norms. Norms say that one doesn't light a cigarette in a private car without first asking permission of the other passengers. They also say, however, that one needn't ask permission to smoke at a picnic. Norms say that others can ask you to stop smoking at a restaurant, or that you never smoke during a meal.

European norms are savagely different. There the presumption is in the smoker's favor; vis-à-vis the smoker, the norms are laissez-faire. But in the States the norms effect a certain constraint, and this constraint, we can say, *regulates* smoking behavior.

Law and norms are still not the only forces regulating smoking behavior. The market too is a constraint. The price of cigarettes is a constraint on your ability to smoke. Change the price, and you change this constraint. Likewise with quality. If the market supplies a variety of cigarettes of widely varying quality and price, your ability to select the kind of cigarette you want increases; increasing choice here reduces constraint.

Finally, there are the constraints created, we might say, by the technology of cigarettes, or by the technologies affecting their supply.[8] Unfiltered cigarettes present a greater constraint on smoking than filtered cigarettes if you are worried about your health. Nicotine-treated cigarettes are addictive and therefore create a greater constraint on smoking than untreated cigarettes. Smokeless cigarettes present less of a constraint because they can be smoked in more places. Cigarettes with a strong odor present more of a constraint because they can be smoked in fewer places. In all of these ways, how the cigarette *is* affects the constraints faced by a smoker. How it is, how it is designed, how it is built—in a word, its *architecture*.

Thus, four constraints regulate this pathetic dot—the law, social norms, the market, and architecture—and the "regulation" of this dot is the sum of these four constraints. Changes in any one will affect the regulation of the whole. Some constraints will support others; some may undermine others. A complete view, however, should consider them together.

So think of the four together like this:

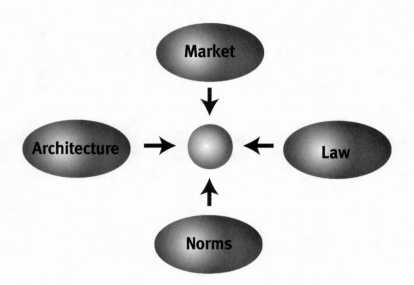

In this drawing, each oval represents one kind of constraint operating on our pathetic dot in the center. Each constraint imposes a different kind of cost on the dot for engaging in the relevant behavior—in this case, smoking. The cost from norms is different from the market cost, which is different from the cost from law and the cost from the (cancerous) architecture of cigarettes.

The constraints are distinct, yet they are plainly interdependent. Each can support or oppose the others. Technologies can undermine norms and laws; they can also support them. Some constraints make others possible; others make some impossible. Constraints work together, though they function differently and the effect of each is distinct. Norms constrain through the stigma that a community imposes; markets constrain through the price that they exact; architectures constrain through the physical burdens they impose; and law constrains through the punishment it threatens.

We can call each constraint a "regulator," and we can think of each as a distinct modality of regulation. Each modality has a complex nature, and the interaction among these four is hard to describe. I've worked through this complexity more completely in the appendix. But for now, it is enough to see that they are linked and that, in a sense, they combine to produce the regulation to which our pathetic dot is subject in any given area.

The same model describes the regulation of behavior in cyberspace.

Law regulates behavior in cyberspace. Copyright law, defamation law, and obscenity laws all continue to threaten *ex post* sanction for the violation of legal rights. How well law regulates, or how efficiently, is a different question: in some cases it does so more efficiently, in some cases less. But whether better or not, law continues to threaten a certain consequence if it is defied. Legislatures enact;[9] prosecutors threaten;[10] courts convict.[11]

Norms also regulate behavior in cyberspace. Talk about democratic politics in the alt.knitting newsgroup, and you open yourself to flaming; "spoof" someone's identity in a MUD, and you may find yourself "toaded";[12] talk too much in a discussion list, and you are likely to be placed on a common bozo filter. In each case, a set of understandings constrain behavior, again through the threat of *ex post* sanctions imposed by a community.

Markets regulate behavior in cyberspace. Pricing structures constrain access, and if they do not, busy signals do. (AOL learned this quite dramatically when it shifted from an hourly to a flat rate pricing plan.)[13] Areas of the Web are beginning to charge for access, as online services have for some time. Advertisers reward popular sites; online services drop low-population forums. These behaviors are all a function of market constraints and market opportunity. They are all, in this sense, regulations of the market.

And finally, an analog for architecture regulates behavior in cyberspace—*code.* The software and hardware that make cyberspace what it is constitute a set of constraints on how you can behave. The substance of these constraints may vary, but they are experienced as conditions on your access to cyberspace. In some places (online services such as AOL, for instance) you must enter a password before you gain access; in other places you can enter whether identified or not.[14] In some places the transactions you engage in produce traces that link the transactions (the "mouse droppings") back to you; in other places this link is achieved only if you want it to be.[15] In some places you can choose to speak a language that only the recipient can hear (through encryption);[16] in other places encryption is not an option.[17] The code or software or architecture or protocols set these features; they are features selected by code writers; they constrain some behavior by making other behavior possible, or impossible. The code embeds certain values or makes certain values impossible. In this sense, it too is regulation, just as the architectures of real-space codes are regulations.

As in real space, then, these four modalities regulate cyberspace. The same balance exists. As William Mitchell puts it (though he omits the constraint of the market):

Architecture, laws, and customs maintain and represent whatever balance has been struck [in real space]. As we construct and inhabit cyberspace communities, we will have to make and maintain similar bargains—though they will be embodied in software structures and electronic access controls rather than in architectural arrangements.[18]

Laws, norms, the market, and architectures interact to build the environment that "Netizens" know. The code writer, as Ethan Katsh puts it, is the "architect."[19]

But how can we "make and maintain" this balance between modalities? What tools do we have to achieve a different construction? How might the mix of real-space values be carried over to the world of cyberspace? How might the mix be changed if change is desired?

ON GOVERNMENTS AND WAYS TO REGULATE

I've described four constraints that I've said "regulate" an individual. But these separate constraints obviously don't simply exist as givens in a social life. They are neither found in nature nor fixed by God. Each can be changed, though the mechanics of changing each is complex. Law can have a significant role in this mechanics, and my aim in this section is to describe that role.

A simple example will suggest the more general point. Say the theft of car radios is a problem—not big in the scale of things, but a frequent and costly enough problem to make more regulation seem necessary. One response might be to increase the penalty for car radio theft until the risk faced by thieves made it such that this crime did not pay. Life in prison for radio theft. If radio thieves realized that they exposed themselves to a lifetime in prison each time they stole a radio, it might no longer make sense to them to steal radios. The constraint constituted by the threatened punishment of *law* would now be enough to stop the behavior we are trying to stop.

But changing the law is not the only possible technique. A second might be to change the radio's architecture. Imagine that radio manufacturers program radios to work only with a single car—a security code that electronically locks the radio to the car, such that if the radio is removed, it will no longer work. This is a *code* constraint on the theft of radios; it makes the radio no longer effective once stolen. It too functions as a constraint on the radio's theft, and like the threatened punishment of life in prison, it could be effective in stopping the radio-stealing behavior.

Thus, the same constraint can be achieved through different means, and the different means are differently costly. The threatened punishment of life in prison may be fiscally more costly than the change in the architecture of radios (depending on how many people actually continue to steal radios, and how many are caught). From this fiscal perspective, it may be more efficient to change code than law. Fiscal efficiency may also align with the expressive content of law—a punishment so extreme would be barbaric for a crime so slight. Thus, the values may well track the efficient response. Code would be the best means to regulate.

The costs, however, need not align so well, in this example or in others. Take the Supreme Court's hypothetical example of life in prison for a parking ticket.[20] It is likely that whatever code constraint might match this law constraint, the law constraint would be more efficient (if reducing parking violations were the only aim).

There would be very few victims of this law before people conformed their behavior appropriately. But the "efficient result" would conflict with other values. If it is barbaric to incarcerate for life for the theft of a radio, it is all the more so as a penalty for a parking violation. The regulator has a range of means to effect the desired constraint, but the values that these means entail need not align with their efficiency. The efficient answer may well be unjust—that is, it may conflict with values inherent in the norms, or law (constitution), of the society.

Law-talk typically ignores these other regulators. It typically ignores how law can affect their regulation. Many speak as if law must simply take the other three constraints as given and fashion itself to them.[21]

I say "as if" because today it takes only a second's thought to see that this narrowness is absurd. There were times when these other constraints were treated as fixed—when the constraints of norms were said to be immovable by governmental action,[22] or the market was thought to be essentially unregulable,[23] or the cost of changing real-space code was so high as to make the thought of using it for regulation absurd.[24] But we see now that these constraints are plastic.[25] That they are, as law is, changeable, and subject to regulation.

The examples are obvious and many. Think first about the market: talk of a "free market" notwithstanding, there is no more heavily regulated aspect of our life.[26] The market is regulated by law not just in its elements—it is law that enforces contracts, establishes property, and regulates currency—but also in its effects. The law uses taxes to increase the market's constraint on certain behaviors and subsidies to reduce its constraint on other behaviors. We tax cigarettes in part to reduce their consumption, but we subsidize tobacco production to increase its supply. We tax alcohol to reduce its consumption. We subsidize child care to reduce the constraint the market puts on raising children. In many such ways the constraint of law is used to change the constraints of the market.

Law can also change the regulation of architecture. Think about the Americans with Disabilities Act (ADA).[27] Many of the "disabled" are cut off from access to much of the world. A building with only stairs is a building that is inaccessible to a person in a wheelchair. The stairs are a constraint on the disabled person's access to that building. But the ADA in part aims to change that constraint by requiring builders to change the design of buildings so that the disabled are not excluded. Here is a regulation of real-space code, by law, to change the constraint that real-space code creates.

Other examples get even better.

- Some of the power of the French Revolution derived from the architecture of Paris: the city's small and winding streets were easily barricaded, making it possible for revolutionaries to take control of the city with relatively little absolute strength. Louis Napoleon III understood this, and in 1853 he took steps to change it.[28] Paris was rebuilt, with wide boulevards and multiple passages, making it impossible for insurgents to take control of the city.

- Every schoolchild learns of Lafayette's design to make an invasion of Washington difficult. But more interesting is the placement of the White House relative to the Capitol. The distance between them is one mile, and at the time it was a mile through difficult terrain. (The mall was a swamp.) The distance was a barrier meant to tilt the intercourse between Congress and the president by making it marginally more difficult for them to connect—and thereby more difficult for the executive to control the legislature.

- This same idea has influenced the placement of constitutional courts in Europe. Throughout Europe constitutional courts were placed in cities other than the capital. In Germany the court is in Karlsruhe rather than Berlin; in the Czech Republic it is in Brno rather than Prague. The reason again is tied to the constraint of geography: placing constitutional courts far away from legislatures and executives was meant to minimize both the pressure the latter two bodies could place on the court and reduce the court's temptation to bow to it.

- The principle is not limited to high politics. Designers of parking garages or streets where children may play place speed bumps in the road so that drivers must slow down. These structures have the same purpose as a speed limit or a norm against driving too fast. But they operate by modifying architecture so that architecture regulates.

- Neither is the principle limited to virtuous regulation: Robert Moses built bridges on Long Island to block buses, so that African Americans, who depended primarily on public transportation, could not easily get to public beaches.[29] That was regulation through architecture, invidious yet familiar.

- Nor is it limited to governments. A major American airline noticed that passengers on early Monday morning flights were frustrated with the time it took to retrieve bags from the plane. They were much more annoyed than other passengers, even though it took no longer than average to retrieve the bags from these flights. The company began parking these flights at gates farther away from baggage claim, so that by the time the passengers arrived at baggage claim, their bags were there. Frustration with the baggage handling system was eliminated.

- A large hotel in an American city received many complaints about the slowness of its elevators. It installed mirrors next to the elevator doors. The complaints ended.

In each example, a constraint of architecture is changed so as to realize a collective or social end. As a sign above one of the portals at the 1933 Chicago World's Fair put it (though it was speaking of science): "Science Explores: Technology Executes: Man Conforms."[30]

Law can change social norms as well, though much of our constitutional jurisprudence seems dedicated to forgetting just how.[31] Education is the most obvious example. As Thurgood Marshall put it, "Education is not the teaching of the three R's. Education is the teaching of the overall citizenship, to learn to live together with fellow citizens, and above all to learn to obey the law."[32] Education is, in part at least, a process through which we indoctrinate children into certain norms of behavior— we teach them how to "say no" to sex and drugs. We try to build within them a sense of what is correct. This sense then regulates them to the law's end.

Plainly, the content of much of this education is regulated by law. Conservatives worry, for example, that by teaching sex education we change the norm of sexual abstinence. Whether that is correct or not, the law is certainly being used to change the norms of children. If conservatives are correct, the law is eliminating abstinence. If liberals are correct, the law is being used to instill a norm of safe sex. Either way, norms have their own constraint, and law is aiming to change that constraint.

To say that law plays a role is not to say that it always plays a positive role. The law can muck up norms as well as improve them, and I do not claim that the latter result is more common than the former.[33] The point is just to see the role, not to praise or criticize it. The aim is descriptive; the normative comes later.

In each case, the law chooses between direct and indirect regulation. The question is: Which means best advances the regulator's goal, subject to the constraints (whether normative or material) that the regulator must recognize? We can represent the point through a modification of the second figure:

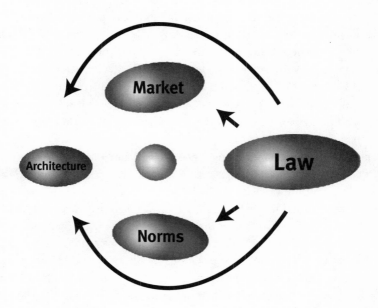

The point should be familiar, and the examples can be multiplied.

Seatbelts: The government may want citizens to wear seatbelts more often.[34] It could pass a law to require the wearing of seatbelts (law regulating behavior directly). Or it could fund public education campaigns to create a stigma against those who do not wear seatbelts (law regulating social norms as a means to regulating behavior). Or it could subsidize insurance companies to offer reduced rates to seatbelt wearers (law regulating the market as a way of regulating behavior). Finally, the law could mandate automatic seatbelts, or ignition-locking systems (changing the code of the automobile as a means of regulating belting behavior). Each action might be said to have some effect on seatbelt use; each has some cost. The question for the government is how to get the most seatbelt use for the least cost.

Discrimination against the disabled: The disabled bear the burden of significant social and physical barriers in daily life.[35] The government might decide to do something about those barriers. The traditional answer is law regulating behavior directly: a law barring discrimination on the basis of physical disability. But the law could do more. It could, for example, educate children so as to change social norms (regulating norms to regulate behavior). It could subsidize companies to hire the disabled (regulating the market to regulate behavior). It could regulate building codes to make buildings more accessible to the disabled (regulating "natural" or real-space codes to regulate behavior). Each of these regulations would have some effect on discrimination and would have a cost. The government would have to weigh the costs against the benefits and select the mode that regulates most effectively.

Drugs: The government is obsessed with reducing the consumption of illicit drugs. Its main strategy has been direct regulation of behavior through the threat of barbaric prison terms for violation of the drug laws. This policy has obvious costs and non-obvious benefits. But most interesting for our purposes are the non-obvious costs. As Tracey Meares persuasively argues, one effective structure for regulating the consumption of illegal drugs is the social structure of the community in which an individual lives.[36] These are what I've called social norm constraints: standards of appropriate behavior enforced by the sanctions of a community—whether through shame, exclusion, or force.

Just as government can act to strengthen these social norm constraints, it should be obvious that government can also act to weaken them.[37] One way to do this is by weakening the communities within which these norms operate. This, says Meares, is what the extreme sanctions of the criminal law do.[38] In their extremity and effect, they undermine the social structures that would support this social policy. This is an indirect effect of the direct regulation of law, and at some point this effect may overwhelm the effect of the law. We might call this the Laffer Curve for criminal law.

The net effect of these different constraints cannot be deduced a priori. The government acts in many ways to regulate the consumption of drugs. It supports extensive public education campaigns to stigmatize the consumption of drugs (regulating social norms to regulate behavior). It seizes drugs at the border, thereby reducing the supply, increasing the price, and presumably reducing demand (regulating the market to regulate behavior). And at times it has even (and grotesquely) regulated the "code" of drugs (by, for example, spraying marijuana fields with paraquat), making them more dangerous and thereby increasing the constraint on their consumption.[39] All of these together influence the consumption of drugs. But as advocates of legalization argue, they also influence the incidence of other criminal behavior as well. The policy maker must assess the net effect—whether on the whole these regulations reduce or increase social costs.

Abortion: One final example will complete the account. Since *Roe v Wade,* the Court has recognized a woman's constitutional right to an abortion.[40] This right, however, has not stopped government from seeking to eliminate or reduce the number of abortions. Again, the government need not rely on direct regulation of abortion (which under *Roe* would be unconstitutional). It can instead use indirect means to the same end. In *Rust v Sullivan,* the Court upheld the power of the government to bias the provision of family planning advice by forbidding doctors in "government-funded" clinics from mentioning abortion as a method of family planning.[41] This is a regulation of social norms (within the social structure of medical care) to regulate behavior. In *Maher v Roe,* the Court upheld the right of the government selectively to disable medical funding for abortion.[42] This is the use of the market to regulate behavior. And in *Hodgson v Minnesota,* the Court upheld the right of the state to force minor women to wait forty-eight hours before getting an abortion.[43] This is the use of real-space code (the constraints of time) to regulate access to abortion. In all these ways, *Roe* notwithstanding, the government can regulate the behavior of women wanting abortions.

In each of these examples, law functions in two very different ways.[44] When its operation is direct, it tells individuals how to behave and threatens punishment if they deviate from that behavior. When its operation is indirect, it aims at modifying one of the other structures of constraint.[45] The regulator selects from among these various techniques according to the return from each—both in efficiency and in the values that each might express.

When we see regulation in this more general way, we can see more clearly how the unregulability of cyberspace is contingent. We get a stronger sense of how the state could intervene to make regulation work. And we should also get a sense of the increased dangers presented by this more expansive sense of regulation. In particular, we should have a stronger sense of the danger it presents to constitutional values. The next section considers one such threat.

THE PROBLEMS OF INDIRECTION

In 1985, after years of inaction, Congress passed the Low Level Radioactive Waste Policy Amendments Act to deal with the problem of nuclear waste.[46] Someone needed to take and store nuclear waste. After sufficient prodding by the government, a number of states formed a compact, which Congress then ratified, implementing a number of requirements and incentives for states to deal with the nuclear waste they produce.

The details of the overall plan are not important here. It is enough to focus on just one part. To induce states to follow federal guidelines for regulating nuclear waste, Congress gave them a choice: either enact certain regulations or "take title" to the spent nuclear fuel. This was a "your money or your life" regulation, for the fuel to which the states would take title was not an asset but a great liability. In a very heavy-handed way, Congress was essentially forcing states to pass the regulations it wanted.

The Supreme Court struck down this part of the law. In effect, the Court held, Congress was commandeering the state legislatures to enact Congress's law. Congress itself, of course, had the power to enact those regulations directly. But it did not have the power to order states to enact laws. Indirection here was not allowed.

This case—*New York v United States*—does not stand for the broad principle that government must regulate only directly, or even for the principle that indirect regulation generally is disfavored. The case was focused quite narrowly on the question of indirection as it involved the states. The most *New York* stands for is the idea that states, as independent sovereigns deserving of special constitutional respect, cannot be co-opted to the federal government's ends—that when the federal government has a program it wants to carry out, it must put its own name behind it.

But while *New York* doesn't establish a general constitutional principle, it does suggest why indirection should be a more general concern. And this general concern is my focus here.

Indirection misdirects responsibility. When a government uses other structures of constraint to effect a constraint it could impose directly, it muddies the responsibility for that constraint and so undermines political accountability. If transparency is a value in constitutional government, indirection is its enemy. It confuses responsibility and hence confuses politics.

Such misunderstandings are possible in other contexts as well. Think again about the case of *Rust*. The federal government helps to fund family planning clinics. ("Helps" fund, not completely funds.)[47] Before 1988 these clinics gave advice on a wide range of birth-related topics, including abortion. Doctors in family planning clinics would advise their patients about abortion whenever they felt such advice was proper.

The Reagan administration wanted to change that. So it ordered (the details of how are not important here) doctors in those clinics to not discuss abortion as a method of family planning with their patients. If asked, the doctors were to say, "The project does not consider abortion an appropriate method of family planning."[48]

The aim of this regulation was clear: to reduce the incidence of abortion. It did this by using doctors to steer patients away from abortion. A doctor has a great deal of power over a patient in a context like this; the patient would most likely understand the doctor to be recommending against abortion.

But notice the technique. The federal government could have stated its own position about abortion. It could have put up posters and billboards saying that abortion is wrong, or it could have used space in its clinics to advertise its view. But it chose instead to bury its policy choice in the words of doctors. It thereby could trade on the professional authority of the doctors to advance its own ends. It could regulate abortion indirectly by regulating the doctors directly.

Just as it tried to use the authority of the states to effect its ends in *New York,* the government trades on a misrepresentation in *Rust.* But worse than in the federalism context, the victim of the misrepresentation here does not even realize that the misrepresentation is a policy choice. The patient is unlikely to hear the doctor's statement as political broadcast from the government. She is most likely to hear it as a medical opinion. Not only is there a confusion about who is responsible for the opinion expressed, but there is also confusion about whether it is an opinion at all.

Rust v Sullivan is one of the great embarrassments of the Supreme Court; the case proving Justice Scalia's rule that any issue gets distorted once it gets near the question of abortion.[49] But my argument here doesn't depend upon whether *Rust* was right. My aim is to bring out a certain sensibility about regulation; *Rust* simply points the way.

Consider a third case. Until 1948 deeds could include covenants (promises) that the property covered by the deed could not be sold to people of a particular race. The purpose of these provisions was clear: to effect and preserve segregation. Their use was extensive. It was estimated, for example, that when *Shelley v Kraemer*[50] struck these provisions down as unconstitutional under the equal protection clause, 25 percent of the properties in south Chicago had been prohibited from sale to African Americans.[51]

As awful as such provisions were, they had a certain integrity. They clearly stated their purpose and were transparent about the values they affirmed. No one could pretend that the segregation they effected was somehow an accidental by-product of decisions made elsewhere. Although they were private covenants, they were enforced by the state and, indeed, derived their meaning from the state. They said: this society is racist.

When the Court struck these provisions down, however, the question became what would replace them. Few expected that the attitudes behind these covenants would suddenly disappear because of a single court judgment. So when the Court ended direct segregation, we should have expected indirect segregation to emerge to replace it.

Sure enough, after 1948 local communities shifted their technique for preserving segregation. Rather than covenants, they used architecture. Communities were designed to "break the flow" of residents from one to another. Highways without easy crossings were placed between communities. Railroad tracks were used to divide. A thousand tiny inconveniences of architecture and zoning replaced the express preferences of covenants. Nothing formally prohibited integration. But informally, much did.[52]

Local governments thus did something very much like what the federal government did in *Rust* and tried to do in *New York:* no longer able to effect segregation directly, they used zoning laws—geographical architecture, or real-space code—to
effect it indirectly. They built their communities and designed their streets to make
it hard for integration to occur. The tiny inconveniences of zoning regulations succeeded in keeping communities separate.

What is most significant is that now, even more than with *Rust,* it becomes very
difficult to see the link between the regulation and its consequence. The continuing
segregation of these communities is described as the product of "choice." Individuals choose to live in one neighborhood rather than another. In a strict sense, that is
correct, but their choices are made in the face of costs that the state has imposed. It
is easier to remain segregated, so people choose to do that. But it is only easier because government has moved mountains to make it that way.

Here the government is regulating indirectly, by using the structures of real-
space code to effect its ends, but this regulation, again, is not seen as regulation. Here
the government gets an effect at no political cost. It gets the benefit of what would
clearly be an illegal and controversial regulation, that is, without even having to admit any regulation exists.

In all three cases, the government is commandeering the power of another
modality—another structure of constraint—to effect its own ends.[53] This in itself is
not necessarily improper. There are plenty of examples that anyone would consider
proper. A requirement that streets be well lit, for instance, is a regulation designed to
reduce crime; it does so indirectly, by regulating the architecture of streets. No one
would think that regulation improper. Nor does all such regulation hide its pedigree.
Think again about speed bumps. They are examples of indirect regulation. Like a
winding road, they use the code of streets to keep down the speed of a car. But no
one is fooled about the source of this regulation; no one believes the bumps are accidental.

Thus, the point is not against indirect regulation generally. The point is instead
about transparency. The state has no right to hide its agenda. In a constitutional
democracy its regulations should be public. And thus, one issue raised by the practice of indirect regulation is the general issue of publicity. Should the state be permitted to use nontransparent means when transparent means are available?

WHERE THIS LEADS

After I published an essay in *The Industry Standard,* arguing that "code is law,"[54] the
following letter was sent to the editor:

> Typical for a Harvard Law Professor. . . . Lessig misses the entire forest while
> dancing among the trees. . . . While his riff on West Coast Code (from Silicon

Valley Programmers) vs. East Coast Code (from government lawyers) is very cleverly crafted, it completely avoids the real difference between the two.

The good professor seems to apply the word "regulation" equally to the efforts of private enterprises to *control the behavior of their customers through market mechanisms and* the efforts of government agencies to *control the behavior of all citizens through force of law.*

So long as the creators and purveyors of West Coast Code (no matter how self-ish, monopolistic, demonic or incompetent they may be) do not carry guns and badges, I will choose them over the enforcers of East Coast Code any time.[55]

Whether or not I've missed the "real difference" between code and law, the ge-nius in this letter is that its author clearly sees the real similarity. The author (the president of an Internet-related business) understands that "private enterprise" tries to "control the behavior of their customers." He writes of "market mechanisms" to achieve that control. (Technically, I was speaking about architectures to achieve that effect, but never mind. Whether markets or architectures, the point is the same.) He therefore sees that there is "regulation" beyond law. He just has his own favorites (corporate executive that he is).

What this author sees is what we all must see to understand how cyberspace is regulated, and to see how law might regulate cyberspace. I've argued in this chapter that government has a range of tools that it uses to regulate. Cyberspace expands that range. The code of cyberspace is becoming just another tool of state regulation. Indirectly, by regulating code writing, the government can achieve regulatory ends, often without suffering the political consequences that the same ends, pursued di-rectly, would yield.

We should worry about this. We should worry about a regime that makes invis-ible regulation easier; we should worry about a regime that makes it easier to regu-late. We should worry about the first because invisibility makes it hard to resist bad regulation; we should worry the second because we don't yet—as I argue in part 3— have a sense of the values put at risk by the increasing scope of efficient regulation.

But the power that government has over cyberspace hangs on an important fea-ture of cyberspace that I have not yet described. We can no longer take that feature for granted—either in this argument or in the world. One feature of the code determines much about the power of government. It is the topic of the chapter that follows.

E I G H T

the limits in open code

I'VE TOLD A STORY OF HOW REGULATION WORKS AND OF INCREASING REGULABILITY—
of changes in the architecture of the Net that will better enable government's control. These changes, I have argued, will emerge even if government does nothing.
They are the by-product of changes made to enable e-commerce.

That was part 1. In this part, I've upped the stakes. My aim has been to give a deeper
account of the values built into a particular architecture of the Net, and thus a deeper
understanding of the ways in which government might act to shape those values.

But now the story changes. I want to introduce a complication on this road to
regulability. While relatively new in Internet time, this complication promises (or
threatens) to bring about an important change in the character of the Net and the
feasibility of regulating it.

This complication is free software, or open source software or, more simply,
open code.[1] Put too simply, everything I have said about the regulability of behavior in cyberspace—or more specifically, about government's ability to affect regulability in cyberspace—crucially depends on whether the application space of
cyberspace is dominated by open code. To the extent that it is, government's power
is decreased; to the extent that it remains dominated by closed code, government's
power is preserved.[2] Open code, in other words, can be a check on state power.

This is a lot to convince you of in a single chapter—especially since the conclusion will seem to be an important reversal on much that I have argued so far. To see
the point, we must back up and understand a bit more about the nature of the code
space that government might regulate and the nature of the actors who might control that space.

CODE ON THE NET

I've spent lots of time talking about the code of cyberspace. For those who know
something about code in cyberspace (and who are still with me here), what I've said

will have been quite frustrating. As they know (and though they doubt it, as I know), there are many different kinds or layers of code on the Internet. When we talk about regulating code, it matters deeply which code we are describing.

The Internet is defined by a set of protocols together referred to as TCP/IP. That label refers to a large number of protocols that feed different "layers" of the network. The standard model for describing layers of a network is the open systems interconnect (OSI) reference model. It describes seven network layers, each representing a "function performed when data is transferred between cooperating applications across" the network. But the TCP/IP suite is not as well articulated. According to Craig Hunt, "most descriptions of TCP/IP define three to five functional levels in the protocol architecture," though it is simplest to describe four functional layers in a TCP/IP architecture.[3] From the bottom of the stack up, we can call these the data link, network, transport, and application layers.[4]

Very few protocols operate at the lowest layer—the data link layer—since that handles local network interactions exclusively. More protocols exist at the next layer up—the network layer, where the IP protocol is dominant. It routes data between hosts and across network links, determining which path the data should take. At the next layer up—the transport layer—two different protocols dominate, TCP and UDP. These negotiate the flow of data between two network hosts. (The difference between the two is reliability—UDP offers no reliability guarantee.)

These three layers are the essential plumbing of the Internet, hidden in the Net's walls. (The faucets work at the next layer; be patient.)

The protocols together function as a kind of odd UPS. Data are passed from the application to the transport layer. There the data are placed in a (virtual) box and a (virtual) label is slapped on. That label ties the contents of the box to particular processes. (This is the work of the TCP or UDP protocols.) That box is then passed to the network layer, where the IP protocol puts the package into another package, with its own label. This label includes the origination and destination addresses. That box then can be further wrapped at the data link layer, depending on the specifics of the local network (whether, for example, it is an Ethernet network).

The whole process is a bizarre packaging game: a new box is added at each layer, and a label on each box describes the process at that layer. At the other end, the packaging process is reversed: like a Russian doll, each package is opened at the proper layer, until at the end the machine recovers the initial application data.

On top of these three layers is the application layer of the Internet. Here protocols "proliferate."[5] These include the most familiar network application protocols, such as FTP (file transfer protocol, a protocol for transferring files), SMTP (simple mail transport protocol, a protocol for transferring mail), and HTTP (hyper text transfer protocol, a protocol to publish and read hypertext documents across the Web). These are rules for how a client (your computer) will interact with a server (where the data are), and the other way around.

These four layers of protocols, then, constitute "the Internet." Building on simple blocks, the system makes possible an extraordinary range of interaction. It is perhaps not quite as amazing as nature—think of DNA—but it is built on the same principle: keep the elements simple, and the compounds will astound.[6]

When I speak about regulating the code, I do not mean that we regulate the TCP/IP protocols. (Though in principle, of course, they could be regulated, and others have suggested that they should be regulated.)[7] Instead, I've had in mind a different part of the code of cyberspace—the part that TCP/IP connects. In the terms of network theory, I've had the "ends" in mind.[8] Not the code at its most basic level of Internet exchange, but the applications (both in hardware and software) that use or implement those protocols.

A different metaphor may help you see the difference. Tim Wu likens the Internet to the electric grid: TCP/IP is the architecture for that grid; programs then "plug into" TCP/IP, or into the Internet. At the top layer, the protocol defines what the plug looks like; lower down, it governs how power flows.[9]

This is a helpful picture. Just as a very large number of appliances can be plugged into the electric grid, so too can a very large number of programs use the Internet. Before doing so, this wide variety need only agree on a simple protocol of data exchange.

My focus is on the code that plugs into the Internet. I will call that code the "application space" of the Internet. This includes all the code that implements TCP/IP protocols at the application layer—browsers, operating systems, encryption modules, Java, e-mail systems, whatever elements you want. This application space code would be the target of regulation in the story of regulability that I have told so far. The question in this chapter is: What is the character of that code that makes it susceptible to regulation?

A SHORT HISTORY OF CODE
ON THE NET

In the beginning, of course, there were very few applications on the Net. The Net was no more than a protocol for exchanging data, and the original programs simply took advantage of this protocol. The file transfer protocol (FTP) was born early in the Net's history;[10] the electronic message protocol (SMTP) was born soon after. It was not long before a protocol to display directories in a graphical way (Gopher) was developed. And in 1991 the most famous of protocols—the hyper text transfer protocol (HTTP) and hyper text markup language (HTML)—gave birth to the World Wide Web.

Each protocol spawned many applications. Since no one had a monopoly on the protocol, no one had a monopoly on its implementation. There were many FTP applications and many e-mail servers. There were even a large number of browsers.[11] The protocols were open standards, gaining their blessing from the standards bodies such as the Internet Engineering Task Force (IETF) and W3C. Once a protocol was specified, programmers could build programs that utilized it.

Much of the software implementing these protocols was "open," at least initially—that is, the source code for the software was available along with the object code.* This openness was responsible for much of the early Net's growth. Others could explore how a program was implemented and learn from that example how better to implement the protocol in the future.

The World Wide Web is the best example of this point. Again, the code that makes a web page appear as it does is called the hyper text markup language, or HTML.† With HTML, you can specify how a web page will appear, and to what it will be linked.

The original HTML was proposed in 1991 by the CERN researcher Tim Berners-Lee[12] It was designed to make it easy to link documents at a research facility, but it quickly became obvious that documents on any machine on the Internet could be linked. Berners-Lee and Cailliau made both HTML and its companion HTTP freely available for anyone to take.

And take them people did, at first slowly, but then at an extraordinary rate. People starting building web pages and linking them to others. HTML became one of the fastest-growing computer languages in the history of computing.

Why? One important reason was that HTML was always "open." Even today, on the two major browsers still in distribution, you can always reveal the "source" of a web page and see what makes it tick. The source remains open: you can download it, copy it, and improve it as you wish. Copyright law may protect the source code of a web page, but in reality it protects it very imperfectly. HTML became as popular as it did primarily because it was so easy to copy. Anyone, at any time, could look under the hood of an HTML document and learn how the author produced it.

Openness—not property or contract but free code and access—created the boom that gave birth to the Internet that we now know. And it was this boom that then attracted the attention of commerce. With all this activity, commerce rightly reasoned, surely there was money to be made.

Historically the commercial model for producing software has been different.[13] Though the history began even as the open code movement continued, commercial software vendors were not about to produce "free" (as in open source) software. Commercial vendors produced software that was closed—that traveled

---

*Source code is the code that programmers write. It is close to a natural language, but not quite a natural language. A program is written in source code, but to be run it must be converted into a language the machine can read. Some source code is converted on the fly—BASIC, for example, is usually interpreted by the computer as the computer runs a BASIC program. But most source code—or the most powerful source code—is "compiled" before it is run. The compiler converts the source code into either assembly code (which mavens can read) or object code (which only geniuses and machines can read). Object code is machine-readable. It is an undifferentiated string of 0s and 1s that instructs the machine about the tasks it is to perform. Programmers do not directly write object code, even if some are able to decipher it; programmers write source code. Object code speaks to the computer; source code speaks to humans and to computers (compilers); assembly code speaks to mavens and computers.

†Hyper text is text that is linked to another location in the same document or in another document located either on the Net or on the same computer.

without its source and was protected against modification both by the law and by its own code.

By the second half of the 1990s—marked most famously by Microsoft's Windows 95, which came bundled Internet-savvy—commercial software vendors began producing "application space" code. This code was increasingly connected to the Net—it increasingly became code "on" the Internet—but for the most part it remained closed.[14] And as we prepare to weather Y2K, most of the most significant software on the market is closed code that has nonetheless found a way to connect to the Net.

It is this balance that we need to track—the balance between open and closed code on the Net. Most of the application space that ordinary users now use is closed. There are many exceptions: Apache, still the number-one server on the Internet whether users realize it or not, and SENDMAIL, still the most widely used program for forwarding mail, are both open code. But if we include within the application space the operating systems that connect to the Net, application space code on the Net is closed.

OPENING CODE ON THE NET

But this balance is changing. From the beginning the trend to enclose code on the Internet has bothered many—some because they believe closed code is less efficient than open code, others because they believe closed code interferes with important values of the Internet.

Richard Stallman is in the latter camp. In 1985 Stallman began the Free Software Foundation, with the aim of fueling the growth of open and free software on the Net. A MacArthur Fellow who gave up his career to commit himself to the cause, Stallman has devoted his life to "free" software. In 1984, years before the Net really took off, he began developing an open source operating system. GNU* was to be the basis of an open code world where, from the operating system on up, code was open.

Despite its many admirers, GNU was a bit ahead of its time. In the world before easy Internet access, it was hard to coordinate a major project, such as developing an operating system. Early in the 1990s, after an injury had slowed Stallman's progress, a different project, devoted to similar ideals, overtook GNU.

In 1991, an undergraduate at the University of Helsinki posted on the Internet the kernel of an operating system. This undergraduate was Linus Torvalds; his kernel was the first step in producing Linux. He posted his kernel and invited the world to help him turn it into an operating system—a free and open operating system that would come with its source code bundled alongside.[15]

---

*GNU is a recursive acronym. The idea was to build an operating system that was not Unix. GNU stands for "GNU's Not Unix." Cute, no?

People took up the challenge, and slowly, through the early 1990s, they built this kernel into an operating system. They did it in part by marrying Linux to Stallman's GNU (which is why it may be most accurate to call it GNU/Linux). But whatever its genealogy, by 1998 it had become apparent to all that Linux was an important competitor to the Microsoft operating system. Microsoft may have imagined in 1995 that by 2000 there would be no other server operating system available except Windows NT, but when 2000 came around, there was GNU/Linux.

GNU/Linux is amazing in many ways. It is amazing first because it is theoretically imperfect but practically superior. Linus Torvalds rejected what computer science told him was the ideal operating system design,[16] and instead built an operating system that was designed for a single processor (an Intel 386) and not cross-platform-compatible. Its creative development, and the energy it inspired, slowly turned GNU/Linux into an extraordinarily powerful system. As of this writing, it has been ported to many different chip platforms—it can run on the Intel chip, the PowerPC chip (used by Apple), and the Sun SPARC chips. Although initially designed to speak only one language, GNU/Linux has become the lingua franca of open source operating systems.

What makes a system open source is a commitment among its developers to keep its core code public—to keep the hood of the car unlocked. That commitment is not just a wish. Stallman encoded it in a contract that sets the terms that control the future use of much open source software. This is the Free Software Foundation's general public license (GPL), which requires that any code licensed with GPL (as Linux is) keep its source free. GNU/Linux was developed by an extraordinary collection of hackers worldwide only because its code was open for others to work on.

Its code, in other words, sits in the commons.[17] Anyone can take it and use it as he wishes. Anyone can take it and come to understand how it works. The code of GNU/Linux is like a research program whose results are always published for others to see. Everything is public; anyone, without having to seek the permission of anyone else, may join the project.

Although the GNU/Linux project is the most important element in the future of open code on the Internet, it is not the only one. Another critical example is Netscape, which in 1998 dedicated its code to the public by giving it over to a company called Mozilla. Anyone can download the Netscape source code from Mozilla; anyone can take it and improve it. With the backing of a company like Netscape and the support of companies like IBM for Linux, it appears quite certain that the near future of application space code on the Internet will in important ways be open source.[18]

REGULATING OPEN SOURCE

So imagine a future in which a significant portion of the application space code is open code. What would that mean for regulability? How would that affect the story I've told of the increasing power of the state to order cyberspace?

In chapter 4, I sketched examples of government regulating code. But think again about those examples: How does such regulation work?

Consider two. The government tells the telephone company something about how its networks are to be designed, and the government tells television manufacturers what kinds of chips TVs are to have. Why do these regulations work?

The answer in each case is obvious. The code is regulable only because the code writers can be controlled. If the state tells the phone company to do something, the phone company is not likely to resist. Resistance would bring punishment; punishment is expensive; phone companies, like all other companies, want to reduce their cost of doing business. If the state's regulation is rational (that is, effective), it will set the cost of disobeying the state above any possible benefit. If, in addition, the target of regulation is within the reach of the state, and a rational actor, then the regulation is likely to have its effect. CALEA's regulation of the network architecture for telephones is an obvious example of this (see chapter 5).

An unmovable, and unmoving, target of regulation, then, is a good start to regulability. And this statement has an interesting corollary: regulable code is closed code. Think again about telephone networks. When the government induces the telephone networks to modify their network software, users have no choice about whether to adopt this modification or not. You pick up the phone, you get the dial tone the phone company gives you. No one I know hacks the telephone company's code to build a different network design. The same with the V-chip—I doubt that many people would risk destroying their television by pulling out the chip, and I am certain that no one re-burns the chip to build in a different filtering technology.

In both cases the government's regulation works because when the target of the regulation complies, customers can do little but accept it.

Open code is different. We can see something of the difference in a story told by Netscape's legal counsel, Peter Harter, about Netscape and the French.[19]

I've described SSL, Netscape's protocol for exchanging encrypted data; it permits secure exchange between a browser and a server. The French were not happy with the security that SSL gave. They wanted to be able to crack SSL transactions. So they requested that Netscape modify SSL to enable their spying.

There are plenty of constraints on Netscape's ability to modify of SSL—not the least of which being that Netscape has given SSL over to the public, in the form of a public standard. But assume for a second that it had not. Assume Netscape really did control the standards for SSL and in theory could modify the code to enable French spying. Would that mean that Netscape could comply with the French demand?

No. Technically, it could comply by modifying the code of Netscape Communicator and then posting a new module that enabled hacking by a government. But just because it posts such a module does not mean it will be adopted. Since Netscape's code is open code, users take only what they want. Although Netscape could offer a feature that the French government wants, there is no reason to believe that users would want this same feature. Another supplier would undoubtedly provide an SSL module without the alteration demanded by the French government.

The point is simple, but its implication profound. To the extent that code is open code, the power of government is constrained. Government can demand, government can threaten, but when the target of its regulation is plastic, it cannot rely on its target remaining as it wants.

Say you are a Soviet propagandist, and you want to get people to read lots of information about Papa Stalin. So you declare that every book published in the Soviet Union must have a chapter devoted to Stalin. How likely is it that such books will actually affect what people read?

Books are open source software: they hide nothing; they reveal their source—they are their source! A user or adopter of a book always has the choice to read only the chapters she wants. If it is a book on electronics, then the reader can certainly choose not to read the chapter on Stalin. There is very little the state can do to modify the reader's power in this respect.

The same idea liberates open source code. The government's rules are rules only to the extent that they impose restrictions that adopters would want. The government may coordinate standards (like "drive on the right"), but it certainly cannot impose standards that constrain users in ways they do not want to be constrained. This architecture, then, is an important check on the government's regulatory power. Open code means open control—there is control, but the user is aware of it.

Closed code functions differently. With closed code, users cannot easily modify the control that the code comes packaged with. Hackers and very sophisticated programmers may be able to do so, but most users would not know which parts were required and which parts were not. Or more precisely, users would not be able to see the parts required and the parts not required because the source code does not come bundled with closed code. Closed code is the propagandist's best strategy—not a separate chapter that the user can ignore, but a persistent and unrecognized influence that tilts the story in the direction the propagandist wants.

WHERE THIS LEADS

My argument so far has taken a simple path. In answer to those who say that the Net cannot be regulated, I've argued that whether it can be regulated depends on its architecture. Some architectures would be regulable, others would not. I have then argued that government could take a role in deciding whether an architecture would be regulable or not. The government could take steps to transform an architecture from unregulable to regulable.

The final step in this progression of regulability is a constraint that is only now becoming significant. Government's power to regulate code, to make behavior within the code regulable, depends in part on the character of the code. Open code is less regulable than closed code; to the extent that code becomes open, government's power is reduced.

This is not, obviously, an absolute claim. I am discussing relative, not absolute, regulability. Even with open code, if the government threatens punishments that are severe enough, it will induce a certain compliance. And even with open code, the techniques of identity, tied to code that has been certified as compliant, will still give government plenty of power. Thus, much of the argument from part 1 survives this point about open code—if the world becomes certificate-rich, regulability still increases.*

But when designing an architecture for cyberspace, the margins matter. The values of a given space are not only the values of speech, autonomy, access, or privacy. They may also be values of limited control. As John Perry Barlow puts it, they are the values of a certain bug being programmed into the architecture of the Net—a bug that inhibits the power of government to control the Net perfectly, even if it does not disable that power entirely.

For some, the objective is to build code that disables any possible governmental control. That is not my objective. I certainly believe that government must be constrained, and I endorse the constraints that open code imposes, but it is not my objective to disable government generally. As I've argued already, and as the next part makes plain, some values can be achieved only if government intervenes. Government has a role, even if not as substantial a role as it would wish. We need to understand this role, as well as how our values might be advanced in the context of the Web.

One constraint seems clear in this account. As I argue more extensively later in the book, even if open code does not disable government's power to regulate completely, it certainly changes that power. On the margin, open code reduces the reward from burying regulation in the hidden spaces of code. It functions as a kind of Freedom of Information Act for network regulation. As with ordinary law, open code requires that lawmaking be public, and thus that lawmaking be transparent. In a sense that George Soros ought to understand, open code is a foundation to an open society.

Even this is an important—some might say an essential—check on the power of government. But whether or not one is for transparency generally, my aim so far is just to map out the links. Regulability is conditional on the character of the code, and open code changes that character. It is a limit on government's power to regulate—not necessarily defeating the power to regulate, but changing it.[20]

---

*Another constraint would arise if more code were burned into hardware rather than existing as software. Then, even if the code were open, it would not be modifiable. I am grateful to Hal Abelson for this point.

PART THREE

applications

Nature doesn't determine cyberspace. Code does. Code is not constant. It changes. It is changing now in a way that will make cyberspace more regulable. It could change in a way that makes cyberspace less regulable. How it changes depends on the code writers. How code writers change it could depend on us.

If we do nothing, the code of cyberspace will change. The invisible hand will change it in a predictable way. To do nothing is to embrace at least that. It is to accept the changes that this change in code will bring about. It is to accept a cyberspace that is less free, or differently free, than the space it was before.

But then, how should the future develop? What values should the space have? I've emphasized the need for choice but have done little to show what that choice should be.

In this part, I practice that choice. I begin with a technique that is familiar to American constitutionalists in cases where constitutional law confronts changed circumstances. This technique, which I call *translation*, decides the present in terms of the past. Its aim is to choose in a way that is faithful to the choices of the past, to translate the commitments of the past into a fundamentally different context. Just as a language translator constructs a text that is different from the source but has the same meaning as the source, so too does the constitutional translator construct an application that, though different from the original application, has the same meaning in the current context as the original did in its context.

Translation will guide in important cases. It will show us how we can go on, consistent with traditions we respect. But in the cases I focus on most extensively, translation alone will not be enough; the past will not resolve the future. The questions raised by the future are issues that were not decided in the past.

These are the *latent ambiguities* that I spoke of at the start, illustrated with searches by worms. My argument in part 3 is that these cases of ambiguity will force us to choose where the framers did not. Cyberspace will make the necessity of this choice patent.

N I N E

translation

AT THE HEIGHT OF OUR LAST WAR ON DRUGS—PROHIBITION, IN THE LATE 1920S—THE federal government began using a technique of police work that startled many but proved quite effective. The technique was wiretapping.[1] Telephones had become a dominant mode of communication, life had just begun to move onto the wires, and in an effort to take advantage of the evidence that this new medium might yield, the government, without warrants, began to tap phones.

Because law enforcement officials themselves were conflicted about the ethics of wiretapping, taps were used sparingly. Nonetheless, for threats perceived to be extremely grave, the technique was deployed. Illegal alcohol, as the obsession of the age, was just such a threat.

The most famous of these taps led to the 1928 Supreme Court case *Olmstead v United States*. The government was investigating one of the largest illegal liquor import, distribution, and sales organizations in the nation. As part of the investigation, the government began to tap the telephones used by dealers and their agents. These were private phones, but the taps were always secured without trespassing on the property of the targets.[2] Instead, the taps were placed on the wires in places where the government had rightful access to the phone lines. Though wiretapping was illegal under many states' laws, the government had not illegally trespassed on the defendants' property while tapping phones.

Using these taps, the government recorded many hours of conversations (775 typewritten pages, according to Justice Louis Brandeis's dissent)[3], and it used these recordings to convict the defendants in the case. The defendants challenged the use of these recordings, claiming that the government had violated the Constitution in securing them. The Fourth Amendment protects "persons, houses, papers, and effects, against unreasonable searches and seizures," and this wiretapping, the defendants argued, was a violation of their right to be protected from unreasonable searches.

Under then-existing law, it was plain that to enter the apartments of Mr. Olmstead and his accomplices and search them (at least while they were gone), the government investigators would have needed a warrant, that is, they would have needed the approval of a judge or magistrate before invading the defendants' privacy. This is what the Fourth Amendment had come to mean—that certain places (persons, houses, papers, and effects) were protected by presumptively requiring a warrant before they could be invaded.[4] Here there had been no warrant, and hence, as the defendants argued, the search had been illegal. The evidence had to be excluded.

We might pause to ask why. If we read the text of the Fourth Amendment carefully, it is hard to see just where a warrant is required:

(a) The right of the people to be secure in their persons, houses, papers, and effects, against unreasonable searches and seizures, shall not be violated, and (b) no Warrants shall issue, but upon probable cause, supported by Oath or affirmation, and particularly describing the place to be searched, and the persons or things to be seized.

The Fourth Amendment is really two commands. (I've added "a" and "b" to help make the point.) The first says that a certain right ("the right of the People to be secure") shall not be violated; the second limits the conditions under which a warrant shall be issued. But the text of the amendment does not state a relationship between the first part and the second part. And it certainly does not say that a search is unreasonable if it is not supported by a warrant. So why "the warrant requirement"?[5]

To make sense of the amendment, we must go back to its framing. At that time, the legal protection against the invasion of privacy was trespass law. If someone entered your property and rifled through your stuff, that person violated your common law rights against trespass. You could sue that person for trespass, whether he was a police officer or private citizen. The threat of such suits gave the police an incentive not to invade your privacy.[6]

Even without a warrant, however, a trespassing police officer might have a number of defenses. These boil down to whether the search was "reasonable." But there were two important facts about this reasonableness. First, the determination of reasonableness was made by a jury. Neighbors and peers of the officer judged whether his behavior had been proper. Second, in some cases reasonableness was found as a matter of law—that is, the judge would instruct the jury to find that the search had been reasonable. (For example, when the officer found contraband on the property of the defendant, whether there was sufficient suspicion before the search or not, the search was reasonable.)[7]

This regime created obvious risks for an officer before he searched someone's property. If he searched and found nothing, or if a jury thought later that his search had not been reasonable, then he paid for his illegal behavior by being held personally liable for the rights he had violated.

But the regime also offered insurance against this liability—the warrant. If the officer secured a warrant from a judge before he made his search, the warrant immunized him against trespass liability. If he then found no contraband or his search turned out to be unreasonable, he still had a defense to a suit.

Creating incentives was one aim of the original system. The law gave an officer an incentive to obtain a warrant before he searched; if he was uncertain, or wanted to avoid all risk of liability, he could first check his judgment by asking a judge. But if the officer was sure, or wanted to hazard the gamble, then not getting a warrant did not make the search automatically unreasonable. He was at risk of increased liability, but his liability was all that was at stake.

The weak link in this system was the judge. If judges were too lax, then warrants would be too easy to get.[8] And weak judges were a concern for the framers. Under British rule judges had been appointed by the Crown, and by the time of the Revolution the Crown was the enemy. Having seen much abuse of the power to issue warrants, the framers were not keen to give judges control in determining whether the government's searches were reasonable.

In particular (as I described in chapter 2), the framers had in mind some famous cases in which judges and the executive had issued "general warrants" giving government officers the power to search generally for objects of contraband.[9] In modern terms, these were "fishing expeditions." Because the officers had warrants, they could not be sued; because the judges were largely immune from suit, they could not be sued. Because no one could be sued, there was a temptation for abuse. The framers wanted to avoid just such judge-made abuse. If there was to be immunity, it would come from a jury, or from a successful search.

This is the origin of clause (b) of the Fourth Amendment. The framers required that judges, when issuing warrants, name particularly "the place to be searched, and the persons or things to be seized," so that judges would not be able to issue warrants of general power. The immunity of the warrant would be limited to particular people and places, and only when probable cause existed to issue the warrant.

This constitutional regime was designed to balance the people's interests in privacy against the legitimate need for the government to search. The officer had an incentive to get a warrant (to avoid the risk of personal liability); the judge had a rule that restricted the conditions under which he could issue a warrant; and together these structures limited official invasions of privacy to cases that presented a strong reason to invade.

So much is background. But notice what follows.

The original regime presupposed a great deal. Most obviously, it presupposed a common law system of trespass law—it was the threat of legal liability from trespass law that created the incentives for officers to seek warrants in the first place. This presupposition placed property at the core of the Constitution's original protections.

Equally important, the regime presupposed much about the technology of the time. The Fourth Amendment focuses on trespass because that was the primary mode of searching at the time. If it had been possible simply to view the contents of a house without going inside, the restrictions of the Fourth Amendment would have made little sense. But the protections of the amendment did make sense as a way to draw the balance between government's power to search and the people's right to privacy *given* the regime of trespass law and privacy-invading technologies that prevailed at the end of the eighteenth century.

Presuppositions—what is taken for granted or considered undebatable—change.[10] How do we respond when such presuppositions change? How do we read a text written against a background of certain presuppositions when those presuppositions no longer apply?

For Americans, or for any nation with a constitution some two hundred years old, this is the central problem for constitutional interpretation. What if the state, for example, were simply to abolish rights against trespass? Would the amendment be read any differently?[11] What if technologies for searching were to change so dramatically that no one would ever need to enter another's property to know just what is kept there? Should the amendment then be read differently?

The history of the Supreme Court's treatment of such questions lacks a perfectly clear pattern, but we can identify two distinct strategies, always competing for the Court's attention. One strategy is focused on what the framers or founders would have done—the strategy of *one-step originalism.* The second strategy aims at finding a current reading of the original Constitution that preserves its original meaning in the present context—a strategy that I call *translation.*

Both strategies are present in the *Olmstead* wiretapping case. When the government tapped the phones of the defendants without any warrant, the Court had to decide whether the use of this kind of evidence was permissible or consistent with the principles of the Fourth Amendment. The defendants said: the government must get a warrant to tap phones. The government said: the Fourth Amendment simply does not apply.

The government's argument was quite simple. The amendment presupposed that the government would be trespassing to search, and it was regulating the conditions under which officers could trespass. But because wiretapping is an invasion of privacy without a trespass, the government is able to tap the defendants' phones without ever entering their property; the amendment therefore does not apply. It simply does not reach to protect invasions that are invasions without trespass.

The Supreme Court agreed. In an opinion written by Chief Justice William H. (and former President) Taft, the Court followed the government.

> The amendment does not forbid what was done here. There was no searching. There was no seizure. The evidence was secured by the use of the sense of hearing and that only. . . . The language of the amendment cannot be extended and expanded to include telephone wires, reaching to the whole world from the defendant's house or office.[12]

This conclusion was received with some surprise, and also with shock. Already much of life had moved to the wires. People were beginning to understand what it meant to have intimate contact "online"; they counted on the telephone system to protect their intimate secrets. Indeed, telephone companies, having strongly fought the authority that the government claimed, pledged not to assist the government except as required by law.[13] This resistance notwithstanding, the Court concluded that the Constitution did not interfere with invasions of this sort. It would not have done so when the Constitution was written; it did not do so at the time when the case was decided.

But the dissent written by Justice Brandeis (there was also a dissent by Justices Holmes, Stone, and Butler) had a different view. Like Taft, the focus was fidelity. But his fidelity was quite differently conceived.

Brandeis acknowledged that the Fourth Amendment, as originally written, applied only to trespass.[14] But it did so, he argued, because when it was written trespass was the technology for invading privacy. That was the framers' presupposition, but that presupposition had now changed. Given this change, Brandeis argued, it was the Court's responsibility to read the amendment in a way that preserved its meaning, changed circumstances notwithstanding. The aim must be to *translate* the original protections into a context in which the technology for invading privacy had changed.[15] This would be done, Brandeis argued, by applying the Fourth Amendment's protection to invasions that were not themselves trespasses.

These two opinions mark two different modes of constitutional interpretation. Taft finds fidelity by simply repeating what the framers did; Brandeis finds fidelity by finding the current equivalent to what the framers did. If we followed Taft, Brandeis argued, we would defeat the protections for privacy that the framers originally set; if we followed Brandeis, Taft implied, we would be adding to the Constitution something that the framers had not written.

Partisans on both sides claimed that the opinion of the other would have "changed" the meaning of the Constitution. But whose opinion, the Court's or Justice Brandeis's, would really "change" the meaning of the Fourth Amendment?

To answer this question, you would first have to ask: Change relative to what? What is the baseline against which this change is a change? Certainly Brandeis would have agreed that in 1791, just after the amendment was passed, any finding by the Court that the amendment reached beyond trespass would have been improper. But when something presupposed by the original amendment has changed, is it clear that the Court's proper response is to act as if nothing has changed at all?

Brandeis's method accounted for the changed presupposition. He offered a reading that changed the scope of the amendment in order to maintain the amendment's protection of privacy. Taft, on the other hand, offered a reading that maintained the scope of the amendment but changed its protection of privacy. Each reading kept something constant; each also changed something. The question is: Which reading preserved what fidelity demands should be preserved?

We might better see the point through a somewhat stylized re-creation. Imagine that we could quantify privacy: we could thus describe the change in the quantity of privacy that any change in technology might bring. (Robert Post has given an absolutely persuasive argument about why privacy is not quantifiable, but my purposes here are simply illustrative.[16]) Imagine then that in 1791 protecting against physical trespass protected 90 percent of personal privacy. The government could still stand on the street and listen through open windows, but the invasion presented by that threat was small, all things considered. For the most part, a regime that protected against trespass also protected privacy.

When telephones came along, however, this protection changed. A lot of private information was put out across the phone lines. Now, if tapping was not trespass, much less of private life was protected from government snooping. Rather than 90 percent being protected by the amendment, only 50 percent was protected.

Brandeis wanted to read the amendment so that it protected what it originally protected—the 90 percent, even though doing so required that it protect against more than simple trespass. He wanted to read it *differently*, we could say, so that it protected the *same*.

This form of argument is common in our constitutional history, and central to the best in our constitutional tradition.[17] It is an argument that responds to changed circumstances by proposing a reading that neutralizes those changes and preserves an original meaning. It is an argument invoked by justices on both the right and the left.[18] It is a way to keep life in a constitutional provision—to make certain that changes in the world do not change the meaning of the Constitution's text. It is an argument, we can say, that aims at *translating* the protections that the Fourth Amendment gave in 1791 into the same set of protections at any time later in our history. It acknowledges that to do this the Court may have to read the amendment differently. But it is not reading the amendment differently to improve the amendment or to add to its protections. It is reading the amendment differently to accommodate the changes in protection that have resulted from changes in technology. It is translation to preserve meaning.

If there is a justice who deserves c-world's praise, if there is a Supreme Court opinion that should be the model for cyberactivists in the future, if there is a first chapter in the fight to protect cyberspace, it is this Justice, this opinion, and this case. Brandeis gave us a model for reading the Constitution to preserve its meaning, and its values, across time and context. It is a method that recognizes what has changed and accommodates that change to preserve something of what the framers originally gave us. It is a method, again, that *translates* the Constitution's meaning across fundamentally different contexts—whether they are as temporally distant as we are from the framers or as distant as cyberspace is from real space.

But it was Taft's opinion that became law, and his narrow view of the Fourth Amendment that prevailed. It took forty years for the Supreme Court to embrace Brandeis's picture of the Fourth Amendment—forty years before *Olmstead* was overruled. The case overruling it was *Katz v United States*.[19]

Charles Katz was suspected of transmitting gambling information to clients in other states by telephone. Federal agents recorded his half of several of his telephone calls by attaching an eavesdropping device to the outside of a public phone booth where he made his calls. Katz was convicted on the basis of this evidence, and the court of appeals upheld the conviction on the basis of *Olmstead.*

Harvard Law School Professor Laurence Tribe was involved in the case at the beginning of his legal career:

> As a [law] clerk to Supreme Court Justice Potter Stewart, I found myself working on a case involving the government's electronic surveillance of a suspected criminal in the form of a tiny device attached to the outside of a public telephone booth. Because the invasion of the suspect's privacy was accomplished without physical trespass into a "constitutionally protected area," the Federal Government argued, relying upon *Olmstead,* that there had been no "search" or "seizure" and therefore the Fourth Amendment "right of the people to be secure in their persons, houses, papers, and effects, against unreasonable searches and seizures" simply did not apply.
>
> At first, there were only four votes to overrule *Olmstead* and to hold the Fourth Amendment applicable to wiretapping and electronic eavesdropping. I'm proud to say that, as a 26-year-old kid, I had at least a little bit to do with changing that number from four to seven—and with the argument, formally adopted by a seven-Justice majority in December 1967, that the Fourth Amendment "protects people, not places" [389 US at 351]. In that decision, *Katz v. United States,* the Supreme Court finally repudiated *Olmstead* and the many decisions that had relied upon it, reasoning that, given the role of electronic telecommunications in modern life, the [First Amendment] purposes of protecting *free speech* as well as the [Fourth Amendment] purposes of protecting *privacy* require treating as a "search" any invasion of a person's confidential telephone communications, with or without physical trespass.[20]

The Court in *Katz* followed Brandeis rather than Taft. It sought a reading of the Fourth Amendment that made sense of the amendment in a changed context. In the framers' context of 1791, protecting against trespass to property was an effective way to protect against trespass to privacy, but in the *Katz* context of the 1960s it was not. In the 1960s much of intimate life was conducted in places where property rules did not reach (in the "ether," for example, of the AT&T telephone network). And so a regime that made privacy hang on property did not protect privacy to the same degree that the framers had intended. Justice Stewart in *Katz* sought to remedy that by linking the Fourth Amendment to a more direct protection of privacy.

The link was the idea of "a reasonable expectation of privacy." The core value, Stewart wrote, was the protection of "people, not places"[21]; hence, the core technique should be to protect people where they have an expectation of privacy, and where that expectation is reasonable. Where people have a reasonable expectation of

privacy, the government cannot invade that space without satisfying the requirements of the Fourth Amendment.

There is much to admire in Stewart's opinion, at least to the extent that he is willing to fashion tools for preserving the Constitution's meaning in changed circumstances—or again, to the extent that he attempts to translate the protections of the
Fourth Amendment into a modern context. There is also much to question.[22] But
we can put those questions aside for the moment and focus on one feature of the
problem that is fairly uncontentious.

While lines will be hard to draw, it is at least fairly clear that the framers made a
conscious choice to protect privacy. This was not an issue off the table of their original debate, or a question they did not notice. And this is not the "right to privacy"
that conservatives complain about in the context of the right to abortion. This is the
right to be free from state intrusion into the "sanctity" of a private home. State-
enforced threats to individual privacy were at the center of the movement that led to
the republic. Brandeis and Stewart simply aimed to effect that choice in contexts
where the earlier structure had grown ineffectual.

Translations like these are fairly straightforward. The original values chosen are
fairly clear; the way in which contexts undermine the original application is easily
grasped; and the readings that would restore the original values are fairly obvious.
Of course, such cases often require a certain interpretive courage—a willingness to
preserve interpretive fidelity by changing an interpretive practice. But at least the direction is clear, even if the means are a bit unseemly.[23]

These are the easy cases. They are even easier when we are not trying to carry values from some distant past into the future but instead are simply carrying values
from one context into another. When we know what values we want to preserve, we
need only be creative about how to preserve them in a different context.

Cyberspace will present many such easy cases. When courts confront them, they
should follow the example of Brandeis: they should translate, and they should push
the Supreme Court to do likewise. Where circumstances have changed to nullify the
protections of some original right, the Court should adopt a reading of the Constitution that restores that right.

But some cases will not be so easy. Sometimes translation will not be an option.
Sometimes the values that translation would track are values we no longer want to
preserve. And sometimes we cannot tell which values translation would select. This
was the problem in chapter 2 with the worm, which made the point about latent
ambiguities. Changing contexts sometimes reveals an ambiguity latent in the original context. We must then choose between two different values, either of which
could be said to be consistent with the original value. Since either way could be said
to be right, we cannot say that the original context (whether now or two hundred
years ago) decided the case.

Professor Tribe describes an example in a founding article in the law of cyberspace, "The Constitution in Cyberspace."[24] Tribe sketches a method of reading the
Constitution in cyberspace that aims to make the Constitution "technologically

neutral." The objective is to adopt readings (or perhaps even an amendment) that make it plain that changes in technology are not to change the Constitution's meaning. We must always adopt readings of the Constitution that preserve its original values. When dealing with cyberspace, judges are to be translators; different technologies are the different languages; and the aim is to find a reading of the Constitution that preserves its meaning from one world's technology to another.[25]

This is fidelity as translation. This kind of translation speaks as if it is just carrying over something that has already been said. It hides the creative in its act; it feigns a certain polite or respectful deference. This way of reading the Constitution insists that the important political decisions have already been made and all that is required is a kind of technical adjustment. It aims at keeping the piano in tune as it is moved from one concert hall to another.

But Tribe then offers an example that may make this method seem empty. The question is about the meaning of the confrontation clause of the Sixth Amendment—the defendant's right in a criminal trial "to be confronted with the witnesses against him." How, Tribe asks, should we read this clause today?

At the time of the founding, he argues, the technology of confrontation was simple—confrontation was two-way. If a witness confronted the accused, the accused, of necessity, confronted the witness. This was a necessity given to us by the technology of the time. But today it is possible for confrontation to be one-way—the witness confronts the accused, but the accused need not confront the witness. The question then is whether the confrontation clause requires one-way or two-way confrontation.[26]

Let us grant that Tribe's descriptions of the available technologies are correct and that the framers embraced the only confrontation clause that their technology permitted. The real question comes in step two. Now that technology allows two possibilities—one-way or two-way confrontation—which does the Constitution *require?*

The Court's answer in its 1990 decision in *Maryland v Craig* was clear: the Constitution requires only one-way confrontation. A confrontation clause regime that permits only one-way confrontation, at least when there are strong interests in not requiring two, is a fair translation of the original clause.[27]

As a matter of political choice, I certainly like this answer. But I do not see its source. It seems to me that this is a question the framers did not decide, and a question that if presented to them might well have divided them. Given the technology of 1791, they did not have to decide between one-way and two-way confrontation; given the conflict of values at stake, it is not obvious how they would have decided it. Thus, to speak as if there were an answer here that the framers simply *gave* us is a bit misleading. The framers gave no answer here, and in my view, no answer can be drawn from what they said.

Like the worm in chapter 2, the confrontation clause presents a *latent ambiguity.*[28] Constitutional law in cyberspace will reveal many such latent ambiguities. And these ambiguities offer us a choice: How will we go on?

Choices are not terrible. It is not a disaster if we must make a decision—so long, that is, as we are capable of it. But here is the nub of the problem that I see. As I argue in more detail in part 4, given the current attitudes of our courts, and our legal culture generally, constitutional choices are costly. We are bad at making these choices; we are not likely to get better at it soon.

When there is no answer about how to proceed—when the translation leaves open a question—we have two sorts of responses in constitutional practice. One response is passive: the court simply lets the legislature decide as it will. This is the response that Justice Scalia presses in the context of the Fourteenth Amendment. On matters that, to the framers, were "undebatable," the Constitution does not speak.[29] In this case, only the legislature can engage, and press, questions of constitutional value and thus say what the Constitution will continue to mean.

The second response is more active: the court finds a way to articulate constitutional values that were not present at the founding. The courts help spur a conversation about these fundamental values—or at least add their voice to this conversation—to focus a debate that may ultimately be resolved elsewhere. The first response is a way of doing nothing; the second is a way of exciting a dialogue about constitutional values as a means to confronting and resolving new questions.

My fear about cyberspace is that we will respond in the first way—that the institutions most responsible for articulating constitutional values will simply stand back while issues of constitutional import are legislatively determined. The institutions most responsible for articulating constitutional values today are the courts. My sense is that they will step back because they feel (as the balance of this book argues) that these are new questions that cyberspace has raised. Their newness will make them feel political, and when a question feels political, courts step away from resolving it.

I fear this not because I fear legislatures, but because in our day constitutional discourse at the level of the legislature is a very thin sort of discourse. The philosopher Bernard Williams has argued that because the Supreme Court has taken so central a role in the articulation of constitutional values, legislatures no longer do.[30] Whether Williams is correct or not, this much is clear: the constitutional discourse of our present Congress is far below the level it must be at to address the questions about constitutional values that will be raised by cyberspace.

How we could reach beyond this thinness of discourse is unclear. We are in a time when constitutional thought has been for too long the domain of lawyers and judges. We have been trapped by a mode of reasoning that pretends that all the important questions have already been answered, that our job now is simply to translate them for modern times. As a result, we do not quite know how to proceed when we think the answers are not already there. As nations across the world struggle to express and embrace constitutional values, we, with the oldest written constitutional tradition, have lost the practice of embracing, articulating, and deciding on constitutional values.

I return to this problem in chapter 15. For now, my point is simply descriptive. Translation is one way to deal with the choices that cyberspace presents. It is one way of finding equivalence across contexts. But in the four applications that follow, I press the question: Is the past enough? Are there choices the framers did not address? Are they choices that we could make?

TEN

intellectual property

HAROLD REEVES IS AMONG THE BEST RESEARCH ASSISTANTS I HAVE HAD. HE WORKED with me to develop the first course I taught on the law of cyberspace. Early into his second year at the University of Chicago Law School, he came to me with an idea he had for a student comment—a student article that would be published in the law review.[1] The topic was trespass law in cyberspace—whether and how the law should protect owners of space in cyberspace from the kinds of intrusions that trespass law protects against in real space. His initial idea was simple: there should be no trespass law in cyberspace.[2] The law should grant "owners" of space in cyberspace no legal protection against invasion. They should be forced to fend for themselves.

Reeves's idea was a bit nutty, and in the end, I think, wrong.[3] But it contained an insight that was quite genius, and that should be central to thinking about law in cyberspace.

The idea—much more briefly and much less elegantly than Reeves has put it—is this: the question that law should ask is what means would bring about the most efficient set of protections for property interests in cyberspace. Two sorts of protections are possible. One is the traditional protection of law—the law defines a space where others should not enter and punishes people who nonetheless enter. The other protection is a fence, a technological device (a bit of code) that (among other things) blocks the unwanted from entering. In real space, of course, we have both—laws and fences that supplement law. No doubt there is some optimal mix between fences and law. Both cost money, and the return from each is not necessarily the same. From a social perspective, we would want the mix that provides optimal protection at the lowest cost. (In economics-speak, we would want a mix such that the marginal cost of an additional unit of protection is equivalent to the marginal benefit.)

The implication of this idea in real space is that it sometimes makes sense to shift the burden of protection to citizens rather than the state. If, for example, a farmer wants to store some valuable seed on a remote part of his farm, it is better for him to bear the cost of fencing in the seed than to require the police to patrol the area more consistently or to increase the punishment for those they catch. The question, then, is always one of balance between the costs and benefits of private protection and state protection.

Reeves's insight about cyberspace follows the same line. The optimal protection for spaces in cyberspace is a mix between public law and private fences. The question to ask in determining the mix is which protection, on the margin, costs less. Reeves argues that the costs of law in this context are extremely high—in part because of the costs of enforcement, but also because it is hard for the law to distinguish between legitimate and illegitimate uses of cyberspaces. There are many "agents" that might "use" the space of cyberspace. Web spiders, which gather data for web search engines; browsers, who are searching across the Net for stuff to see; hackers (of the good sort) who are testing the locks of spaces to see that they are locked; and hackers (of the bad sort) who are breaking and entering to steal. It is hard, *ex ante,* for the law to know which agent is using the space legitimately and which is not. Legitimacy depends on the intention of the person granting access.

So that led Reeves to his idea: since the intent of the "owner" is so crucial here, and since the fences of cyberspace can be made to reflect that intent cheaply, it is best to put all the incentive on the owner to define access as he wishes. The right to browse should be the norm, and the burden to lock doors should be placed on the owner.[4]

Now put Reeves's argument aside, and think for a second about something that will seem completely different but is very much the same idea. Think about "theft" and the protections that we have against it.

I have a stack of firewood behind my house. No one steals it. If I left my bike out overnight, it would be gone.

A friend told me that, in a favorite beach town, the city used to find it impossible to plant flowers—they would immediately be picked. But, he now proudly reports, after a long "community spirit" campaign, the flowers are no longer picked.

There are special laws about the theft of automobiles, planes, and boats. There are no special laws about the theft of skyscrapers. Cars, planes, and boats need protection. Skyscrapers pretty much take care of themselves.

Many things protect property against theft—differently. The market protects my firewood (it is cheaper to buy your own than it is to haul mine away); the market is a special threat to my bike (which if taken is easily sold). Norms sometimes protect flowers in a park; sometimes they do not. Nature sometimes conspires with thieves (cars, planes, and boats) and sometimes against them (skyscrapers).

These protections are not fixed. I could lock my bike and thereby use real-space code to make it harder to steal. There could be a shortage of firewood, increasing demand and making it harder to protect. Public campaigns about civic beauty might stop flower theft; selecting a distinctive flower might do the same. Sophisticated locks might make stolen cars useless; sophisticated bank fraud might make sky-scrapers vulnerable. The point is not that protections are given, or unchangeable, but that they are multiplied and their modalities different.

Property is protected by the sum of the different protections that law, norms, the market, and real-space code yield. This is just an application of the point made in chapter 7. From the point of view of the state, we need law only when the other three modalities leave property vulnerable. From the point of view of the citizen, real-space code (such as locks) is needed when laws and norms alone do not protect enough. Understanding how property is protected means understanding how these different protections work together.

Reeves's idea and these reflections on firewood and skyscrapers point to the different ways that law might protect "property" and suggest the range of kinds of property that law might try to protect. They also invite a question that has been asked by Justice Stephen Breyer and many others: Should law protect some kinds of property—in particular, intellectual property—at all?[5]

Among the kinds of property law might protect, my focus in this chapter will be on just one—"intellectual property," or more particularly, the property protected by copyright. Of all the different types of property, this type is said to be the most vulnerable to the changes that cyberspace would bring. Intellectual property, it is said, cannot be protected in cyberspace. And in the terms that I've sketched, we can begin to see why—and more important, why what is said must be wrong.

ON THE REPORTS OF COPYRIGHT'S DEMISE

Roughly put, copyright gives a copyright holder the right to control the copying of that to which the right extends.[6] I have a copyright in this book. That means, subject to some important exceptions, you cannot copy this book without my permission. The right is protected to the extent that laws (and norms) support it, and it is threatened to the extent that technology makes it easy to copy. Strengthen the law, holding technology constant, and the right is stronger. Strengthen the technology, holding the law constant, and the right is weaker.[7]

In this sense, copyright has always been at war with technology. Before the printing press (and especially the availability of paper[8]), there was not much need to protect an author's copyright. Copying was so expensive that nature itself protected that right. But as the cost of copying decreased, the threat to the author's control increased. As each generation has delivered a technology better than the last, the ability of the copyright holder to protect her intellectual property has been weakened.

But up to now, the law could respond quite easily. If photocopying machines in libraries posed a new threat to the right, then the law could be modified to better deal with photocopying machines.[9] If videotape allowed TV viewers to tape a show to view at a different time, the law could be modified to deal with time shifting.[10] In all these cases, the real protection accorded to property is the sum of these different kinds of constraints; we can see that increases in legal protection, in response to increased threats to copying,[11] may on balance simply restore the power an author once held rather than increase the author's right.[12]

Fortunately, from law's perspective at least, technological changes have always been gradual. Copies have become better and cheaper, but only by degrees, and over a relatively extended period. There have been shocks to the system, but the law has had time to react when the old system seemed out of step—by slowly modifying its protections and extending them where technology seemed to be eroding them.[13]

It is said by some that cyberspace changes not only the technology of copying but also (and more important) the power of law to protect against illegal copying.[14] It does both simultaneously, and extremely quickly. Not only does the Net promise perfect copies of digital originals at practically no cost,[15] but it also threatens to impose an almost impossible task on law enforcers: tracing and punishing copyright violators. In the terms of chapter 7: the effective constraint of law (against copying) disappears just at the time when the constraints of technology disappear as well. The threat posed by technology is maximal, while the protection promised by law is minimal. For the holder of the copyright, cyberspace appears to be the worst of both worlds—a place where the ability to copy could not be better, and where the protection of law could not be worse.

Talk like this gave birth to the panic of copyright holders, who wanted to see legislative changes made to better protect the copyright. For of course, the predictions of cyberspace mavens notwithstanding, not everyone was willing to concede that copyright law was dead. Intellectual property lawyers and interest groups pushed early on to have law shore up the protections of intellectual property that cyberspace would erase.

LAW TO THE RESCUE

The product of the original push was a White Paper produced by the Commerce Department in 1995 after soliciting comments for more than two years about how cyberspace threatened copyright.[16] The White Paper outlined a series of modifications aimed, it said, at restoring "balance" in intellectual property law. Entitled "Intellectual Property and the National Information Infrastructure," the report sought to restate existing intellectual property law in terms that anyone could understand, as well as recommend changes in the law in response to the changes the Net would bring. But as scholars quickly pointed out, the first part was a bust.[17] The report no more "restated" existing law than Soviet historians "retold" stories of Stalin's administration. The restatement had a tilt, very definitely in the direction of increased intellectual property protection, but it pretended that its tilt was the natural lay of the land.

For our purposes, however, it is the recommendations that are most significant. The government proposed four responses to the threat presented by cyberspace. In the terms of chapter 7, these responses should be familiar.

The first response was traditional. The government proposed changes in the law of copyright to "clarify" the rights that it was to protect.[18] These changes were intended to better define the rights granted under intellectual property law and to further support these rights with clarified (and possibly greater) legal penalties for their violation.

But the proposal went far beyond these traditional means. A second recommendation was for increased educational efforts, both in the schools and among the general public, about the nature of intellectual property and the importance of protecting it. In the terms of chapter 7, this is the use of law to change norms so that norms will better support the protection of intellectual property. It is an indirect regulation of behavior by direct regulation of norms.

Education was not, however, the most significant indirect regulation. More interesting for our purposes was the government's financial and legal support for the development of copyright management schemes—software that would make it easier to control access to and use of copyrighted material. We will explore these schemes at some length later in this chapter, but I mention it now as another example of indirect regulation—using the market to subsidize the development of a certain software tool, and using law to regulate the properties of other software tools. Copyright management systems are supported by government funding, and the threat of felony conviction hangs over anyone interested in designing software to crack them.[19]

The 1995 package of proposals was a scattershot of techniques—some changes in law, some support for changing norms, and lots of support for changing the code of cyberspace to make it better able to protect intellectual property. Perhaps nothing better than this could have been expected in 1995. The law promised a balance of responses to deal with the shifting balance brought on by cyberspace.

Balance is attractive. Moderation seems right. But something is missing from this approach. The White Paper proceeds as if the problem of protecting intellectual property in cyberspace were just like the problem of protecting intellectual property in real space. It proceeds as if the four constraints would operate in the same proportions as in real space, as if nothing fundamental had changed.

But something fundamental *has* changed: the role that code plays in the protection of intellectual property has changed. Code can, and increasingly will, displace law as the primary defense of intellectual property in cyberspace. Private fences, not public law.

The White Paper does not see this. Built into its scattershot of ideas is one that is crucial to its approach but fundamentally wrong—the idea that the nature of cyberspace is anarchy. The White Paper promises to strengthen law in every area it can. But it approaches the question like a ship battening down for a storm: whatever happens, the threat to copyright is real, damage will be done, and the best we can do is ride it out.

This is fundamentally wrong. We are not entering a time when copyright is more threatened than it is in real space. We are instead entering a time when copyright is more effectively protected than at any time since Gutenberg. The power to regulate access to and use of copyrighted material is about to be perfected. Whatever the mavens of the mid-1990s may have thought, cyberspace is about to give holders of copyrighted property the biggest gift of protection they have ever known.

In such an age—in a time when the protections are being perfected—the real question for law is not, how can law aid in that protection? but rather, is the protection too great? The mavens were right when they predicted that cyberspace will teach us that everything we thought about copyright was wrong.[20] But the lesson in the future will be that copyright is protected far too well. The problem will center not on copy-right but on copy-*duty*—the duty of owners of protected property to make that property accessible.

That's a big claim. To see it, however, and to see the consequences it entails, we need consider only two small examples. The first is a vision of a researcher from Xerox PARC (appropriately enough), Mark Stefik, and his idea of "trusted systems."[21] The second is an implication of a world dominated by trusted systems. Both examples will throw into relief the threat that these changes present for values that our tradition considers fundamental. Both should force us to make a choice about those values, and about their place in our future.

THE PROMISE FOR INTELLECTUAL
PROPERTY IN CYBERSPACE

It all depends on whether you really understand the idea of trusted systems. If you don't understand them, then this whole approach to commerce and digital publishing is utterly unthinkable. If you do understand them, then it all follows easily.

Ralph Merkle, quoted in Stefik, "Letting Loose the Light" (1996)

Given the present code of the Internet, you can't control well who copies what. If you have a copy of a copyrighted photo, rendered in a graphics file, you can make unlimited copies of that file with no effect on the original. When you make the one-hundredth copy, nothing indicates that it is the one-hundredth copy rather than the first. There is very little in the code as it exists now that regulates the distribution of and access to material on the Net.

This problem is not unique to cyberspace. We have already seen a technology that presented the same problem; a solution to the problem was subsequently built into the technology.[22] Digital audio technology (DAT) tape was a threat to copyright, and a number of solutions to this threat were proposed. Some people argued for higher penalties for illegal copying of tapes (direct regulation by law). Some argued for a tax on blank tapes, with the proceeds compensating copyright holders (indirect regulation of the market by law). Some argued for better education to stop illegal copies of tapes (indirect regulation of norms by law). But some argued for a change in the code of tape machines that would block unlimited perfect copying.

With the code changed, when a machine is used to copy a particular CD, a serial number from the CD is recorded in the tape machine's memory. If the user tries to copy that tape more than a limited number of times, the machine adjusts the quality of the copy. As the copies increase, the quality is degraded. This degradation is deliberately created. Before DAT, it was an unintended consequence of the copying technologies—each copy was unavoidably worse than the original. Now it has been reintroduced to restore a protection that had been eroded by technology.

The same idea animates Stefik's vision, though his idea is not to make the quality of copies decrease but rather to make it possible to track and control the copies that are made.[23]

Think of the proposal like this. Today, when you buy a book, you may do any number of things with it. You can read it once or one hundred times. You can lend it to a friend. You can photocopy pages in it or scan it into your computer. You can burn it, use it as a paperweight, or sell it. You can store it on your shelf and never once open it.

Some of these things you can do because the law gives you the right to do them—you can sell the book, for example, because the copyright law explicitly gives you that right. Other things you can do because there is no way to stop you. A book seller might sell you the book at one price if you promise to read it once, and at a different price if you want to read it one hundred times, but there is no way for the seller to know whether you have obeyed the contract. In principle, the seller could sell a police officer with each book to follow you around and make sure you use the book as you promised, but the costs would plainly be prohibitive.

But what if each of these rights could be controlled, and each unbundled and sold separately? What if, that is, the software itself could regulate whether you read the book once or one hundred times; whether you could cut and paste from it or simply read it without copying; whether you could send it as an attached document to a friend or simply keep it on your machine; whether you could delete it or not; whether you could use it in another work, for another purpose, or not; or whether you could simply have it on your shelf or have it and use it as well?

Stefik describes a network that makes such unbundling of rights possible. He describes an architecture for the network that would allow owners of copyrighted materials to sell access to those materials on the terms they want and would enforce those contracts.

The details of the system are not important here[24] (it builds on the encryption architecture I described in chapter 4), but its general idea is easy enough to describe.

As the Net is now, basic functions like copying and access are crudely regulated in an all-or-nothing fashion. You generally have the right to copy or not, to gain access or not.

But a more sophisticated system of rights could be built into the Net—not into a different Net, but on top of the existing Net. This system would function by discriminating in the intercourse it has with other systems. A system that controlled access in this more fine-grained way would grant access to its resources only to another system that controlled access in the same way. A hierarchy of systems would develop, and copyrighted material would be traded only among systems that properly controlled access.

In such a world, then, you could get access, say, to the *New York Times* and pay a different price depending on how much of it you read. The *Times* could determine how much you read, whether you could copy portions of the newspaper, whether you could save it on your hard disk, and so on. But if the code you used to access the *Times* site did not enable the control the *Times* demanded, then the *Times* would not let you onto its site at all. In short, systems would exchange information only with others that could be trusted, and the protocols of trust would be built into the architectures of the systems.

Stefik calls this "trusted systems," and the name evokes a helpful analog. Think of bonded couriers. Sometimes you want to mail a letter with something particularly valuable in it. You could simply give it to the post office, but the post office is not a terribly reliable system; it has relatively little control over its employees, and theft and loss are not uncommon. So instead of going to the post office, you could give your letter to a bonded courier. Bonded couriers are insured, and the insurance is a cost that constrains them to be reliable. This reputation then makes it possible for senders of valuable material to be assured about using their services.

This is what a structure of trusted systems does for owners of intellectual property. It is a bonded courier that takes the thing of value and controls access to and use of it according to the orders given by the principal.

Imagine for a moment that such a structure emerged generally in cyberspace. How would we then think about copyright law?

An important point about copyright law is that, though designed in part to protect authors, its protection was not to be absolute—the copyright is subject to "fair use," limited terms, and first sale. The law threatened to punish violators of copyright laws—and it was this threat that induced a fairly high proportion of people to comply—but the law was never designed to simply do the author's bidding. It had public purposes as well as the author's interest in mind.

Trusted systems provide authors with the same sort of protection. Because authors can restrict unauthorized use of their material, they can extract money in exchange for access. Trusted systems thus achieve what copyright law achieves. But it can achieve this protection *without the law doing the restricting*. It permits a much more fine-grained control over access to and use of protected material than law permits, and it can do so without the aid of the law.

What copyright seeks to do using the threat of law and the push of norms, trusted systems do through the code. Copyright orders others to respect the rights of the copyright holder before using his property. Trusted systems give access only if rights are respected in the first place. The controls needed to regulate this access are built into the systems, and no users (except hackers) have a choice about whether to obey these controls. The code displaces law by codifying the rules, making them more efficient than they were just as rules.

Trusted systems in this scheme are an alternative for protecting intellectual property rights—a privatized alternative to law. They need not be exclusive; there is no reason not to use both law and trusted systems. Nevertheless, the code in effect is doing the work that the law used to do. It implements the law's protection, through code, far more effectively than the law did.

What could be wrong with this? We do not worry when people put double bolts on their doors to supplement the work of the neighborhood cop. We do not worry when they lock their cars and take their keys. It is not an offense to protect yourself rather than rely on the state. Indeed, in some contexts it is a virtue. Andrew Jackson's mother, for example, told him, "Never tell a lie, nor take what is not your own, nor sue anybody for slander, assault and battery. Always settle them cases yourself."[25] Self-sufficiency is often seen as a sign of strength, and going to the law as a sign of weakness.

There are two steps to answering this question. The first rehearses a familiar but forgotten point about the nature of property; the second makes a less familiar, but central, point about the nature of intellectual property. Together they suggest why perfect control is not the control that law has given owners of intellectual property.

THE LIMITS ON THE PROTECTION OF PROPERTY

The realists in American legal history (circa 1890–1930) were scholars who (in part) emphasized the role of the state in what was called "private law."[26] At the time they wrote, it was the "private" in private law that got all the emphasis. Forgotten was the "law," as if "property" and "contract" existed independent of the state.

The realists' aim was to undermine this view. Contract and property law, they argued, was *law* that gave private parties power.[27] If you breach a contract with me, I can have the court order the sheriff to force you to pay; the contract gives me access to the state power of the sheriff. If your contract with your employer says that it may dismiss you for being late, then the police can be called in to eject you if you refuse to leave. If your lease forbids you to have cats, then the landlord can use the power of the courts to evict you if you do not get rid of the cats. These are all instances where contract and property, however grounded in private action, give a private person an entitlement to the state.

No doubt this power is justified in many cases; to call it "law" is not to call it unjust. The greatest prosperity in history has been created by a system in which private parties can order their lives freely through contract and property. But whether justified in the main or not, the realists argued that the contours of this "law" should be architected to benefit society.[28]

This is not communism. It is not an attack on private property. It is not to say that the state creates wealth. Put your Ayn Rand away. These are claims about the relationship between private law and public law, and they should be uncontroversial.

Private law creates private rights to the extent that these private rights serve some collective good. If a private right is harmful to a collective good, then the *state* has no reason to create it. The state's interests are general, not particular. It has a reason to create rights when those rights serve a common, rather than particular, end.

The institution of private property is an application of this point. The state has an interest in defining rights to private property because private property helps produce a general, and powerful, prosperity. It is a system for ordering economic relations that greatly benefits all members of society. No other system that we have yet devised better orders economic relations. No other system, some believe, could.[29]

But even with ordinary property—your car, or your house—property rights are never absolute. There is no property that does not have to yield at some point to the interests of the state. Your land may be taken to build a highway, your car seized to carry an accident victim to the hospital, your driveway crossed by the postman, your house inspected by health inspectors. In countless ways, the system of property we call "private property" is a system that balances exclusive control by the individual against certain common state ends. When the latter conflict with the former, it is the former that yields.

This balance, the realists argued, is a feature of all property. But it is an especially important feature of intellectual property. The balance of rights with intellectual property differs from the balance with ordinary real or personal property. "Information," as Boyle puts it, "is different."[30] And a very obvious feature of intellectual property shows why.

When property law gives me the exclusive right to use my house, there's a very good reason for it. If you used my house while I did, I would have less to use. When the law gives me an exclusive right to my apple, that too makes sense. If you eat my apple, then I cannot. Your use of my property ordinarily interferes with my use of my property. Your consumption reduces mine.

The law has a good reason, then, to give me an exclusive right over my personal and real property. If it did not, I would have little reason to work to produce it. Or if I did work to produce it, I would then spend a great deal of my time trying to keep you away. It is better for everyone, the argument goes, if I have an exclusive right to my (rightly acquired) property, because then I have an incentive to produce it and not waste all my time trying to defend it.[31]

Things are different with intellectual property. If you "take" my idea, I still have it. If I tell you an idea, you have not deprived me of it.[32] An unavoidable feature of intellectual property is that its consumption, as the economists like to put it, is "nonrivalrous." Your consumption does not lessen mine. If I write a song, you can sing it

without making it impossible for me to sing it. If I write a book, you can read it
(please do) without disabling me from reading it. Ideas, at their core, can be *shared*
with no reduction in the amount the "owner" can consume. This difference is fundamental, and it has been understood since the founding.

Jefferson put it better than I:

> If nature has made any one thing less susceptible than all others of exclusive
> property, it is the action of the thinking power called an idea, which an individ-
> ual may exclusively possess as long as he keeps it to himself; but the moment it is
> divulged, it forces itself into the possession of every one, and the receiver cannot
> dispossess himself of it. Its peculiar character, too, is that no one possesses the
> less, because every other possess the whole of it. He who receives an idea from
> me, receives instruction himself without lessening mine; as he who lites his taper
> at mine, receives light without darkening me. That ideas should freely spread
> from one to another over the globe, for the moral and mutual instruction of
> man, and improvement of his condition, seems to have been peculiarly and
> benevolently designed by nature, when she made them, like fire, expansible over
> all space, without lessening their density at any point, and like the air in which we
> breathe, move, and have our physical being, incapable of confinement or exclu-
> sive appropriation. Inventions then cannot, in nature, be a subject of property.[33]

Technically, Jefferson is confusing two different concepts. One is the possibility
of excluding others from using or getting access to an idea. This is the question
whether ideas are "excludable"; Jefferson suggests that they are not. The other concept is whether my using an idea lessens your use of the same idea. This is the question of whether ideas are "rivalrous";[34] again, Jefferson suggests that they are not.
Jefferson believes that nature has made ideas both nonexcludable and nonrivalrous,
and that there is little that man can do to change this fact.[35]

But in fact, ideas are not both nonexcludable and nonrivalrous. I can exclude
people from my ideas or my writings—I can keep them secret, or build fences to
keep people out. How easily, or how effectively, is a technical question. It depends on
the architecture of protection that a given context provides. But given the proper
technology, there is no doubt that I can keep people out.

What I cannot do, however, is change the nature of my ideas as "nonrivalrous"
goods. No technology (that we know of) will erase an idea from your head as it
passes into my head. No technology will make it so that I cannot share your ideas
with no harm to you. My knowing what you know does not lessen your knowing of
the same thing. That fact is given in the world, and it is that fact that makes intellectual property different. Unlike apples, and unlike houses, ideas are something I can
take from you without diminishing what you have.

It does not follow, however, that there is no need for property rights over expressions or inventions.[36] Just because you can have what I have without lessening

what I have does not mean that the state has no reason to create rights over ideas, or over the expression of ideas.

If a novelist cannot stop you from copying (rather than buying) her book, then she has very little incentive to produce more books. She may have as much as she had before you took the work she produced, but if you take it without paying, she has no monetary incentive to produce more.

Now in fact, of course, the incentives an author faces are quite complex, and it is not possible to make simple generalizations about the incentives authors face.[37] But generalizations do not have to be perfect to make a point: even if some authors write for free, it is still the case that the law needs some intellectual property rights. If the law did not protect the author at all, there would be fewer authors. The law has a reason to protect the rights of authors, *at least insofar as doing so gives them an incentive to produce.* With ordinary property, the law must both create an incentive to produce and protect the right of possession; with intellectual property, the law need only create the incentive to produce.

This is the difference between these two very different kinds of property, and this difference affects fundamentally the nature of intellectual property law. While we protect real and personal property to protect the owner from harm and give the owner an incentive, we protect intellectual property only to ensure that we create a sufficient incentive to produce it. "Sufficient incentive," however, is something less than "perfect control." And in turn we can say that the ideal protections of intellectual property law are something less than the ideal protections for ordinary or real property.

This difference between the nature of intellectual property and ordinary property was recognized by our Constitution, which in article I, section 8, clause 8, gives Congress the power "to promote the Progress of Science and useful Arts, by securing for limited Times to Authors and Inventors the exclusive Right to their respective Writings and Discoveries."

Note the special structure of this clause. First, it sets forth the precise reason for the power—to promote the progress of science and useful arts. It is for those reasons, and those reasons only, that Congress may grant an exclusive right—otherwise known as a monopoly. And second, note the special temporality of this right: "for limited Times." The Constitution does not allow Congress to grant authors and inventors permanent exclusive rights to their writings and discoveries, only limited rights. It does not give Congress the power to give them "property" in their writings and discoveries, only an exclusive right over them for a limited time.

The Constitution's protection for intellectual property then is fundamentally different from its protection of ordinary property. I've said that all property is granted subject to the limit of the public good. But even so, if the government decided to nationalize all property after a fifteen-year term of ownership, the Constitution would require it to compensate the owners. By contrast, if Congress set the copyright term at fifteen years, there would be no claim that the government pay compensation after the fifteen years were up. Intellectual property rights are a monopoly that the state gives to producers of intellectual property in exchange for their producing intellectual property. After a limited time, the product of their work becomes the public's to use as it wants. This *is* Communism, at the core of our Constitution's protection of intellectual property. This "property" is not property in the ordinary sense of that term.

And this is true for reasons better than tradition as well. Economists have long understood that granting property rights over information is dangerous (to say the least).[38] This is not because of leftist leanings among economists. It is because economists are pragmatists, and their objective in granting any property right is simply to facilitate production. But there is no way to know, in principle, whether increasing or decreasing the rights granted under intellectual property law will lead to an increase in the production of intellectual property. The reasons are complex, but the point is not: increasing intellectual property's protection is not guaranteed to "promote the progress of science and useful arts"—indeed, often doing so will stifle it.

The balance that intellectual property law traditionally strikes is between the protections granted the author and the public use or access granted everyone else. The aim is to give the author sufficient incentive to produce. Built into the law of intellectual property are limits on the power of the author to control use of the ideas she has created.[39]

A classic example of these limits and of this public use dimension is the right of "fair use." Fair use is the right to use copyrighted material, regardless of the wishes of the owner of that material. A copyright gives the owner certain rights; fair use is a limitation on those rights. Under the right of fair use, you can criticize this book, cut sections from it, and reproduce them in an article attacking me. In these ways and in others, you have the right to use this book independent of how I say it should be used.

Fair use does not necessarily work against the author's interest—or more accurately, fair use does not necessarily work against the interests of authors as a class. When fair use protects the right of reviewers to criticize books without the permission of authors, then more critics criticize. And the more criticism there is, the better the information is about what books people should buy. And the better the information is about what to buy, the more people there are who will buy. Authors as a whole benefit from the system of fair use, even if particular authors do not.

The law of copyright is filled with such rules. Another is the "first sale" doctrine. If you buy this book, you can sell it to someone else free of any constraint I might impose on you.[40] This doctrine differs from the tradition in, for example, Europe, where there are "moral rights" that give the creator power over subsequent use.[41] I've already mentioned another example—limited term. The creator cannot extend the term for which the law will provide protection; that is fixed by the statute and runs when the statute runs.[42]

Taken together, these rules give the creator significant control over the use of what he produces, but never perfect control. They give the public some access, but not complete access. They are balanced by design, and different from the balance the law strikes for ordinary property. They are constitutionally structured to help build an intellectual and cultural commons.

The law strikes this balance. It is not a balance that would exist in nature. Without the law, and before cyberspace, authors would have very little protection; with the law, they have significant, but not perfect, protection. The law gives authors something they otherwise would not have in exchange for limits on their rights, secured to benefit the intellectual commons as a whole.

PRIVATE SUBSTITUTES FOR PUBLIC LAW

But what happens when code protects the interests now protected by copyright law? What happens when Mark Stefik's vision is realized, and when what the law protects as intellectual property can be protected through code? Should we expect that any of the limits will remain? Should we expect code to mirror the limits that the law imposes? Fair use? Limited term? Would private code build these "bugs" into its protections?

The point should be obvious: when intellectual property is protected by code, nothing requires that the same balance be struck. Nothing requires the owner to grant the right of fair use. She might, just as a bookstore allows individuals to browse for free, but she might not. Whether she grants this right depends on whether it profits her. Fair use becomes subject to private gain.[43]

As privatized law, trusted systems regulate in the same domain where copyright law regulates, but unlike copyright law, they do not guarantee the same public use protection. Trusted systems give the producer maximum control—admittedly at a cheaper cost, thus permitting many more authors to publish. But they give authors more control (either to charge for or limit use) in an area where the law gave less than perfect control. Code displaces the balance in copyright law and doctrines such as fair use.

Some will respond that I am late to the party: copyright law is already being displaced, if not by code then by the private law of contract. Through the use of click-wrap, or shrink-wrap, licenses, authors are increasingly demanding that purchasers, or licensees, waive rights that copyright law gave them. If copyright law gives the right to reverse-engineer, then these contracts might extract a promise not to reverse-engineer. If copyright law gives the right to dispose of the book however the purchaser wants after the first sale, then a contract might require that the user waive that right. And if these terms in the contract attached to every copyright work are enforceable merely by being "attached" and "knowable," then already we have the ability to rewrite the balance that copyright law creates. Already, through contract law, copyright holders can defeat the balance that copyright law intends.

I agree that this race to privatize copyright law through contract is already far along, fueled in particular by decisions such as Judge Frank Easterbrook's in *ProCD v Zeidenberg*[44] and by the efforts in some quarters to push a new uniform code that would facilitate these contracts.[45]

But contracts are not as bad as code. Contracts are a form of law. If a term of a contract is inconsistent with a value of copyright law, you can refuse to obey it and let the other side get a court to enforce it. The ultimate power of a contract is a decision by a court—to enforce the contract or not. Although courts today are relatively eager to find ways to enforce these contracts, there is at least hope that if the other side makes its case very clear, courts could shift direction again.[46]

The same is not true of code. Whatever problems there are when contracts replace copyright law, the problems are worse when code displaces copyright law. Again—where do we challenge the code? When the software protects in a particular way without relying in the end on the state, where can we challenge the nature of the protection? Where can we demand balance when the code takes it away?

The rise of contracts modifying copyright law (due in part to the falling costs of contracting) and the rise of code modifying copyright law (promised as trusted systems become all the more common) raise for us a question that we have not had to answer before. We have never had to choose whether authors should be permitted perfectly to control the use of their intellectual property independent of the law, for such control could only be achieved through law.[47] The balance struck by the law was the best that authors could get. But now the code gives authors a better deal. And thus we must now decide whether this better deal makes public sense.

Some argue that it does, and that this increased power to control use in fact is not inconsistent with fair use.[48] Fair use, these commentators argue, defined the rights in an area where it was not possible to meter and charge for use. In that context, fair use set a default rule that parties could always contract around. The default rule was that use was free.

But as the limits of what it is possible to meter and charge for changes, the scope of fair use changes as well.[49] If it becomes possible to license every aspect of use, then no aspect of use would have the protections of fair use. Fair use, under this conception, was just the space where it was too expensive to meter use. By eliminating that space, cyberspace merely forces us to recognize the change in the context within which fair use functions.

There are then, from this view, two very different conceptions of fair use.[50] One conception views it as inherent in the copyright—required whether technology makes it possible to take it away or not; the other views it as contingent—needed where technology makes it necessary. We can choose between these two conceptions, if indeed our constitutional commitment is ambiguous.

A nice parallel to this problem exists in constitutional law. The framers gave Congress the power to regulate interstate commerce and commerce that affects interstate commerce.[51] At the founding, that was a lot of commerce, but because of the inefficiencies of the market, not all of it. Thus, the states had a domain of commerce that they alone could regulate.[52]

Over time, however, the scope of interstate commerce has changed so that much less commerce is now within the exclusive domain of the states. This change has produced two sorts of responses. One is to find other ways to give states domains of exclusive regulatory authority. The justification for this response is the claim that these changes in interstate commerce are destroying the framers' vision about state power.

The other response is to concede the increasing scope of federal authority, but to deny that it is inconsistent with the framing balance.[53] Certainly, at the founding, some commerce was not interstate and did not affect interstate commerce. But that does not mean that the framers intended that there must always be such a space. They tied the scope of federal power to a moving target; if the target moves completely to the side of federal power, then that is what we should embrace.[54]

In both contexts, the change is the same. We start in a place where balance is given to us by the mix of frictions within a particular regulatory domain: fair use is a balance given to us because it is too expensive to meter all use; state power over commerce is given to us because not all commerce affects interstate commerce. When new technology disturbs the balance, we must decide whether the original intent was that there be a balance, or that the scope of one side of each balance should faithfully track the index to which it was originally tied. Both contexts, in short, present ambiguity.

Many observers (myself included) have strong feelings one way or the other. We believe this latent ambiguity is not an ambiguity at all. In the context of federal power, we believe either that the states were meant to keep a domain of exclusive authority[55] or that the federal government was to have whatever power affected interstate commerce.[56] In the context of fair use, we believe that either fair use is to be a minimum of public use, guaranteed regardless of the technology,[57] or that it is just an inefficient consequence of inefficient technology, to be removed as soon as efficiency can be achieved.[58]

But in both cases, this may make the problem too easy. The best answer in both contexts may be that the question was unresolved at the time: perhaps no one thought of the matter, and hence there is no answer to the question of what they would have intended if some central presupposition had changed. And if there was no original answer, we must decide the question by our own lights. As Stefik says of trusted systems—and, we might expect, of the implications of trusted systems—"It is a tool never imagined by the creators of copyright law, or by those who believe laws governing intellectual property cannot be enforced."[59]

The loss of fair use is a consequence of the perfection of trusted systems. Whether you consider it a problem or not depends on your view of the value of fair use. If you consider it a public value that should exist regardless of the technological regime, then the emergence of this perfection should trouble you. From your perspective, there was a value latent in the imperfection of the old system that has now been erased.

But even if you do not think that the loss of fair use is a problem, trusted systems threaten other values latent in the imperfection of the real world. Consider now a second.

THE ANONYMITY THAT IMPERFECTION ALLOWS

I was a student in England for a number of years, at an English university. In the college I attended, there was a "buttery"—a shop that basically sold alcohol. During the first week I was there I had to buy a large amount of Scotch (a series of unimaginative gifts, as I remember). About a week after I made these purchases, I received a summons from my tutor to come talk with him in his office. When I arrived, the tutor asked me about my purchases. This was, to his mind, an excessive amount of alcohol, and he wanted to know whether I had a good reason for buying it.

Needless to say, I was shocked at the question. Of course, formally, I had made a purchase at the college, and I had not hidden my name when I did so (indeed, I had charged it on my college account), so formally, I had revealed to the college and its agents my alcohol purchases. Still, it shocked me that this information would be monitored by college authorities and then checked up on. I could see why they did it, and I could see the good that might come from it. It just never would have occurred to me that this data would be used in this way.

If this is an invasion, of course it is a small one. Later it was easy for me to hide my binges simply by buying from a local store rather than the college buttery. (Though I later learned that the local store rented its space from the college, so who knows what deal they had struck.) And in any case, I was not being punished. The college was just concerned. But the example suggests a more general point: we reveal to the world a certain class of data about ourselves that we ordinarily expect the world not to use.

Trusted systems depend on such data—they depend on the ability to know how people use the property that is being protected. To set prices most efficiently, the system ideally should know as much about individuals and their reading habits as possible. It needs to know this data because it needs an efficient way to track use and so to charge for it.[60]

But this tracking involves a certain invasion. We live now in a world where we think about what we read in just the way that I thought about what I bought as a student in England—we do not expect that anyone is keeping track. We would be shocked if we learned that the library was keeping tabs on the books that people checked out and then using this data in some monitoring way.

Such tracking, however, is just what trusted systems require. And so the question becomes: Should there be a right against this kind of monitoring? The question is parallel to the question of fair use. In a world where this monitoring could not effectively occur, there was, of course, no such right against it. But now that monitoring can occur, we must ask whether the latent right to read anonymously, given to us before by imperfections in technologies, should be a legally protected right.

Julie Cohen argues that it should, and we can see quite directly how her argument proceeds.[61] Whatever its source, it is a value in this world that we can explore intellectually on our own. It is a value that we can read anonymously, without fear that others will know or watch or change their behavior based on what we read. This is an element of intellectual freedom. It is a part of what makes us as we are.[62]

Yet this element is potentially erased by trusted systems. These systems need to monitor, and this monitoring destroys anonymity. We need to decide whether, and how, to preserve values from today in a context of trusted systems.

This is a matter of translation.[63] The question is, how should changes in technology be accommodated to preserve values from an earlier context in a new context? It is the same question that Brandeis asked about wiretapping.[64] It is the question the Court answers in scores of contexts all the time. It is fundamentally a question about preserving values when contexts change.

In the context of both fair use and reading, Cohen has a consistent answer to this question of translation. She argues that there is a right to resist, or "hack," trusted systems to the extent that they infringe on traditional fair use. (Others have called this the "Cohen Theorem.") As for reading, she argues that copyright management schemes must protect a right to read anonymously—that if they monitor, they must be constructed so that they preserve anonymity. The strategy is the same: Cohen identifies a value yielded by an old architecture but now threatened by a new architecture, and then argues in favor of an affirmative right to protect the original value.

THE PROBLEMS THAT PERFECTION MAKES

These two examples reveal a common problem—one that will reach far beyond copyright. At one time we enjoy a certain kind of liberty, but that liberty comes from the high costs of control.[65] That was the conclusion we drew about fair use—that when the cost of control was high, the space for fair use was great. So too with anonymous reading: we read anonymously in real space not so much because laws protect that right as because the cost of tracking what we read is so great.

When those costs fall, the liberty is threatened. That threat requires a choice—do we allow the erosion, or do we erect other limits to re-create the original space for liberty?

The law of intellectual property is the first example of this general point. The architectures of property will change; they will allow for a greater protection for intellectual property than real-space architectures allowed; and this greater protection will force a choice on us that we do not need to make in real space. Should the architecture allow perfect control over intellectual property, or should we build into the architecture an incompleteness that guarantees a certain aspect of public use? Or a certain space for individual freedom?

Ignoring these questions will not make them go away. Pretending that the framers answered them is no solution either. In this context (and this is just the first) we will need to make a judgment about which values the architecture will protect.

CHOICES

I've argued that cyberspace will open up at least two important choices in the context of intellectual property: whether to allow intellectual property in effect to become completely propertized (for that is what a perfect code regime for protecting intellectual property would do), and whether to allow this regime to erase the anonymity latent in less efficient architectures of control. These choices were not made by our framers. They are for us to make now.

I have a view, in this context as in the following three, about how we should exercise that choice. But I am a lawyer, trained to be shy about saying "how things ought to be." Lawyers are taught to point elsewhere—to the framers, to the United Nations charter, to an act of Congress—when arguing about how things ought to be. Having said that there is no such authority here, I feel as if I ought therefore to be silent.

Cowardly, not silent, however, is how others might see it. I should say, they say, what I think. So in each of these four applications (intellectual property, privacy, free speech, and sovereignty), I will offer my view about how these choices should be made. But I do this under some duress and encourage you to simply ignore what I believe. It will be short, and summary, and easy to discard. It is the balance of the book—and, most importantly, the claim that *we* have a choice to make—that I really want to stick.

Anonymity

Cohen, it seems to me, is plainly right about anonymity, and the Cohen Theorem inspirational. However efficient the alternative may be, we should certainly architect cyberspaces to ensure anonymity—or more precisely, pseudonymity—first. If the code is going to monitor just what I do, then at least it should not know that it is "I" that it is monitoring. I am less troubled if it knows that "14AH342BD7" read such and such; I am deeply troubled if that number is tied back to my name.

Cohen is plainly right for a second reason as well: all of the good that comes from monitoring could be achieved while protecting privacy as well. It may take a bit more coding to build in routines for breaking traceability; it may take more planning to ensure that privacy is protected. But if those rules are embedded up front, the cost would not be terribly high. Far cheaper to architect privacy protections in now rather than retrofit for them later.

The Commons

An intellectual commons I feel much more strongly about.

We can architect cyberspace to preserve a commons or not. (Jefferson thought that nature had already done the architecting, but Jefferson wrote before there was code.[66]) We should choose to architect it with a commons. Our past had a commons that could not be designed away; that commons gave our culture great value. What value the commons of the future could bring us is something we are just beginning to see. Intellectual property scholars saw it—long before cyberspace came along—and laid the groundwork for much of the argument we need to have now.[67] The greatest work in the law of cyberspace has been written in the field of intellectual property. In a wide range of contexts, these scholars have made a powerful case for the substantive value of an intellectual commons.[68]

James Boyle puts the case most dramatically in his extraordinary book *Shamans, Software, and Spleens.*[69] Drawing together both cyberspace and noncyberspace questions, he spells out the challenge we face in an information society—and particularly the political challenge we face.[70] Elsewhere he identifies our need for an "environmental movement" in information policy—a rhetoric that gets people to see the broad range of values put at risk by this movement to propertize all information.[71]

We are far from that understanding just now, and this book, on its own, won't get us much closer. It is all that I can do here to point to the choice we will have to make, and hint, as I have, about a direction.

E L E V E N

p r i v a c y

THE CONCLUSION OF PART 1 WAS THAT CODE COULD ENABLE A MORE REGULABLE CY-berspace and that this is cause for concern. The conclusion of the last chapter was that code could enable a more regulable regime of intellectual property, and again, that this is cause for concern. In both cases, code resets a traditional balance between freedom and constraint, and we need to ask whether the new balance is consistent with our tradition or with how we want the space to be.

With "privacy," the story is a bit different. Here the code has already upset a traditional balance. It has already changed the control that individuals have over facts about their private lives. The question now is: Could code re-create something of that traditional balance? I argue that it can.[1]

There's a story from early MUD history that will introduce this debate about privacy.[2] You recall that MUDs are text-based virtual realities where people build characters and those characters come to represent who their creators are. In the early history of MUDs the community of MUDers was relatively small, and certain characters became well known across MUD communities. Famous characters became known to everyone.

There is a behavior in MUDs and MOOs called "tinySex"—text-based virtual sex in which (at least) two people talk through a sexual encounter. Sometimes this talking is just talk. Sometimes something more is going on. But in any case, tinySex is a significant part of the history of MUDs, as its cognates are in other parts of cyberspace and in real space as well.[3]

In an early and prominent MUD, there appeared a character who was particularly interested in tinySex, and especially in tinySex with famous MUD characters. This character (a man in real space) "was" a woman, and he proceeded to "seduce" (tinySeduce?) a string of famous characters. Off they would go to some "private room" and engage in a tinySex affair. Many famous MUDers were seduced by this character, who engaged in quite a bit of tinySex.

We know this because the character recorded these tinySex trysts, both the se-
duction and the sex that followed. After collecting a large number of victims, he
posted the recordings. Now sitting in the MUD space of this previously flourishing
community were the transcripts of sexual encounters by some of the most prominent members of the community. All Monica, all the time, but long before any Monica existed.

Now of course, there have always been affairs. People have always raced off to
some corner to engage in sex, whether tiny or not. And there have always been
people who just love to kiss and tell. But rather than the similarities, think about
some of the differences. It is not just the fact that an affair has occurred, but that
every twist of the event is replayed. And it is not just that a recording exists, but that
this "recording" is posted in a prominent and searchable space. The private goings-
on were monitored, in a space that makes monitoring extremely easy. The product
of this monitoring is then searchable—the design makes that easy as well. Every
move is captured; only some are discarded; the rest remain out there to be searched.

This event destroyed this MUD community. People could not quite face each
other in the same way again. They moved on, took different characters, or left MUD
space entirely. No laws had been broken, but the space was destroyed.

And so it should be, you might be tempted to say. Perhaps it is best that a bit of
light flushed out this sort of "deviant" behavior, that we live in a world where our actions accord with our words, where we are who we seem to be. Perhaps we are better
off living in such a world, and maybe it is good that cyberspace makes this possible.

There is a part of anyone's life that is *monitored,* and there is a part that can be
searched. The monitored is that part of one's daily existence that others see or notice
and that others can respond to, if response is appropriate. As I walk down the street,
my behavior is monitored. If I walked down the street in a small village in western
China, my behavior would be monitored quite extensively. This monitoring in both
cases would be transitory. People would notice, for example, if I were walking with
an elephant or walking in a dress, but if there were nothing special about my walk,
if I simply blended into the crowd, then I might be noticed for the moment but forgotten soon after—more quickly in Cambridge, perhaps, than in China.

The searchable is the part of your life that leaves, or is, a record. Scribblings in
your diary leave a record of your thoughts. Stuff in your house is a record of what
you possess. The recordings on your telephone answering machine are a record of
who called and what they said. These parts of your life are not so ephemeral. They
instead remain to be reviewed—if technology and the law permit.

Privacy, as Ethan Katsh defines it, is the power to control what others can come
to know about you.[4] People gain knowledge about you in only two ways—through
monitoring or searching (or by reports relying on the results of monitoring and
searching). One can do little about gossip, and the law can do little about reporting.
So to understand the real privacy that you have, we must understand something
about these two ideas of monitoring and searching. What are the constraints in real

space on others' ability to monitor and search, and how do those constraints change as we move to cyberspace?

I begin by examining these two questions separately, marking out the changes that cyberspace might bring and identifying the latent ambiguities that these changes reveal.[5] Then, as in the last chapter, I will consider arguments on both sides of these ambiguities. Again, in the end I will push one side. But whether you accept my position is not as important to me as whether you accept the idea that an argument for a position is required. Here too we do not have a decision of the framers to follow. We must make our own.

SPACES   PROTECTED   BY   LAW

Recall the worm from the start of this book: a bit of code works itself onto your machine, scans your disk, and reports back to some central place facts about your machine. "Illegal copy of Word 98," or, "Multiple copies of Now Utilities," or, "NSA Document 5G67K13"—such facts are reported if they are true; nothing is reported if they are not.

This example may have seemed oddly removed from the mainstream of privacy issues. After all, we do not really think the government has a set of worms working themselves across the Net, spying on people (though it is alleged by some that the NSA installs sniffers at various network switches).

But whether or not the specifics of the example convince you, the general form should. We can imagine a host of contexts where the burdens of a search have been eliminated and its perfection increased, and where the constitutional question raised by the search is thus made all the more difficult.

In each of these contexts, the same question presents itself: Is the constitutional value a protection against unjustified burdens imposed by the state, or is it a substantive value of privacy? When the burden decreases, does the protected privacy decrease? Is the protection against state trespass or against incursions into a particular space? This is the same question that Louis Brandeis and William Howard Taft confronted in the wiretapping case of 1928.[6] It is a question we must now ask in an increasingly large range of our own private lives.

I consider some of that range in the section that follows. My aim is to explore the *constitutional* question that this change presents; I am not talking about statutory protections, which are in fact quite rich. My question is: What would the Constitution protect absent the protections of a statute?[7]

I am also not considering any technological steps that the individual might take to protect privacy on her own. I consider that in a section that follows.

E-mail

Electronic mail is a text-based message stored in digital form. It is like a transcribed telephone call. When sent from one person to another, e-mail is copied and transmitted from machine to machine; it sits on these different machines until removed either by routines—decisions by machines—or by people.

The content of many e-mail messages is like the content of an ordinary telephone call—unplanned, unthinking, the ordinary chatter of friends. But unlike a telephone call, this content is saved, and once saved, it is monitorable, archivable, and searchable. Companies can build routines that watch the interactions between employees, that watch what is said to others, and that collect and organize what is said, to be used as the company sees fit.

Can, and do. The single greatest invasion of any sensible space of privacy that cyberspace has produced is the extraordinary monitoring of employees in which corporations now engage. On the theory that they "own the computer," employers increasingly snoop in the e-mail of employees, looking for stuff they deem improper.

To be sure, in principle, such monitoring and searching are possible with telephone calls or letters. But in practice, they are not. To monitor telephones or regular mail requires time and money—that is, human intervention. And this cost means that most won't do it. Here again, the costs of control yield a certain kind of freedom.

This freedom is reduced as the costs of searching fall. More content can be searched without imposing any burden on the target of the search. Should protections against searching therefore fall as well?

V-mail

If e-mail, why not v-mail? Voice mail systems archive messages and record the communication attributes of the conversations.[8] As technologies for voice recognition improve, so does the ability to search voice records. These records exist in archives and could be searched, just as the NSA scans international telephone calls, for example.[9] And thus, we could well imagine technologies that would allow us to scan v-mail, looking for key words or topics and pulling out from a general archive only those keys.

This search would also impose no burden on the user. It could be targeted on and limited to specific topics, and it could operate in the background without anyone ever knowing. Does a constitutional privacy speak to these practices?

Video

A picture might be worth a thousand words, but Hewlett-Packard has found a way to represent a face in less than a hundred bytes.[10] A face can be captured, stored, and matched against video archives of locations. Hewlett-Packard estimates that even at one hundred yards its technologies could identify the face in a videotape. Using video cameras located around a city, the government could begin to monitor where people go by attempting to identify the people captured by the cameras.

But that is the future. Even now video technologies are used to identify license plates in the Channel Tunnel[11] or vehicles entering airport parking garages.[12] Using these technologies, and others, it will become increasingly easy to monitor movements in public.

Telephones

Cell phones need to locate themselves so that transmitters can follow the caller as she moves from one zone to another. These data about location are collected by systems that service the call. But obviously these data could be put to other uses, such as monitoring and tracking. And as I described in chapter 5, the FBI is now pushing for this data to be made readily available so that the government, if it wants, can track who it wants.

Of course, the FBI justifies such tracking not by arguing that it wants the ability to spy but by citing public safety reasons. If we could track your cell phone's location, the argument goes, then when you call 911, it would be easier for emergency relief services to be dispatched to find you. True enough, though of course, the system could also be programmed to report locations *only* when 911 was dialed. The FBI, not surprisingly, overlooked that possibility.[13]

In each case, there is a question about whether to protect the space against invasions by the government (the constitutional question). Textually, the Constitution seems to require that we answer that question by asking what is "reasonable." Historically, we have determined what is reasonable by weighing the burdens, taking the technologies that produce them for granted. It was a given that searching a house is invasive, and a given that listening to phone calls is too expensive. These givens have governed what kind of privacy seemed reasonable. We took the world as we found it, and then built our privacy around that.

But in the digital world these burdens are not givens. Burdens are determined by the architectures of the space, and these architectures are plastic. If the protection turns on how burdensome a search is, then we can design the space to eliminate the burden. And if we do that, then the question rightly becomes whether the protection for privacy is eliminated as well.

The answer to that question depends, of course, on the conception of privacy at stake. The kind of privacy I have spoken of already—as a way to minimize intrusion—is only the first of at least three conceptions.

Privacy to Minimize Burden

The first conception, which we could call the utility conception, seeks to minimize intrusion. We want to be left alone, not interfered with, not troubled. And so we want a protection that minimizes the extent to which tranquillity is disturbed. Sometimes the state will have reason to search us or to interfere with our peace. But we want this interference kept at a minimum. The test then is the burden of the state's intervention; when an intervention can be made less burdensome, the protection against it decreases as well.

Privacy as Dignity

The second conception tracks dignity. Even if a search does not bother you at all, or even if you do not notice the search, this conception of privacy holds that the very idea of a search of your possessions is an offense to your dignity. From this perspective, if the state wants to search your house, it had better have a good reason. Its search harms your dignity whether it interferes with your life or not.

I saw these two conceptions of privacy play out against each other in a tragically common encounter in Washington, D.C. A friend and I had arranged a "police ride-along"—riding with District police during their ordinary patrol. The neighborhood we patrolled was among the poorest in the city, and around 11:00 P.M. a report came in that a car alarm had been tripped in a location close to ours. When we arrived near the scene, at least five police officers were attempting to hold three youths; three of the officers were holding the suspects flat against the wall, with their legs spread and their faces pressed against the brick.

These three were "suspects"—they were near a car alarm when it went off—and yet, from the looks of things, you would have thought they had been caught holding the Hope diamond.

And then an extraordinary disruption broke out. To the surprise of everyone, and to my terror (for this seemed a tinder box, and what I am about to describe seemed a match), one of the three youths, no older than seventeen, turned around in a fit of anger and started screaming at the cops. "Every time anything happens in this neighborhood, I get thrown against the wall, and a gun pushed against my head. I've never done anything illegal, but I'm constantly being pushed around by cops with guns."

His friend then turned around and tried to calm him down. "Cool it, man, they're just trying to do their job. It'll be over in a minute, and everything will be cool."

"I'm not going to cool it. Why the fuck do I have to live this way? I am not a criminal. I don't deserve to be treated like this. Someday one of these guns is going to go off by accident—and then I'll be a fucking statistic. What then?"

At this point the cops intervened, three of them flipping the indignant youth around against the wall, his face again flat against the brick. "This will be over in a minute. If you check out, you'll be free to go. Just relax."

In the voice of rage of the first youth was the claim of dignity denied. Whether reasonable or not, whether minimally intrusive or not, there was something insulting about this experience—all the more insulting when repeated, one imagines, over and over again. I was reminded of an opinion by Justice Scalia (an odd association, I realize, but I had worked for the man), who wondered whether the framers of the Constitution would have considered constitutional the police practice known as a "Terry stop"—stopping and frisking any individual whenever the police have a reasonable suspicion. As Justice Scalia wrote: "I frankly doubt . . . whether the fiercely proud men who adopted our Fourth Amendment would have allowed themselves to be subjected, on mere *suspicion* of being armed and dangerous, to such indignity."[14]

And yet, on the other hand, there is the argument of minimal intrusion. If privacy is a protection against unjustified and excessive disruption, then this was no invasion of privacy. As the second youth argued, the intrusion was minimal; it would pass quickly (as it did—five minutes later, after their identification checked out, we had left); and it was reasonably related to some legitimate end. Privacy here is simply the protection against unreasonable and burdensome intrusions, and this search, the second youth argued, was not so unreasonable and burdensome as to justify the fit of anger (which also risked a much greater danger).

Privacy as Substantive

These two conceptions of privacy, however, are distinct from a third, which is about neither preserving dignity nor minimizing intrusion but instead is substantive— privacy as a way to constrain the power of the state to regulate. Here the work of William Stuntz is a guide.[15] Stuntz argues that the real purpose of the Fourth and Fifth Amendments is to make some types of regulation too difficult to effect by making the evidence needed to prosecute violations unavailable.

This is a hard idea for us to imagine, for in our world the sources of evidence are many—credit card records, telephone records, video cameras at 7-Elevens, and so on. But put yourself back two hundred years, when the only real evidence was testimony and things. Imagine that in that time the state wanted to punish you for "sedition." The only good evidence of sedition would be your writings or your own testimony about your thoughts. If those two sources were eliminated, then it would be practically impossible to prosecute sedition successfully.

As Stuntz argues, this is just what the Fourth and Fifth Amendments do. Combined, they make collecting the evidence for a crime like sedition impossible, thereby making a crime like sedition impossible. And not just sedition—as Stuntz argues, the effect of the Fourth, Fifth, and Sixth Amendments was to restrict the scope of regulation that was practically possible. As he captures the idea: "Just as a law banning the use of contraceptives would tend to encourage bedroom searches, so also would a ban on bedroom searches tend to discourage laws prohibiting contraceptives."[16]

But were not such searches already restricted by, for example, the First Amendment? Would not a law punishing seditious libel have been unconstitutional in any case? In fact, it was not clear at the founding; indeed, it was so unclear that in 1798 Congress passed the Alien and Sedition Acts, which in effect punished sedition quite directly.[17] Many thought these laws unconstitutional. But the Fourth and Fifth Amendments would have been effective limits on their enforcement, whether the substantive laws were constitutional or not.

On this conception, privacy is a substantive limit on government's power.[18] As a restriction on the power of government to enforce certain laws, it provides a substantive limit on the kinds of regulation that government can effectively impose. Understood this way, privacy does more than protect dignity or limit intrusion; privacy limits what government can do.

Choosing a Conception of Privacy

In principle, these three distinct conceptions of privacy could yield different results depending on the case. A search, for example, might not be intrusive but might offend dignity. In that case, we would have to choose a conception of privacy that we believed best captured the Constitution's protection.

At the time of the founding, however, these different conceptions of privacy probably would not, for the most part, have yielded different conclusions. Any search that reached beyond the substantive limits of the amendment, or beyond the limits of dignity, would also have been a disturbance. Half of the framers could have held the dignity conception and half the utility conception, but because every search would have involved a violation of both, all the framers could have endorsed the protections of the Fourth Amendment.

Today, however, these three conceptions could yield different results. The utility conception could permit efficient searches that are forbidden by the dignity and substantive conceptions. The correct translation (as Brandeis employed the term in the *Olmstead* wiretapping case) depends on selecting the proper conception to translate.

In this sense, our original protections were the product of what Cass Sunstein calls an "incompletely theorized agreement."[19] Given the technology of the time, there was no reason to work out which theory underlay the constitutional text; all three were consistent with existing technology. But as the technology has changed, the original context has been challenged. Now that technologies such as the worm can search without disturbing, there is a conflict about what the Fourth Amendment protects.

This conflict is the other side of Sunstein's incompletely theorized agreement. We might say that in any incompletely theorized agreement ambiguities will be latent, and we can describe contexts where these latencies emerge. The latent ambiguities about the protection of privacy, for example, are being rendered patent by the evolution of technology. And this in turn forces us to choose.

Some will once again try to suggest that the choice has been made—by our Constitution, in our past. This is the rhetoric of much of our constitutional jurisprudence, but it is not very helpful here. I do not think the framers worked out what the amendment would protect in a world where perfectly noninvasive searches could be conducted. They did not establish a constitution to apply in all possible worlds. They established a constitution for their world. When their world differs from ours in a way that reveals a choice they did not have to make, then we need to make that choice.[20]

CONTROLLED USE

Two years ago I received in my mailbox a letter from AT&T. It was addressed to an old girlfriend, but the letter had not been forwarded. The address was my then-current apartment. AT&T wanted to offer her a new credit card. They were a bit late: she and I had broken up eight years before. Since then, she had moved to Texas, and I had moved to Chicago, to Washington, back to Chicago, on to New Haven, back to Chicago, and finally to Boston, where I had moved twice. My peripateticism, however, did not deter AT&T. With great faith in my constancy, it believed that living with me in this apartment was a woman I had not even seen in three years.

How did AT&T maintain such a belief? Well, floating about in cyberspace is lots of data about me. It has been collected ever since I began using credit cards, telephones, and who knows what else. The system continuously tries to update and refine this extraordinary data set—that is, it profiles who I am and, using that profile, determines how it will interact with me.

What exactly should we think about this constant electronic monitoring?[21]

The lawyer's unthinking response might be this: it has always been possible for people to be monitored and profiled. Governments do it all the time; so do corporations. More important, so do small communities. Not long ago most people lived in communities that constantly monitored everyone's behavior. Your comings and goings, who you were with, how much you spent at the market—all this was known by your neighbors, nosey or not. There may have been no video camera watching you when you went to the market to buy groceries. But something worse—your neighbors—did. They saw when you went, and with whom, and they, unlike video cameras, could gossip. So what we have now is just the same as what we had then. Maybe more entities are able to monitor, and maybe more activity is monitored. But the fact that monitoring goes on has not changed at all.

This type of argument is ubiquitous in law—"it's the same sort of thing as in 1791, so nothing is different"—and as an argument it is universally bad. The question is not whether there was something then *like* what happens now. The question is whether what happens now is substantially different. (A tiger is like a kitten, but unlike a kitten a tiger is not a pet.) If it is different, then we must ask whether we ought to treat it differently.

The monitoring of modern life is indeed different in substance from the monitoring at the time of the founding. There is no doubt that life then was monitored, that it was hard to hide yourself from others, but that monitoring was different. It was done by people whose memories were imperfect and who were likely to notice only behavior out of the ordinary. These memories, moreover, could not be searched, or collected, or produced as records. A private eye might interview the neighbors to learn what they saw, but as any investigator knows, what people saw is an extraordinarily imperfect record of what actually happened. Gossipy neighbors might have watched, but their watching produced nothing as lasting or as reliable as videotape, a toll booth's electronic records of when you entered and when you left, a credit card system's endless collection of data about your purchases, or the telephone system's records of who you called when and for how long.

Today's monitoring is different because the technologies of monitoring—their efficiency and their power—are different. In the 1790s the technology was humans; now it is machines. Then the technology noticed only what was different; now it notices any transaction. Then the default was that searchable records were not collected; now the default is that all monitoring produces searchable records.

These differences add up.[22] Together they constitute monitoring of potentially far greater significance. What exactly is the threat posed by this greater monitoring? Why is it troubling if all the information in the world about me is collected? What possible harm could it do to me—assuming (and of course you should assume this) that I have done nothing bad? What are the consequences of a perfectly monitorable world?

I am considering here only collecting that is perfectly legal. I am not talking about breaking into someone's house and reading her diary, or stealing information from bank records. I am not discussing invasions of privacy in the traditional sense. My focus here is on the data collected about an individual in day-to-day interactions, data that an individual, in a sense, displays to the world. What could be wrong with collecting what is publicly displayed?

Arguments rage on both sides of this question, one side arguing that there is no harm from this sort of monitoring, the other side arguing the opposite.

The latter argument assumes that the balance of privacy is struck at the line where you reveal information about yourself to the public. Sure, information kept behind closed doors, or written in a private diary, should be protected by the law. But when you go out in public, when you make transactions there or send material there, you give up any right to privacy. Others now have the right to collect data about your public behavior and do with it what it suits them to do.[23]

Why is that idea not troubling to these theorists? The reasons are many:

- First, the harm is actually not very great. You get a discount card at your local grocery store; the store then collects data about what you buy. With that data, the store may market different goods to you or figure out how better to price its products; it may even decide that it should offer different mixes of discounts to better serve customers. These responses, the argument goes, are the likely ones, because the store's business is only to sell groceries more efficiently.
- Second, it is an unfair burden to force others to ignore what you show them. If data about you are not usable by others, then it is as if you were requiring others to discard what you have deposited on their land. If you do not like others using information about you, do not put it in their hands.

- Third, these data actually do some good. I do not know why Nike thinks I am a good person to tell about their latest sneakers, and I do not know why Keds does not know to call. In both cases, I suspect the reason is bad data about me. I would love it if Nike knew enough to leave me alone. And if these data were better collected and sorted, it would.
- Finally, no one spends money collecting these data to actually learn anything about *you*. They want to learn about people *like* you. They want to know your type. In principle, they would be happy to know your type even if they could not then learn who you are. What the merchants want is a way to discriminate—only in the sense of being able to tell the difference between *sorts* of people.

The other side of this argument, however, also has a point.[24] It begins, as we have done elsewhere, by noticing the values that were originally protected by the imperfection of monitoring technology. This imperfection helped preserve important substantive values. One such value is the benefit of innocence. At any given time, there are innocent facts about you that may appear, in a particular context or to a particular set, guilty. Peter Lewis, in a *New York Times* article called "Forget Big Brother," puts the point well:

Surveillance cameras followed the attractive young blond woman through the lobby of the midtown Manhattan hotel, kept a glassy eye on her as she rode the elevator up to the 23rd floor and peered discreetly down the hall as she knocked at the door to my room. I have not seen the videotapes, but I can imagine the digital readout superimposed on the scenes, noting the exact time of the encounter. That would come in handy if someone were to question later why this woman, who is not my wife, was visiting my hotel room during a recent business trip. The cameras later saw us heading off to dinner and to the theater—a middle aged, married man from Texas with his arm around a pretty East Village woman young enough to be his daughter.

"As a matter of fact," Lewis writes, "she is my daughter."[25]

One lesson of the story is the burden of these monitored facts. The burden is on you, the monitored, first to establish your innocence, and second, to assure all who might see these ambiguous facts that you are innocent. Both processes, however, are imperfect; say what you want, doubts will remain. There are always some who will not believe your plea of innocence.

Modern monitoring only exacerbates this problem. Your life becomes an ever-increasing record; your actions are forever held in storage, open to being revealed at any time, and therefore at any time demanding a justification.

A second value follows directly from this modern capacity for archiving data. We all desire to live in separate communities, or among or within separate normative spaces. Privacy, or the ability to control data about yourself, supports this desire. It enables these multiple communities and disables the power of one dominant community to norm others into oblivion. Think, for example, about a gay man in an intolerant small town.

The point comes through most clearly when contrasted with an argument recently advanced by David Brin.[26] Brin argues against this concern with privacy—at least if privacy is defined as the need to block the production and distribution of data about others. He argues against it because he believes that such an end is impossible; the genie is out of the bottle. Better, he suggests, to find ways to ensure that this data-gathering ability is generally available. The solution to your spying on me is not to block your spying, but to let me spy on you—to hold you accountable, perhaps for spying, perhaps for whatever else you might be doing.

There are two replies to this argument. One asks: Why do we have to choose? Why can't we both control spying and build in checks on the distribution of spying techniques?

The other is more telling. Brin assumes that this counterspying would be useful to hold others "accountable." But according to whose norms? "Accountable" is a benign term only so long as we have confidence in the community doing the accounting. When we live in multiple communities, accountability becomes a way for one community to impose its view of propriety on another. And because we do not live in a single community; we do not live by a single set of values; and perfect accountability can only undermine this mix of values.

The imperfection in present monitoring enables this multiplication of normative communities. The ability to get along without perfect recording enables a diversity that perfect knowledge would erase.

A third value arises from a concern about profiling. If you search on "mortgage" in a web search engine, advertising for mortgages appears on your computer screen. The same for sex and for cars. Advertising is linked to the search you submit. Data about the search are collected—and not just about the search. The site collects every bit of personal information about you that it can.[27]

Data collection is the dominant activity of commercial web sites. Some 92 percent of them collect personal data from web users, which they then aggregate, sort, and use.[28] Oscar Gandy calls this the "panoptic sort"—a vast structure for collecting data and discriminating on the basis of that data—and it is this discrimination, he says, that ought to concern us.[29]

But why should it concern us? Put aside an important class of problems—the misuse of the data—and focus instead on its ordinary use. As I said earlier, the main effect is simply to make the market work more smoothly: products are matched to people, and interests to people, in a way that is better targeted and less intrusive than what we have today. Imagine a world where advertisers could tell which venues paid and which did not; where it was inefficient to advertise with billboards and on broadcasts; where most advertising was targeted and specific. Advertising would be more likely to go to those people for whom it would be useful information. Or so the argument goes. This is discrimination, no doubt, but not the discrimination of Jim Crow. It is the wonderful sort of discrimination that spares me Nike ads.

But beyond a perhaps fleeting concern about how such data affect the individual, profiling raises a more sustained collective concern about how it might affect a community.

That concern is about manipulation. You might be skeptical about the power of television advertising to control people's desires. Television is so obvious, the motives so clear. But what happens when the motive is not so obvious? When options just seem to appear right when you happen to want them? When the system seems to know what you want better and earlier than you do, how can you know where these desires really come from?

Whether this possibility is a realistic one, or whether it should be a concern, are hard and open questions. Steven Johnson argues quite effectively that in fact these agents of choice will facilitate a much greater range and diversity—even, in part, chaos—of choice.[30] But there's another possibility as well—profiles will begin to normalize the population from which the norm is drawn. The observing will affect the observed. The system watches what you do; it fits you into a pattern; the pattern is then fed back to you in the form of options set by the pattern; the options reinforce the pattern; the cycle begins again.

A second concern is about equality. Profiling raises a question that was latent in the market until quite recently. For much of the nineteenth century in the United States economic thought was animated by an ideal of equality. In the civil space individuals were held to be equal. They could purchase and sell equally; they could approach others on equal terms. Facts about individuals might be known, and some of these facts might disqualify them from some economic transactions—your prior bankruptcy, for example, might inhibit your ability to make transactions in the future. But in the main, there were spaces of relative anonymity, and economic transactions could occur within that anonymity.[31]

Over time this space of equality has been displaced by economic zonings that aim at segregation.[32] They are laws, that is, that promote distinctions based on social or economic criteria.[33] The most telling example is zoning itself. It was not until this century that local law was used to put people into segregated spaces.[34] At first, this law was racially based, but when racially based zoning was struck down, the techniques of zoning shifted.[35]

It is interesting to recall just how contentious this use of law was.[36] To many, rich and poor alike, it was an affront to the American ideal of equality to make where you live depend on how much money you had. It always does, of course, when property is something you must buy. But zoning laws add the support of law to the segregation imposed by the market. The effect is to re-create in law, and therefore in society, distinctions among people.

There was a time when we would have defined our country as a place that aimed to erase these distinctions. The historian Gordon Wood describes this goal as an important element of the revolution that gave birth to the United States.[37] The enemy was social and legal hierarchy; the aim was a society of equality. The revolution was an attack on hierarchies of social rank and the special privileges they might obtain.

All social hierarchies require information before they can make discriminations of rank. Having enough information about people required, historically, fairly stable social orders. Making fine class distinctions—knowing, for instance, whether a well-dressed young man was the gentleman he claimed to be or only a dressed-up trades-man—required a knowledge of local fashions, accents, customs, and manners. Only where there was relatively little mobility could these systems of hierarchy be imposed.

As mobility increased, then, these hierarchical systems were challenged. Beyond the extremes of the very rich and very poor, the ability to make subtle distinctions of rank disappeared as the mobility and fluidity of society made them too difficult to track.

Profiling changes all this. An efficient and effective system for monitoring makes it possible once again to make these subtle distinctions of rank. Collecting data cheaply and efficiently will take us back to the past. Think about frequent flyer miles. Everyone sees the obvious feature of frequent flyer miles—the free trips for people who fly frequently. This rebate program is quite harmless on its own. The more interesting part is the power it gives to airlines to discriminate in their services.

When a frequent flyer makes a reservation, the reservation carries with it a customer profile. This profile might include information about which seat she prefers or whether she likes vegetarian food. It also tells the reservation clerk how often this person flies. Some airlines would then discriminate on the basis of this information. The most obvious way is through seat location—frequent flyers get better seats. But such information might also affect how food is allocated on the flight—the frequent flyers with the most miles get first choice; those with the fewest may get no choice.

In the scheme of social justice, of course, this is small potatoes. But my point is more general. Frequent flyer systems permit the re-creation of systems of status. They supply information about individuals that organizations might value, and use, in dispensing services.[38] They make discrimination possible because they restore information that mobility destroyed. They are ways of defeating one benefit of anonymity—the benefit of equality.

Economists will argue that in many contexts this ability to discriminate—in effect, to offer goods at different prices to different people—is overall a benefit.[39] On average, people are better off if price discrimination occurs than if it does not. So we are better off, these economists might say, if we facilitate such discrimination when we can.

But these values are just one side of the equation. Weighed against them are the values of equality. For us they may seem remote, but we should not assume that because they are remote now they were always remote.

Take tipping: as benign (if annoying) as you might consider the practice of tipping, there was a time at the turn of the century when the very idea was an insult. It offended a free citizen's dignity. As Viviana Zelizer describes it:

In the early 1900s, as tipping became increasingly popular, it provoked great moral and social controversy. In fact, there were nationwide efforts, some successful, by state legislatures to abolish tipping by turning it into a punishable misdemeanor. In countless newspaper editorials and magazine articles, in etiquette books, and even in court, tips were closely scrutinized with a mix of curiosity, amusement, and ambivalence—and often open hostility. When in 1907, the government officially sanctioned tipping by allowing commissioned officers and enlisted men of the United States Navy to include tips as an item in their travel expense vouchers, the decision was denounced as an illegitimate endorsement of graft. Periodically, there were calls to organize anti-tipping leagues.[40]

There is a conception of equality animating the history that Zelizer recounts that would be corrupted by the efficiency that profiling embraces. In both cases, there is a value that is weighed against efficiency. Although I believe this value is relatively weak in American life, who am I to say? The important point is not about what is strong or weak, but about the tension or conflict that lay dormant until revealed by the emerging technology of profiling.

The pattern should be familiar by now, for the change is the change we have seen elsewhere. Once again, the code changes, throwing into relief a conflict of values. Whereas before there was relative equality because the information that enabled discrimination was too costly to acquire, now it pays to discriminate. The difference—what makes it pay—is the emergence of a code. The code changes, the behavior changes, and a value latent in the prior regime is displaced.

We could react by hobbling the code, thus preserving this world. We could create constitutional or statutory restrictions that prevent a move to this world. Or we could find ways to reconcile this emerging world with the values we think are fundamental.

S O L U T I O N S

I've identified two distinct threats to the values of privacy that we might imagine cyberspace presenting. No doubt there are others. And no doubt it is an open question how seriously we will take these threats. But I want to end by considering a few responses. How might we, if convinced of the danger or committed to privacy values, act to restore in the individual a kind of control over these personal data that are collected and searchable by the architectures of cyberspace?

The problems are of two sorts. The first is the question of "efficient invasion": technologies now enable searching with none of the burdens that searches ordinarily entailed. Second is the question of monitoring, and the control over data that monitoring produces. These two problems invite different solutions. I touch on the first, and then focus on the second.

One note in advance: even this distinction is ambiguous. It presumes some natural division between searching and monitoring. No doubt, *given a particular architecture,* there is such a division. But when architectures are plastic, the line between monitoring and searching is plastic as well. An architecture can be designed to make a certain behavior monitorable, or it can be designed to necessitate a search to find that behavior.

Telephones are an easy example. One could design telephone networks to report with each call who was called, where that person lives, how long the call lasted, and from which line it was made. Indeed, this is how telephone networks today *are* designed. Given this design, this information is now *monitorable,* whereas under an earlier design obtaining the same information required a *search.*

If changing the architecture can change data from searchable to monitorable, then the values that are being protected in both contexts must be consistent. My aim in the next two sections is to articulate a structure that might support this consistency.

SEARCHABLE: THE POWER OF CODE AND THE PROMISE OF PROCEDURE

Remember the problem: systems that can invade, or search, without anyone knowing or being disturbed. To this (and any) problem, we might imagine two sorts of solutions. One solution is code-based: make it harder to search effectively. The other solution is law-based: add legal protections to inhibit improper searches. I consider the code-based solution first, since it is the more familiar and more easily summarized.

Encryption. As we saw in chapter 4, the primary use of technologies of encryption is to hide your words from the eyes of others. Encrypted communication creates a private language between the listener and the speaker. While arguments rage about whether an encrypted communication can actually be cracked,[41] for most of what most of us would want to say, existing encryption is perfectly adequate.

But it is not common. Thus, one solution to improve privacy is a far greater deployment of encryption code. This is already happening, though the deployment has been hampered by the government's efforts to control encryption. But slowly— and again, as a (good) by-product of commerce—the Net is becoming encryption-rich.

But encryption will not solve the problem of privacy. Encrypted communication would be harder for the government to overhear, but it would not disable the government's legitimate demands for data. If the government has the right to force you to reveal the contents of a document, then it also has the right to force you to reveal the key that locks the document.[42] Moreover, not all electronic communication is easily encrypted. Some people therefore will demand a solution beyond code.

This solution should track two particular values protecting real-space privacy. First, any burden must be minimal, and any search that creates more than a minimal burden must be justified by individualized suspicion.[43] Second, any search must be disclosed—individuals must be given notice that their space has been searched.[44]

It might be said that the principle behind the second idea is to ban all of these inoffensive and invisible searches. Perhaps that should be done. But if we understand this second idea to be about checking the abuse of power (since by giving notice you give someone opportunity to complain), then we might imagine substitutions that protect the same value without sacrificing the benefit these technologies might bring.

A translation, therefore, might well look like this. Although the technology would enable these costless searches, they should be deployed only when adequate and strong procedural limits have been met. And adequate and strong procedural limits would include the requirement that two branches of government (not just the executive) concur before any invasion occurs.[45]

But what would invasion mean? Again, architectures could be designed to make data accessible without an invasion; they could be designed, that is, to make data monitorable, so that a search of the records of monitoring would involve no invasion at all.

The choice we must make is between two conceptions of law enforcement that today are mixed. One conception is reactive, responding to an event; the other is preventive, predicting an event. The reactive model would define invasion as any sifting to identify a culprit; this sifting, the argument goes, should be allowed only when there is cause to suspect. Scanning the innocent, on this view, would not be permitted, though collecting data to enable a subsequent scan might be.

The preventive conception would allow constant monitoring. The values of procedure here would simply control how much you would have to know about the people you are monitoring in order to commence monitoring; but you could still design this space to enable monitoring, and you could monitor for patterns suggesting misbehavior.

For a real-space example not far from present technology, think about airport searches. Technology is now being developed to enable something called body scans. These would enable an official to peer through your clothes to see whether you are concealing weapons. We might imagine any number of ways to deploy this technology. In a purely reactive mode, we might say that only the suspicious can be subjected to the body scan, though a fear about selective suspiciousness might push us to make the scan general. There is no insult in being scanned, the argument goes, if everyone else is; there is only an insult if you have been picked out from the crowd.

But even if everyone were scanned, there would be questions about how the system should be designed. Would the officials see the people whose bodies they were scanning? Imagine, in one version, officers watching people enter a booth, seeing what is under their clothes, and then watching (leering) as they leave. Contrast that system with one in which the officers are located elsewhere, the images they see are cut up by the computer, and though they still see what is under people's clothes, they cannot automatically connect what they are seeing to particular individuals.

Whatever you think about this procedure in general, the second design is a more effective balance of interests than the first. Still, even with this second design there remains this latent question of how far we will push the preventive over the exceptional. Airports are exceptional, though this technology could be extended beyond airports. Whether it should be is the choice pressed on us by these changes in code.

MONITORING: THE RE-SOLUTION THROUGH PROPERTY

Control over the results of monitoring is a more ambitious project. The traditional solution is to enact laws to deal with the problem. That has been Europe's solution, for example—extensive and sustained support for legal protections against the misuse of data. The substance of such law is, I think, uncontroversial. Its values are essentially "notice" and "choice"—companies will inform consumers about how data will be used and not use it for any other purpose. Its aim is to restore to the individual control over the use of data about herself.[46]

But in the United States we have turned to law less often. Although sensational abuses have at times produced targeted federal laws, they have not led to comprehensive legal protection.[47]

This is not to say, of course, that we have no protections for privacy. As we have seen throughout, there are other laws besides federal ones, as well as regulators besides the law. At times these other forms of protection may protect privacy better than law does. Obviously, if we want to understand the protections for privacy, we should understand how these interventions matter.

The U.S. government has argued for a type of industry "self-regulation" expressed through industrial codes of conduct. An old idea strangely called "new" (the same practices were popular during the New Deal), self-regulation lets industries set the rules about how data ought to be protected. Once they set the rules, the argument goes, pressure from other members of the industry, or from the market itself, could force a sustained compliance.

Of course, norms can be effective regulators. But a necessary condition of their success is that the community of norm enforcers include those who bear the cost of the behavior being regulated. And I confess to being skeptical that this is in fact happening here. The industry that would develop the norms to regulate itself does not bear the relevant costs of the use of the data it collects. That cost—the privacy cost—is borne by individuals, not corporations; they are not part of the community building the norm.

So rather than norms, I want to suggest a different regulatory mechanism—one that relies on code rather than good behavior. In a world where the dimensions of decision have been so radically multiplied, we need a more effective way to control what we collectively do.

The standard response to this question of data practices is choice—to give the individual the right to choose how her data will be used. And the standard way we have pushed individuals to choose is through text—through privacy statements that report a site's privacy practices and then give the consumer the right to opt in or out of those practices.[48]

But the processing costs for text are wildly high. No one has the time or patience to read through cumbersome documents describing obscure rules for controlling data. What is needed is a way for the machine to negotiate our privacy concerns for us, a way to delegate the negotiating process to a smart agent—an electronic but-ler—who, like the butler, knows well what we like and what we do not like.

What is needed, that is, is a machine-to-machine protocol for negotiating pri-vacy protections.[49] The user sets her preferences once—specifies how she would ne-gotiate privacy and what she is willing to give up—and from that moment on, when she enters a site, the site and her machine negotiate. Only if the machines can agree will the site be able to obtain her personal data.

The kernel to this architecture is a project sponsored by the World Wide Web Consortium.[50] Dubbed P3P, the project's aim is to facilitate an architecture within which users can express their preferences and negotiate the use of data about them. "P3P products will allow users to be informed of site practices (in both machine and human readable formats), to delegate decisions to their computer when appropri-ate, and allow users to tailor their relationship to specific sites."[51]

My aim is not to endorse this particular privacy architecture. P3P has its prob-lems, not all of them clearly resolvable.[52] My point instead is the same one made throughout this book: we could imagine an architecture, tied to a market, that pro-tects privacy rights in a way that real space cannot, but that architecture will not emerge on its own. It needs the push of law.

The law would be a kind of property right in privacy. Individuals must have both the ability to negotiate easily over privacy rights and the entitlement to privacy as a default. That is property's purpose: it says to those who want, you must negotiate before you can take. P3P is the architecture to facilitate that negotiation; the law is the rule that says negotiation must occur.

But why property? What is the benefit of a property regime? Why is it superior to a regime that simply enforces rules (as the Europeans do)?

A property regime is fundamentally different from what we have now.[53] Privacy now is protected through liability rules—if you invade someone's privacy, they can sue you and you must then pay. There are two important differences between liabil-ity rules and property rules.

The first difference is that a property regime requires negotiation before taking; a liability regime allows a taking, and payment later. The key to a property regime is to give control, and power, to the person holding the property right; the key in a li-ability regime is to protect the right but facilitate the transfer of some asset from one person to another. There can be holdouts (people who will not agree to transfer) with a property regime; there can be no holdouts in a liability regime. There is individual control or autonomy with a property regime, but not with a liability regime. Property protects choice; liability protects transfer.

The second difference follows directly from the first. With a liability rule, a court, jury, or statute determines how valuable certain privacy is to you. Ordinarily, you are compensated only for what a reasonable person would have suffered. It is like a regime for buying and selling cars in which, rather than negotiating up front, people simply take other people's cars and a court later determines what they must pay.

Property regimes work very differently. When you have a property right, before someone takes your property they must negotiate with you about how much it is worth. If you have a sentimental attachment to your 1974 Nova, there is little the buyer can do about it. The car's market value might be $200, but if you will not sell it for less than $1,000, the buyer is stuck. You cannot be forced to give up your Nova unless you get your minimum price.

A property regime thus protects both those who value their privacy more than others and those who value it less, by requiring that someone who wants to take a given resource must ask. Such a regime gives us confidence that if a trade occurs, it will be at a price that makes neither party worse off.

There are those, especially on the left, who are radically skeptical about a property regime to protect privacy.[54] Property is said to commodify, to marketize, to monetize relations that are valuable on a very different scale. The last thing we need, these skeptics argue, is to have another sphere of our lives ruled by the market.[55]

My impulse is to sympathize with this argument. But I am not convinced that anything is ultimately gained by this insistence on theory. We are not debating whether to move into a world where data are collected, used, and sold. We already live in that world. Given that we are here, how can we ensure that at least some control is granted to those whom these data are about? I advocate a property regime not because of the sanctity of property as an ideal, but because of its utility in serving a different but quite important ideal.

Those who take this ideal of privacy to an extreme have a very different view about how the architecture should support it. The action group Privacy Now!, for example, threatens terrorist action to disable the systems of data gathering and control.[56] Marc Rotenberg of the Electronic Privacy Information Center (EPIC) argues strongly against any architecture that enables the trading or exchange of privacy rights.[57] Both groups view privacy as a kind of inalienable right—one whose dignity deserves the respect that we give the right to vote or the freedom to engage in sexual relations. They believe that none of these rights ought to be sold, and that exchange of any of them should be criminalized.

We could certainly construct a world where privacy was so viewed, and we could build walls that the police defended. But I doubt that this extreme is actually our view—or more important, that it ought to be.

A world where privacy is commodified in this sense might turn out to be radically inferior. Or it might be fine. My argument is not from first principles; it is intended only as a pragmatic response to an emerging issue. If the world turns out not to our liking, then of course we should modify the architectures.

But the key is to see the relationship between these architectures and the possibilities for exchange. As Justice Breyer argued about intellectual property, it may well be that constructing the architectures for exchange is all we need to do to ensure the protection appropriate to the context.[58] We will just have to see.

PRIVACY COMPARED

The reader who was dissatisfied with my argument in the last chapter is likely to begin asking pointed questions. "Didn't you reject in the last chapter the very regime you are endorsing here? Didn't you reject an architecture that would facilitate perfect sale of intellectual property? Isn't that what you've created here?"

The charge is accurate enough. I have endorsed an architecture here that is essentially the same architecture I questioned for intellectual property. Both are regimes for trading information; both make information "like" "real" property. Yet with copyright, I argued against a fully privatized property regime; with privacy, I am arguing in favor of it. What gives?

The difference is in the underlying values that inform, or that should inform, information in each context. In the context of intellectual property, our bias should be for freedom. Who knows what "information wants";[59] whatever it wants, we should read the bargain that the law strikes with holders of intellectual property as narrowly as we can. We should take a grudging attitude to property rights in intellectual property; we should support them only as much as necessary to build and support information regimes.

But (at least some kinds of) information about individuals should be treated differently. You do not strike a deal with the law about personal or private information. The law does not offer you a monopoly right in exchange for your publication of these facts. That is what is distinct about privacy: individuals should be able to control information about themselves. We should be eager to help them protect that information by giving them the structures and the rights to do so. We value, or want, our peace. And thus, a regime that allows us such peace by giving us control over private information is a regime consonant with public values. It is a regime that public authorities should support.

This conclusion is subject to important qualifications, only two of which I will describe here.

The first is that nothing in my regime would give individuals final or complete control over the kinds of data they can sell, or the kinds of privacy they can buy. The P3P regime would in principle enable upstream control of privacy rights as well as individual control. If we lived, for example, in a regime that identified individuals based on jurisdiction, then transactions with the P3P regime could be limited based on the rules for particular jurisdictions.

Second, there is no reason such a regime would have to protect all kinds of private data, and nothing in the scheme so far tells us what should and should not be considered "private" information. There may be facts about yourself that you are not permitted to hide; more important, there may be claims about yourself that you are not permitted to make ("I am a lawyer," or, "Call me, I'm a doctor"). You should not be permitted to engage in fraud or to do harm to others. This limitation is an analog to fair use in intellectual property—a limit to the space that privacy may protect.

I started this chapter by claiming that with privacy the cat is already out of the bag. We already have architectures that deny individuals control over what others know about them; the question is what we can do in response.

My response has been: look to the code. We must build into the architecture a capacity to enable choice—not choice by humans but by machines. The architecture must enable machine-to-machine negotiations about privacy so that individuals can instruct their machines about the privacy they want to protect.

But how will we get there? How can this architecture be erected? Individuals may want cyberspace to protect their privacy, but what would push cyberspace to build in the necessary architectures?

Not the market. The power of commerce is not behind any such change. Here, the invisible hand would really be invisible. Collective action must be taken to bend the architectures toward this goal, and collective action is just what politics is for. Laissez-faire will not cut it.

T W E L V E

---

free speech

THE RIGHT TO FREE SPEECH IS NOT THE RIGHT TO SPEAK FOR FREE. IT IS NOT THE RIGHT to free access to television, or the right that people not hate you for what you have to say. Strictly speaking—legally speaking—the right to free speech in the United States means the right to be free from punishment by the government in retaliation for at least some (probably most) speech. You cannot be jailed for criticizing the president, though you can be jailed for threatening him; you cannot be fined for promoting segregation, though you will be shunned if you do; you cannot be stopped from speaking in a public place, though you can be stopped from speaking with an FM transmitter. Speech in the United States is protected—in a complex, and at times convoluted, way—but its constitutional protection is a protection against the government.

Nevertheless, a constitutional account of free speech that thought only of government would be radically incomplete.[1] Two societies could have the same "First Amendment"—the same protections against government's wrath—but if within one dissenters are tolerated while in the other they are shunned, the two societies would be very different free speech societies. More than government constrains speech, and more than government *protects* free speech. A complete account of this—and any—right must consider the full range of burdens and protections.

Consider, for example, the "rights" of the disabled to protection against discrimination. The law protects the disabled; social norms don't, neither does the market, and until the law intervened, neither did architectures. The net of these four modalities would describe the protection, in any particular context, that the disabled have. Law might intervene to strengthen the protection—regulating architecture, for example, so that it better protects against discrimination in access. But for any given mix we could understand these four modalities working together to protect (however slightly) the disabled from discrimination.

In the terms of chapter 7, we could then use the same four modalities to consider within each context the protection *from* constraint, as well as the imposition *of* regulatory constraints. Modalities of constraint (powers) function as a sword against the object regulated; modalities of protection (rights) function as a shield for the regulated against constraint. The following figure captures the point.

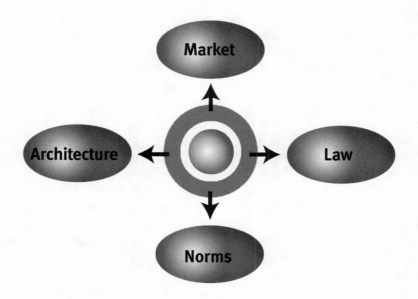

In the center is the object regulated—the pathetic dot from chapter 7. Surrounding the individual now is a shield of protection, the net of law/norms/market/architecture that limits the constraints these modalities would otherwise place on the individual. I have not separated the four in the sphere of the shield because obviously there is no direct match between the modality of constraint and the modality of protection. When law as protector conflicts with law as constraint, constitutional law overrides ordinary law.

These modalities function together. Some might undercut others, meaning that the sum of protections might seem to be less significant than the parts. The "right" to promote the decriminalization of drugs in the present context of the war on drugs is an example. The law protects your right to advocate the decriminalization of drugs. The state cannot lock you up if, like George Soros, you start a campaign for the decriminalization of marijuana or if, like the Nobel Prize–winning economist Milton Friedman or the federal judge Richard Posner, you write articles suggesting it. If the First Amendment means anything, it means that the state cannot criminalize speech about law reform.

But that legal protection does not mean that I would suffer no consequences for promoting legalization of drugs. My neighbors would be appalled at the idea, and some no doubt would shun me. Nor would the market necessarily support me. It

would be quite difficult to buy time on television for a speech advocating such a reform. Television stations have the right to select their ads (within some limits); they
do not like controversial or tasteless ads.[2] Mine would most likely be deemed too
controversial. Stations also have the FCC—an active combatant in the war on
drugs—looking over their shoulders. And even if I were permitted to advertise, I am
not George Soros. I do not have millions to spend on such a campaign. I might manage a few off-hour spots on a local station, but I could not afford, for instance, a
campaign on the networks during prime time.

Finally, architecture wouldn't protect my speech very well either. In the United
States at least, there are few places where you can stand before the public and address them about some matter of public import without most people thinking you
a nut or a nuisance. There is no speakers' corner in every city; most towns do not
have a town meeting. "America offline," in this sense, is very much like America
Online—not designed to give individuals access to a wide audience to address
public matters. Only professionals get to address Americans on public issues—
politicians, scholars, celebrities, journalists, and activists, most of whom are confined to single issues. The rest of us have a choice—listen, or be dispatched to the
gulag of social lunacy.

Thus, the protection for controversial speech is more conditional than a narrow
legal view would suggest. The right to be a dissenter is on balance less protected than
it could be when more than law is reckoned.

Let's take this example now to cyberspace. How is the "right" to promote the legalization of drugs in cyberspace protected? Here too, of course, the law protects my
right of advocacy—at least in the United States. It is quite possible that the same
speech would be illegal elsewhere and that perhaps I could be prosecuted for uttering such speech in cyberspace "in" another country. Speech promoting the Nazi
Party, for example, is legal in the United States but not in Germany.[3] Uttering such
speech in cyberspace may make one liable in German space as well.

The law therefore is an imperfect protection. Do norms help to protect
speech? With the relative anonymity of cyberspace and its growing size, norms do
not function well there to restrain controversial speech. Even in cyberspaces
where people know each other well, they are likely to be more tolerant of dissident views when they know (or believe, or hope) the dissident lives thousands of
miles away.

The market provides a major protection to speech—relative to real space, market constraints on speech in cyberspace are tiny. Recall how easily Jake Baker became
a publisher, with a potential readership greater than the readership of all law books
(like this one) published in the last decade.

But on top of this list of protectors of speech in cyberspace is architecture. Relative anonymity, decentralized distribution, multiple points of access, no necessary
tie to geography, no simple system to identify content, tools of encryption[4]—all
these features and consequences of the Internet protocol make it difficult to control
speech in cyberspace. The architecture of cyberspace is the real protector of speech

there; it is the real "First Amendment in cyberspace," and this First Amendment is no local ordinance.[5]

Just think about what this means. For over fifty years the United States has been the exporter of a certain political ideology, at its core a conception of free speech. Many have criticized this conception: some found it too extreme, others not extreme enough. Repressive regimes—China, North Korea—rejected it directly; tolerant regimes—France, Hungary—complained of cultural decay; egalitarian regimes—the Scandinavian countries—puzzled over how we could think of ourselves as free when only the rich can speak and pornography is repressed.

This debate has gone on at the political level for a long time. And yet, as if under cover of night, we have now wired these nations with an architecture of communication that builds within their borders a far stronger First Amendment than our ideology ever advanced. Nations wake up to find that their telephone lines are tools of free expression, that e-mail carries news of their repression far beyond their borders, that images are no longer the monopoly of state-run television stations but can be transmitted from a simple modem. We have exported to the world, through the architecture of the Internet, a First Amendment *in code* more extreme than our own First Amendment *in law*.

This chapter is about the regulation of speech and the protection of speech in cyberspace—and therefore also in real space. My aim is to obsess about the relationship between architecture and the freedom it makes possible, and about the significance of law in the construction of that architecture. It is to get you to see how this freedom is built—the constitutional politics in the architectures of cyberspace.

I say "politics" because this building is not over. As I have argued (over and over again), there is no single architecture for cyberspace; there is no given or necessary structure to its design. The first-generation Internet might well have breached walls of control. But there is no reason to believe that architects of the second generation will do so, or not to expect a second generation to build in control. There is no reason to think, in other words, that this initial flash of freedom will not be short-lived. And there is certainly no justification for acting as if it will not.

We can already see the beginnings of this reconstruction. Already the architecture is being remade to reregulate what real-space architecture before made regulable. Already the Net is changing from free to controlled.

Some of these steps to reregulate are inevitable; some shift back is unavoidable. Before the change is complete, however, we must understand the freedoms the Net now provides and determine which freedoms we mean to preserve.

And not just preserve. The architecture of the Internet, as it is right now, is perhaps the most important model of free speech since the founding. This model has implications far beyond e-mail and web pages. Two hundred years after the framers ratified the Constitution, the Net has taught us what the First Amendment means. If we take this meaning seriously, then the First Amendment will require a fairly radical restructuring of the architectures of speech off the Net as well.

But all that is to get ahead of the story. In the balance of this chapter, I want to tell three stories—one about publication, one about access, and one about distribution. With each, I want to consider how "free speech" is regulated.

These stories do not all have the same constitutional significance. My aim in the first is to illustrate a relationship between architectures and institutions of free speech; the second identifies another latent ambiguity in our constitutional regime; and the third is a straightforward translation of the framing design. It is the third story that, if correct, would prove the most fundamental, though all three illustrate the relationship between values, architectures, and the choices they now present.

THE REGULATORS OF SPEECH: PUBLICATION

Floyd Abrams is one of America's leading First Amendment lawyers. In 1971 he was a young partner at the law firm of Cahill, Gordon.[6] Late in the evening of Monday, June 14, he received a call from James Goodale, in-house counsel for the *New York Times*. Goodale asked Abrams, together with Alexander Bickel, a Yale Law School professor, to defend the *New York Times* in a lawsuit that was to be filed the very next day.

The *New York Times* had just refused the government's request that it cease all publication of what we now know as the "Pentagon Papers" and return the source documents to the Department of Defense.[7] These papers, mostly from the Pentagon's "History of U.S. Decision Making Process on Vietnam Policy," evaluated U.S. policy during the Vietnam War.[8] Their evaluation was extremely negative, and their conclusions were devastating. The papers made the government look extremely bad and made the war seem unwinnable.

The papers had been given to the *New York Times* by someone who did think the war was unwinnable; who had worked in the Pentagon and helped write the report; who at first did not believe the war was unwinnable but who over time had come to see the impossibility that the Vietnam War was.

This someone was Daniel Ellsberg. Ellsberg smuggled one of the fifteen copies of the papers from a safe at the RAND Corporation to an offsite photocopier. There, he and a colleague, Anthony Russo, photocopied the papers over a period of several weeks.[9] Ellsberg tried without success to make the papers public by having them read into the *Congressional Record*. He eventually contacted the *New York Times* reporter Neil Sheehan in the hope that the *Times* would publish them. Ellsberg knew that this was a criminal act, but for him the war itself was a criminal act; his aim was to let the American people see just what kind of a crime it was.

For two and a half months the *Times* editors pored over the papers, working to verify their authenticity and accuracy. After an extensive review, the editors determined that they were authentic and resolved to publish the first of a ten-part series of excerpts and stories on Sunday, June 13, 1971.[10]

On Monday afternoon, one day after the first installment appeared, Attorney General John Mitchell sent a telegraph to the *New York Times* stating:

> I respectfully request that you publish no further information of this character and advise me that you have made arrangements for the return of these documents to the Department of Defense.[11]

When the *Times* failed to comply, the government filed papers to enjoin the paper from continuing to publish stories and excerpts from the documents.[12]

The government's claims were simple: these papers contained government secrets; they were stolen from the possession of the government; to publish them would put many American soldiers at risk and embarrass the United States in the eyes of the world. This concern about embarrassment was more than mere vanity: embarrassment, the government argued, would weaken our bargaining position in the efforts to negotiate a peace. Because of the harm that would come from further publication, the Court should step in to stop it.

The argument was not unprecedented. Past courts had stopped the publication of life-threatening texts, especially in the context of war. As the Supreme Court said in *Near v Minnesota*, for example, "no one would question but that a government might prevent actual obstruction to its recruiting service or the publication of the sailing dates of transports or the number and location of troops."[13]

Yet the question was not easily resolved. Standing against precedent was an increasingly clear command: if the First Amendment meant anything, it meant that the government generally cannot exercise the power of prior restraint.[14] "Prior restraint" is when the government gets a court to stop publication of some material, rather than punish the publisher later for what was illegally published. Such a power is thought to present much greater risks to a system of free speech.[15] Attorney General Mitchell was asking the Court to exercise this power of prior restraint.

The Court struggled with the question, but resolved it quickly. It struggled because the costs seemed so high,[16] but when it resolved the question, it did so quite squarely against the government. In the Court's reading, the Constitution gave the *New York Times* the right to publish without the threat of prior restraint.

The Pentagon Papers is a First Amendment classic—a striking reminder of how powerful a constitution can be. But even classics get old. In a recent speech, Abrams asked an incredible question: Is the case really important anymore?

For the government to succeed in a claim that a printing should be stopped, it must show "irreparable harm"—harm so significant and irreversible that the Court must intervene to prevent it.[17] But the showing depends on the publication not occurring—if the Pentagon Papers had already been published by the *Chicago Tribune*, the government would have claimed no compelling interest to stop its publication in the *New York Times*. When the cat is already out of the bag, preventing further publication cannot prevent the cat from getting out of the bag.

This point is made clear in a case that came after *New York Times*—a case that could have been invented by a law professor. *The Progressive* was a left-wing magazine that in the late 1970s commissioned an article by Howard Morland about the workings of an H-bomb. *The Progressive* first submitted the manuscript to the Department of Energy, and the government in turn brought an injunction to block its publication. The government's claim was compelling: to give to the world the secrets of how to build a bomb would make it possible for any terrorist to annihilate any city. On March 26, 1979, Judge Robert Warren of the Western District of Wisconsin agreed and issued a temporary restraining order enjoining *The Progressive* from publishing the article.[18]

Unlike the Pentagon Papers case, this case stewed, no doubt in part because the district judge hearing the case understood the great risk this publication presented. The judge did stop the publication while he thought through the case. And for two and a half months he thought. The publishers went to the Court of Appeals, and to the Supreme Court, asking each to hurry the thinking along. No one did anything.

Until Chuck Hansen, a computer programmer, ran a "Design Your Own H-Bomb" contest and circulated an eighteen-page letter in which he detailed his understanding of how an H-Bomb works. On September 16, 1979, the *Press-Connection* of Madison, Wisconsin, published the letter. The next day the government moved to withdraw its case, conceding that it was now moot. The compelling interest of the government ended once the secret was out.[19]

Note what this sequence implies. There is a need for the constitutional protection that the Pentagon Papers case represents only because there is a real constraint on publishing. Publishing requires a publisher, and a publisher can be punished by the state. But if the essence or facts of the publication are published elsewhere first, then the need for *constitutional* protection disappears. Once the piece is published, there is no further *legal* justification for suppressing it.

So, Abrams asks, would the case be important today? Is the constitutional protection of the Pentagon Papers case still essential?

Surprisingly, Floyd Abrams suggests not.[20] Today there's a way to ensure that the government never has a compelling interest in asking a court to suppress publication. If the *New York Times* wanted to publish the Pentagon Papers today, it could ensure that the papers had been previously published simply by leaking them to a USENET newsgroup. More quickly than its own newspaper is distributed, the papers would then be published in millions of places across the world. The need for the constitutional protection would be erased, because the architecture of the system gives anyone the power to publish, quickly and anonymously.

The architecture of the Net, Abrams argues, eliminates the need for the constitutional protection; even better, the Net protects against prior restraint just as the Constitution did—by ensuring that strong controls on information can no longer be achieved. Abrams argues that the Net does what publication of the Pentagon Papers was designed to do—ensure that the truth does not remain hidden.

But there's a second side to this story.

On July 17, 1996, TWA Flight 800 fell from the sky ten miles off the southern coast of Center Moriches, New York. Two hundred and thirty people were killed. Immediately after the accident the United States launched the largest investigation of an airplane crash in the history of the National Transportation Safety Board (NTSB), spending $27 million to discover the cause of the crash, which eventually was determined to have been a mechanical failure.[21]

This was not, however, the view of the Internet. From the beginning stories circulated about missiles—people said they saw a streaking light shoot toward the plane just before it went down. There were also stories about missile tests conducted by the Navy seventy miles from the crash site.[22] And then there were reports of a cover-up by the U.S. government to hide its involvement in one of the worst civil air disasters in American history.

The government denied these reports, yet the more the government denied them, the more contrary "evidence" appeared on the Net.[23] There were repeated reports of sightings of missiles by witnesses on the ground. These reports, writers on the Net claimed, were being "suppressed" by the government. The witnesses were being silenced. And then, as a final straw in the story, there was a report, purportedly by a government insider, claiming that indeed there was a conspiracy— because evidence suggested that friendly fire had shot down TWA 800.[24]

A former press secretary to President John F. Kennedy believed it. In a speech in France, Pierre Salinger announced that his government was hiding the facts of the case, and that he had the proof.

I remember this event well. I was talking to a colleague just after I heard Salinger's report. I recounted Salinger's report to this colleague, a leading constitutional scholar from one of the top American law schools. We both were at a loss about what to believe. There were cross-cutting intuitions about credibility. Salinger was no nut, but the story was certainly loony.

Salinger, it turns out, had been caught by the Net. He had been tricked by the flip side of the point that everyone can publish. In a world where everyone can publish, it is very hard to know what to believe. For publishers are also editors, and editors make decisions about what to publish—decisions that ordinarily are driven at least in part by the question, is it true? Statements cannot verify themselves. We cannot always tell, from a sentence reporting a fact about the world, whether that sentence is true.[25] So in addition to our own experience and knowledge of the world, we must rely on structures of reputation that build credibility. When something is published, we associate the claim with the publisher. If the *New York Times* says that aliens have kidnapped the president, that is a different story from a story with the identical words published in the *National Enquirer*.

When a new technology comes along, however, we are likely to lose our bearings. This is nothing new. It is said that the word *phony* comes from the birth of the telephone—the phony was the con artist who used the phone to trick people who were familiar with face-to-face communication only. We should expect the same uncertainty in cyberspace, and expect that it too, at first, will shake expectations of credibility.

Abrams's argument then depends on a feature of the Net that we cannot take for granted. If there were credibility on the Net, the importance of the Pentagon Papers would indeed be diminished. But if speech on the Net lacks credibility, the protections of the Constitution again become important.

"Credibility," however, is not a quality that is legislated; nor is it coded. It comes from institutions of trust that help the reader separate reliable from unreliable sources. Flight 800 thus raises an important question: How can we reestablish credibility in this space so that it is not lost to the loons?[26]

Two solutions are possible. One, a top-down solution, would empower editors—people who select what should be published based on a host of considerations, including the truth of what is said. The other, bottom-up, would facilitate the construction of reputation—a measure of the significance of the speech that turns on who is actually uttering it. In real space, of course, the two go together—editing goes with publishing, and hence, because of the selections made by the editors at the *New York Times,* the reputation of the *New York Times* is different from the reputation of the *National Enquirer.* We might have thought that the *New York Times* sold newspapers. But cyberspace is teaching us that it sells editing services that happen to be delivered on paper.

In cyberspace, these two functions could be distinct. Editing could be separate from distribution, which means that there could be a greater competition among editors. And credibility would be one of the values that editing services would sell.

Traditionally such credibility has been created by an institution of some stability—the *New York Times,* for example—serving a credentialing function. Being hired as a reporter by the *New York Times* says something important about your status; the *Times* then has an interest in policing you—your misadventures would reflect negatively on the *Times.* The public gets the benefit of a clear structure of responsibility.

We could see just this kind of reintermediation—restoration of intermediaries—on the Net.[27] But it could happen in other ways too. Imagine a kind of rating service that, as with bonds or with medical malpractice insurance, rates the reputation of each reporter and source through some formula of its own determination. We could imagine any number of such agencies, each providing reporters with ratings that serve as their credential. The reporter's rating would become part of every story published on the Net. And the same with any source, anonymous or not, since any source could also receive a rating.

In this example, an architecture of trust would replace institutions of trust.[28] A reporter could gain credibility as a good and accurate reporter whether employed by the *New York Times* or not. Hence, reintermediation on the Net need not involve the re-creation of the relatively few trusted publishers in real space but instead could focus on the relocation of the credentialing service from the publisher to independent agencies.

The difference between these reregulations is a difference in the power of institutions. Without preferring one over the other, we may note the trade-off between an architecture and a market structure.

THE REGULATORS OF SPEECH: ACCESS

Pornography, in real space, is regulated extensively. Porn—not obscenity and not child porn, but what the Supreme Court calls sexually explicit speech that is "harmful to minors."[29] Obscenity and child porn are regulated too, but their regulation is different from that of porn. Obscenity and child porn are banned for all people in real space (United States); porn is banned only for kids.

We can understand porn's regulation by considering the four modalities of regulation. All four are directed to a common end: to keep porn away from kids while (sometimes) ensuring adults' access to it.

First, laws do this. Laws in many jurisdictions require that porn not be sold to kids.[30] Since at least 1968, when the Supreme Court decided *Ginsberg v New York*,[31] such regulation has been consistently upheld. States can require vendors of porn to sell it only to adults; they can also require vendors to check the ID of buyers.

But not only laws channel. Social norms do as well. Norms restrict the sale of porn generally—society for the most part sneers at consumers of porn, and this sneer undoubtedly inhibits its sale. Norms also support the policy of keeping porn away from kids. Porn dealers don't like to think of themselves as people who corrupt. Selling porn to kids is universally seen as corrupting, and this is an important constraint on dealers, as on anyone else.

The market too keeps porn away from kids. Porn in real space costs money. Kids, on average, do not have much money. Because sellers discriminate on the basis of who can pay, they thus help to discourage children from getting porn.

But the regulations of law, market, and norms all presuppose another regulation that makes the first three possible: the regulation of real-space architecture. In real space it is hard to hide that you are a child. A kid can don a mustache and climb onto stilts, but it would still be pretty hard for him to convince a salesperson that he's not a kid. Thus, because a kid cannot hide his age, and because porn is largely sold face to face, the architectures of real space make it relatively cheap for laws and norms to be effective.

This constellation of regulations in real space has the effect of controlling, to a reasonable degree, the distribution of porn to kids. It is not perfect—any child who really wants the stuff can get it—but regulation does not need to be perfect to be effective. It is enough that these regulations make porn generally unavailable—as they do in real space.

In cyberspace the regulation of porn is different. The first difference is the market. In real space porn costs money, but in cyberspace it need not—at least not much. If you want to distribute one million pictures of "the girl next door" in real space, it is not unreasonable to say that distribution will cost close to $1,000,000. In cyberspace distribution is practically free. So long as you have access to cyberspace and a scanner, you can scan a picture of "the girl next door" and then distribute the digital image across USENET to many more than one million people for just the cost of an Internet connection.

With this market for supply, much more porn can be produced for cyberspace than for real space. But there is also the market for demand. Porn in cyberspace can be retrieved—often and in many places—for free. Not from commercial porn sites, but from USENET servers, for example. Thus, the constraint of the market is absent in cyberspace.

More important than the market, however, is the difference in architectures. A crucial feature that makes regulation in real space possible is the difficulty of disguising who you are. In cyberspace there is no fact about your identity to disguise. You enter without an identity, and you identify only what you want to identify. Thus, a kid in cyberspace need not disclose that he is a kid. And therefore he need not suffer the discriminations applied to a child in real space. No one needs to know that Jon is Jonny; therefore no one needs to know the necessary preconditions for applying the restrictions of law, norms, and the market.

The result is what we all know: there are few limits on the distribution of porn to children in cyberspace. And this fact, in turn, gave birth to the "porn scare."[32]

Just about the time the Net was coming into the popular consciousness, a particularly seedy part of the Net came into view first. This was the extraordinary growth of sex available on the Net. This concern became widespread in the United States early in 1995.[33] Its source was an extraordinary rise in the number of ordinary users of the Net, and therefore a rise in use by kids and an even more extraordinary rise in the availability of what many call porn on the Net. An extremely controversial (and deeply flawed) study published in the *Georgetown University Law Review* reported that the Net was awash in porn.[34] *Time* ran a cover story about its availability.[35] Senators and congressmen were bombarded with demands to do something to regulate "cybersmut."

Congress responded in 1996 with the Communications Decency Act (CDA). A law of extraordinary stupidity, it practically impaled itself on the First Amendment. The law made it a felony to transmit "indecent" material on the Net to a minor, or to a place where a minor could observe it. But it gave speakers on the Net a defense—if they took good-faith, "reasonable, effective" steps to screen out children, then they could speak "indecently."[36]

There were at least three problems with the CDA, any one of which should have doomed it to well-deserved extinction.[37] The first was the scope of the speech it addressed: "indecency" is not a category of speech that Congress has the power to regulate (at least not outside the context of broadcasting.)[38] As I have already described,

Congress *can* regulate speech that is "harmful to minors," or *Ginsberg* speech, but that is very different from speech called "indecent." Thus, the first strike against the statute was that it reached too far.

Strike two was vagueness.[39] The form of the allowable defenses was clear: so long as there was an architecture for screening out kids, the speech would be permitted. But the architectures that existed at the time for screening out children were relatively crude, and in some cases quite expensive. It was unclear whether, to satisfy the statute, they had to be extremely effective or just reasonably effective given the state of the technology. If the former, then the defenses were no defense at all, because an extremely effective block was extremely expensive; the cost of a reasonably effective block would not have been so high.

Strike three was the government's own doing. In arguing its case before the Supreme Court in 1997, the government did little either to narrow the scope of the speech being regulated or to expand the scope of the defenses. It stuck with the hopelessly vague, overbroad definition Congress had given it, and it displayed a poor understanding of how the technology might have provided a defense. As the Court considered the case, there seemed to be no way that an identification system could satisfy the statute without creating an extreme burden on Internet speakers.

But let's step back from the CDA for a moment and clarify just what is possible in a regulation of this kind. Since the case of *Ginsberg v New York,* it has been assumed that there is a class of speech that adults have a right to but children do not. States can regulate that class to ensure that such speech is channeled to the proper user.

Conceptually, then, before such a regulation could be applied, two questions must be answered:

1. Is this speech within the class of "regulable" speech?
2. Is this listener under a minimum age?

Clearly, the sender is in a better position to answer question one, and the receiver is in a better position to answer question two. Yet the CDA imposed the full burden of the regulation on the sender—he must determine both whether his speech is subject to regulation and whether the recipient is above the minimum age.

An alternative would be to place the burden on the receiver—or more precisely, on his parents. Parents know whether they have children who should be protected from porn; if they do, they arguably should take steps to block out speech they consider inappropriate for their children.

Both solutions—placing the burden on the recipient or on the sender—require a new architecture for the Net, not at the level of the TCP/IP protocol, but in the application space (see chapter 8). Both require that changes be built into the most common suite of applications in a way that users can depend on.

What might these applications look like? Let's call the first a *zoning* solution. Speakers are zoned into a space from which children are excluded. The second is a *filtering* solution. Listeners are empowered to block speech they want to block. We could describe each as a version of the other—with zoning, people are filtered; with filtering, the listener zones speech. But let's keep the kinds distinct and consider what each would require.

Architectures That Zone Speech

Two kinds of zoning solutions are conceptually equivalent, but constitutionally distinct. One, that is, is constitutional; the other, not. Both solutions require a change in the architecture of the Net to facilitate the production of a certain kind of information. One solution requires a signal that the user is a kid (call this a "kids-ID"). The other requires a signal that the user is an adult (call this an "adult-ID").

The difference is crucial, but let's see first how each might work. With the kids-ID solution, we could imagine the government requiring browser manufacturers to modify their browsers to permit users to set up profiles. One option in that profile would be a check-off box where the user signals that he is a minor. If this check-off box is selected in a profile on a given machine, the other profiles on the machine would require a password. Many people could share a single machine, but if any of them were minors, the adult profiles would be secured with a password.

Take an example from a hypothetical family. Say a family of three shares a single computer. One member of that family is a minor. Using this modified browser, the adults would set up a profile for each member of the family. With the child's profile, the kids-ID box would be checked, and a password would be used to access that profile. Any member of the family using the system would select his or her own profile and browse according to the rules of that profile. (Netscape already provides something close to this. With Navigator Communicator 4.5, for example, you can set up profiles just as I have described, though they do not have a kids-ID option.)

Armed with such a browser, a kid-identified user would then transmit this fact to a web site when accessing the site. This scheme would require that the web site block *Ginsberg* speech to any self-identified minor.[40] The burden on the child (or more accurately, the burden on his parents) would be slight, and the burden on the web site would also be slight.

That is one kind of zoning solution. A second would require the opposite identification: rather than guaranteeing everyone access except those who identify themselves as children, this version would grant access to adult material only to those users who could certify that they were adults.

We have seen such a system already: an architecture of digital certificates. Users wanting to enter a regulable site would have their credentials checked automatically. Those holding the right certificate would be permitted to enter; those without one would be denied entry. Web sites would then bear the burden of verifying that certificates were authentic, and would also bear the burden of determining which elements, if any, of their speech were regulable. But they would bear this burden only when the site had *Ginsberg* speech.

This second zoning solution is the model of the first CDA and Congress's more recent (and constitutionally troubled) Child Online Protection Act (COPA).[41] The burden is placed on both the adult site and the adult who wants adult speech. He must secure an ID; the site must verify the ID.

These two ID systems both effect zoning, but at different costs. One burdens the parents of children slightly and web sites practically not at all; the other burdens adults significantly and web sites significantly as well.

This difference should be constitutionally significant. It should incline the Court against upholding a statute like COPA, while disposing it to uphold a statute that requires kid-IDs. If a zoning solution is selected, the Court should uphold the solution that imposes the least cost on free speech interests.

But both statutes are different from a filtering solution. Both zone the Net according to features of the users. A filtering solution zones the Net according to features of the speech. Would a zoning solution impose fewer costs on free speech interests than a filtering solution?

Architectures That Filter Speech

The filtering system is a bit more complex, though a ready model exists: the architecture of the World Wide Web Consortium's platform for Internet content selection (PICS).[42]

We have already seen a relative (actually, a child) of PICS in the chapter about privacy. P3P, like PICS, is a protocol for rating and filtering content on the Net. In the context of privacy, the content was assertions about privacy practices, and the regime was designed to help individuals negotiate those practices.

With online speech the idea is much the same. PICS divides the problem of filtering into two parts—labeling (rating content) and then filtering the content according to those labels. Software authors would compete to write software that could filter according to the ratings; content providers and rating organizations would compete to rate content. Users would then pick their filtering software and rating system. If you wanted the ratings of the Christian Right, for example, you could select its rating system; if I wanted the ratings of the Atheist Left, I could select that. By picking our raters, we would pick the content we wanted the software to filter.

This regime requires a few assumptions. First, software manufacturers would have to write the code necessary to filter material. (This has already been done—both Netscape and Microsoft have PICS-compliant filters within their browser software.) Second, rating organizations would actively have to rate the Net. This, of course, would be no simple task; organizations are only slowly taking up the challenge.[43] Third, organizations that rated the Net in a way that allowed for a simple translation from one rating system to another would have a competitive advantage over other raters. They could, for example, sell a rating system to the government of Taiwan and then easily develop a slightly different rating system for the "government" of IBM.

If all three assumptions held true, any number of ratings could be applied to the Net. As envisioned by its authors, PICS would be neutral among ratings and neutral among filters; the system would simply provide a language with which content on the Net could be rated, and with which decisions about how to use that rated material could be made from machine to machine.[44]

Neutrality sounds like a good thing. It sounds like an idea that policymakers should embrace. Your speech is not my speech; we are both free to speak and listen as we want. We should establish regimes that protect that freedom; PICS seems to be just such a regime.

But PICS contains more "neutrality" than we might like. PICS is not just *horizontally* neutral—allowing individuals to choose from a range of rating systems the one he or she wants; PICS is also *vertically* neutral—allowing the filter to be imposed at any level in the distributional chain. Most people who first endorsed the system imagined the PICS filter sitting on a user's computer, filtering according to the desires of that individual. But nothing in the design of PICS prevents organizations that provide access to the Net from filtering content as well. Filtering can occur at any level in the distributional chain—the user, the company through which the user gains access, the ISP, or even the jurisdiction within which the user lives. Nothing in the design of PICS requires that such filters announce themselves. Filtering in an architecture like PICS can be invisible, and indeed, in some of its implementations invisibility is part of its design.[45]

From a free speech perspective, how should we evaluate these two architectures? One regime—either the zoning regime of the CDA or the alternative kids-ID regime—requires those who have zonable speech to place that speech behind walls; the second regime permits listeners to adopt filters that block offending speech. The blockings of the first follow requirements in a law; the filterings of the second, while perhaps induced by law, follow from individual choice. One (zoning) looks like "censorship"; the other looks like "choice" (PICS). Thus, most people embrace the second while trashing the first.[46]

But from a free speech perspective, this is exactly backward. As a (perhaps) unintended consequence, the PICS regime not only enables nontransparent filtering but, by producing a market in filtering technology, engenders filters for much more than *Ginsberg* speech. That, of course, was the complaint against the original CDA. But here the market, whose tastes are the tastes of the community, facilitates the filtering. Built into the filter are the norms of a community, which are broader than the narrow filter of *Ginsberg*. The filtering system can expand as broadly as the users want, or as far upstream as sources want.

The zoning solution is narrower. There would be no incentive for speakers to block out listeners; the incentive of a speaker is to have more, not fewer, listeners. The only requirements to filter out listeners would be those that may constitutionally be imposed—*Ginsberg* speech requirements. Since they would be imposed by the state, these requirements could be tested against the Constitution, and if the state were found to have reached too far, it could be checked.

The difference, then, is in the generalizability of the regimes. The filtering regime would establish an architecture that could be used to filter any kind of speech, and the desires for filtering then could be expected to reach beyond a constitutional minimum; the zoning regime would establish an architecture for blocking that would not have this more general purpose.

Which regime should we prefer?

Notice the values implicit in each regime. Both are general solutions to particular problems. The filtering regime does not limit itself to *Ginsberg* speech; it can be used to rate, and filter, any Internet content. And the zoning regime is not limited to facilitating zoning only for *Ginsberg* speech. The CDA zoning solution could be used to certify any number of attributes of the user—not only age but citizenship or credit-worthiness. The kids-ID zoning solution could be used to advance other child protective schemes. Both have applications far beyond the specifics of porn on the Net.

In principle at least. We should be asking, however, what the incentives are to extend the solution beyond the problem. In addition, what resistance is this extended solution likely to encounter?

Here we begin to see an important difference between the two regimes. When your access is blocked because of a certificate you are holding, you want to know why. When you are told you cannot enter a certain site, the claim to exclude is checked at least by the person being excluded. Sometimes the exclusion is justified, but when it is not, it can be challenged. Zoning, then, builds into itself a system for its own limitation. A site cannot block someone from the site without that individual knowing it.[47]

Filtering is different. If you cannot see the content, you cannot know what is being blocked. In principle at least, content could be filtered by a PICS filter somewhere upstream and you would not necessarily know this was happening. Nothing in the PICS design requires truth in blocking in the way that the zoning solution does. Thus, upstream filtering becomes easier, less transparent, and less costly with PICS.

This effect is even clearer if we take apart the components of the filtering process. Recall the two elements of filtering solutions—labeling content, and then blocking based on that labeling. We might well argue that the labeling is the more dangerous of the two elements. If content is labeled, then it is possible to monitor who gets what without even blocking access. That might well raise greater concerns than blocking, since blocking at least puts the user on notice.

These possibilities should trouble us only if we have reason to question the value of filtering generally, and upstream filtering in particular. I believe we do. But I must confess that my concern grows out of yet another latent ambiguity in our constitutional past.

There is an undeniable value in filtering. We all filter out much more than we process, and in general it is better if we can select our filters rather than have others select them for us. If I read the *New York Times* rather than the *Wall Street Journal*, I am selecting a filter according to my understanding of the values both newspapers bring to the process of filtering. Obviously, in any particular case, there cannot be a problem with this.

But there is also a value in confronting the unfiltered. We individually may want to avoid issues of poverty or of inequality, and so we might prefer to tune those facts out of our universe. But from the standpoint of society, it would be terrible if citizens could simply tune out problems that were not theirs. Those same citizens have to select leaders to manage these very problems.[48]

In real space we do not have to worry about this problem too much because filtering is usually imperfect. However much I'd like to ignore homelessness, I cannot go to my bank without confronting homeless people on the street; however much I'd like to ignore inequality, I cannot drive to the airport without passing through neighborhoods that remind me of how unequal a nation the United States is. All sorts of issues I'd rather not think about force themselves on me. They demand my attention in real space, regardless of my filtering choices.

This is not true for everyone. The very rich can cut themselves off from what they do not want to see. Think of the butler on a nineteenth-century English estate, answering the door and sending away those he thinks should not trouble his master. Those people lived perfectly filtered lives. And so do some today.

But on balance, most of us do not. We must confront the problems of others and think about problems that affect our society. This exposure makes us better citizens.[49] We can better deliberate and vote on issues that affect others if we have some sense of the problems they face.

What happens, then, if the imperfections of filtering disappear? What happens if everyone can, in effect, have a butler? Would such a world be consistent with the values of the First Amendment?

Some believe that it would not be. Cass Sunstein, for example, has argued quite forcefully that the framers embraced what he calls a "Madisonian" conception of the First Amendment.[50] This Madisonian conception rejects the notion that the mix of speech we see should solely be a function of individual choice. It insists, Sunstein claims, on ensuring that we are exposed to the range of issues we need to understand if we are to function as citizens. It therefore would reject any architecture that makes consumer choice trump. Choice is not a bad circumstance in the Madisonian scheme, but it is not the end of the matter. Ithiel de Sola Pool makes a very similar point:

> What will it mean if audiences are increasingly fractionated into small groups with special interests? What will it mean if the agenda of national fads and concerns is no longer effectively set by a few mass media to which everyone is exposed? Such a trend raises for society the reverse problems from those posed by mass conformism. The cohesion and effective functioning of a democratic society depends upon some sort of public agora in which everyone participates and where all deal with a common agenda of problems, however much they may argue over the solutions.[51]

On the other side are scholars such as Geoffrey Stone, who insists just as strongly that any such paternalistic ideal is nowhere found in the conception of free speech embraced by our framers.[52] The amendment, he says, is merely concerned with banning state control of private choice. Since enabling private choice is no problem under this regime, perfect filtering is likewise no problem.

This is another latent ambiguity, and as with others, I do not think we get far by appealing to Madison. To use Sunstein against Sunstein, the framers' First Amendment was an incompletely theorized agreement, and it is better simply to confess that it did not cover the case of perfect filtering.[53] The framers couldn't imagine a PICS-enabled world; they certainly didn't agree upon it. If we are to support one regime over another, we must do so by asserting the values we want to embrace rather than claiming they have already been embraced.

So what values should we choose? In my view, we should not opt for perfect filtering. We should not design for the most efficient system of censoring—or at least, we should not do this in a way that allows invisible upstream filtering. Nor should we opt for perfect filtering so long as the tendency worldwide is to overfilter speech. If there is speech the government has an interest in controlling, then let that control be obvious to the users. Only when regulation is transparent is a political response possible.

Thus, between the two, my vote is for the least transformative regime. A zoning regime that enables children to self-identify is less transformative than a filtering regime that in effect requires all speech to be labeled. A zoning regime is not only less transformative but less enabling (of other regulation)—it requires the smallest change to the existing architecture of the Net and does not easily generalize to a far more significant regulation.

I would opt for a zoning regime even if it required a law and the filtering solution required only private choice. If the state is pushing for a change in the mix of law and architecture, I do not care that it is pushing with law in one context and with norms in the other. From my perspective, the question is the result, not the means—does the regime produced by these changes protect free speech values?

Others are obsessed with this distinction between law and private action. They view regulation by the state as universally suspect and regulation by private actors as beyond the scope of constitutional review. And, to their credit, most constitutional law is on their side.

But as I've hinted before, and defend more below, I do not think we should get caught up in the lines that lawyers draw. Our question should be the values we want cyberspace to protect. The lawyers will figure out how.

The annoying skeptic who keeps noting my "inconsistencies" will like to pester me again at this point. In the last chapter, I embraced an architecture for privacy that is in essence the architecture of PICS. P3P, like PICS, would enable machine-to-machine negotiation about content. With P3P the content is rules about privacy practices, and with PICS it is rules about content. But how, the skeptic asks, can I oppose one yet favor the other?

The answer is the same as before: the values of speech are different from the values of privacy; the control we want to vest over speech is less than the control we want to vest over privacy. For the same reasons that we disable some of the control over intellectual property, we should disable some of the control over content. A little bit of messiness, or friction, is a value, not a cost.[54]

But are these values different just because I say they are? No. They are only different if *we* say they are different. In real space we treat them as different, and my only argument is that we choose what we want in cyberspace.

THE REGULATORS OF SPEECH: DISTRIBUTION

So far my arguments about architectures have been about architectures in cyberspace. In this final story, I blur the borders a bit. I want to use the architecture of cyberspace to show something important about the regulation of broadcasting.

The Federal Communications Commission regulates speech. If I wanted to broadcast a political speech on FM radio at a frequency of 98.6 MHz in Boston, the FCC would have me prosecuted.[55] To speak on 98.6 in Boston I need a license; I do not have such a license; to speak without a license is a crime. It is a crime despite the fact that the Constitution says, "Congress shall make no law . . . abridging the freedom of speech, or of the press." What gives?

The answer rests on a deeply held assumption at the core of our jurisprudence governing broadcasting technologies: only a fixed amount of spectrum is available for broadcasting, and the only way to facilitate broadcasting is to allocate slices of the spectrum to users, who are then solely entitled to use their allocated spectrum. Without allocation, there would be chaos, in which event there would be no broadcasting.

This view first came on the constitutional scene after Congress passed the Radio Act of 1927.[56] In 1926 Secretary of Commerce Herbert Hoover gave up the practice of controlling broadcasting after a number of circuit courts held that he did not have the power to do so. If he did not have the power, he said, then the invisible hand would have to govern. But Hoover was no friend of the invisible hand. He predicted what would happen if radio were left to the invisible hand (chaos), and some suggest that he helped bring about what he predicted. Stations would override other stations, he said; broadcasting would be a mess. When some confusion did arise, Hoover used this to justify new federal regulation.[57]

Congress then rode to the rescue by authorizing the FCC to regulate in a massively invasive way. Only the licensed could speak; what they said would be controlled by their license; they had to speak in the public interest; they had to share their resource with their opponents. In short, Congress said, broadcasting had to be regulated in the same way the Soviet Union regulated its economy.[58] We had no choice. As Justice Felix Frankfurter said in upholding the regime, it was compelled by the "nature" of broadcasting.[59]

From the beginning, however, there have been skeptics—not about the idea that spectrum must be regulated but about the means by which it is regulated. Was it necessary to have a central agency to allocate property? The common law, these skeptics argued, had done just fine.[60] Ronald Coase in 1959 proposed that if the spectrum were auctioned rather than licensed, it would be allocated to the highest-value users.[61] Coase's idea caught on—fifty years later. In the United States the FCC has just begun to auction huge chunks of the broadcasting spectrum. Soon much of the decision about who gets to say what will be made by private interests—but private interests backed by the force of the state.

Think for a second about the architecture implied by this development. If spectrum must be allocated, the argument goes, a governmental body should do the allocation. If this body licenses, then its right to do so must be extensive and powerful as it reviews the practices of licensees and allocates renewals accordingly. But even if the government simply auctions spectrum, it must still do extensive policing. Channels must be kept clear; interlopers must be punished. Under either regime—licensing or auctioning—both strong government and a great deal of private power are required. They are justified—indeed compelled—by the nature of broadcasting technology.

Many have noticed how different this architecture is from that of the press at the founding. The "press" in 1791 was not the *New York Times* or the *Wall Street Journal*. It did not comprise large organizations of private interests, with millions of readers associated with each organization. Rather, the press then was much like the Internet today. The cost of a printing press was low, the readership was slight, and anyone (within reason) could become a publisher—and in fact an extraordinary number did.[62] When the Constitution speaks of the rights of the "press," the architecture it has in mind is the architecture of the Internet.[63]

The market has erased this architecture in the print press; nature, we are told, has eliminated it in broadcasting. And so we are left with a world where the dominant architectures of free speech are fundamentally different from those the framers embraced.

In chapter 4, I said that architectures could differ both in the values they embrace and in the regulability of behavior within their space. But here we see a third way in which architectures differ. As the example of broadcasting shows, architectures differ in the justifications of regulation that they entail. Given an architecture of spectrum allocation, more regulation is justified, since someone must make choices about allocation.

So we have an architecture for broadcasting that is fundamentally different from the framers' design. It justifies a massive amount of state regulation over core areas of speech. Yet it is an architecture, we are told, that we are compelled to accept because nature gives us no other choice. Spectrum must be allocated if broadcasting is to occur.

But what if this assumption were no longer true?[64] Whatever the state of radio technology was in 1927, there's an emerging view that broadcasting today does not require spectrum allocation. There is a second architecture for broadcasting (which I will call "Spread Spectrum"—it has a few different names) that would not require any spectrum allocation at all.[65] If broadcasting were done through this technology, the extensive governmental regulation would no longer be justified.

How could this be? Your intuition about broadcasting is likely to that when two transmitters transmit on the same frequency, the signals "interfere" with each other in the sense that both are distorted. But in fact, the distortion we hear is caused by dumb receivers, not by conflicting signals. A dumb receiver needs a clear channel— or a clear difference between the channel it is receiving and everything else. If it does not receive a clear channel, then it does not know which signal to focus on. Thus, it sounds as if it were moving between the two, as if the transmissions were themselves mixed.

But a smart receiver could distinguish the transmissions. It could tell which it was to receive and ignore all others, without any coordination of the transmissions. The only requirement would be an agreement about the protocols for receivers. Receivers would wait until they received the proper packet, and only then would they open it.

This is the architecture of the Internet. Machines have addresses; they collect from the Net packets addressed to that machine.[66] No one allocates a particular channel to your machine; your machine shares the Net with every other machine on the Net. But the Net has a protocol about sharing this commons. Once this protocol is agreed on, no further regulation is required.

Broadcasting, many now argue, could be set up the same way. Broadcasts could be made using a spread spectrum design, and no one would have to allocate a particular bit of spectrum to a particular sender. Although this architecture in effect turns spectrum into a commons, there would be no tragedy of the commons since the technology of the receivers would regulate their use depending on global demand. Everyone could be a broadcaster.

So here we have an alternative architecture for broadcasting, one that does not require massive government regulation or state-supported oligopolies like NBC. It is an architecture that would facilitate far wider use of broadcast spectrum, and it would put those uses in competition with other ways of transmitting packets— copper and glass. All modes of transmission would compete with each other, and speakers would have the benefit of the most competitive mode.

Two architectures (spread spectrum and spectrum allocation), two structures of regulation (small and large), and two structures for industry (small and large broadcasters): Which, we might ask, is more consistent with the First Amendment's design?

Here, finally, we have an example of a translation that works. We have a choice between an architecture that is the functional equivalent of the architecture of the American framing and an architecture equivalent to the Soviet framing. One architecture distributes power and facilitates speech; the other concentrates power and raises the price of speech. Between these two choices, the American framers made a choice. The state was not to be in the business of licensing speakers either directly or indirectly. Yet that is just the business that spectrum allocation allows.

A faithful reading of the framers' Constitution, my colleague Yochai Benkler and I have argued,[67] would strike down the regime of spectrum allocation.[68] A faithful reading would reject an architecture that so strongly concentrates power. The model for speech that the framers embraced was the model of the Internet—distributed, noncentralized, fully free and diverse. Of course, we should choose whether we want a faithful reading—translation does not provide its own normative support. But if fidelity is our aim, this is its answer.

SPEECH LESSONS

What I described at the start of the book as modalities of constraint I have re-described in this chapter as modalities of protection. While modalities of constraint can be used as swords against the individual (powers), modalities of protection can be used as shields (rights).

In principle we might think about how the four modalities protect speech, but I have focused here on architectures. Which architectures protect what speech? How does changing an architecture change the kind of speech being protected?

I have not tried to be comprehensive. But I have pushed for a view that addresses the relationship between architectures and speech globally and uses constitutional values to think not just about what is permitted, given a particular architecture, but also about which architectures are permitted. Our real-space constitution should inform the values of our cyberspace constitution. At the least, it should constrain the state in its efforts to architect cyberspace in ways that are inconsistent with those values.

T H I R T E E N

interlude

LET'S PAUSE FOR A MOMENT AND LOOK BACK OVER THESE THREE CHAPTERS. THERE IS a pattern to the problems they present—a way of understanding how all three problems are the same.

In one sense, each has asked: How much control should we allow over information, and by whom should this control be exercised? There is a battle between code that protects intellectual property and fair use; there is a battle between code that might make a market for privacy and the right to report facts about individuals regardless of that market; there is a battle between code that enables perfect filtering and architectures that ensure some messiness about who gets what. Each case calls for a balance between control and no control.

My vote in each context may seem to vary. With respect to intellectual property, I argue against code that tracks reading and in favor of code that guarantees a large space for an intellectual commons. In the context of privacy, I argue in favor of code that enables individual choice—both to encrypt and to express preferences about what personal data is collected by others. Code would enable that choice; law could inspire that code. In the context of free speech, however, I argue against code that would perfectly filter speech—it is too dangerous, I claim, to allow perfect choice there. Better choice, of course, is better, so code that would empower better systems of reputation is good, and code that would widen the legitimate range of broadcasting is also good.

The aim in all three contexts is to work against centralized structures of choice. In the context of filtering, however, the aim is to work against structures that are too individualized as well.

You may ask whether these choices are consistent. I think they are, but it's not important that you agree. You may believe that a different balance makes sense—more control for intellectual property or filtering perhaps, and less for privacy. My real interest is in conveying the necessity of such balancing and of the values implicit in the claim that we will always require a balance. Always there is a competition between the public and private; always the rights of the private must be balanced against the interests of the public. Always a choice must be made about how far each side will be allowed to reach. These questions are inherently questions of public law: How will a particular constellation of constitutional values be reckoned? How will a balance be struck in particular factual contexts?

I have argued this point while neglecting to specify who is responsible for any given imbalance. There are those who would say that there is too much filtering, or not enough privacy, or too much control over intellectual property, but these are not public concerns unless the government is responsible for these imbalances. Constitutional value in the United States extends only so far as state action extends. And I have not shown just how state action extends to these contexts.

I do not intend to. In my view, our tradition reveals at least an ambiguity about how far constitutional values are to extend. In a world where only governments are regulators, keeping the Constitution's authority limited to state action makes some sense. But when the modalities of regulation are multiplied, there is no reason to limit the reach of constitutional values. Our framers made no choice about this; there is no reason why regulation through code cannot be informed by constitutional values. No argument has been made for why this part of our life should be cut off from the limitations and protections traditionally provided by the Constitution.

Code strikes the balance between individual and collective rights that I have highlighted so far. In the final chapter of part 3, a different balance is struck—one again made salient by code. However, this time the balance is not between the state and the individual but between the state and the implicit regulations of the architectures of cyberspace. Now the threat is to a traditional sovereignty. How do we translate that tradition to fit a world where code is law?

FOURTEEN

s o v e r e i g n t y

VIETNAM IS A COMMUNIST NATION—ONE OF THE FEW REMAINING, AND OF COURSE not anything like the communism that gave birth to the cold war, but nonetheless, it is a sovereign nation that still links its identity to Marx and Lenin (through Chairman Ho).

The United States is not a Communist nation. Defeated by Vietnam yet a victor in the cold war, we are a nation that in large part defines itself in opposition to the ideology of Marx and Lenin.[1] Vietnam sets as its ideal the state in service of the withering of the state; the United States sets as its ideal the withered state in the service of liberty. Control is the model of communism; freedom is the model of the United States.

Or so we are to think.

I confess a certain fascination with Communist states. In the early 1980s I wandered through every European Communist state that would let me in. I spent much of the summer of 1996 wandering through Vietnam. Alone and e-mail-free, I tried to understand this place that in my childhood fell victim to my nation's exported struggle with the cold war.

I've been to many places—traveling is a hobby of mine—but never to a place more spectacular. One is always overwhelmed by forgiveness, and an American can't help being overwhelmed by this nation's warmth and welcome. Perhaps had we "won" the war forgiveness would not be so forthcoming. But it apparently comes easily to those who did win.

I was not there to understand forgiveness, however, but to learn something about how the place ran. I wanted to understand how this state exercises control over its citizens; how it continues to regulate; how it qualifies as one of the last remaining Communist states. So I spent time talking to lawyers, businessmen, and managers of the emerging Net in Vietnam ("NetNam"). Very quickly, a surprising picture emerged.

Though Vietnam is a "Communist" state whose ideology, as understood in the West, admits very little limitation on the power of the state; though the Vietnamese state sets as its ideal a common good rather than the good of individuals or individual liberty; though on paper there is no "liberty" in Vietnam in the sense that we in the West like to imagine it—though all this is true, I could not escape the feeling that people in Vietnam, in their day-to-day existence, are far less "regulated" than people in the United States. Not all people, of course: political opponents undoubtedly feel the power of the state quite forcefully. But I sensed that ordinary people in their ordinary lives, many running small shops, had no conception of the control that government can exercise; no experience of having their wages reported to a central bureaucracy once a quarter; no understanding of what it is like to live under the (relative) efficiency of the regulation we have here. Life there is remarkably free from governmental control. It was hard to imagine how it would have been different had Nixon won the war. Pornography was banned and hippies were harassed, but in the main, people and business got on with very little direct or effective regulation by government.

This fact (if you'll allow random observations of an untrained anthropologist to count as fact) is not hard to understand. The "law" on the books in Vietnam may or may not be a stricter or more extensive regulator than the "law" in the United States. But the architecture of life in Vietnam clearly makes any real regulation by the state impossible. There is no infrastructure of control—there is barely any infrastructure at all. Whatever the regulations of the state may be, there is no architecture that could make them effective. Even if there is more regulation there than here (and frankly I doubt that there is), Vietnam has an effective "freedom."

This makes perfect sense. The power to regulate is a function of architecture as much as of ideology; architectures enable regulation as well as constrain it. To understand the power a government might have, we must understand the architectures within which it governs.

The preceding chapters have all been about this very point. We can have an idea of sovereign power—the right of the sovereign to regulate or control behavior—but our idea is meaningful only when we place it within a particular regulatory context, or within particular architectures of control. The state's power may be "absolute," but if the architecture does not support regulation, the state's effective power is quite slight. On the other hand, the state's power may be limited, but if the architectures of control are very efficient, this limited power can be extraordinarily extensive. To understand a state's power to regulate we must ask: How well does its infrastructure support a structure of regulation?

This is the question we should ask about the regulation of cyberspace—about sovereignty there. We should ask this question first about real-space governments: What power do they have to regulate life in cyberspace? How does the architecture of cyberspace support the regulation of real-space governments there? And then we should ask it about the "sovereignty" of cyberspace itself.

In the end, I want to argue that there *is* a sovereignty in cyberspace; that this sovereignty competes with real-space sovereigns; and that control of that sovereign is essential if we are to achieve democratic control over an extraordinarily important aspect of real-space life. *Real-space* life, not just cyberspace life, since in the end, and in the beginning, life there is always also life here.

THE SOVEREIGN OF THE SPACE

Cyberspace is a place. People live there. They experience all the sorts of things that they experience in real space there. Some experience more. They experience this not as isolated individuals playing some high-tech computer game. They experience it in groups, in communities, among strangers, and among people they come to know and sometimes like—or love.

While they are in that place, cyberspace, they are also here. They are at a terminal screen, eating chips, ignoring the phone. They are downstairs on the computer, late at night, while their husbands are asleep. They are at work, at cyber-cafés, and in computer labs. They live this life there, while here, and then at some point in the day they jack out and are only here. They rise from the machine, in a bit of a daze, and turn around. They have returned.

So *where* are they when they are in cyberspace?

We have this desire to pick. We want to say that they are either in cyberspace or in real space. We have this desire because we want to know which space is responsible. Which space has *jurisdiction* over them? Which space rules?

The answer is both. Whenever anyone is *in* cyberspace, she is also here, in real space. Whenever one is subject to the norms of a cyberspace community, one is also living within a community in real space. You are always in both places if you are there, and the norms of both places apply. The problem for law is to work out how the norms of the two communities are to apply given that the subject to whom they apply may be in both places at once.

Think again about Jake Baker. The problem with Jake was not that he went to a different place where the norms were different. The problem was that he was simultaneously in a Michigan dorm room and on the Net. He was subject to the norm of civility in the dorm, and he was subject to the norm of indecency in cyberspace. He was subject, that is, to two sets of norms as he sat in that single chair.

So whose norms would apply? How would real-space governments deal with the conflict between these two communities?

Some examples might help. Ordinarily, when you go to Europe you do not bring the federal government with you. You do not carry along a set of rules for Americans while in Europe. In Germany you are generally subject to German law. The United States ordinarily has very little reason to worry about regulating your behavior there—so long, at least, as you are there.

But sometimes the U.S. government does have a reason to regulate American citizens abroad. When it does, nothing in international law can stop it.[2] For example, there are jurisdictions where pedophilia is not regulated. For a time they became target tourist spots for pedophiles from around the world. The U.S. government, in 1994, passed a law to forbid Americans from engaging in child sex while outside the United States, even in jurisdictions where child sex is permitted.[3]

What justification could there have been for such a law? Obviously, the sense of Congress was that if a person engages in such behavior in a foreign country, they are more likely to do it here as well. If they visit a community where the norms permit such behavior, they are more likely to carry those norms back to their life here. Thus, while the American government generally doesn't much care what you do elsewhere, it does begin to care when what you do elsewhere has an effect on your life here. When it does, it will regulate your life elsewhere.

Regulations like this are the exception, of course, but only because the threat of these alternative communities is relatively slight. The frictions of real-space life make it less likely that the norms of an alien culture will bleed into our own; the distance between us and alien cultures is so great that very few can afford to have a life in both places.

But the Net changes this. As the Baker case suggests, and as any number of other cases will press, with cyberspace these other communities are no longer elsewhere. They can be brought home, and real-space communities no longer have the buffer of friction to protect them. Another community can now capture the attention of their citizens without their citizens' ever leaving. People may be in both places at the same time. The question for government is how far to allow this alien force to go.

In an important sense, this is a very old story. Cultures at one time isolated are later invaded when the barriers to invasion fall. Think about the plea from Europeans to stop the invasion of American culture, which pours over satellite television into the living rooms of European citizens.[4] Or even more extreme, the Middle East. These are places that have for some time been thinking about the barriers they might erect to protect their culture from the invasions of an alien culture.

Still, there is a difference here. The invasions these cultures resist are relatively passive. *Dallas* and *Baywatch*[5] are not sets of rules that people in Hungary or Singapore must follow. They display a certain (im)moral universe, which Hungarians and Singaporeans are able to see. But they don't draw people into a different form of life. The alternatives offered by TV are alternatives of the imagination. But the interactive life of cyberspace offers more than watching: it offers alternative ways of living (or at least some cyberspaces do).

Thus, the story is old, but as with each latent ambiguity, the twist is new. The question now is not just about what powers a state should have given that its citizens can travel; the question is about what power a state should have given that its citizens can live in two places at once.

How can governments accept these alternative ways of living while the people living them are also living within the jurisdiction of these governments?

We should begin by putting the problem in context.

"Sovereignty" is the sovereign's power to set rules that govern the behavior of people rightfully within its reach. The power to set *rules*—for of course I could affect people's behavior simply by stalling a bus in a busy intersection. And the power *rightfully* to set rules—for an invading army might set rules, but that wouldn't necessarily make the invader a sovereign.

Beyond this minimum, the concept has undergone significant change. At one time "logic" said that you could be subject to only one sovereign at a time.[6] Anything else, it was thought, violated the very idea of "sovereignty." But the United States changed that. In the United States, citizens are subject to two sovereigns at the same time—the nation and the state. Dual sovereignty is our contribution to the theory of sovereignty. However radical it was at the founding, it is now quite commonplace in sovereignty talk.

But dual sovereignty creates its own problems. How do dual sovereigns deal with the problem of conflicting authority? In matters of justice as well as of constitutional politics, dual sovereigns must have a simple way to resolve conflicts in authority.

In the United States these conflicts are resolved by the principle of supremacy: when proper laws of the federal government conflict with proper laws of the states, the federal laws prevail.[7] By design, these conflicts were to be infrequent, but if in practice they emerged, the U.S. Constitution provided a simple resolution.

But as conflicts among laws from outside a single sovereign (or outside a structure of dual sovereignty) grow in number and significance, another problem emerges. People have never really been subject to the laws of only one sovereign. Behavior across borders, or behavior that had effects across borders, has always risked running afoul of competing rules. As the integration of international life has increased, so have these conflicts. Behavior has effects in many places; how many places legitimately have a claim to regulate in these spaces? How, in other words, could it be *just* that a single act is subject to the control of many sovereigns?[8]

Cyberspace has exploded this third stage of the debate. What was once the exception will become the rule. Behavior was once governed ordinarily within one jurisdiction, or within two coordinating jurisdictions. Now it will systematically be governed within multiple, noncoordinating jurisdictions. How can law handle this?

This question has produced a ferocious argument between two extremes. At one end is the work of David Post and David Johnson. Johnson and Post argue that the multiplicity of jurisdictions in which your behavior is subject to regulation (since anything you do in cyberspace has an effect in every other context) should mean that much behavior is presumptively not subject to regulation anywhere. Anywhere, that is, save cyberspace.[9] The inconsistency of any other solution, they argue, would be absurd. Rather than embracing the absurd, we should embrace something far more sensible: life in cyberspace, as Milan Kundera might put it, is life elsewhere.

At the other extreme is the work of scholars such as Jack Goldsmith, who claims there is nothing new here.[10] For many years the law has worked through these conflicts of authority. Cyberspace may increase the incidence of these conflicts, but it does not change their nature. Old structures may have to be molded to fit this new form, but the pattern of the old will suffice.

While both sides embrace partial truths, in my view both are mistaken. It is true, as Johnson and Post argue, that there is something new here. But what is new is not a difference in kind, only a difference in degree. And it is true, as Goldsmith argues, that we have always had disputes of this form. But we have not had conflicts at this level of actor. We have not had a time when we could say that people are actually living in two places at once, with no principle of supremacy between them. This is the challenge that we will face in the future.

This duality is a problem because the legal tools we have used to resolve these questions before were not designed to deal with conflicts among citizens. They were designed to deal with conflicts among institutions, or relatively sophisticated actors. They are rules made for businesses interacting with businesses, or businesses interacting with governments. They were not designed for disputes between citizens.

Jessica Litman makes an analogous point in her work on copyright.[11] For much of the last century, Litman argues, copyright has worked fairly well as a compromise between publishers and authors. It is a law that has largely been applied to institutions. Individuals were essentially outside copyright's purview since individuals didn't really "publish."

The Internet, of course, changes all this. Now everyone is a publisher. And Litman argues (convincingly, in my view) that copyright's rules do not necessarily work well when applied to individuals.[12] More precisely, the ideal rules for individuals would not necessarily be the ideal rules for institutions. The rules of copyright need to be reformed to make them better suited to a world where individuals are publishers.

The same is true of conflicts between sovereigns. The rules for dealing with these conflicts work well when the parties are repeat players—corporations that must do business in two places, for example, or individuals who constantly travel between two places. These people can take steps to conform their behavior to the limited range of contexts in which they live, and the existing rules help them to that end. But it does not follow (as it does not follow in the context of copyright) that the same mix of rules would work best in a world where anyone could be a multinational.

The solution to this change will not come from insisting either that everything is the same or that everything is different. It will take more work than that. When a large number of citizens live in two different places, and when one of those places is not solely within the jurisdiction of a particular sovereign, then what kinds of claims should one sovereign be able to make on others, and what kinds of claims can these sovereigns make on cyberspace?

This question is not yet answered. It is another latent ambiguity in our Constitution's past—but in this case there is no founding international constitutional moment that could have answered the question. Even if there had been, it would not have answered this question. At the founding ordinary people were not routinely living in multiple noncoordinating jurisdictions. This is something new.

There are already some examples of how the law deals with conflicts between the norms of the virtual community and the rules of the real-space community. What lesson can we learn from these?

"Hackers" are an obvious first example. Originally, hackers were relatively harmless cyber-snoops whose behavior was governed by the norms of the hacker community.[13] A hacker was not to steal; he was not to do damage; he was to explore, and if he found a hole in a system's security, he was to leave a card indicating the problem.[14] He was a bit more invasive than a security guard, who checks office doors to make sure they are locked. The hacker of this earlier era not only checked the locks but let himself in, took a quick peek around, and left a cute (or sarcastic) note saying, in effect, "Hey, stupid, you left your door open."

All this may seem quite bizarre to you. But you have to put yourself into the culture of the early Net to understand (and hence to have the right to judge) this behavior. At this early stage the Net was a world of open software and open systems. The basic operating system was some flavor of UNIX, an open (as in transparent) system that had many different versions brewing on different parts of the Net.[15] As in any evolutionary model, these versions were genetically related but slightly different. Hackers took on the role of snooping about to sniff out problems with the evolving genetic code.

This was also a world where terribly valuable stuff was not really "on the Net." Separate networks for defense and finance were not part of the Internet proper.[16] While some famous efforts were made to hack those places, most hacking was benign.[17] People within the hacking community understood the benefit of their naggingly smart invasions.

That was the world that was. It didn't take much to see that this world would not survive for long. This community of people who thought it fair to test the locks, enter someone else's machine if they could, and snoop their file structure—this community was not going to mesh with a Net where commerce could survive. It may have been fine to play these games in a world of geeks, but when money came online a better system of security was inevitable.

As these cultures came into conflict, real-space law quickly took sides. Law worked ruthlessly to kill a certain kind of online community. The law made the hackers' behavior a "crime," and the government took aggressive steps to combat it. A few prominent and well-publicized cases were used to redefine the hackers' "harmless behavior" into what the law would call "criminal." The law thus erased any ambiguity about the "good" in hacking.

A good example of this is the story of Robert Tappin Morris, a graduate student at Cornell.[18] Morris was studying Internet mail—the protocols that govern the transfer of mail between two computers on the Net—when he discovered, and then exploited, flaws in two programs that were and still are widely used to transfer mail and information about users: Sendmail and Fingerdaemon. Morris was convinced that both left open certain doors on the system, thereby allowing people to use the protocols for improper purposes. The protocols governed, for example, when a computer would open its door to allow mail to be deposited onto its disk, but they had no good way to distinguish between knocks on the door by postmen and knocks by burglars.

In real space, if you discover that the door of the local bank is unlocked, you might simply call the bank (if you're a decent sort), or maybe the police, and let them know. If you discover a certain flaw in software made by Novell, you might send a letter to Novell. But when you discover a flaw in Sendmail, it's not so clear what to do. Sendmail, the dominant program for distributing mail on the Net, is free.[19] Sites have an incentive to keep the program up to date, but because doing so can be difficult and time-consuming, most do not update the program until they have had a scare. And a scare comes best from a demonstration. A self-respecting hacker *demonstrates* a problem, but in a very particular way. He shows what is wrong, but without doing any harm.

That was Morris's aim. He used a worm—which, you remember, is a bit of code spit onto the Net and designed to copy itself over and over, without affecting the operation of anyone's machine. Its purpose is simply self-replication. It does not aim to do any particular damage. It simply attaches itself to e-mail messages and thus copies itself everywhere, so that at a certain point its author can declare: "See, I told you. There's a hole in Sendmail and in Fingerdaemon."

But things didn't quite go as planned. The worm was not as harmless as Morris thought. He had made it multiply much too fast, and very soon it was clogging the whole Net. It had copied itself so many times that it froze the machines exposed to its spread. Machines by the hundreds were taken down, and thousands of dollars of damage incurred. Morris tried quickly to stop the mess he had started, but he didn't start quickly enough. The worm won; Morris lost.

It was not hard to find the culprit; too many people knew of Morris's plan. He was charged with violation of the Computer Fraud and Abuse Act of 1986, a federal law that made it illegal to access intentionally "federal interest computers" without authorization if that access damages or prevents authorized use of those computers causing a loss of more than $1,000.[20] Morris was convicted and sentenced to three years' probation, four hundred hours of community service, and a fine of $10,050 plus the costs of his supervision.[21]

The government had an objective—to vilify the hacker. Its aim was to turn the hacker into a criminal. And thus, rather than reading any lenity into the statute, the government insisted that it be applied strictly—not only against Morris but against a scad of other high-profile hackers as well. This was a war whose aim was to remake the hacker community into outlaws. Phiber Optik,[22] David LaMaccia,[23]Steve Jackson Games,[24] and others were the victims of this war. Real-space communities could not tolerate these sorts in their midst. So the hackers were banished.[25]

Should this be our standard response? Does life in cyberspace have no legitimacy against the view of real-space sovereigns? Does it have no claim? If it should, how could it make its claim? What would be its power?

The fate of the hackers is an example of real-space law taking over when cyberspace and real-space communities conflict. The example seems to say that real space will necessarily win this conflict—that cyberspace cannot bend the rules of real space. I don't believe that is true. Cyberspace will have an effect. For all the prominence of these efforts at reclaiming real-space sovereign authority, they are dwarfed by the examples of real-space sovereigns losing regulatory power and effect. Real-space sovereigns are in competition with cyberspace and, long before they realize it, cyberspace will have won.

To see how, we must look to how emerging architectures in cyberspace change effective regulation. The simplest example, but not the most significant, is one we have seen in the context of free speech. A nation in 1980 might have had fairly effective control over what was published within its borders. The government, for example, might be fairly confident that no newspapers would be too critical, since it could effectively punish its critics. State television would be under government control. The state could not really control what people said on telephones, but telephones were too crude, and the audience too small, to matter. The mix of architecture and law in this hypothesized state kept speech effectively regulated.

The Internet changed this mix. Now there can be speech critical of the government without governmental sanction. Publishing can go on without government intervention. The effective regulation of speech has changed. The values of the Internet—the free speech built into its architecture—now trump the values of control that our hypothetical nation embraced.

But this is just the most obvious example. Consider some others.

Imagine a nation with a well-developed balance of rights built into its law of contract. These rights protect consumers in some cases; they set the terms for business relations in others. Some of these rights are default, in the sense that the parties could agree to change them. But some are mandatory for a certain class of contractor or for a certain kind of contract.[26] (Many U.S. cities, for example, require a standard landlord-tenant agreement for apartment rentals.)

These rules of contract law would be effective in real space to define the rights of one individual making a claim against another. The enforcement of any contract in this space would be subject to these rules.

Enter cyberspace, where the architecture of interaction, or the architecture of a particular cyberspace, determines a host of rules about contracts. These rules—about how an offer is accepted, when it is effective, how it can be canceled, what terms must be bargained for, whether terms are enforceable, whether there must be a written agreement, and so on—may or may not be consistent with the contract rules of a particular jurisdiction. But a citizen from a particular jurisdiction can now enter into an agreement subject to these terms. These terms governing the agreement are the effective rules of contract for that particular agreement, and if they are inconsistent with the rules of the local jurisdiction from which the person comes, then so much the worse for the local rules. The terms of the contract are those agreed to in the text of the agreement, or implicit in the architecture that regulates dealings about the agreement.

One might say this is nothing new. One might say, following Goldsmith, that people have always been able to enter into international agreements.[27] These agreements have always implied a choice of law, and the law chosen may or may not be consistent with local law. If it is inconsistent, then there are restrictions on a local jurisdiction's ability to enforce it against a local citizen. So the same structure would constrain in this context.

But this analytical similarity should not obscure a substantive difference. Again, international agreements for the most part are agreements between sophisticated actors. Before cyberspace, ordinary consumers were not international actors. We can assume that sophisticated actors are able to defend themselves against rules inconsistent with their interest, or with the requirements of their local jurisdictions. Consumers, individuals, and ordinary cyber-contractors are not in the same position. When people lack the competence or advice to negotiate effectively, the effect is to shift control over such agreements from local courts and administrators to whatever rule is built into the code. Thus, local governments lose control over the rules and the effective rule-maker shifts to cyberspace.

A third example pushes the public law dimension of this conflict more strongly. Think again about copyright law. The law of copyright establishes a set of rights that individuals have against the copyright owner. We have seen these described in chapter 10, but for convenience, we can lump them under the label "fair use." There is some controversy in the United States about the extent to which fair use rights can legitimately be modified by contract. In an important opinion, Judge Easterbrook of the 7th Circuit Court of Appeals said, in effect, that these rights can plainly be modified through contract.[28] Thus, if you buy a piece of copyrighted work and promise to waive your rights of fair use, that promise, on this theory, can be held against you.

Easterbrook's conclusion might well make sense in real space, where there are real costs to contracting. In real space these costs prevent most copyrighted material from being wrapped in these anti–fair use agreements. The cost of real-space contracting creates a balance, tilting the result toward the protection of fair use.

But in cyberspace—especially when we consider the international dimensions to cyberspace—this balance is again skewed. If it becomes one of the rules of the space to click away fair use rights, then the balance of property and fair use so important to copyright's very design becomes skewed. Again, the architecture, and the rules it makes possible, conflict with real-space regimes. Once again, real-space sovereigns must decide how far they will allow this conflict to reach.

Contract and copyright are not the only laws that will compete with the code of cyberspace. Think about the rules of access through the mail, and its equivalent in cyberspace, e-mail. In real space, even in gated communities, the mail gets through. You can send advertisements or political commentary to people within these communities. Rules about trespass and private property might block you from entering the community and leafleting door to door.[29] But in real space you can use the mail.[30]

In cyberspace gated communities are different. The code of AOL, for example, gives subscribers tools that filter advertisements or block messages from certain people or servers. The rules about access in that space are different from the rules about access in this space.

So what? Again, the skeptic insists, the rules of contract law in Denmark are not the same as in Dallas. Why should the fact that two places have different rules *matter* any more, or less?

The key again is simultaneity, and here again, the metaphor of space is confusing. Ordinarily, you are in one space at a time, and when there are two sets of rules, this real-space rule offers an acceptable resolution. The rules for gambling are different in Nevada and in New Mexico; citizens from New Mexico must travel to Nevada to spend an evening subject to Nevada's rules. From the perspective of New Mexico, that might not be ideal, but it is not terrible. On balance, the opportunity to escape is not without cost, so there will not be so many of these escapes as to offend New Mexico's regulatory objectives.

But recall Jake Baker. The problem with Baker was that while he was in one place, he was living under the rules of a second. While in Ann Arbor, he was living within the norms of a radical community in cyberspace. Or forget Jake Baker (what a relief that would be); think about the wife having an affair with someone "in cyberspace." Can she really say to her husband, "That is there, this is here"? Couldn't he rightfully say—"Look, even if you are there, you are also here." Should we really view the effect of life in cyberspace as irrelevant to life here?[31]

To the extent that architectures in cyberspace are rules that affect behavior, the space is sovereign.[32] In the sense that any set of normative commitments is sovereign, cyberspace is sovereign. But this sovereignty produces perpetual competition. The rules that govern cyberspace may be different from those that govern real space. As the rules that govern real space compete, cyberspace increasingly wins out. It is the norms, the freedom, the rules, and the law of the place that in an increasingly large range of cases govern the norms, the freedom, the rules, and the law of people also living here.

There is little question about how real-space sovereigns will respond to this. They will come to see that the power of another sovereign is wired into their telephones, and they will struggle (as the United States has done with the hackers) as the rules and norms of this other sovereign affect the behavior of their citizens in their space. They have the tools at their disposal to resist the architecture of the Net to protect their regulatory power.

But now I want to make a stronger claim: not only can the government take these steps to reassert its power to regulate, but that it should. Government should push the architecture of the Net to facilitate its regulation, or else it will suffer what can only be described as a loss of sovereignty.

This is not some blind paeon to government. In fact, I am not concerned about "government" at all. My concern is accountability—these architectures and the values they embed should be architectures and values that we have chosen. They are political in the most ordinary way: they are structures that order real life, and they ought therefore to be structures that we have in some sense chosen.

In some sense—but which sense? From the bottom up or the top down?[33] From elected officials dictating the terms of code? Or from wired individuals choosing their own sets of code? Here ultimately is the hardest problem that cyberspace will present. But to see its complexity, we must put it in context.

Our history of self-government has a particular form, with two importantly contingent features. Before our founding, life was geographically based—a nation was a society located in a physical space, with a single sovereign allegiance. As I've mentioned, the conceptual revolution of the American republic was that citizens could have two sovereigns—more precisely, that they (as the ultimate sovereign) could vest their sovereign power in two different delegates. Their state government was one delegate, the federal government was another; individuals living in a single geographic location could be citizens of both governments. That was the idea of the founding document, and the Fourteenth Amendment made it explicit: "All persons born or naturalized in the United States, and subject to the jurisdiction thereof, are citizens of the United States and of the State wherein they reside."

Citizenship in this sense did not always mean a right to contribute to the self-government of whatever community you were a citizen of.[34] Even today children are citizens but they have no right to vote. For those recognized as members of civil and political society, citizenship is an entitlement: it is a right to participate in the governing of the political community of which they are members. As a citizen of the United States, I have the right to vote in U.S. elections; as a citizen of Massachusetts, I have the right to vote in Commonwealth of Massachusetts elections. And I have both rights at the same time.

At this level, the link between entitlement and geography makes sense. But as we work down the hierarchy of "communities," it makes less sense. As we move down the chain, where I live seems less and less determinative of membership. I am a member of the Boston community, yet because I live in Cambridge, I have no right to participate in the governance of Boston. If I moved away from Cambridge yet continued to work here, I would have given up my right to participate in the governance of Cambridge, even though I would continue to have an extremely strong interest in Cambridge and its development.

Political theorists have noted this problem for some time.[35] Scholars such as Richard Ford have contributed significantly to the view that we need a way to understand community and the right to participate in its governance that is not directly tied to geography.

These troubles with geography at the local level are nothing, however, compared with the problem in cyberspace. No one really lives in cyberspace; people who are "in" cyberspace are always also "in" real space. That they are in cyberspace should entitle them to some say over its architectures, and that they are in real space should give their real-space communities a right to some control over the architectures in cyberspace, at least to the extent that cyberspace architectures have an effect on the citizens in real space.

But why? Why do real-space citizens need to have any control over cyber-places or their architectures? You might spend most of your life in a mall, but no one would say you have a right to control the mall's architecture. Or you might like to visit Disney World every weekend, but it would be odd to claim that you therefore have a right to regulate Disney World. Why isn't cyberspace like a mall or a theme park?

Your relationship to a mall, or to Disney World, is the relationship of consumer to merchant. If you don't like two-all-beef-patties-special-sauce-lettuce-cheese-pickles-onions-on-a-sesame-seed-bun, then you can go to Burger King; McDonald's has no duty to let you vote on its hamburgers. If you don't like the local mall, you can go to another. The power you have over these institutions is your ability to exit. They compete for your attention, your custom, and your loyalty; if they compete well, you will give them your custom; if they don't, you will go somewhere else. What makes this system work, then, is the competition among these potential sources for your custom.

This part of our life is crucial; it is where we spend most of our time. Most people are more satisfied with this part of their lives than they are with the part within which they get to vote. In a sense, all these places are governments; they all impose rules on us. But our recourse under the rules of the market is to take our business elsewhere.

Still, an important part of our life is not like this. There are no states that say to their citizens—you have no right to vote here; if you don't like it, leave. At least no democratic state does this. Our role in relation to our governments is that of a stakeholder with a voice. We have a right—if the government is to be called democratic—to participate in its structuring.

And not just governments. It would be an odd university that gave its faculty no right to vote on issues central to the university (though it is an odd corporation that gives its employees a right to vote on issues related to employment). It would be an odd social club that did not give members some control over its functions—though again, there are such clubs, just as there are nondemocratic governments. The point is not that we have this relationship with most of the organizations in our lives, or even with the most important ones. The point is that much of our lives are spent in these two alternative modes—either as consumers, or as members.

Some theorists have tried to collapse these two modes into one. Some have tried to carry the member model into every sphere of social life—the workplace, the mall, the local pub.[36] Others have tried to carry the consumer model into every sphere of social life—followers of Charles Tiebout, for example, have tried to explain competition among governments along the lines of the choices we make among toothpastes.[37] But even if we cannot articulate perfectly the justifications for treating these choices differently, it would be a mistake to collapse these different spheres into one. It would be hell to have to vote on the design of toothpaste, and tyranny if our only recourse against a government we didn't like was to move to a different land.

Some have nonetheless urged that we think of cyberspace in the consumer mode. If we don't like a particular cyber community, we can move—far more easily, in fact, than we can in real space. Because exit is so cheap, we should use exit as our ballot. Some communities in cyberspace can choose to make members, others not; architectures in cyberspace can be constructed with little worry about sanction from real space. The world of cyberspace would become a virtual menu, and if you don't like one selection, you simply pick something else.

The best work in this line are the writings of David Post and his sometime coauthor David Johnson.[38] Post's article "Anarchy, State, and the Internet" best sets the stage here. Communities in cyberspace, Post argues, are governed by "rule-sets." We can understand these rule-sets to be the requirements, whether embedded in the architecture or promulgated in a set of rules, that constrain behavior in a particular place. The world of cyberspace, he argues, will be composed of these rule-sets. Individuals will choose to enter one rule-set or another. As rule-sets compete for our attention, the world of cyberspace will come to be defined by this competition of sovereigns for customers.

Post's argument rests on an important insight about the nature of governmental power. He views government's power in the same sense in which we now understand a firm's market power in antitrust law. By "market power" antitrust lawyers and economists mean a firm's ability to raise prices profitably. In a perfectly competitive market, a firm with no market power is the one that cannot raise its prices because it would lose so much in sales as to make the increase not worth it.[39] The firm that does have market power can raise prices and see its profits increase. The firm with market power also has the ability to force consumers to accept a price for a good that is higher than the price in a competitive market.

We might imagine an analogous constraint operating on government. Governments, like firms, can get away with only so much. As they become more repressive, or as they regulate more harshly, other governments, or other rule-sets, become competitors. At some point it is easier for citizens to leave than to put up with the burdens of regulation,[40] or easier to evade the law than to comply with it.

Because in real space such moves are costly, governments—or rule-sets—at least in the short run can get away with a lot. In cyberspace, the claim is, moving is not so hard. If you do not like the rule-set of your ISP, you can change ISPs. If you do not like the amount of advertising on one Internet portal, then in two seconds you can change your default portal. Life in cyberspace is about joining without ever leaving your home. If the group you join does not treat you as you want to be treated, you can leave. Because competitive pressure is greater in cyberspace, governments and other propagators of rule-sets must behave like firms in a competitive market.

This is an important conception of governance in cyberspace. It argues for a world of volunteers, one where rules are not imposed but selected. It is a world that minimizes the power of any particular government, by making governments competitors for citizens. It is government like McDonald's or Coca-Cola—eager to please, fearful of revolt.

Nonetheless, I have disagreements. I want to question the model—by questioning first its positive and then, its normative claims.

First, consider the claim that exit costs are lower in cyberspace than in real space; in doing so, we should distinguish between commodities and communities. When you switch to a different ISP or Internet portal, you no doubt confront a different set of "rules." And these rules no doubt compete for your attention. This is just like going from one restaurant or shopping mall to another. There are competing rule-sets; they are among several factors you consider in choosing an ISP; and to the extent that there is easy movement among these rule-sets, this movement is undoubtedly a competition among them.

Communities are different. Consider the "competition" among, say, MUDs. You join a MUD and spend months building a character in that community. At the end of this time, you have probably become well known in that community—you have well-developed social capital. That social capital—the set of experiences and understandings that individuals in that space have of you—is built through time and repeated interactions.

You have social capital in real space too. You have the set of relationships that define your friendships, your reputation, and your status. But you also have other capital—a house perhaps, a car, a savings account. When you move in real space, you can, for the most part, transfer your assets. You can sell your house and then buy another in the place you are moving to; you can move your money from one bank to another; if you move into a community as, for example, a doctor, you have a certain status based on that.

In cyberspace no assets are transferable. You can move from one community to another, but with each move you must start over again.[41] You do not enter a MUD with money or social status. You enter as a character whom you must then construct.

Paradoxically, then, we might say that it is harder to change communities in cyberspace than it is in real space. It is harder because you must give up everything in a move from one cyber-community to another, whereas in real space you can bring much of it with you.[42] Communities in cyberspace, then, may in the short run have more power over their citizens than real-space communities do.

This suggests a picture of competing rule-sets in cyberspace that is more complex than Post believes. It is not clear that markets will function more competitively there (since it is easier to build in these loyalty programs).[43] Nor is it clear that communities will function more competitively there (since it is harder to transfer social capital).[44]

There is a second, more fundamental criticism. Even if we could construct cyberspace on the model of the market—so that we relate to spaces in cyberspace the way we relate to toothpaste in real space—we should not want to do it. An important and long-standing tradition argues that beyond their role as consumers humans need to increase the contexts where they are members. Both as a matter of justice and as a matter of human flourishing, we need these parts of our lives where we have control over the architectures under which we live.

In at least some ways, then, we should relate to cyberspace as members rather than as customers. In an odd but wholly familiar sense, we need to take responsibility for what cyberspace is; we must become citizens of cyberspace just as we are simultaneously citizens of, say, the United States and Massachusetts. Being all three at once will force us to work out how these various political communities should interact.

At times these different roles will conflict, but this is a conflict we in the United States know well. A conscientious white southerner in the 1960s, for example, must have felt the conflict between being an American citizen and a citizen of a southern state. The vision of equality in these two different communities differed, and a white citizen had to select the one to which he would be loyal.

But how then do we act in these multiple roles as citizen? How do we respect the multiple roles while permitting the different jurisdictions to flourish?

One way of thinking about this problem is what in legal jargon is called subsidiarity.[45] Subsidiarity suggests that local issues should be dealt with locally, and that multiple jurisdictions should respect other jurisdictions dealing with whatever issues are properly their own. A community has the right to regulate its members, but only insofar as its regulation affects their membership in that community. Regulation should not extend beyond that narrow range.

But subsidiarity is not a determinative concept; there is no independent way of deciding what is "local."[46] A community and a state could both have the objective of providing "equal and excellent" education for their citizens, but nothing in the concept of subsidiarity tells us at which level this objective should be pursued.

The same will be the case in cyberspace. What Arab states consider "local" is not what Americans will see as local; what poor nations see as universal access will be more comprehensive than what many rich ones see as universal access. Subsidiarity alone will not determine the proper scope of political action. Political decisions have to do that.

Therefore, we need to be able to make political decisions at the level of the Net. A political judgment needs to be made about the kind of freedom that will be built into the Net. Our problem is imagining how that decision could be made.

In a sense, as I argued in chapter 3, the decision was made when the Net was built. The Net imposed on the world an architecture of freedom that was more robust and important than any political structure the United States had ever exported.

Some would call this a kind of imperialism—the imposition of our values on other nations—and insist that we create an architecture that does not impose the First Amendment on the world. Who are we to insist on free speech as a worldwide value? Or on free markets as the organizing structure for economies the world over? Isn't this just the sort of decision that local governments ought to make? Why are we making it for them?

There was a time when the United States was really "these united States," a time when the dominant political reality was local and there were real differences of culture and values between New York and Virginia. Despite these differences, in 1789 these states united to establish a relatively thin national government. This government was to be minimal and limited; it had a number of narrow, strictly articulated purposes. Beyond them, the national government was not to go.

These limits made sense in the limited community that the United States was. At the time there was very little that the states shared *as a nation*. They shared a history of defeating the strongest army in the world,[47] and a purpose of growing across an almost endless continent. But they did not share a social or political life. Life was local, exchange was rare, and in such a world limited national government made sense.

Nevertheless, there were national questions to be articulated and resolved. Slavery, for example, was a mark on our country as a whole, even though the practice was limited to a few states. There had been arguments at the founding about whether slavery should be left to local regulation.

But the Constitution was founded on a compromise about that question. Congress was not permitted to address the question of the "importation" of slaves until 1808.[48] After that, it could, and people, increasingly, said that it should. Slavery continued, however, to be a stain on the moral standing of our nation. Congress could eliminate it in the territories at least, and some argued that it should do so in the southern states as well.

Opponents to this call for Congress to cleanse our nation of slavery were of two sorts. One type supported the institution of slavery and believed it was central to southern life. They are not my focus here. My focus is a second type—those who, with perfect integrity and candor, argued that slavery was a local issue, not a national issue; that the framers had understood it not to be a national issue; and that the national government should let it alone.

However true that claim might have been in 1791 or 1828, it became less plausible over time. As the nation became socially and economically more integrated, the plausibility of saying, "I am a Virginian first," declined, and the significance of being a citizen of the nation as a whole increased.[49]

This change came about not through some political decision but as a result of a changing economic and social reality. Our sense of being members of a national community increased until, at a certain stage, it became impossible to deny our national citizenship. The Fourteenth Amendment wrote it into the Constitution; economic and social intercourse made it completely real. And as this change took hold, the claim that issues like slavery were local became absurd.

The very same process is happening to us now, internationally, and it is making an important cyberspace contribution. It has been slowly gaining momentum, of course, since the end of World War II, but the Internet has wildly accelerated the pace. Ordinary citizens are connected internationally and can make international transactions as never before. The presence of a community that is beyond any individual state is increasingly undeniable.

As this international community develops in cyberspace, its citizens will find it increasingly difficult to stand neutral in this international space. Just as a principled sort of citizen in 1791 might have said that slavery in Virginia was irrelevant to a citizen in Maine, so in 1991 the control of speech in Singapore may have been irrelevant to a citizen of the United States. But just as the claim about slavery's local relevance became implausible in the course of the nineteenth century, the claim about speech on the Net will become equally implausible in the next century. Cyberspace is an international community; there are constitutional questions for it to answer; and increasingly, we cannot simply stand back from this international space and say that these questions are local issues.

At least, we could not say that once we effectively invaded this international space with the Internet of 1995. We put into the world an architecture that facilitated extraordinarily free speech and extraordinary privacy; that enabled secure communications through a protocol that permitted encryption; and that encouraged free communications through a protocol that resisted censorship. That was the speech architecture that the Net gave the world—that *we* gave the world.

Now we are changing that architecture. We are enabling commerce in a way we did not before; we are contemplating the regulation of encryption; we are facilitating identity and content control. We are remaking the values of the Net, and the question is: Can we commit ourselves to neutrality in this reconstruction of the architecture of the Net?[50]

I don't think that we can. Or should. Or will. We can no more stand neutral on the question of whether the Net should enable centralized control of speech than Americans could stand neutral on the question of slavery in 1861. We should understand that we are part of a worldwide political battle; that we have views about what rights should be guaranteed to all humans, regardless of their nationality; and that we should be ready to press these views in this new political space opened up by the Net.

I am not arguing for world government. Indeed, the impossibility of such an idea is the focus of much of the next chapter. My argument instead is that we must take responsibility for the politics we are building into this architecture because this architecture is a kind of sovereign governing the community that lives in that space. We must consider the politics of the architectures of the life there.

I have argued that we should understand the code in cyberspace to be its own sort of regulatory regime, and that this code can sometimes be in competition with the law's regulatory regime. In copyright, for example, we saw how copyright law could be inconsistent with the regulatory regime of trusted systems. My argument is that we should understand these to be two regulatory regimes in competition with each other. We need a way to choose between them. We need a way to decide which should prevail.

As this system of regulation by code develops, it will contain its own norms, which it will express in its structures or in the rules it imposes. If the predictions of law and economics are correct, these norms will no doubt be efficient, and they may well be just. But to the extent that justice does not track efficiency, they will be efficient and unjust. The question will then be: How do we react to this gap?

There is an important pattern in this competition between code and law. Law, at least as it regulates international relations, is the product of extended negotiations. Countries must come to an agreement about how law will regulate and about any norms that they will impose on private ordering. As their work relates to cyberspace in particular, this agreement is quite significant. It will require the nations of the world to come to a common understanding about this space and to develop a common strategy for dealing with its regulation.

Meanwhile, of course, the space is regulating itself. While nations argue about what regulation there should be, the code of cyberspace continues to develop with a certain kind of sovereign authority. Its regulations need fewer agreements, and its structure alone admits new protocols.

What we will see, I suggest, is the emergence of a fairly unified regulation through code while law remains in flux. This development will cause a shift in effective regulatory power—from law to code, from sovereigns to software. Just as there was a push toward convergence on a simple set of network protocols, there will be a push toward convergence on a uniform set of rules to govern network transactions. This set of rules will include not the law of trademark that many nations have, but a unified system of trademark, enforced by a single committee;[51] not a diverse set of policies governing privacy, but a single set of rules, implicit in the architecture of Internet protocols; not a range of contract law policies, implemented in different ways according to the values of different states, but a single, implicit set of rules decided through click-wrap agreements and enforced where the agreement says. As Walter Wriston, the former Citibank chairman and author of *The Twilight of Sovereignty*, puts it, "The government can't do much about it. It's another thing slipping through their fingers."[52]

We should pause to consider just what this will mean.

We have governments for a purpose—in democratic states, we might even say, for good purpose. For much of human history governments could do very little. The cost of doing anything was, on the margin, extremely high. Much of the world operated under an effective laissez-faire; little of the world was really regulated.

The nineteenth and twentieth centuries were the centuries of government. For the first time, and brutally in many cases, government took control of both itself and the market. It became activist, focused on changing the status quo, antilibertarian. It could take control this way in large part because of the economies of its regulation and the diseconomies of escaping its regulations. Borders keep people in, and hence governments could regulate.

Cyberspace undermines this balance. Regulation does not become more costly, but escape from regulation becomes easier. The shift is away from the power of government to regulate, and toward the power of individuals to escape government regulation.

Effective regulation then shifts from lawmakers to code writers. The question for us is whether this shift should be unchecked. And the answer should depend first upon who the code writers are, and second upon what values they bring to their work.

We are just leaving a time when the code writers are a relatively independent body of experts and code is the product of a consensus formed in forums like the Internet Engineering Task Force (IETF). These were regulatory bodies whose standards set policy, but they were in one sense disinterested in the outcomes: they wanted to produce nothing more than code that would work.

We are entering a very different world where code is written within companies; where standards are the product of competition; where standards tied to a dominant standard have advantages. We are entering a world where code is corporate in a commercial sense, and leaving a world where code was corporate in a very different sense.

To the extent that this code is law, to the extent that it is a chosen structure of constraint, we should worry about how it is structured and whose interests may define its constraint, just as we worry when any lawmaking power is assumed by a private body. If code is law, who are the lawmakers? What values are being embedded into the code?

Both questions are fundamentally about sovereignty. Who should be building this world, and who should be specifying the values that this world will build into itself?

We have already seen one response to this shift. I have argued that local rules will become less significant because it is hard to enforce local rules relative to global rules. But doing so is hard only because the architecture makes it hard. We do not have a simple system for distinguishing natives of Canada from natives of New York, so it is burdensome to apply different rules to each.

But as I discussed in chapter 5, local rules need not be difficult to enforce. A certificate-rich Internet, for example, would enable sovereigns to reclaim some of their authority. In a cyberspace where everyone carried citizenship IDs, the Net could be zoned to apply citizen-specific rules. If you come from the United States and are under the age of seventeen, a Swedish server could block you; if you come from Russia, it could not. A world where certificates were generally available would be a world where states could again insist that their rules be applied, not the rules of the dominant nation (the United States) or the Net.

Sovereigns will get this.[53] They will come to understand that there is a different architecture for the Net that would re-enable their own control. When they do, they will push to facilitate the predicate to this architecture of regulability—certificates.

And when they do, we again will have to decide whether this architecture of regulability is creating the cyberspace we want.

A choice.

A need to make a choice.

My claim in part 1 was that commerce would help make this choice. Commerce,
I argued, will push for a certificate architecture that would enable its own form of
control. That architecture would enable some forms of state control. But the precise
control would depend on the architecture.

I have not argued against government. I have not said that we should architect
the space to disable collective control. Indeed, I have argued just the opposite. I have
marked myself as one of those loons who actually thinks that collective choice can
do some good.

But I am not a statist. I don't think the best of us is given to us from top-down.
There is a proper space for collective life, and an important space for private life. A
good constitution helps us navigate that balance.

We could architect the system of identification in cyberspace to enable some
forms of local control; we could build it so that some forms of local control would
matter. But the simple answers here are not answers: it would be a disaster if cyberspace became a place where localities again completely controlled—if geography,
that is, were simply mapped onto the space—just as it would be a disaster if no local (and hence no collective) control existed.

The answer steers a different course.

The last four chapters have told the story of a certain kind of displacement. In each,
a type of liberty has been transformed. In the first three, the liberty is displaced by a
more efficient architecture of control: fair use is coded away; privacy becomes too
cumbersome; filters become predominant. Architectures emerge that displace a liberty that had been sustained simply by the inefficiency of doing anything different.

In the last story, the liberty of the state to regulate is displaced by a more efficient
architecture of mobility. Here efficiency works on the side of freedom from regulation. Under this architecture, it becomes too costly to track and control citizens; it
becomes too easy for citizens to live subject to a different set of rules. Local control
declines; the Net's control increases.

The key is to see that these different changes are structurally the same. In each
case, the increase in a kind of efficiency throws into relief a value that had been latent. The conflict is between that efficiency (different in each case) and the value latent in the less efficient regime. This is not a value in inefficiency but instead a value
made possible by a particular inefficiency.

I don't mean this as a criticism of the notion of efficiency. To identify a value that
has been lost by efficiency is only to raise the question of whether in fact the "efficient" is efficient, or efficient to a particular end. The question is what the end
should be. If the value that is lost is of value, then it may no longer be efficient to

sacrifice it. Compare: driving on highways is a quicker way to get between two cities, but you lose a sense of the countryside when you drive only on interstate highways.

Nor do I mean to claim that this argument is new. It is practically trite to remark the values of a slower and quieter time, displaced by the rush of modern life. But to remark these values is not to say that they should be accorded infinite weight. The mad rush of modern life has no doubt moved many people out of poverty. That is an undoubted good, and one that weighs heavily against the "loss" of a quieter time.

But the values at stake in these four applications are at the core of who we are and who we understand ourselves to be, both as a people and as individuals. If we believe that the regulations of cyberspace will displace these values, then the efficiency of these regulations in gaining some ends may be inefficient in gaining the ends we collectively want.[54] The decision then is not about choosing between efficiency and something else, but about which values should be efficiently pursued. My claim in each of these cases is that to preserve the values we want, we must act against what cyberspace otherwise will become. The invisible hand, in other words, will produce a different world. And we should choose whether this world is one we want.

How we go about making these choices is the question of part 4. It is the pathology of modern politics that we have become so disgusted with self-government that our automatic response to government is criticism. Freedom is always freedom from government; liberty is always liberty from what government would otherwise do. These were also the thoughts of the people who suffered under the most oppressive governments of our time—the people of post-Communist Europe. They too, just after the fall of communism, were keen to find ways to minimize government, to create spaces not regulated by government.

But their lessons should be our lessons. What they learned was that liberty does not necessarily follow from having a space of no government. Freedom from governmental tyranny may be a necessary condition for liberty, but it is not sufficient. More important, government is necessary to help establish the conditions necessary for liberty to exist. This is because there are collective values that, acting as individuals, we will not realize. These collective values are sometimes values of liberty, which governments can act to establish and support. The freedom to contract, to own property, to travel, to vote—all of these rights require massive governmental support.

Sometimes these collective values deny or restrict liberty in the name of some other value that is weighed more strongly than liberty. The examples that follow canvass both kinds of values, and the threat that cyberspace will present to each. The lesson that should emerge from the collection is a lesson about how to respond: what disciplines we must relearn if we are to preserve these values against changes that we now only imperfectly control.

PART FOUR

responses

The lesson of part 1 was that the Net won't take care of itself. There is no nature that will protect cyberspace against change, and there is a tremendous amount of pressure for cyberspace to change. If the change continues along the lines it has taken so far, it will become a highly regulable space—not the locus of liberty, not a space of no control, but a technology of government and commercial power wired into every aspect of our lives.

But that's just one possible spin. The aim of part 2 was to suggest others. The built environments of cyberspace could be many, because the choices are many. And the potential power of government over these choices is great. Government has many tools with which to bend, or perfect, the architectures of this space. It has many techniques with which to make cyberspace what it wants cyberspace to be. These powers, however, are constrained—sometimes by law, more importantly by the code itself. Open code is one such constraint. But the possibilities of constraint are not themselves constraints. The message of part 2 was that little is determined, and much is possible. Choice is possible.

Part 3 exercised that choice. I began with a traditional legal technique for deciding how to go on—let the framers decide. Though the framers knew little about TCP/IP, the argument was that they established a tradition that can be translated into the context of cyberspace. They gave us the values, and our task is to carry those values into cyberspace.

But translation does not deal well with latent ambiguities. My argument in the balance of part 3 was that there are many such ambiguities. In four crucial areas of social and political life in cyberspace, the words of the framers will not carry us far in making the necessary choices. Where translation gives out, a choice must be made.

The question for this part is whether we're capable of that choice. My argument is that we're not. We have so completely passed off questions of principle to the judicial branch, and so completely corrupted our legislative process with the backhand of handouts, that we confront this moment of extraordinary importance incapable of making any useful decisions. We have been caught off-guard, drunk on the political indulgence of an era, and the most we may be able to do is stay on our feet until we have time to sober up.

F I F T E E N

the problems we face

I'VE ARGUED THAT THERE IS A CHOICE ABOUT HOW CYBERSPACE SHOULD BE, BUT THAT we're disabled from making that choice. We are disabled for three very different reasons. One is tied to the limits we place on courts, the second to the limits we have realized in legislatures, and the third to the limits in our thinking about code. If choice must be made, these limits mean we will not be making that choice. We are at a time when the most significant decisions about what this space will be must be made, yet we haven't the institutions, or practice, to make them.

In part 4, I describe these problems, and in chapter 16, I sketch three types of solutions to them. Neither part will be complete, but both should be suggestive. The problems that cyberspace reveals are not problems with cyberspace. They are realspace problems that cyberspace shows us we must now resolve.

PROBLEMS WITH COURTS

There are two types of constitutions, one we could call *codifying,* and the other *transformative.* A codifying constitution tries to preserve something essential from the constitutional or legal culture in which it is enacted—to protect that culture against changes in the future. A transformative constitution (or amendment) does the opposite: it tries to change something essential in the constitutional or legal culture in which it is enacted—to make life different in the future, to remake some part of the culture. The symbol of the codifying regime is Ulysses tied to the mast; the symbol of the transformative is revolutionary France.

Our Constitution has both regimes within it. The Constitution of 1789—before the first ten amendments—was a transformative constitution. It "called into life" a new form of government and gave birth to a nation.[1] The Constitution of 1791— the Bill of Rights—was a codifying constitution. Against the background of the new constitution, it sought to entrench certain values against future change.[2] The Civil

War amendments were transformative again. They aimed to remake part of what the American social and legal culture had become—to rip out from the American soul a tradition of inequality and replace it with a tradition and practice of equality.[3]

Of these two regimes, the transformative is clearly the more difficult to realize. A codifying regime at least has inertia on its side; a transformative regime must fight. The codifying regime has a moment of self-affirmation; the transformative regime is haunted with self-doubt. Constitutional moments die, and when they do, the institutions charged with enforcing their commands, such as courts, face increasing political resistance. Flashes of enlightenment notwithstanding, the people go back to their old ways, and courts find it hard to resist.

Our own constitutional history reveals just this pattern. The extraordinary moment after the Civil War—when three amendments committed to civil equality were carved into our Constitution's soul—had passed by 1875. The nation gave up the struggle for equality and turned to the excitement of the industrial revolution. Laws enforcing segregation were upheld;[4] the right of African Americans to vote was denied;[5] laws enforcing what was later seen to be a new kind of slavery were allowed.[6] Only after one hundred years of continued inequality did the Supreme Court again take up the cause of the Civil War amendments. It would not be until *Brown v Board of Education,* in 1954, that the Court again recognized the transformative idea of the Civil War amendments.[7]

One could criticize the Court for this century of weakness. I think it is more important to understand its source. Courts operate within a political context. They are the weakest branch of resistance within that political context. For a time they may be able to insist on a principle greater than the moment. But that time will pass. If the world returns to its racist ways, even a strong statement of principle enacted within our Constitution's text permits a court only so much freedom to resist. Courts are subject to the constraints of what "everyone" believes is right, even if what "everyone" believes is inconsistent with basic constitutional texts.

Life is easier with a codifying constitution. For here there is a tradition that the text is just meant to entrench. If this tradition is long-standing, then there is hope that it will remain solid as well.

But even a codifying constitution faces difficulties. Codification notwithstanding, if the passions of a nation become strong enough, there is often little a court can do. The clarity of the First Amendment's protection of freedom of speech notwithstanding, when the speech was that of communists and anarchists, the government was allowed the power to punish.[8] The presumption of innocence and equality notwithstanding, when Japan bombed Pearl Harbor, the government was allowed to shuttle every West Coast American of Japanese descent into concentration camps.[9]

These are the realities of courts in a democratic system. We lawyers like to romanticize the courts, to imagine them as above influence. But they have never been so, completely, or forever. They are subject to a political constraint that matters. They are an institution within a democracy. No institution within a democracy can be the enemy of the people for long.

It is against this background that we should think about the problems raised in part 3. In each case, my argument was that we will need to choose the values we want cyberspace to embrace. These questions are not addressed by any clear constitutional text or tradition. In the main, they are questions affecting the codifying part of our tradition, but they are also cases of latent ambiguity. There is no "answer" to them in the sense of a judgment that *seems* to have been made and that a court can simply report. An answer must be fixed upon, not found; made, not discovered; chosen, not reported.

This creates difficulties for an American court. We live in the shadow of the Supreme Court of Chief Justice Earl Warren. Many people think (but I am not one of this crowd) that his was a wildly activist court, that it "made up" constitutional law and imposed its own "personal values" onto the political and legal system. Many view the Rehnquist Court as providing a balance to this activism of old.

I think this view is wrong. The Warren Court was not "activist" in any sense inconsistent with a principle of interpretive fidelity, and the Rehnquist Court is no less activist than the Warren Court. The question, however, is not what was true; the question is what people believe. What we believe is that the past was marked by activism, and that this activism was wrong.

Wrong *for a court,* at least. The opponents of the Warren Court are not just conservatives. Some are liberals who believe that the Court was not acting judicially.[10] These opponents believe that the Court was making, not finding, constitutional law—that it was guided by nothing more than whether it could muster a majority.

Any court risks seeming like a "Warren Court" when it makes judgments that don't *seem* to flow plainly or obviously from a legal text. Any court is vulnerable when its judgments *seem* political. Against the background of history, our Supreme Court is particularly vulnerable to this view. The Court will feel the reaction when its actions *seem* political.

My point is not that the Court fears retaliation; our Court is secure within our constitutional regime.[11] The Court feels the reaction to its seemingly political decisions because of its own image of its proper role. In its view, its role is not to be "political"; its conception is that it is to be a faithful agent, simply preserving founding commitments until they have changed.[12]

But when—as in the cases of latent ambiguity—there are no founding commitments to preserve, then any attempt at translation will seem to be something more. And whenever it seems as if the Court is doing more than simply preserving founding commitments, the perception is created that the Court is simply acting to ratify its own views of a proper constitutional regime rather than enforcing judgments that have been constitutionalized by others.[13] In a word, it seems to be acting "politically."

But what does "political" mean here? It does not mean simply that the Court is making value or policy choices. The claim is not that values are improper reasons for a court to decide a case. To the contrary: value choices or policy choices, *properly ratified by the political process,* are appropriate for judicial enforcement. (The problem with the choices in cases of latent ambiguity is that they do not seem to have been properly ratified by the political process. They reflect values, but the values do not seem to be taken from the Constitution.)

"Political" thus refers to judgments not clearly ratified and presently contested.[14] When the very foundations of a judgment are seen to be fundamentally contested, and when there is no reason to believe that the Constitution takes a position on this contest, then enforcing a particular outcome of translation will appear, in that context, political.[15]

Cyberspace will press this problem intensely. When a framing value can be translated with some clarity or certainty, the Court can act in a way that resists present majorities in the name of founding commitments. But when ambiguities are latent and a choice really seems to be a *choice,* translation will not suffice. My claim is that the Court will not be the locus for that choice.

This might seem overly pessimistic, especially when we consider the success in striking down the Communications Decency Act.[16] But that case itself reveals the instability that I fear will soon resolve itself into passivity.

Throughout both lower court opinions, the courts spoke as if they were "finding" facts about the nature of cyberspace. The "findings" determined the constitutional result, and both courts reported their findings with a confidence that made them seem set in stone.

These findings, for the most part, were exceptionally good descriptions of where cyberspace was in 1996. But they did not tell us anything about where cyberspace is going or *what it could be.* The courts spoke as if they were telling us about the *nature* of cyberspace, but as we've seen, cyberspace has no intrinsic nature. It is as it is designed. By striking down Congress's efforts to zone cyberspace, the courts were not telling us what cyberspace *is* but what it *should be.* They were making, not finding, the nature of cyberspace; their decisions are in part responsible for what cyberspace will become.

At first it will not seem this way. When we confront something new, it is hard to know what is natural, or given about it, and what part can be changed. But over time courts will see that there is little in cyberspace that is "natural." Limits on the architecture of cyberspace that they have reported as findings in one opinion will be seen to have been "design choices" later on. What was "impossible" will later become possible, and as these shifts in the possible occur, courts will more and more feel that they cannot really say what cyberspace is. They will see that their findings affect what they find. They will see that they are in part responsible for what cyberspace has become.

This is Heisenberg applied to constitutional law. And as courts notice it, as they have in other areas, they will increasingly defer to the political branches: if these judgments are policy, they will be left to policy makers, not judges.[17]

One can hardly blame judges for this. Indeed, in some cases their deference should be encouraged.[18] But we should not underestimate its consequences. In the future legislatures will act relatively unconstrained by courts; the values that we might call constitutional—whether enacted into our Constitution or not—will constrain these legislatures only if they choose to take them into account.

Before we turn to what we might expect from legislatures, consider one other problem with courts—specifically, the problem confronting our constitutional tradition as the Constitution moves into the context of cyberspace. This is the problem of "state action."

Architectures constitute cyberspace; these architectures are varied; they variously embed political values; some of these values have constitutional import. Yet for the most part—and fortunately—these architectures are private. They are constructed by universities or corporations and implemented on wires no longer funded by the Defense Department. They are private and therefore traditionally outside the scope of constitutional review. The constitutional values of privacy, access, rights of anonymity, and equality need not trouble this new world, since this world is "private" and the Constitution is concerned only with "state action."

Why this should be is not clear to me. If code functions as law, then we are creating the most significant new jurisdiction since the Louisiana Purchase, yet we are building it just outside the Constitution's review. Indeed, we are building it just so that the Constitution will not govern—as if we want to be free of the constraints of value embedded by that tradition.

So far in this book, I have not relied very much on this private/public distinction. You might say I have ignored it. But I have ignored it not because it makes no sense, but because I don't know how it could be carried over to the regulation of cyberspace. The concept of state action itself presents a latent ambiguity, and I don't think we have a clear idea of how to resolve it.

The ambiguity is this: the Constitution was drawn at a time when basic architectures were set. The framers *found* the laws of nature, the laws of economics, the "natural law" of man; they were not made by government or man.

These architectures constrained, of course, and their constraint was a "regulation." But the degree to which they could be used as tools of self-conscious control was limited. Town planning was not limited,[19] but beyond laying out a space, there was little these founders could do about the rules that would govern the built environment of this space.

Cyberspace, however, has different architectures, whose regulatory power is not so limited. An extraordinary amount of control can be built into the environment that people know there. What data can be collected, what anonymity is possible, what access is granted, what speech will be heard—all these are choices, not "facts." All these are designed, not found.

Our context, therefore, is very different. That the scope of constitutional review was limited in the first context does not compel it to be similarly limited in the second. It could be, but we cannot know that merely from its being so limited in a very different context.

We have no answer from the framers, then, about the scope of state action. We must decide on our own what makes better sense of our constitutional tradition. Is it more faithful to our tradition to allow these structures of control, the functional equivalent of law, to develop outside the scope of constitutional review? Or to extend constitutional review to the structures of private regulation, to preserve those fundamental values within our tradition?

These are hard questions, though it is useful to note that they are not as hard to ask in other constitutional regimes. The German tradition, for example, would have less trouble with the idea that private structures of power must ultimately be checked against fundamental constitutional values.[20] The German tradition, of course, is not our own. But the fact that they have sustained this view suggests that we may make space for the constraint of the Constitution without turning everything into a constitutional dispute. Nevertheless, it will take a revolution in American constitutional law for the Court, self-consciously at least, to move beyond the limits of state action.

It is in these two ways then that courts are stuck. They cannot be seen to be creative, and the scope of their constitutional review has been narrowed (artificially, I believe) to exclude the most important aspect of cyberspace's law—code. If there are decisions about where we should go, and choices about the values this space will include, then these are choices we can't expect our courts to make.

PROBLEMS WITH LEGISLATORS

At a conference in former Soviet Georgia, sponsored by some Western agency of democracy, an Irish lawyer was trying to explain to the Georgians what was so great about a system of judicial review—the system by which courts can strike down the acts of a parliament. "Judicial review," he enthused, "is wonderful. Whenever the court strikes down an act of parliament, the people naturally align themselves with the court, against the parliament. The parliament, people believe, is just political; the supreme court, they think, is principled." A Georgian friend, puppy-democrat that he is, asked, "So why is it that in a democracy the people are loyal to a nondemocratic institution and repulsed by the democratic institution in the system?" "You just don't understand democracy," said the lawyer.

When we think about the question of governing cyberspace—when we think about the questions of choice I've sketched, especially those raised in part 3—we are likely to get a sinking feeling. This seems impossibly difficult, this idea of governing cyberspace. Who is cyberspace? Where would it vote? The very idea seems abhorrent to cyberspace itself. As John Perry Barlow put it in his "Declaration of the Independence of Cyberspace":

> Governments of the Industrial World, you weary giants of flesh and steel, I come from Cyberspace, the new home of Mind. On behalf of the future, I ask you of the past to leave us alone. You are not welcome among us. You have no sovereignty where we gather.

But our problem is not with governance *in cyberspace*. Our problem is simply with governance. There is no special set of dilemmas that cyberspace will present;

there are only the familiar dilemmas of modern governance, but in a new place. Some things are different; the target of governance is different; the scope of international concerns is different. But the difficulty with governance will not come from this different target; the difficulty comes from our problem with governance.

Throughout this book, I've worked to identify the choices that cyberspace will present. I've argued that its very architecture is up for grabs and that, depending on who grabs it, there are several different ways it could turn out. Clearly some of these choices are collective—about how we collectively will live in this space. One would have thought that collective choices were problems of governance. Yet very few of us would want government to make these choices. Government seems the solution to no problem we have, and we should understand why this is. We should understand the Irish in us.

Our skepticism is not a point about principle. Most of us are not libertarians. We may be antigovernment, but for the most part we believe that there are collective values that ought to regulate private action. We are also committed to the idea that collective values should regulate the emerging technical world. Our problem is that we do not know how it should be regulated, or by whom.

Like the Irish, we are weary of governments. We are profoundly skeptical about the product of democratic processes. We believe, rightly or not, that these processes have been captured by special interests more concerned with individual than collective values. Although we believe that there is a role for collective judgments, we are repulsed by the idea of placing the design of something as important as the Internet into the hands of governments.

The examples here are many, and the pattern arresting. The single unifying message in the government's own description of its role in cyberspace is that it should simply get out of the way. In the area of Internet commerce, the government says, commerce should take care of itself. (At the same time, of course, the government is passing all sorts of laws to increase the protections for intellectual property.)

A perfect example of this point is the government's recent hand-off of control of the management of the domain name system.[21] For some time the government had been thinking about how best to continue the governance or control of the domain name system. It had originally farmed the work out under National Science Foundation contracts, first to a California nonprofit organized by the late Jon Postel, and then to a private for-profit corporation, Network Solutions.

The contracts were due to lapse in 1998, however, and for a year the government thought in earnest about what it should do. In June 1998 it released a White Paper calling for the establishment of a nonprofit corporation devoted to the collective interest of the Internet as a whole and charged with deciding the policy questions relating to governing the domain name system. Policy-making power was to be taken away from government and placed with an organization outside its control.

Think about the kinds of questions my Georgian friend might ask. A "nonprofit corporation devoted to the collective interest"? Isn't that just what government is supposed to be? A board composed of representative stakeholders? Isn't that what a

Congress is? Indeed, my Georgian friend might observe that this corporate structure differs from government in only one salient way—there is no ongoing requirement of elections.

This is policy making vested in what is in effect an independent agency, but one wholly outside the democratic process. And what does this say about us? What does it mean when our natural instinct is to put policy-making power in bodies outside the democratic process?

First, it reflects the pathetic resignation that most of us feel about the products of ordinary government. We have lost faith in the idea that the product of representative government might be something more than mere interest—that, to steal the opening line from Justice Marshall's last Supreme Court opinion, power, not reason, is the currency of deliberative democracy.[22] We have lost the idea that ordinary government might work, and so deep is this despair that not even government thinks the government should have a role in governing cyberspace.

I understand this resignation, but it is something we must overcome. We must isolate the cause and separate it from the effect. If we hate government, it is not because the idea of collective values is anathema. If we hate government, it is because we have grown tired of our own government. We have grown weary of its betrayals, of its games, of the interests that control it. We must find a way to get over it.

We stand on the edge of an era that demands we make fundamental choices about what life in this space, and therefore life in real space, will be like. These choices will be made; there is no nature here to discover. And when they are made, the values we hold sacred will either influence our choices or be ignored. The values of free speech, privacy, due process, and equality define who we are. If there is no government to insist on these values, who will do it?

When government steps aside, it is not as if nothing takes its place. Paradise does not prevail. It's not as if private interests have no interests, as if private interests don't have ends they will then pursue. To push the antigovernment button is not to teleport us to Eden. When the interests of government are gone, other interests take their place. Do we know what those interests are? Are we so certain they are better?

If there are choices to be made, they will be made. The question is only by whom. If there is a decision to be made about how cyberspace will grow, then that decision will be made. The only question is by whom. We can stand by and do nothing as these choices are made—by others, by those who will not simply stand by. Or we can try to imagine a world where choice can again be made collectively, and responsibly.

PROBLEMS WITH CODE

At a recent workshop, Jean Camp, a Harvard computer scientist who teaches in the Kennedy School of Government, said that I had missed the point. The problem, she said, is not that "code is law" or that "code regulates." The problem is that "we haven't had a conversation about how code regulates." And then to the rest of the audience, she said, "Did all of you like the debate we had about whether Microsoft Word documents would carry in them a unique identifying number? Was that a satisfying debate?"[23]

Her irony carried with it an important insight, and an interesting mistake. Of course, for the computer scientist code is law. And if code is law, then obviously the question we should ask is: Who are the lawmakers? Who writes this law that regulates us? What role do we have in defining this regulation? What right do we have to know of the regulation? And how might we intervene to check it?

All that is perfectly obvious for someone who thinks and breathes the regulations of code. But to a lawyer, both Camp and I, throughout this book, have made a very basic mistake. Code is not law, any more than the design of an airplane is law. Code does not regulate, any more than buildings regulate. Code is not public, any more than a television is public. Being able to debate and decide is an opportunity we require of public regulation, not of private action.

Camp's mistake is a good one. It is a mistake more of us should make more of the time. Because while of course code is private, and of course different from the U.S. Code, its differences don't mean there are not similarities as well. "East Coast Code"—law—regulates by enabling and limiting the options that individuals have, to the end of persuading them to behave in a certain way. "West Coast Code" does the same. East Coast Code does this by increasing the cost to those who would deviate from the rules required by the code. West Coast Code does the same. And while we might argue that East Coast Code is more prevalent—that it regulates and controls a far larger part of our lives—that is a difference in degree, not kind. It's a reason to be balanced in our concern, not to be unconcerned.

Of course there are differences between law and code. I don't think that everything is necessarily public, or that the Constitution should regulate every aspect of private life. I don't think it is a constitutional issue when I turn off Rush Limbaugh. But to say that there should be a difference is not to say that the difference should be as dramatic or absolute as present constitutional thinking makes it. When we lawyers tell the Jean Camps of the world that they are simply making a "mistake" when they bring to code the values of public law, it is we who are making the mistake. Whether code should be tested with these constraints of public value is a question, not a conclusion. It needs to be decided by argument, not definition.

The formalism in American law, which puts beyond review these structures of control, is a third pathology that inhibits choice. Courts are disabled, legislatures pathetic, and code untouchable. That is our present condition. It is a combination that is deadly for action—a mix that guarantees that little good gets done.

S I X T E E N

---

r e s p o n s e s

WE NEED A PLAN. I'VE TOLD A DARK STORY ABOUT THE CHOICES THAT A CHANGING cyberspace will present, and about our inability to respond to these choices. I've linked this inability to three features of our present legal and political culture. In this short chapter, I consider three responses. Of necessity these responses are nothing more than sketches, but they should be enough to suggest the nature of the changes we need to make.

RESPONSES OF A JUDICIARY

I've said that we should understand the courts' hesitancy as grounded in prudence. When so much seems possible, and when a rule is not clearly set, it is hard for a court to look like a court as it decides what policies seem best.[1]

Although I agree with this ideal of prudence in general, we need to move its counsel along—to place it in context and limit its reach. We should isolate the source of the judge's difficulty. Sometimes a certain hesitation before resolving the questions of the Constitution in cyberspace finally, or firmly, or with any pretense to permanence, is entirely appropriate. But in other cases, judges—especially lower court judges—should be stronger. Lower court judges, because there are many of them and because many are extraordinarily talented and creative. Their voices would teach us something here, even if their rulings were temporary or limited in scope.

In cases of simple translation (where there are no latent ambiguities and our tradition seems to speak clearly), judges should firmly advance arguments that seek to preserve original values of liberty in a new context. In these cases there is an important space for activism. Judges should identify our values and defend them, not necessarily because these values are right, but because if we are to ignore them, we should do so only because they have been rejected—not by a court but by the people.

In cases where translation is not so simple (cases that have latent ambiguities), judges, especially lower court judges, have a different role. In these cases, judges (especially lower court judges) should kvetch. They should talk about the questions these changes raise, and they should identify the competing values at stake. Even if the decision they must adopt in a particular case is deferential or passive, it should be deferential in protest. These cases may well be a place for prudence, but to justify their passivity and compensate for allowing rights claims to fail, judges should raise before the legal culture the conflict presented by them. Hard cases need not make bad law, but neither should they be treated as if they were easy.

That is the simplest response to the problem of latent ambiguity. But it is incomplete. It forces us to confront questions of constitutional value and to choose. A better solution would help resolve these questions. While it will never be the job of the courts to make final choices on questions of value, by raising these questions the courts may inspire others to decide them.

This is the idea behind the doctrine of a second look, outlined twenty years ago by Guido Calabresi, a professor at the time who is now a judge.[2] Brutally simplified, the idea is this: when the Supreme Court confronts questions that present open, yet fundamental questions of value, it should be open about the conflict and acknowledge that it is not plainly resolved by the Constitution. But the Court should nonetheless proceed to resolve it in the way most likely to induce democratic review of the resolution. If the resolution induces the proper review, the Court should let stand the results of that review. The most the Court should do in such cases is ensure that democracy has its say; its job is not to substitute its values for the views of democrats.

Many ridicule this solution.[3] Many argue that the framers clearly had nothing like this in mind when they established a Supreme Court and permitted judicial review. Of course they did not have this in mind. The doctrine of a second look is not designed for the problems the framers had in mind. As a response to the problems of latent ambiguities, it itself reveals a latent ambiguity.

We might deny this ambiguity. We might argue that the framers envisioned that the Court would do nothing at all about latent ambiguities; that in such contexts the democratic process, through Article V, would step in to correct a misapplication or to respond to a changed circumstance. That may well have been their view. But I don't think this intent is clear enough to foreclose our consideration of how we might best confront the coming series of questions on the application of constitutional value to cyberspace. I would rather err on the side of harmless activism than on the side of debilitating passivity. It is a tiny role for courts to play in the much larger conversation we need to have—but to date have not started.

RESPONSES FOR CODE

A second challenge is confronting the law in code—resolving, that is, just how we think about the regulatory power of code. Here are a number of ideas that together would push us toward a world where regulation imposed through code would have to satisfy constitutional norms.

Here again is the link to open code. In chapter 8, when I described a kind of check that open code would impose on government regulation, I argued that it was harder for government to hide its regulations in open code, and easier for adopters to disable any regulations the government imposed. The movement from closed to open code was a movement from regulable to less regulable. Unless you are simply committed to disabling government's power, this change cannot be unambiguously good.

But there are two parts to the constraint that open code might impose; one is certainly good, and the other is not necessarily terrible. The first part is transparency—the regulations would be known. The second part is resistance—that known regulations could be more easily resisted. The second part need not follow from the first, and it need not be debilitating. It may be easier to disable the regulations of code if the code is in the open. But if the regulation is legitimate, the state can require that it not be disabled. If it wants, it can punish those who disobey.

Compare the regulation of seatbelts. For a time the federal government required that new cars have automatic seatbelts. This was the regulation of code—the car would be made safer by regulating the code to force people to use seatbelts. Many people hated seatbelts, and some disabled them. But the virtue of the automatic seatbelt was that its regulation was transparent. No one doubted who was responsible for the rule the seatbelt imposed. If the state didn't like it when people disabled their seatbelts, it was free to pass laws to punish them. In the end the government did not press the issue—not because it couldn't, but because the political costs would have been too high. Politics checked the government's regulation, just as it should.

This is the most we can expect of the regulation of code in cyberspace. There is a trade-off between transparency and effectiveness. Code regulation in the context of open code is more transparent but also less binding. Government's power to achieve regulatory ends would be constrained by open code.

But there is a benefit as well. Closed code would make it easier for the government to hide its regulation and thus achieve an illicit regulatory end. Thus, there is no simple defeat of government's ends but instead a trade-off—between publicity and power, between the rules' transparency and people's obedience. It is an important check on government power to say that the only rules it should impose are those that would be obeyed if imposed transparently.

Does this mean that we should push for open rather than closed code? Does it mean that we should ban closed code?

No. It does not follow from these observations that we should ban closed code or that we must have a world with only open code. But they do point to the values we should insist on for any code that regulates. If code is a lawmaker, then it should embrace the values of a particular kind of lawmaking.

The core of these values is transparency. What a code regulation does should be at least as apparent as what a legal regulation does. Open code would provide that transparency—not for everyone (not everyone reads code), and not perfectly (badly written code hides its functions well), but more completely than closed code would.

Some closed code would provide this transparency. If code were more modular—if a code writer simply pulled parts off the shelf to plug into her system, as if she were buying spark plugs for a car—then even if the code for these components was closed, the functions and regulation of the end product would be open.[4] Componentized architecture could be as transparent as an open code architecture, and transparency could thus be achieved without opening the code.

The best code (from the perspective of constitutional values) is both modular and open. Modularity ensures that better components could be substituted for worse. And from a competitive perspective, modularity permits greater competition in the development of improvements in a particular coding project.

It is plausible, however, that particular bits of code could not be produced if it were produced as open code, that closed code may sometimes be necessary for competitive survival. If so, then the compromise of a component system would permit something of the best of both worlds—some competitive advantage along with transparency of function.

I've argued for transparent code because of the constitutional values it embeds. I have not argued against code as a regulator or against regulation. But I have argued that we insist on transparency in regulation and that we push code structures to enhance that transparency.

The law presently does not do this. Indeed, as Mark Lemley and David O'Brien argue, the existing structure of copyright protection for software tends to push the development of software away from a modular structure.[5] The law prefers opaque to transparent code; it constructs incentives to hide code rather than to make its functionality obvious.

Many have argued that the law's present incentives are inefficient—that they tend to reduce competition in the production of software.[6] This may well be right. But the greater perversity is again constitutional. Our law creates an incentive to enclose as much of an intellectual commons as possible. It works against publicity and transparency, and helps to produce, in effect, a massive secret government.

Here is a place for concrete legal change. Without resolving the question of whether closed or open code is best, we could at least push closed code in a direction that would facilitate greater transparency. Yet the inertia of existing law—which gives software manufacturers effectively unlimited terms of protection—works against change. The politics is just not there.

RESPONSES OF A DEMOCRACY

In his rightly famous book *Profiles in Courage,* then-Senator John F. Kennedy tells the story of Daniel Webster, who, in the midst of a fight over a pact that he thought would divide the nation, said on the floor of the Senate, "Mr. President, I wish to speak today, not as a Massachusetts man, nor as a Northern man, but as an American. . . . "[7]

When Webster said this—in 1850—the words "not as a Massachusetts man" had a significance that we are likely to miss today. To us, Webster's statement seems perfectly ordinary. What else would he be but an American? How else would he speak?

But these words came on the cusp of a new time in the United States. They came just at the moment when the attention of American citizens was shifting from their citizenship in a state to their citizenship in the nation. Webster spoke just as it was becoming possible to identify yourself, apart from your state, as a member of a nation.

As I've said, at the founding citizens of the United States (a contested concept itself) were citizens of particular states first. They were loyal to their own states because their lives were determined by where they lived. Other states were as remote to them as Tibet is to us—indeed, today it is easier for us to go to Tibet than it was then for a citizen of South Carolina to visit Maine.

Over time, of course, this changed. In the struggle leading up to the Civil War, in the battles over Reconstruction, and in the revolution of industry that followed, individual citizens' sense of themselves as Americans grew. In those national exchanges and struggles, a national identity was born. Only when citizens were engaged with citizens from other states was a nation created.

It is easy to forget these moments of transformation, and even easier to imagine that they have happened only in the past. Yet no one can deny that the sense of being "an American" shifted in the nineteenth century, just as no one can deny that the sense of being "a European" is shifting in Europe today. Nations are built as people experience themselves inside a common political culture. This change continues for us today.

We stand today just a few years before where Webster stood in 1850. We stand on the brink of being able to say, "I speak as a citizen of the world," without the ordinary person thinking, "What a nut." We stand just on the cusp of a time when ordinary citizens will begin to feel the effects of the regulations of other governments, just as the citizens of Massachusetts came to feel the effects of slavery and the citizens of Virginia came to feel the effects of a drive for freedom. As Nicholas Negroponte puts it, "Nations today are the wrong size. They are not small enough to be local and they are not large enough to be global."[8] This misfit will matter.

As we, citizens of the United States, spend more of our time and money in this space that is not part of any particular jurisdiction but subject to the regulations of all jurisdictions, we will increasingly ask questions about our status there. We will begin to feel the entitlement Webster felt, as an American, to speak about life in another part of the United States. For us, it will be the entitlement to speak about life in another part of the world, grounded in the feeling that there is a community of interests that reaches beyond diplomatic ties into the hearts of ordinary citizens.

What will we do then? When we feel we are part of a world, and that the world regulates us? What will we do when we need to make choices about how that world regulates us, and how we regulate it?

The weariness with government that I described at the end of the last chapter is not a condition without cause. But its cause is not the death of any ideal of democracy. We are all still democrats; we simply do not like what our democracy has produced. And we cannot imagine extending what we have to new domains like cyberspace. If there were just more of the same there—more of the excesses and betrayals of government as we have come to know it—then better that there should be less.

There are two problems here, though only one that is really tied to the argument of this book, and so only one that I will discuss in any depth. The other is much deeper—a sense of a basic corruption in any system that would allow so much political influence to be peddled by those who hand out money. This is the corruption of campaign financing, a corruption not of people but of process. Even good souls in Congress have no choice but to spend an ever-increasing amount of their time raising an ever-increasing amount of money to compete in elections. This is an arms race, and our Supreme Court has effectively said that the Constitution requires it.[9]

But there is a second, oddly counterintuitive reason for this increasing failure of democracy. This is not that government listens too little to the views of the public. It is that government listens too much. Every fancy of the population gets echoed in polls, and these polls in turn pulse the democracy. Yet the message the polls transmit is not the message of democracy; their frequency and influence is not the product of increased significance. The president makes policy on the basis of overnight polling only because overnight polling is so easy.

This is partly a technology problem. Polls mark an interaction of technology and democracy that we are just beginning to understand. As the cost of monitoring the current view of the population drops, and as the machines for permanent monitoring of the population are built, we are producing a perpetual stream of data about what "the people" think about every issue that government might consider.

A certain kind of code perfects the machine of monitoring—code that automates perfect sample selection, that facilitates databases of results, and that simplifies the process of connecting. We rarely ask, however, whether perfect monitoring is a good.

It has never been our ideal—constitutionally at least—that democracy be a perfect reflection of the present temperature of the people. Our framers were keen to design structures that would mediate the views of the people. Democracy was to be more than a string of excited utterances of the people. It was to be deliberative, reflective, and balanced by limitations imposed by a constitution.

But maybe, to be consistent with the arguments from part 3, I should say that at least there was a latent ambiguity about this question. In a world where elections were extremely costly and communication was complicated, democracy had to get by with infrequent elections. Nevertheless, we cannot really know how the framers would have reacted to a technology that allows perfect and perpetual polling.

There is an important reason to be skeptical of the flash pulse of the people. The flash pulse is questionable not because the people are uneducated or incapable of good judgment, and not because democracy needs to fail, but because it is often the product of ignorance. People often have ill-informed or partially informed views that they simply repeat as judgments when they know that their judgments are not being particularly noticed or considered.

Technology encourages this sort of judgment. As a consequence of the massive increase in reporting on news, we are exposed to a greater range of information about the world today than ever before. This exposure, in turn, gives us confidence in our judgment. Never having heard of East Timor, people when asked might well have said, "I don't know." But having seen ten seconds on TV, or thirty lines on a web portal news page, gives them a spin they didn't have before. And they repeat this spin, with very little value added.

The solution to this problem is not less news, or a ban on polling. The solution is a better kind of polling. The government reacts to bad poll data because that is the only data we have. But these polls are not the only possible kinds of polls. There are techniques for polling that compensate for the errors of the flash poll and produce judgments that are both more considered and more stable.

An example is the "deliberative" poll devised by Professor James Fishkin.[10] Rather than a pulse, Fishkin's polls seek an equilibrium. They bring a cross-section of people together for a weekend at a time. These people, who represent all segments of a society, are given information before the poll that helps ensure that they know something about the subject matter. After being introduced to the topic of the poll, they are then divided into small juries and over the course of a couple of days argue about the topic at issue and exchange views about how best to resolve it. At the end they are asked about their views, and their responses at this point form the "results" of the poll.

The great advantage of this system is not only that information is provided but that the process is deliberative. The results emerge out of the reasoning of citizens debating with other citizens. People are not encouraged to just cast a ballot. They give reasons for their ballot, and those reasons will or will not persuade.

We could imagine (we could dream) of this process extending generally. We could imagine it becoming a staple of our political life. And if it did, it might well do good, as a counterweight to the flash pulse and the perpetually interested process that ordinary government is. It would be a corrective to the process we now have, and one that might bring hope.

Cyberspace might make this process where reasons count more possible; it certainly makes it even more necessary. It is possible to imagine using the architecture of the space to design deliberative forums, which could be used to implement Fishkin's polling. But my message throughout is that cyberspace makes the need all the more urgent.[11]

There is a magic in a process where reasons count—not where experts rule or where only smart people have the vote, but where power gets set in the face of reason. The magic is in a process where citizens give reasons, and citizens understand that power is constrained by these reasons.

This was the magic that Tocqueville wrote of when he told the world of the amazing system of juries in the United States. Citizens serving on juries must make reasoned, persuasive arguments in coming to decisions that often have extraordinary consequences for social and political life. Writing in 1835, Tocqueville said of juries:

> The jury . . . serves to communicate the spirit of the judges to the minds of all the citizens; and this spirit, with the habits which attend it, is the soundest preparation for free institutions. It imbues all classes with a respect for the thing judged and with the notion of right. . . . It teaches men to practice equity; every man learns to judge his neighbor as he would himself be judged. . . . The jury teaches every man not to recoil before the responsibility of his own actions and impresses him with that manly confidence without which no political virtue can exist. It invests each citizen with a kind of magistracy; it makes them all feel the duties which they are bound to discharge towards society and the part which they take in its government. By obliging men to turn their attention to other affairs than their own, it rubs off that private selfishness which is the rust of society.[12]

It wasn't Tocqueville, however, or any other theorist, who sold me on this ideal. It was a lawyer who first let me see the power of this idea—a lawyer from Madison, Wisconsin, my uncle, Richard Cates.

We live in a time when the sane vilify lawyers. No doubt lawyers are in part responsible for this. But I can't accept it, and not only because I train lawyers for a living. I can't accept it because etched into my memory is a picture my uncle sketched, explaining why he was a lawyer. In 1974 he had just returned from Washington, where he worked for the House Committee on Impeachment—of Nixon, not Clinton, though Hillary Rodham was working with him. I pressed him to tell me everything; I wanted to hear about the battles. It was not a topic that we discussed much at home. My parents were Republicans. My uncle was not.

My uncle's job was to teach the congressmen about the facts in the case—to first learn everything that was known, and then to teach this to the members of the committee. Although there was much about his story that I will never forget, the most compelling part was not really related to the impeachment. My uncle was describing for me the essence of his job—both for the House and for his clients:

> It is what a lawyer does, what a good lawyer does, that makes this system work. It is not the bluffing, or the outrage, or the strategies and tactics. It is something much simpler than that. What a good lawyer does is tell a story that persuades. Not by hiding the truth or exciting the emotion, but using reason, through a story, to persuade.
>
> When it works, it does something to the people who experience this persuasion. Some, for the first time in their lives, see power constrained by reason. Not

by votes, not by wealth, not by who someone knows—but by an argument that persuades. This is the magic of our system, however rare the miracles may be.

This picture stuck—not in its elitist version, of experts deciding what's best, nor in its Rikki Lake version, of excited crowds yelling opponents down. But in its simple version that juries know. And it is this simple picture that our current democracy misses. Where through deliberation, and understanding, and a process of building community, judgments get made about how to go on.

We could build some of this back into our democracy. The more we do, the less significant the flash pulses will be. And the less significant these flash pulses are, the more we might have faith again in that part of our tradition that made us revolutionaries in 1791—the commitment to a form of government that respects deliberation, and the people, and that stands opposed to corruption dressed in aristocratic baubles.

SEVENTEEN

what declan doesn't get

DECLAN MCCULLAGH IS A WRITER WHO WORKS FOR *WIRED NEWS*. HE ALSO RUNS A "listserve" that feeds to subscribers the bulletins that he has decided to forward and facilitates a discussion among these members. The list was originally called "Fight Censorship," and it initially attracted a large number of subscribers who were eager to organize to resist the government's efforts to "censor" the Net.

But Declan uses the list now for more than a discussion of censorship. He feeds to the list other news that he imagines his subscribers will enjoy. So in addition to news about efforts to eliminate porn from the Net, Declan includes reports on FBI wiretaps, or efforts to protect privacy, or the government's efforts to enforce the nation's antitrust laws. I'm a subscriber; I enjoy the posts.

Declan's politics are clear. He's a smart, if young, libertarian whose first reaction to any suggestion that involves government is scorn. In one recent message, he cited a story about a British provider violating fax spam laws; this, he argued, showed that laws regulating e-mail spam are useless. There is one unifying theme to Declan's posts: let the Net alone. And with a sometimes self-righteous sneer, he ridicules those who question this simple, if powerful, idea.

I've watched Declan's list for some time. For a brief time I watched the discussion part of the list as well. But the most striking feature about this list to me is the slow emergence of a new topic of concern—one that now gets more posts than "censorship."

This topic is Y2K—the "year 2000 problem" that threatens to disrupt much in our social and economic life as computers discover that the new millennium does not compute. As clearly as Declan's libertarianism comes through, so too does his obsession with Y2K. He is either terrified or perversely amused by what the new millennium will bring to the computer next door.

From the perspective of this book, these twin concerns—with regulation by the state and regulation by code—are quite consistent. Just as we should worry about the bad regulations of law, so too should we worry about the bad regulations of code. And from the perspective of this book, Y2K is our first real crisis in code. It is the first time that the culture as a whole will have to confront the environmental damage done by shortsighted coders. Like shortsighted lawmakers, they have created a crisis whose proportions we cannot yet see.

But from the perspective of Declan's libertarianism, these twin concerns are harder to reconcile. Y2K is the product of a certain kind of libertarianism. It is the product of not thinking through the regulation of code, and of law not properly holding coders responsible for their code. Thousands of coders went about their work thinking their actions were simply their own. The culture and the legal system essentially treated those actions as those of individuals acting alone. Now, years after the first bad code was compiled, we are faced with a kind of environmental disaster: we are surrounded by code that in critical and unpredictable ways will misfire—at a minimum causing the economy millions of dollars, and under some doomsday scenarios costing much worse damage.

It is a lack of a certain kind of regulation that produced the Y2K problem, not too much regulation. An overemphasis on the private got us here, not an overly statist federal government. Were the tort system better at holding producers responsible for the harms they create, code writers and their employers would have been more concerned with the harm their code would create. Were contract law not so eager to allow liability in economic transactions to be waived, the licenses that absolved the code writers of any potential liability from bad code would not have induced an even greater laxity in what these code writers were producing. And were the intellectual property system more concerned with capturing and preserving knowledge than with allowing private actors to capture and preserve profit, we might have had a copyright system that required the lodging of source code with the government before the protection of copyright was granted, thus creating an incentive to preserve source code and hence create a resource that does not now exist but that we might have turned to in undoing the consequences of this bad code. If in all these ways government had been different, the problems of Y2K would have been different as well.[1]

Y2K is just one example of a more general point that has been at the core of this book. We've had technology in our lives forever, and people have written about the consequences of technology for society since there has been technology. But this continuity should not blind us to an important disconnect we are about to see. Code may be only a difference in degree, but a difference in degree at some point becomes a difference in kind. The unintended consequence of private coding behavior is a time-bomb set to explode over the next year or so. The Y2K problem should awaken us to other time-bombs in our lives—that is, to the general effect that code will have on our lives.

For here is a reality that all this "code talk" obscures. By speaking as I have about the code in cyberspace, by describing how government might regulate that code, by making it seem as if the worlds I am describing were in some sense elsewhere, I have obscured an obvious and critical point that the Y2K crisis makes real: code is not elsewhere, and we are not elsewhere when we feel its effects. As Andrew Shapiro puts it: "Seeing cyberspace as elsewhere . . . misconstrue[s] its legal significance. It . . . keep[s] us from seeing the way that regulatory forces like . . . code, which some say are 'there,' are actually affecting us here."[2]

We live life in real space, subject to the effects of code. We live ordinary lives, subject to the effects of code. We live social and political lives, subject to the effects of code. Code regulates all these aspects of our lives, more pervasively over time than any other regulator in our life. Should we remain passive about this regulator? Should we let it affect us without doing anything in return?

And thus again the odd juxtaposition of Declan's two obsessions. Governments should intervene, at a minimum, when private action has public consequences; when shortsighted actions threaten to cause long-term harm; when failure to intervene undermines significant constitutional values and important individual rights; and when a form of life emerges that may threaten values we believe to be fundamental.

Yet so pervasive is our sense of the failure of government that a writer as intelligent as Declan cannot see the implications of these two great evils that he does so much to report. If we believe that government cannot do anything good, then Declan's plea—that it do nothing—makes sense. And if government can do nothing, then it follows that we should treat these man-made disasters as natural. Just as we speak of the disaster of the West Coast sliding into the Pacific, so too should we speak of a disaster of code sliding us into another dark age. Neither can we do anything about, yet both are great topics for growing audiences.

I've advocated a different response. We need to think collectively and sensibly about how this emerging reality will affect our lives. Do-nothingism is not an answer; something can and should be done.

I've argued this, but not with much hope. So central are the Declans in our political culture today that I confess I cannot see a way around them. I have sketched small steps; they seem very small. I've described a different ideal; it seems quite alien. I've promised that something different could be done, but not by any institution of government that I know. I've spoken as if there could be hope. But Hope was just a television commercial.

The truth, I suspect, is that the Declans will win—at least for now. We will treat code-based environmental disasters—like Y2K, like the loss of privacy, like the censorship of filters, like the disappearance of an intellectual commons—as if they were produced by gods, not by Man. We will watch as important aspects of privacy and free speech are erased by the emerging architecture of the panopticon, and we will speak, like modern Jeffersons, about nature making it so—forgetting that here, we are nature. We will in many domains of our social life come to see the Net as the product of something alien—something we cannot direct because we cannot direct anything. Something instead that we must simply accept, as it invades and transforms our lives.

Some say this is an exciting time. But it is the excitement of a teenager playing chicken, his car barreling down the highway, hands held far from the steering wheel. There are choices we could make, but we pretend that there is nothing we can do. We *choose* to pretend; we shut our eyes. We build this nature, then are constrained by this nature we have built.

It is the age of the ostrich. We are excited by what we cannot know. We are proud to leave things to the invisible hand. We make the hand invisible by looking the other way.

But it is not a great time, culturally, to come across revolutionary technologies. We are no more ready for this revolution than the Soviets were ready for theirs. We, like the Soviets, have been caught by a revolution. But we, unlike they, have something to lose.

A P P E N D I X

In chapter 7, I sketched briefly an argument for how the four modalities I described constrain differently. In this appendix, I want to extend that argument. My hope is to provide a richer sense of how these modalities—law, the market, norms, and architecture—interact as they regulate. Such an understanding is useful, but not necessary, to the argument of this book. I've therefore put it here, for those with an interest, and too much time. Elsewhere I have called this approach "the New Chicago School."[1]

Law is a command backed up by the threat of a sanction. It commands you not to commit murder and threatens a severe penalty if you do so anyway. Or it commands you not to trade in cocaine and threatens barbaric punishments if you do. In both cases, the picture of law is fairly simple and straightforward: don't do this, or else.

Obviously law is much more than a set of commands and threats.[2] Law not only commands certain behaviors but expresses the values of a community (when, for example, it sets aside a day to celebrate the birth of Martin Luther King, Jr.);[3] constitutes or regulates structures of government (when the Constitution, for example, establishes in Article I a House of Representatives distinct from a Senate); and establishes rights that individuals can invoke against their own government (the Bill of Rights). All these are examples of law; by focusing on just one kind of law, I do not mean to diminish the significance of these other kinds. Still, this particular aspect of law provides a well-defined constraint on individuals within the jurisdiction of the law giver, or sovereign. That constraint—objectively—is the threat of punishment.

Social *norms* constrain differently. By social norms, I mean those normative constraints imposed not through the organized or centralized actions of a state, but through the many slight and sometimes forceful sanctions that members of a community impose on each other. I am not talking about patterns of behavior: it may be that most people drive to work between 7:00 and 8:00 A.M., but this is not a norm. A norm governs socially salient behavior, deviation from which makes you socially abnormal.[4]

Life is filled with, constituted by, and defined in relation to such norms—some of which are valuable, and many of which are not. It is a norm (and a good one) to thank others for service. Not thanking someone makes you "rude," and being rude opens you up to a range of social sanctions, from ostracism to criticism. It is a norm to speak cautiously to a seatmate on an airplane, or to stay to the right while driving slowly. Norms discourage men from wearing dresses to work and encourage all of us to bathe regularly. Ordinary life is filled with such commands about how we are to behave. For the ordinarily socialized person, these commands constitute a significant portion of the constraints on individual behavior.

What makes norms different, then, is the mechanism and source of their sanction: they are imposed by a community, not a state. They are similar to law in that, at least objectively, their constraint is imposed after a violation has occurred.

The constraints of the *market* are different again. The market constrains through price. A price signals the point at which a resource can be transferred from one person to another. If you want a Starbucks coffee, you must give the clerk two dollars. The constraint (the two dollars) is simultaneous with the benefit you want (the coffee). You may, of course, bargain to pay for the benefit later ("I'd gladly pay you Tuesday for a hamburger today"), but the obligation is incurred at the time you receive the benefit. To the extent that you stay in the market, this simultaneity is preserved. The market constraint, then, unlike law and norms, does not kick in after you have taken the benefit you seek; it kicks in at the same time.

This is not to say that market transactions cannot be translated into law or norm transactions. Indeed, market transactions do not exist except within a context of law and norms. You must pay for your coffee; if you do not, the law of theft applies. Nothing in the market requires that you tip the waiter, but if you do not, norms kick in to regulate your stinginess. The constraints of the market exist *because* of an elaborate background of law and norms defining what is buyable and sellable, as well as rules of property and contract for how things may be bought and sold. But given these laws and norms, the market still constrains in a distinct way.

The constraint of our final modality is neither so contingent nor, in its full range, so dependent. This is the constraint of *architecture*—the way the world is, or the ways specific aspects of it are. Architects call it the *built environment;* those who don't give out names just recognize it as the world around them.

Plainly some of the constraints of architecture are constraints we have made (hence the sense of "architecture") and some are not. A door closes off a room. When locked, the door keeps you out. The constraint functions not as law or norms do—you cannot ignore the constraint and suffer the consequence later. Even if the constraint imposed by the door is one you can overcome—by breaking it down perhaps, or picking the lock—the door still constrains, just not absolutely.

Some architectural constraints, however, *are* absolute. Star Trek notwithstanding, we cannot travel at warp speed. We can no doubt travel fast, and technology has enabled us to travel faster than we used to. Nonetheless, we have good reason (or at least physicists do) for believing that there is a limit to the speed at which we can travel. As an old T-shirt put it, "186,282 miles per second. It's not just a good idea. It's the law."

But whether absolute or not, or whether man-made or not, we can consider these constraints as a single class—as the constraints of architecture, or real-space code. What unites this class is the agency of the constraint: no individual or group imposes the constraint, or at least not directly. Individuals are no doubt ultimately responsible for much of the constraint, but in its actual execution the constraint takes care of itself. Laws need police, prosecutors, and courts to have an effect; a lock does not. Norms require that individuals take note of nonconforming behavior and respond accordingly; gravity does not. The constraints of architecture are self-executing in a way that the constraints of law, norms, and the market are not.

This feature of architecture—self-execution—is extremely important for understanding its role in regulation. It is particularly important for unseemly or unjust regulation. For example, to the extent that we can bring about effects through the automatic constraints of real-space code, we need not depend on the continued agency, loyalty, or reliability of individuals. If we can make the machine do it, we can be that much more confident that the unseemly will be done.

The launching of nuclear missiles is a nice example. In their original design, missiles were to be launched by individual crews located within missile launch silos. These men would have been ordered to launch their missiles, and the expectation was that they would do so. Laws, of course, backed up the order—disobeying the order to launch subjected the crew to court-martial.[5]

But in testing the system, the army found it increasingly unreliable. Always the decision to launch was checked by a judgment made by an individual, and always that individual had to decide whether the order was to be obeyed. Plainly this system is less reliable than a system where all the missiles are wired, as it were, to a single button on the president's desk. But we might believe that there is value in this second check, that the agency of the action by the soldier ensures some check on the decision to launch.[6]

This is an important consequence of the automatic nature of the constraints of architecture. Law, norms, and the market are constraints checked by judgment. They are enacted only when some person or group chooses to do so. But once instituted, architectural constraints have their effect until someone stops them.

Agency, then, is one distinction between the four constraints. The *temporality* of the constraint—*when* it is imposed—is a second one.

Here I should distinguish between two different perspectives: that of someone observing when a constraint is imposed (the objective perspective), and that of the person who experiences the constraint (the subjective perspective). So far my description of the four constraints in this single model has been from the objective perspective. From that perspective they are quite different, but from a subjective perspective they need not differ at all.

From the objective perspective the difference is between constraints that demand payment up front and constraints that let you play and then pay. Architecture and the market constrain up front; law and norms let you play first. For example, think of the constraints blocking your access to the air-conditioned home of a neighbor who is gone for the weekend. Law constrains you—if you break in, you will be trespassing. Norms constrain you as well—it's unneighborly to break into your neighbor's house. Both of these constraints, however, would be imposed on you *after* you broke into the house. They are prices you might have to pay later.[7] The architectural constraint is the lock on the door—it blocks you *as you are trying* to enter the house. The market constrains your ownership of an air conditioner in the same way—it demands money before it will give you one. From an objective perspective what distinguishes these two classes of constraints is their temporality—when the sanction is imposed.

From a subjective perspective, however, all these differences may disappear. Subjectively, you may well *feel* a norm constraint long before you violate it. You may feel the constraint against breaking into your neighbor's house just at the thought of doing so. Whatever the temporality of the constraint from an objective perspective, you may experience the constraint differently. A constraint may be *objectively* ex post, but experienced *subjectively* ex ante.

The point is not limited to norms. Think about a child and fire. Fire is a bit of real-space code: the consequences are felt as soon as the constraint it imposes is violated. A child learns this the first time he puts his hand near a flame. Thereafter, the child internalizes the constraint of fire before putting his hand in a fire. Burned once, the child knows not to put his hand so near the flame a second time.[8]

We can describe this change as the development of a subjective constraint on the child's behavior. We can then see how the idea extends to other constraints. Think about the stock market. For those who do not shop very much, the constraints of the market may indeed be only the objective constraint of the price demanded when they make a purchase. However, for those who experience the market regularly—who have, as it were, a sense of the market—the constraints of the market are quite different. Such people come to know them as second nature, which guides or constrains their actions. Think of a stockbroker on the floor of an exchange. To be a great broker in that context is to come to know the market "like the back of your hand," to let it become second nature. In the terms that we've used, this broker has let the market become subjectively part of who she is.

Each constraint, then, has a subjective and an objective aspect. Laws are objectively ex post, but for most of us, the fact that a law directs us in a particular way is usually sufficient to make it a subjective constraint. (It is not the objective threat of jail that constrains me from cheating on my taxes; instead, I have made subjective the constraints of the law with respect to taxes. Honest, IRS. This is true.) As a subjective constraint, it constrains us before we act.

For those who are fully mature, or fully integrated, all objective constraints are subjectively effective prior to their actions. They feel the constraints of real-space code, of law, of norms, and of the market, before they act. For the completely immature, or totally alienated, few objective constraints are subjectively effective. They step in the mud and only then learn about the constraint of mud; they steal bread and only then learn about the punishments of the law; they show up at a wedding in cut-offs and only then learn about the scorn of their friends; they spend all their money on candy and only then learn of the constraint of market scarcity. These two types mark out the extremes; most of us are somewhere in between.

The more subjective a constraint, then, the more effective it is in regulating behavior. It takes work to make a constraint subjective. An individual must choose to make it a part of who he or she is. To the extent that the norm is made subjective, it constrains simultaneously with the behavior it regulates.

This points to one final distinction between law and norms, on the one hand, and real-space code, on the other. Law and norms are more efficient the more subjective they are, but they need some minimal subjectivity to be effective at all. The person constrained must know of the constraint. A law that secretly punishes people for offenses they do not know exist would not be effective in regulating the behavior it punishes.[9]

But this is not the case with architecture. Architecture can constrain without any subjectivity. A lock constrains the thief whether or not the thief knows that it is a lock blocking the door. The distance between two places constrains the intercourse between those two places whether or not anyone in those places understands that constraint. This point is a corollary of the point about agency: just as a constraint need not be imposed by an agent, neither does the subject need to understand it.

Architectural constraints, then, work whether or not the subject knows they are working, while law and norms work only if the subject knows something about them. If the subject has internalized them, they can constrain whether or not the expected cost of complying exceeds the benefit of deviating. Law and norms can be made more codelike the more they are internalized. But internalization takes work.

Though I have used language invoking architects, my language is not the language of architects. It is instead stolen, and bent. I am not a scholar of architecture, but I have taken from architecture its insight about the relationship between the built environment and the practices that environment creates.[10] Neither architects nor I take this relationship to be determinative. Structure X does not determine behavior Y. Instead, these forms are always simply influences that can change, and when they are changed, they change the affected behavior.

Like Michael Sorkin, I believe that "meanings inhere in forms, and that the settings for social life can aid its fulfillment." His book *Local Code: The Constitution of a City at 42ºN Latitude* suggests each feature of the model I am describing, including the ambiguity between law and architecture (building codes) and the constitution the two enable. Whatever the source of the content of these codes, he writes, "their consequences are built."[11] This is the feature to focus on.

My suggestion is that if we relativize regulators—if we understand how the different modalities regulate and how they are subject, in an important sense, to law—then we will see how liberty is constructed not simply through the limits we place on law. Rather, liberty is constructed by structures that preserve a space for individual choice, however that choice may be constrained.

We are entering a time when our power to muck about with the structures that regulate is at an all-time high. It is imperative, then, that we understand just what to do with this power. And, more important, what not to do.

NOTES

PREFACE

1. See http://mit.edu/cfp6.

CHAPTER ONE

1. Paulina Borsook, "How Anarchy Works," *Wired* 110 (October 1995): 3.10, available on-line at http://www.wired.com/wired/archive/3.10/ietf.html (visited May 30, 1999), quoting Netlander, David Clark.

2. James Boyle, talk at Telecommunications Policy Research Conference (TPRC), Washington, D.C., September 28, 1997. David Shenk discusses the libertarianism that cyberspace inspires (as well as other, more fundamental problems with the age) in a brilliant cultural how-to book that responsibly covers both the technology and the libertarianism; see *Data Smog: Surviving the Information Glut* (San Francisco, Harper Edge, 1997), esp. 174–77. The book also describes technorealism, a responsive movement that advances a more balanced picture of the relationship between technology and freedom.

3. See Kevin Kelley, *Out of Control: The New Biology of Machines, Social Systems, and the Economic World* (Reading, Mass.: Addison-Wesley, 1994), 119.

4. As Stephen Holmes has put it, "Rights depend upon the competent exercise of . . . legitimate public power. . . . The largest and most reliable human rights organization is the liberal state. . . . Unless society is politically well organized, there will be no individual liberties and no civil society"; "What Russia Teaches Us Now: How Weak States Threaten Freedom," *American Prospect* 33 (1997): 30, 33.

5. This is a dark picture, I confess, and it contrasts with the picture of control drawn by Andrew Shapiro in *The Control Revolution* (New York: Public Affairs, 1999). As I discuss later, however, the difference between Shapiro's view and my own turns on the extent to which architectures enable top-down regulation. In my view, one highly probable architecture would enable greater regulation than Shapiro believes is likely.

6. See "We Know Where You Will Live," Computers, Freedom, and Privacy Conference, March 30, 1996, audio link available at http://www-swiss.ai.mit.edu/~switz/cfp96/#audio.

7. See William J. Mitchell, *City of Bits: Space, Place, and the Infobahn* (Cambridge, Mass.: MIT Press, 1995), 111. In much of this book, I work out Mitchell's idea, though I drew the metaphor from others as well. Ethan Katsh discusses this notion of software worlds in "Software Worlds and the First Amendment: Virtual Doorkeepers in Cyberspace," *University of Chicago Legal Forum* (1996): 335, 338. Joel Reidenberg discusses the related notion of "lex informatica" in "Lex Informatica: The Formulation of Information Policy Rules Through Technology," *Texas Law Review* 76 (1998): 553. I have been especially influenced by James Boyle's work in the area.

I discuss his book in chapter 9, but see also "Foucault in Cyberspace: Surveillance, Sovereignty, and Hardwired Censors," *University of Cincinnati Law Review* 66 (1997): 177. For a recent and powerful use of the idea, see Shapiro, *The Control Revolution.* Mitch Kapor is the father of the meme "architecture is politics" within cyberspace talk. I am indebted to him for this.

8. Mark Stefik, "Epilogue: Choices and Dreams," in *Internet Dreams: Archetypes, Myths, and Metaphors,* edited by Mark Stefik (Cambridge, Mass.: MIT Press, 1996), 390.

9. *Missouri v Holland,* 252 US 416, 433 (1920).

10. Richard Stallman, for example, organized resistance to the emergence of passwords at MIT. Passwords are an architecture that facilitates control by excluding users not "officially sanctioned." Steven Levy, *Hackers* (Garden City, N.Y.: Anchor Press/Doubleday, 1984), 416–17.

CHAPTER TWO

1. See, for example, Stanley Fish, *Doing What Comes Naturally* (Durham, N.C.: Duke University Press, 1989), ch. 17.

2. It is also hypothetical. I have constructed this story in light of what could be, and in places is. But I'm a law professor; I make up hypotheticals for a living.

3. One gets a good sense of the possibilities in this space from a how-to manual; one of my favorites is Bruce Damer's *Avatars!* (Berkeley, Calif.: Peachpit Press, 1998). The range of experiences and the possibilities outlined by Damer don't yet match the hypothetical I have based this section on, but any difference is just a matter of coding.

4. "MUD" has had a number of meanings, originally Multi-User Dungeon, or Multi-User Domain. A MOO is a "MUD, object-oriented." Sherry Turkle's analysis of life in a MUD or MOO, *Life on the Screen: Identity in the Age of the Internet* (New York: Simon & Schuster, 1995), is still a classic. See also Elizabeth Reid, "Hierarchy and Power: Social Control in Cyberspace," in *Communities in Cyberspace,* edited by Marc A. Smith and Peter Kollock (New York: Routledge, 1999), 107. The father—or god—of a MUD named LamdaMOO is Pavel Curtis. See his account in "Mudding: Social Phenomena in Text-Based Virtual Realities," in Stefik, *Internet Dreams,* 265–92. For two magical pages of links about the history of MUDs, see Lauren P. Burka, "The MUDline," available at http://www.apocalypse.org/pub/u/lpb/mud-dex/mudline.html (visited May 30, 1999); and Lauren P. Burka, "The MUDdex," available at http://www.apocalypse.org/pub/u/lpb/muddex/ (visited May 30, 1999).

5. A pareto superior move requires that at least one person be made better off and that no one be made worse off. See Robert Cooter and Thomas Ulen, *Law and Economics,* 2d ed. (Reading, Mass.: Addison-Wesley, 1997), 12, 41–42.

6. Jake Baker's given name was Abraham Jacob Alkhabaz, but he changed his name after his parents' divorce. See Peter H. Lewis, "Writer Arrested After Sending Violent Fiction Over Internet," *New York Times,* February 11, 1995, 10.

7. The seven are comp, misc, news, rec, sci, soc, and talk. See Henry Edward Hardy, "The History of the Net, v8.5," September 28, 1993, available at http://www.grin.net/~cturley/gsezine/GS.WorldView/*HISTORY.OF.THE.NET/ (visited May 30, 1999).

8. I have drawn from Jonathan Wallace and Mark Mangan's vivid account in *Sex, Laws, and Cyberspace* (New York: M&T Books, 1996), 63, though more interesting variations on this story circulate on the Net (I'm playing it safe).

9. See *United States v Baker,* 890 FSupp 1375, 1390 (EDMich 1995); see also Wallace and Mangan, *Sex, Laws, and Cyberspace,* 69–77.

10. See Mike Godwin, *CyberRights: Defending Free Speech in the Digital Age* (New York: Times Books, 1998), 117–32.

11. No doubt the worm would interact with the operation of the machine, as it would interact with, for example, the operating system at least.

12. My example is drawn from Michael Adler, "Cyberspace, General Searches, and Digital Contraband: The Fourth Amendment and the Net-Wide Search," *Yale Law Journal* 105 (1996): 1093; cf. Laura B. Riley, "Concealed Weapon Detectors and the Fourth Amendment: The Constitutionality of Remote Sense Enhanced Searches," *UCLA Law Review* 45 (1997): 281, 325–27. Adler's example provides a nice parallel to Arnold H. Loewy, "The Fourth Amendment as a Device for Protecting the Innocent," *Michigan Law Review* 81 (1983): 1229, 1244—though they reach opposite conclusions.

13. See William J. Stuntz, "The Substantive Origins of Criminal Procedure," *Yale Law Journal* 105 (1995): 393, 406–7.

14. See, for example, Thomas A. Clancy, "The Role of Individualized Suspicion in Assessing the Reasonableness of Searches and Seizures," *University of Memphis Law Review* 25 (1995): 483, 632. "Individualized suspicion . . . has served as a bedrock protection against unjustified and arbitrary police actions."

15. See *United States v Place*, 462 US 696, 707 (1983).

16. James Boyle, *Shamans, Software, and Spleens: Law and the Construction of the Information Society* (Cambridge, Mass.: Harvard University Press, 1996), 4.

17. See Susan Freiwald, "Uncertain Privacy: Communication Attributes After the Digital Telephony Act," *Southern California Law Review* 69 (1996): 949, 951, 954.

18. Cf. John Rogers, "Bombs, Borders, and Boarding: Combatting International Terrorism at United States Airports and the Fourth Amendment," *Suffolk Transnational Law Review* 20 (1997): 501, n.201.

19. See Mitchell Kapor, "The Software Design Manifesto," available at http://www.kei.com/homepages/mkapor/Software_Design_Manifesto.html (visited May 30, 1999); David Farber, "A Note on the Politics of Privacy and Infrastructure," November 20, 1993, available at http://icg.pobox.com/cis590/reading.045.txt (visited May 30, 1999); "Quotations," available at http://www.cs.yorku.ca/~peter/4361/quotes.html (visited May 30, 1999); see also Pamela Samuelson et al., "A Manifesto Concerning the Legal Protection of Computer Programs," *Columbia Law Review* 94 (1994): 2308. Steven Johnson powerfully makes a similar point: "All works of architecture imply a worldview, which means that all architecture is in some deeper sense political"; see *Interface Culture: How New Technology Transforms the Way We Create and Communicate* (San Francisco: Harper Edge, 1997), 44. The Electronic Frontier Foundation, originally cofounded by Mitch Kapor and John Perry Barlow, has updated Kapor's slogan "architecture is politics" to "architecture is policy." I prefer the original.

20. See Steve Silberman, "We're Teen, We're Queer, and We've Got E-Mail," *Wired* (November 1994): 76, 78, 80, reprinted in *Composing Cyberspace: Identity, Community, and Knowledge in the Electronic Age,* edited by Richard Holeton (Boston: McGraw-Hill, 1998), 116.

21. Cf. *United States v Lamb*, 945 FSupp 441 (NDNY 1996).

22. Jed Rubenfeld has developed most extensively an interpretive theory that grounds meaning in a practice of reading across time, founded on paradigm cases; see "Reading the Constitution as Spoken," *Yale Law Journal* 104 (1995): 1119, 1122; and "On Fidelity in Constitutional Law," *Fordham Law Review* 65 (1997): 1469.

23. See *Minnesota v Dickerson*, 508 US 366, 380 (1993) (Justice Antonin Scalia concurring: "I frankly doubt . . . whether the fiercely proud men who adopted our Fourth Amendment would have allowed themselves to be subjected, on mere *suspicion* of being armed and dangerous, to such indignity. . . . ").

CHAPTER THREE

1. My use of the term "architecture" is somewhat idiosyncratic, but not completely. I use it in the sense spoken of by Charles Morris and Charles Ferguson in "How Architecture Wins

Technology Wars," *Harvard Business Review* (March-April 1993): 86. My usage is not quite the usage of computer scientists, except in the sense of a "structure of a system"; see the definition of architecture in Pete Loshin, *TCP/IP Clearly Explained*, 2d ed. (Boston: AP Professional, 1997).

2. J. C. Herz, *Surfing on the Internet: A Nethead's Adventures On-Line* (Boston: Little, Brown, 1995), 2–3.

3. This account of Chicago's network design may well be dated. I can verify its accuracy only up to 1996.

4. The University of Chicago is a private university, so on its own force, the First Amendment would not constrain it. That distinguishes it from a public university, such as the University of California.

5. See Helen Nissenbaum, "Values in the Design of Computer Systems," *Computers and Society* (March 1998): 38.

6. For an extremely readable description, see Loshin, *TCP/IP Clearly Explained*, 15–23; see also Craig Hunt, *TCP/IP Network Administration*, 2d ed. (Sebastopol, Calif.: O'Reilly & Associates, 1998), 8–22; *Trust in Cyberspace*, edited by Fred B. Schneider (Washington, D.C.: National Academy Press, 1999), 29–36.

7. Peter Steiner, cartoon, *New Yorker*, July 5, 1993, 61.

8. See Nicholas Negroponte, *Being Digital* (New York: Alfred A. Knopf, 1995), 18, 179–80.

9. This was the hope, as Justice Sandra Day O'Connor saw it, of the Communications Decency Act (CDA) of 1996. See *Reno v American Civil Liberties Union*, 117 SCt 2329, 2351–57 (1997) (Justice Sandra Day O'Connor concurring in part and dissenting in part). Its objective, in her view, was to require the use of technologies that would make it feasible to zone kids out of parts of the Net where pornography was present. While O'Connor thought the CDA unconstitutional, she suggested that another statute, more narrowly tailored, would pass constitutional review; see Lawrence Lessig, "Reading the Constitution in Cyberspace," *Emory Law Journal* 45 (1996): 869, 883–95; Lawrence Lessig, "The Zones of Cyberspace," *Stanford Law Review* 48 (1996): 1403.

10. In some contexts we call a network architecture that solves some of these "imperfections"—that builds in these elements of control—an intranet. Intranets are the fastest-growing portion of the Internet today. They are a strange hybrid of two traditions in network computing—the open system of the Internet, based on TCP/IP, and the control-based capability of traditional proprietary networks layered onto the Internet. Intranets mix values from each to produce a network that is interoperable but gives its controller more control *over access* than anyone would have over the Internet. My argument in this book is that an "internet" with control is what our Internet is becoming. According to the reporter Steve Lohr ("Netscape Taking on Lotus with New Corporate System," *New York Times,* October 16, 1996, D2), "Netscape executives pointed to studies projecting that the intranet market will grow to $10 billion by 2000." Lohr had also reported ("Internet Future at IBM Looks Oddly Familiar," *New York Times*, September 2, 1996, 37) that "investment in the United States in intranet software for servers, the powerful computers that store network data, would increase to $6.1 billion by 2000 from $400 million this year. By contrast, Internet server software investment is projected to rise to $2.2 billion by 2000 from $550 million."

CHAPTER FOUR

1. Though I do think it is necessarily the case that how commerce is architected affects fundamental values. In this, I agree with David Chaum, who argued early on that payment systems would be crucial for "achieving electronic privacy"; see, for example, "Achieving Electronic Privacy," *Science* (August 1992): 96, 96–97, available at http://ganges.cs.tcd.ie/mepeirce/Project/Chaum/sciam.html (visited May 30, 1999). Payment systems are crucial, and they can be crucially different.

2. As in *United States* v *O'Brien,* 391 US 367 (1968), in which the Court upheld a statute that made burning a draft card a crime. The state interest was in preserving a usable credential.

3. See Ed Krol, *The Whole Internet: User's Guided Catalogue* (Sebastopol, Calif.: O'Reilly & Associates, 1992), 23–25; Loshin, *TCP/IP Clearly Explained,* 3–83; Hunt, *TCP/IP,* 1–22; see also Ben M. Segal, "A Short History of Internet Protocols at CERN," available at http://wwwinfo.cern.ch/pdp/ns/ben/TCPHIST.html (visited May 30, 1999).

4. See Jerome H. Saltzer et al., "End-to-End Arguments in System Design," in *Integrated Broadband Networks,* edited by Amit Bhargava (New York: Elsevier Science Publishing Co., 1991), 30.

5. By "layering" I don't mean that such architectures would change the basic TCP/IP protocol suite. The changes I am describing here are within the application space—not the application layer—of Internet applications. I define "application space" in chapter 8.

6. There is also the disadvantage of securing the password, especially if the password is transmitted as plain text. I am simplifying brutally in my consideration of that issue here.

7. For a description of the privacy and security threats posed by cookies ("essentially nonexistent"), see U.S. Department of Energy, "Computer Incident Advisory Capability," *Information Bulletin, I–034: Internet Cookies,* available at http://www.ciac.org/ciac/bulletins/i–034.shtml (visited May 30, 1999); see also Carl W. Chamberlin, "To the Millennium: Emerging Issues for the Year 2000 and Cyberspace," *Notre Dame Journal of Law, Ethics, and Public Policy* 13 (1999): 131, 173; "Developments in the Law—The Law of Cyberspace: IV. Internet Regulation Through Architectural Modification: The Property Rule Structure of Code Solutions," *Harvard Law Review* 112 (1999): 1634, 1644, n.57; Neil Randall, "How Cookies Work," *PC Magazine Online,* available at http://www.zdnet.com/pcmag/features/cookie/cks1.htm (visited May 30, 1999).

8. Any security problem comes not from the cookies directly (since they are simply passive data) but from applets (smaller applications) that might misuse the data collected. David Wille, in "Personal Jurisdiction and the Internet: Proposed Limits on State Jurisdiction over Data Communications in Tort Cases" (*Kentucky Law Journal* 87 [1999]: 95, 198–99), describes the security dangers with cookies. For a second description of the possible risks from cookies, see Jerry Kang, "Information Privacy in Cyberspace Transactions," *Stanford Law Review* 50 (1998): 1193, 1227–29.

9. Stewart A. Baker and Paul R. Hurst, *The Limits of Trust: Cryptography, Governments, and Electronic Commerce* (Boston: Kluwer Law International, 1998), xv.

10. Ibid.

11. See Hal Abelson et al., "The Risks of Key Recovery, Key Escrow, and Trusted Third-Party Encryption," *World Wide Web Journal* 2 (1997): 241, 245: "Although cryptography has traditionally been associated with confidentiality, other cryptographic mechanisms, such as authentication codes and digital signatures, can assure that messages have not been tampered with or forged."

12. Whitfield Diffie and Martin E. Hellman, "New Directions in Cryptography," *IEEE Transactions on Information Theory* IT–22 (November 1976): 644–54. The idea had apparently been discovered earlier by James Ellis at the British Government Communication Headquarters, but it was not then published; see Baker and Hurst, *The Limits of Trust,* xvii.

13. A symmetric key algorithm is an encryption routine that requires the same key to encrypt and decrypt a message. An asymmetric key algorithm is one that uses a different key to encrypt and decrypt.

14. There are other issues as well; see Bruce Schneier, *Applied Cryptography: Protocols, Algorithms, and Source Code in C,* 2d ed. (New York: Wiley, 1996), 4–5; Conference, "The Development and Practice of Law in the Age of the Internet," *American University Law Review* 46 (1996): 327.

15. For a comprehensive analysis of the legal issues surrounding PKI, see "Public Key Infrastructure Symposium," *Jurimetrics Journal* 38 (1998): 241.

16. "Digital ID Center," available at http://www.verisign.com/products/individual/index.html (visited May 30, 1999).

17. As Baker and Hurst point out, certifications supporting the secure electronic transaction (SET) protocol are not identity certificates; *The Limits of Trust,* 252–53.

18. See A. Michael Froomkin, "Flood Control on the Information Ocean: Living with Anonymity, Digital Cash, and Distributed Databases," *Journal of Law and Communication* 15 (1996): 395, 505.

19. See Gail L. Grant, *Understanding Digital Signatures: Establishing Trust over the Internet and Other Networks* (New York: McGraw-Hill, 1998), 5.

20. Jane Kaufman Winn, "Open Systems, Free Markets, and Regulation of Internet Commerce," *Tulane Law Review* 72 (1998): 1177, 1238.

21. Once again, of course, even that idea is not new. Telephones have been used to sell things since the birth of phones; they too are an open and insecure network. The same was true of telegraphs before them; see Tom Standage, *The Victorian Internet* (New York: Walker & Co., 1998).

22. See Mark A. Lemley and David McGowan, "Legal Implications of Network Economic Effects," *California Law Review* 86 (1998): 479, 484, 552–53.

23. See Richard E. Smith, *Internet Cryptography* (Reading, Mass.: Addison-Wesley, 1997), 218–28.

24. Winn ("Open Systems," 1210) reports that the SET "protocol developed by Visa and MasterCard [is] currently being marketed . . . as a secure Internet application for any type of bank or credit card." See also the introduction to the concept of "secure electronic commerce" on the Visa web site at http://www.visa.com/cgi-bin/vee/nt/ecomm/main.html (visited May 30, 1999).

25. See Winn, "Open Systems," 1210–11.

26. See C. Bradford Biddle, "Legislating Market Winners: Digital Signature Laws and the Electronic Commerce Marketplace," *San Diego Law Review* 34 (1997): 1225, 1242, n.37.

27. See Grant, *Understanding Digital Signatures,* 14; see also Smith, *Internet Cryptography,* 295–319.

28. See Richard L. Field, "1996: Survey of the Year's Developments in Electronic Cash Law and the Laws Affecting Electronic Banking in the United States," *American University Law Review* 46 (1997): 967, 988 (discussing a federal PKI steering committee to "coordinate efforts by executive agencies to use public key digital signature technology"); see also Baker and Hurst, *The Limits of Trust,* 275–83.

29. See Donna N. Lampert et al., "Overview of Internet Legal and Regulatory Issues," *Practicing Law Institute/Patents, Copyrights, Trademarks, and Literary Property* 544 (1998): 179, 220; see also Grant, *Understanding Digital Signatures,* 66–93.

30. In the United States mandated IDs are extremely rare. It was not until the late 1950s that citizens returning from abroad were required to carry a passport; see David Brin, *The Transparent Society: Will Technology Force Us to Choose Between Privacy and Freedom?* (Cambridge, Mass.: Perseus Books, 1998), 68.

31. There are many digital certificate vendors serving as certificate authorities. The more well-known include VeriSign (www.verisign.com), Thawte (www.thawte.com), GTE's CyberTrust (www.cybertrust.gte.com), Entrust (www.entrust.com), Frontier Technologies (www.frontiertech.com), and Xcert (www.xcert.com). Some are tailored to a particular industry, such as TradeWave (www.tradewave.com), and some are region-specific, such as KeyWitness (www.keywitness.ca) in Canada and BelSign International (www.belsign.be) in Europe. Network Solutions has teamed up with VeriSign so that anyone who registers his or her domain name has an option to obtain a digital server certificate from VeriSign; see "Our

Partners," available at http://www.netsol.com/partners/ (visited May 30, 1999). For a more exhaustive list of certificate authorities, see "The PKI Page," available at http://www.pca.dfn.de/eng/team/ske/pem-dok (visited May 30, 1999).

CHAPTER 5

1. See generally *Trust in Cyberspace,* edited by Fred B. Schneider (Washington, D.C.: National Academy Press, 1999), 27–29.

2. See Katie Hafner and Matthew Lyon, *Where Wizards Stay Up Late: The Origins of the Internet* (New York: Simon & Schuster, 1996), 62–63.

3. Communications Assistance for Law Enforcement Act, Public Law 103–414, 108 Stat 4279, 47 USC § 1001 et seq., and in scattered sections of 18 USC.

4. See Richard A. Posner, "The Cost of Rights: Implications for Central and Eastern Europe—and for the United States," *Tulsa Law Journal* 32 (1996): 1, 7–9; cf. William J. Stuntz, "The Uneasy Relationship Between Criminal Procedure and Criminal Justice," *Yale Law Journal* 107 (1997): 1, 4.

5. "Without such limits, the government's natural incentive is to evade or exploit the procedural civil-criminal line by changing the substantive civil-criminal line"; Stuntz's point, made earlier, is about overcriminalization, not increased punishments; see William J. Stuntz, "Substance, Process, and the Civil-Criminal Line," *Journal of Contemporary Legal Issues* 7 (1996): 1.

6. From an economic perspective, this kind of regulation makes sense if it is the cheapest means to a social end. Obviously, if the government simply mandated this change in architecture, it would be inexpensive for the government. What is interesting about the act is its mandate that the government pay for the change in architecture. The government is thus internalizing the costs of change, and we might think about this as a useful technique to ensure that social value is increased by this type of regulatory technique. Put another way: the government is "taking" the regulatory power of the telephone network's code, and as is generally true with takings, it might make sense to require that this taking be funded by the government.

7. As of this writing, the proposals are still being reviewed; see John Hanchette, "'Big Brother' Going Too Far?: Privacy Rights Eroding, Critics Say," *Florida Today,* February 15, 1999, 10A, available at 1999 WL 7000142.

8. See Center for Democracy and Technology, "FBI Seeks to Impose Surveillance Mandates on Telephone System; Balanced Objectives of 1994 Law Frustrated: Status Report," March 4, 1999, available at http://www.cdt.org/digi_tele/status.html (visited May 30, 1999).

9. For a good description of the Audio Home Recording Act of 1992, see Christine C. Carlisle, "Recent Development: The Audio Home Recording Act of 1992," *Journal of Intellectual Property Law* 1 (1994): 335, 336–38. For an analysis of the act and its effect on copyright, see Joel L. McKuin, "Home Audio Taping of Copyrighted Works and the Audio Home Recording Act of 1992: A Critical Analysis," *Hastings Communications and Entertainment Law Journal* 16 (1994): 311.

10. See Audio Home Recording Act, 17 USC § 1002 (1994) (requiring the serial copy management system); see also U.S. Department of Commerce, *Intellectual Property and the National Information Infrastructure: Report of the Working Group on Intellectual Property Rights* (Washington, D.C.: Information Infrastructure Task Force, 1995), 179, 189–90.

11. See 47 CFR § 15.120; see also Telecommunications Act of 1996 Pub.L. 104–104, § 551, 110 Stat. 56, 139–42 (1996), 47 USC § 303 (1998) (providing for study and implementation of video blocking devices and rating systems).

12. For a review of the evidence considered, see U.S. Senate Committee on Commerce, Subcommittee on Communications, *Hearings on Violence on Television,* 93d Cong., 2d sess.

(1974); U.S. Senate Committee on Commerce, Subcommittee on Communications, *Hearings in Review of Policy Matters of Federal Communications Commission and Inquiry into Crime and Violence on Television and a Proposed Study Thereof by the Surgeon General,* 91st Cong., 1st sess., pt. 2 (1969); see also Surgeon General's Scientific Advisory Committee on Television and Social Behavior, *Television and Growing Up: The Impact of Televised Violence: Report to the Surgeon General* (Washington, D.C.: U.S. Government Printing Office, 1972); Matthew L. Spitzer, *Seven Dirty Words and Six Other Stories* (New Haven, Conn.: Yale University Press, 1986), 95–118; *Television and Social Behavior: Media Content and Control,* edited by George Comstock and Eli A. Rubinstein (1972); George Comstock, "Television and American Social Institutions," in *Children and Television,* 3d ed., edited by John C. Wright and Aletha C. Huston (1983), 27; George Comstock, "Violence in Television Content: An Overview," in *National Institute of Mental Health: Television and Behavior: Scientific Progress and Implications for the Eighties: Technical Reviews* 2 (1982), 110; Harry T. Edwards and Mitchell N. Berman, "Regulating Violence on Television," *Northwestern University Law Review* 89 (1995): 1487, 1535; E. Barrett Prettyman Jr. and Lisa A. Hook, "The Control Of Media-Related Imitative Violence," *Federal Communications Law Journal* 38 (1987): 317.

13. See *Red Lion Broadcasting Company v Federal Communications Commission,* 395 US 367 (1969) (ruling that the FCC's orders requiring radio stations to provide time for response to personal attack do not violate the First Amendment); see also *Turner Broadcasting System, Inc., v Federal Communications Commission,* 512 US 622, 637–38 (1994). But see *Denver Area Educational Telecommunications Consortium, Inc. v Federal Communications Commission,* 518 US 727 (1996) (ruling that provisions permitting cable operator to filter content on leased access channels are consistent with First Amendment, but that similar provisions with regard to public access channels are not).

14. Increasingly the opinion is that the rationale behind *Red Lion* (scarcity of spectrum justifies certain regulation) is no longer valid; see Roxana Wizorek, "Children's Television: The FCC's Attempt to Educate America's Children May Force the Supreme Court to Reconsider the *Red Lion* Rationale," *Catholic University Law Review* 47 (1997): 153, 182–86; but see Laurence H. Winer, "The Red Lion of Cable, and Beyond?–*Turner Broadcasting v FCC*," *Cardozo Arts and Entertainment Law Journal* 15 (1997): 1, 21–25 (arguing *Turner* may revive gatekeeper aspect of *Red Lion*).

15. The consequence of an efficient v-chip on most televisions would be the removal of the standard justification for regulating content on broadcasting. If users can self-filter, then the FCC need not do it for them; see Peter Huber, *Law and Disorder in Cyberspace: Abolish the FCC and Let Common Law Rule the Telecosm* (New York: Oxford University Press, 1997), 172–73.

16. For a good discussion of the Clipper controversy, see Laura J. Gurak, *Persuasion and Privacy in Cyberspace: The Online Protests over Lotus Marketplace and the Clipper Chip* (New Haven, Conn.: Yale University Press, 1997), 32–43. For a sample of various views, see Kirsten Scheurer, "The Clipper Chip: Cryptography Technology and the Constitution," *Rutgers Computer and Technology Law Journal* 21 (1995): 263; cf. Howard S. Dakoff, "The Clipper Chip Proposal: Deciphering the Unfounded Fears That Are Wrongfully Derailing Its Implementation," *John Marshall Law Review* 29 (1996): 475. "Clipper was adopted as a federal information-processing standard for voice communication" in 1994; see Gurak, *Persuasion And Privacy in Cyberspace,* 125.

17. See Electronic Frontier Foundation (EFF), *Cracking DES: Secrets of Encryption Research, Wiretap Politics, and Chip Design* (Sebastopol, Calif.: Electronic Frontier Foundation, 1998), ch. 1.

18. For a good summary of the Clipper scheme, see Baker and Hurst, *The Limits of Trust,* 15–18; A. Michael Froomkin, "The Metaphor Is the Key: Cryptography, the Clipper Chip, and the Constitution," *University of Pennsylvania Law Review* 143 (1995): 709, 752–59. For a more technical discussion, see Bruce Schneier, *Applied Cryptography: Protocols, Algorithms, and Source Code in C,* 2d ed. (New York: Wiley, 1996): 591–93.

19. See Field, "1996: Survey of the Year's Developments in Electronic Cash Law . . . ," 967, 993, n.192.

20. See A. Michael Froomkin, "It Came from Planet Clipper: The Battle over Cryptographic Key 'Escrow,'" *University of Chicago Legal Forum* 1996 (1996): 15, 32.

21. This was the purpose of the proposed Oxley-Manton Amendment to the Security and Freedom Through Encryption (SAFE) Act of 1997, NR 695, 105th Cong., 1st sess. Baker and Hurst (*The Limits of Trust*, 21–22) note that "1997 saw remarkable change in the nature of the encryption debate. The beginning of the legislative session saw industry pushing for export liberalization and the closing weeks saw industry defending against domestic controls."In 1996 the government implemented a policy to allow firms to export encryption technologies using the government's DES (digital encryption standard) so long as a key recovery system is built in; see EFF, *Cracking DES*, 1–4–1–5. As EFF's "Cracking DES" project makes clear, however, DES is an unreliable encryption standard.There was some hope for the government's encryption policy after the 1996 publication of the National Research Council's report, the product of a committee appointed by the NRC to study national cryptography policy. The committee, chaired by University of Chicago Law Professor Kenneth Dam, was made up of major leaders in both the industrial and research sectors. The report's conclusions were clear—and damning for the government's anti-encryption policy. The report argued strongly for liberalization of encryption regulations; see *Cryptography's Role in Securing the Information Society*, edited by Kenneth W. Dam and Herbert S. Lin (Washington, D.C.: National Academy Press, 1996). Some believed that the report would have a significant effect, but there were doubts early on. As Froomkin says ("It Came from Planet Clipper," 69), the battle is far from over.

22. This is one reading of the decision in *Bernstein v U.S. Department of Justice*, 176 F3d 1132 (9th Cir 1999). There were dissents from the view of the rights of programmers (Judge Thomas Nelson: "I am still inevitably led to conclude that encryption source code is more like conduct than speech"). See also Laura M. Pilkington, "First and Fifth Amendment Challenges to Export Controls on Encryption: Bernstein and Karn," *Santa Clara Law Review* 37 (1996): 159, 210; Thinh Nguyen, "Cryptography, Export Controls, and the First Amendment in *Bernstein v U.S. Department of Justice*," *Harvard Journal of Law and Technology* 10 (1997): 667, 677–78; in "Cryptic Controversy: U.S. Government Restrictions on Cryptography Exports and the Plight of Philip Zimmermann," *Georgia State University Law Review* 13 (1997): 581, 603). Ronald J. Stay claims that the right to speak cryptographically is supported as much as the right to speak Navajo.

23. The idea was suggested in the Clinton administration's 1995 White Paper; see Pamela Samuelson, "Regulation of Technologies to Protect Copyrighted Works," *Communications of the ACM* [Association for Computing Machinery] 39 (1996): 17.

24. Digital Millennium Copyright Act, Public Law 105–304, 112 Stat 2860 (1998).

25. Former Attorney General Richard Thornburgh, for example, has called a national ID card "an infringement on rights of Americans"; see Ann Devroy, "Thornburgh Rules Out Two Gun Control Options; Attorney General Objects to Registration Card for Gun Owners, National Identification Card," *Washington Post*, June 29, 1989, A41. The Immigration Reform and Control Act of 1986 (Public Law 99–603, 100 Stat 3359 [1986], 8 USC § 1324a[c] [1988]) eschews it: "Nothing in this section shall be construed to authorize directly or indirectly, the issuance or use of national identification cards or the establishment of national identification cards." Given the power of the network to link data, however, this seems to me an empty protection.

26. Notice that this would be an effective end-run around the protections that the Court recognized in *Reno v American Civil Liberties Union*, 117 SCt 2329 (1997). There are many "activities" on the Net that Congress could easily regulate (such as gambling). Regulation of

these activities could require IDs before access to these activities would be permitted. To the extent that such regulation increases the incidence of IDs on the Net, other speech-related access conditions would become easier to justify.

27. Arthur Cordell and T. Ran Ide have proposed the consideration of a bit tax; see Arthur J. Cordell et al., *The New Wealth of Nations: Taxing Cyberspace* (Toronto: Between the Lines, 1997). Their arguments are compelling from the perspective of social justice and economics, but what they do not account for is the architecture that such a taxing system would require. A Net architected to meter a bit tax could be architected to meter just about anything.

28. Countries with such a requirement include Argentina, Australia, Belgium, Greece, Italy, and Switzerland; see Richard L. Hasen, "Law, Economics, and Norms: Voting Without Law?" *University of Pennsylvania Law Review* 144 (1996): 2135.

29. See Baker and Hurst, *The Limits of Trust*, 255–73.

30. See the description in Scott Bradner, "The Internet Engineering Task Force," in *Open Sources: Voices from the Open Source Revolution*, edited by Chris DiBona et al. (Sebastopol, Calif.: O'Reilly & Associates, 1999).

31. Michael Froomkin makes a similar point: "Export control rules have had an effect on the domestic market for products with cryptographic capabilities such as e-mail, operating systems, and word processors. Largely because of the ban on export of strong cryptography, there is today no strong mass-market standard cryptographic product within the U.S. even though a considerable mathematical and programming base is fully capable of creating one"; "It Came from Planet Clipper," 19.

32. See "Network Associates and Key Recovery," available at http://www.nai.com/products/security/key.asp (visited May 30, 1999).

33. Cisco has developed products that incorporate the use of network-layer encryption through the IP Security (IPSec) protocol. For a brief discussion of IPSec, see Cisco Systems, Inc., "IP Security–IPSec Overview," available at http://www.cisco.com/warp/public/732/Security/ipsec_ov.htm (visited May 30, 1999). For a more extensive discussion, see Cisco Systems, Inc., "Cisco IOS Software Feature: Network-Layer Encryption—White Paper," available at http://www.cisco.com/warp/public/cc/cisco/mkt/security/encryp/tech/encrp_wp.htm (visited May 30, 1999); Cisco Systems, Inc. "IPSec—White Paper," available at http://www. cisco.com/warp/public/cc/cisco/mkt/security/encryp/tech/ipsec_wp.htm (visited May 30, 1999); see also Dawn Bushaus, "Encryption Can Help ISPs Deliver Safe Services," *Tele.Com.* March 1, 1997; Beth Davis and Monua Janah, "Cisco Goes End-to-End," *Information Week,* February 24, 1997, 22.

34. See Internet Architectural Board statement on "private doorbell" encryption, available at http://www.ietf.org/mail-archive/ietf-announce/msg01937.html (visited May 31, 1999).

35. Little, but not nothing. Through conditional spending grants, the government was quite effective initially in increasing Net participation, and it was effective in resisting the development of encryption technologies; see Whitfield Diffie and Susan Eva Landau, *Privacy on the Line: The Politics of Wiretapping and Encryption* (Cambridge, Mass.: MIT Press, 1998). Steven Levy tells of a more direct intervention. When Richard Stallman refused to password-protect the MIT AI (artificial intelligence) machine, the Department of Defense threatened to take the machine off the Net unless the architectures were changed to restrict access. For Stallman, this was a matter of high principle; for the Department of Defense, it was business as usual; see Steven Levy, *Hackers: Heroes of the Computer Revolution* (Garden City, N.Y.: Anchor Press/Doubleday, 1984), 417–18.

36. See Minnesota Statute §§ 609.75, subd. 2–3, 609.755(1) (1994), making it a misdemeanor to place a bet unless done pursuant to an exempted, state-regulated activity, such as licensed charitable gambling or the state lottery. Internet gambling organizations are not exempted.

37. See Scott M. Montpas, "Gambling Online: For a Hundred Dollars, I Bet You Government Regulation Will Not Stop the Newest Form of Gambling," *University of Dayton Law Review* 22 (1996): 163.

38. Or at least it could work like this. Depending on the design, it could reveal much more.

39. See 18 USC § 1955 (regulating businesses, defining interstate "illegal gambling" as gambling that occurs in a state in which it is illegal).

40. See *Biometrics: Personal Identification in Networked Society,* edited by Anil Jain, Ruud Bolle, and Sharath Pankanti (Boston: Kluwer Academic Publishers, 1999); see also Amanda Lang in "Mytec Braced for Lucent's Challenge," *Financial Post* (Toronto), May 15, 1997, 6. At a conference where these technologies were described, a participant recalled a question he had asked the manufacturer of a device that identified people based on their hand: "Does it have to be a live hand?" The company representative turned white. "No," was the response.

41. On virtual private networks, see Smith, *Internet Cryptography,* chs. 6, 7; on biometric techniques for security, see *Trust in Cyberspace,* edited by Fred B. Schneider (Washington, D.C.: National Academy Press, 1999), 123–24, 133–34.

42. Roberto Mangabeira Unger, *Social Theory: Its Situation and Its Task* (New York: Cambridge University Press, 1987).

43. In Bruce Ackerman, *Social Justice in the Liberal State* (New Haven, Conn.: Yale University Press, 1980), the core analytic device is dialogue: every assertion of power is met with a demand for justification.

44. Mitchell, *City of Bits,* 112.

45. Brin, *The Transparent Society,* 324.

CHAPTER 6

1. Mike Godwin, *Cyber Rights: Defending Free Speech in the Digital Age* (New York: Times Books, 1998), 15. See also Esther Dyson, *Release 2.0: A Design for Living in the Digital Age* (New York: Broadway Books, 1997), who asserts: "Used right, the Internet can be a powerful enabling technology fostering the development of communities because it supports the very thing that creates a community—human interaction" (32); see also Stephen Doheny-Farina, *The Wired Neighborhood* (New Haven, Conn.: Yale University Press, 1996), 121–37. For a recent and important collection examining community in cyberspace, see Marc A. Smith and Peter Kollock, *Communities in Cyberspace* (New York: Routledge, 1999). The collection ranges across the social issues of community, including "social order and control," "collective action," "community structure and dynamics," and "identity." The same relationship between architecture and norms assumed in this chapter guides much of the analysis in Smith and Kollock's collection.

2. The newest "communitarian" on the Net might be business. A number of influential works have argued that the key to success with online businesses is the development of "virtual communities"; see, for example, Larry Downes and Chunka Mui, *Unleashing the Killer App: Digital Strategies for Market Dominance* (Boston: Harvard Business School Press, 1998), 101–9; John Hagel and Arthur G. Armstrong, *Net Gain: Expanding Markets Through Virtual Communities* (Boston: Harvard Business School Press, 1997).

3. For a detailed study of Internet demographics, see Matrix Information and Directory Services, "Internet Demographics: The Third MIDS Internet Demographic Survey" (MIDS ids3, October 1995), available at http://www.mids.org/ids3/index.html (visited May 30, 1999).

4. For a great sense of how it was, see the articles by Rheingold, Barlow, Bruckman, and Ramo in part 4 of Richard Holeton, *Composing Cyberspace: Identity, Community, and Knowl-*

edge in the Electronic Age (Boston: McGraw-Hill, 1998). Howard Rheingold's book (the first chapter of which is excerpted in Holeton's book) is also an early classic; see *The Virtual Community: Homesteading on the Electronic Frontier* (Reading, Mass.: Addison-Wesley, 1993). Stacy Horn's book is a brilliant text taken more directly from the interchange (and more) online; see *Cyberville: Clicks, Culture, and the Creation of an Online Town* (New York: Warner Books, 1998).

5. For an excellent description, see Jonathan Zittrain, "The Rise and Fall of Sysopdom," *Harvard Journal of Law and Technology* 10 (1997): 495.

6. As Steven Johnson puts it: "In theory, these are examples of architecture and urban planning, but in practice they are bound up in broader issues: each design decision echoes and amplifies a set of values, an assumption about the larger society that frames it"; *Interface Culture: How New Technology Transforms the Way We Create and Communicate* (San Francisco: Harper, 1997), 44. See also Nelson Goodman, "How Buildings Mean," in *Reconceptions in Philosophy and Other Arts and Sciences*, edited by Nelson Goodman and Catherine Z. Elgin (London: Routledge, 1988), 31–48.

7. Cf. Godwin, *Cyber Rights:* "If you're face-to-face with someone, you're exposed to countless things over which the other person may have had no conscious control—hair color, say, or facial expressions. But when you're reading someone's posted ASCII message, *everything you see is a product of that person's mind*" (42, italics in original); see also ibid., 44.

8. See Martha Minow, *Making All the Difference: Inclusion, Exclusion, and American Law* (Ithaca, N.Y.: Cornell University Press, 1990), 74–97.

9. See Laura J. Gurak, *Persuasion and Privacy in Cyberspace: The Online Protests over Lotus, Marketplace, and the Clipper Chip* (New Haven, Conn.: Yale University Press, 1997), 4–15. Gurak notes that "pseudonyms, for example, can be used to mask the name of a speaker, so that often it is the ethos of the *texts,* not the character of the speaker, that does or does not convince others." Cf. Lori Kendall, "MUDder? I Hardly Know 'Er!: Adventures of a Feminist MUDder," in *Wired Women: Gender and New Realities in Cyberspace,* edited by Lynn Cherny and Elizabeth Reba Weise (Seattle: Seal Press, 1996), 207. Godwin describes another possibility, as the ASCII channel on the Net shuts down: "Then, perhaps, the world of ASCII communications will become a preserve for the edgy exchanges of tense text maniacs. Like me"; *CyberRights,* 45.

10. This is what economists would call a "separating equilibrium": "players of different types adopt different *strategies* and thereby allow an uninformed player to draw inferences about an informed player's type from that player's actions"; Douglas G. Baird, Robert H. Gertner, and Randal C. Picker, *Game Theory and the Law* (Cambridge, Mass.: Harvard University Press, 1994), 314. William Mitchell argues that the advance back to synchronous communication is not necessarily an advantage: "As much more efficient asynchronous communications systems have become commonplace, though, we have seen that strict synchrony is not always desirable; controlled asynchrony may have its advantages"; *City of Bits,* 5–16.

11. On making the Web accessible, see Judy Brewer and Daniel Dardailler, "Web Accessibility Initiative (WAI)," available at http://www.w3.org/WAI (visited May 30, 1999); cf. "Note: Facial Discrimination: Extending Handicap Law to Employment Discrimination on the Basis of Physical Appearance," *Harvard Law Review* 100 (1987): 2035.

12. See AOL, "About the Company: Profile," available at http://www.aol.com/corp/profile/ (visited May 30, 1999).

13. See Kara Swisher, *Aol.com: How Steve Case Beat Bill Gates, Nailed the Netheads, and Made Millions in the War for the Web* (New York: Times Business, 1998), 65.

14. As stated in AOL's Terms of Service (TOS): "As an AOL member you are required to follow our TOS no matter where you are on the Internet." Some of the other terms of service include the following rules:"Language: Mild expletives and nonsexual anatomical references are allowed, but strong vulgar language, crude or explicit sexual references, hate speech, etc.,

are not. If you see it, report it at Keyword: Notify AOL.Nudity: Photos containing revealing attire or limited nudity in a scientific or artistic context are okay in some places (not all). Partial or full frontal nudity is not okay. If you see it, report it at Keyword: Notify AOL.Sex/Sensuality: There is a difference between affection and vulgarity. There is also a difference between a discussion of the health or emotional aspects of sex using appropriate language, and more crude conversations about sex. The former is acceptable, the latter is not. For example, in a discussion about forms of cancer, the words *breast* or *testicular* would be acceptable, but slang versions of those words would not be acceptable anywhere."Violence and Drug Abuse: Graphic images of humans being killed, such as in news accounts, may be acceptable in some areas, but blood and gore, gratuitous violence, etc., are not acceptable. Discussions about coping with drug abuse in health areas are okay, but discussions about or depictions of illegal drug abuse that imply it is acceptable are not."

15. See Amy Harmon, "Worries About Big Brother at America Online," *New York Times,* January 31, 1999, 1.

16. Swisher, *Aol.com,* 314–15.

17. Ibid., 96–97.

18. See Robert C. Post, *Constitutional Domains: Democracy, Community, Management* (Cambridge, Mass.: Harvard University Press, 1995), 199–267.

19. See *CyberPromotions, Inc. v America Online, Inc.,* 948 FSupp 436 (EDPa 1996) (holding that a company has no free speech right under the United States, Pennsylvania, or Virginia Constitutions to send unsolicited e-mail over the Internet to a competitor's customers).

20. See Elizabeth Reid, "Hierarchy and Power: Social Control in Cyberspace," in *Communities in Cyberspace,* edited by Marc A. Smith and Peter Kollock (London: Routledge, 1999), 109.

21. See Josh Quittner, "Johnny Manhattan Meets the Furry Muckers," *Wired* (March 1994): 92, available at http://www.wired.com/wired/archive/2.03/muds.html (visited May 30, 1999).

22. See Julian Dibbell, "A Rape in Cyberspace," *Village Voice,* December 23, 1993, 36, 37, available at http://www.levity.com/julian/bungle_vv.html (visited May 30, 1999).

23. Ibid.

24. In particular, see Dibbell's extraordinary *My Tiny Life: Crime and Passion in a Virtual World* (London: Fourth Estate, 1998).

25. Ibid., 13–14.

26. If anything, the sexuality of the space invited adolescent responses by adolescents; see Scott Bukatman, *Terminal Identity: The Virtual Subject in Postmodern Science Fiction* (Durham, N.C.: Duke University Press, 1993), 326. On MOOs in particular, see Dibbell, *My Tiny Life.* The challenge for the community was to construct norms that would avoid these responses without destroying the essential flavor of the space.

27. Dibbell, *My Tiny Life,* 24–25.

28. See Haakon (Pavel Curtis), "Petition System Implemented and in Force," message 773 on *social-issues (#7233), LambdaMOO Bulletin Board, May 1, 1993, available at http://vesta.physics.ucla.edu/~smolin/lambda/laws_and_history/ballothistory (visited May 30, 1999).

29. See Haakon (Pavel Curtis), "How to Make a Vote Binding on the Wizards" (first draft), message 511 on *social-issues (#7233), LambdaMOO Bulletin Board, April 8, 1993, available at http://vesta.physics.ucla.edu/~smolin/lambda/laws_and_history/ballothistory (visited May 30, 1999).

30. For a rich account of both the democracy and how it functions, and the implications for self-regulation with a MUD, see Jennifer Mnookin, "Virtual(ly) Law: The Emergence of Law on LambdaMOO," *Journal of Computer-Mediated Communication* 2 (1996): 1.

31. Hafner and Lyon, *Where Wizards Stay Up Late,* 216. "Flaming" is e-mail or other electronic communication that expresses exaggerated hostility; see Gurak, *Persuasion and Privacy in Cyberspace,* 88.

32. Mnookin, "Virtual(ly) Law," 14.

33. One student of mine studied this behavior and concluded that the difference was significant. That study was limited, however, by a relatively small sample. On the question more generally, Gurak reaches a different conclusion about whether cyberspace remedies gender imbalances; *Persuasion and Privacy in Cyberspace*, 104–13.

34. Mike Godwin makes a similar point about the construction of any virtual community: "What most of us will want in the future, I think, is a place where we're known and accepted on the basis of what Martin Luther King Jr. called 'the content of our character.' But without planning, without a deliberate architectural vision about shaping virtual communities—and, most of all, without true freedom of speech—the incoming hordes of cyberspace inhabitants will continue to be alienated, isolated, without any sense of belonging. Virtually homeless"; *Cyber Rights*, 41.

CHAPTER SEVEN

1. Or more precisely, against a certain form of government regulation. The more powerful libertarian arguments against regulation in cyberspace are advanced, for example, by Peter Huber in *Law and Disorder in Cyberspace: Abolish the FCC and Let Common Law Rule the Telecosm*. Huber argues against agency regulation and in favor of regulation by the common law. See also Thomas Hazlett in "The Rationality of U.S. Regulation of the Broadcast Spectrum," *Journal of Law and Economics* 33 (1990): 133, 133–39. For a lawyer, it is hard to understand precisely what is meant by "the common law." The rules of the common law are many, and the substantive content has changed. There is a common law process, which lawyers like to mythologize, in which judges make policy decisions in small spaces against the background of binding precedent. It might be this that Huber has in mind, and if so, there are, of course, benefits to this system. But as he plainly understands, it is a form of *regulation* even if it is constituted differently.

2. The primary examples are the convictions under the 1917 Espionage Act; see, for example, *Schenck v United States*, 249 US 47 (1919) (upholding conviction for distributing a leaflet attacking World War I conscription); *Frohwerk v United States*, 249 US 204 (1919) (upholding conviction based on newspaper alleged to cause disloyalty); *Debs v United States*, 249 US 211 (1919) (conviction upheld for political speech said to cause insubordination and disloyalty).

3. See, for example, the work of John R. Commons, *Legal Foundations of Capitalism* (1924), 296–98, discussed in Herbert Hovenkamp, *Enterprise and American Law, 1836–1937* (Cambridge, Mass.: Harvard University Press, 1991), 235; see also John R. Commons, *Institutional Economics: Its Place in Political Economy* (1934).

4. The general idea is that the tiny corrections of space enforce a discipline, and that this discipline is an important regulation. Such theorizing is a tiny part of the work of Michel Foucault; see *Discipline and Punish: The Birth of the Prison* (1979), 170–77, though his work generally inspires this perspective. It is what Oscar Gandy speaks about in *The Panoptic Sort: A Political Economy of Personal Information* (Boulder, Colo.: Westview Press, 1993), 23. David Brin makes the more general point that I am arguing—that the threat to liberty is broader than a threat by the state; see *The Transparent Society*, 110.

5. See, for example, *The Built Environment: A Creative Inquiry into Design and Planning*, edited by Tom J. Bartuska and Gerald L. Young (Menlo Park, Calif.: Crisp Publications, 1994); *Preserving the Built Heritage: Tools for Implementation*, edited by J. Mark Schuster et al. (Hanover, N.H.: University Press of New England, 1997). In design theory, the notion I am describing accords with the tradition of Andres Duany and Elizabeth Plater-Zyberk; see, for example, William Lennertz, "Town-Making Fundamentals," in *Towns and Town-Making Principles*, edited by Andres Duany and Elizabeth Plater-Zyberk (New York: Rizzoli, 1991): "The

work of . . . Duany and . . . Plater-Zyberk begins with the recognition that design affects be-havior. [They] see the structure and function of a community as interdependent. Because of this, they believe a designer's decisions will permeate the lives of residents not just visually but in the way residents live. They believe design structures functional relationships, quantita-tively and qualitatively, and that it is a sophisticated tool whose power exceeds its cosmetic at-tributes" (21).

6. Elsewhere I've called this the "New Chicago School"; see Lawrence Lessig, "The New Chicago School," *Journal of Legal Studies* 27 (1998): 661. It is within the "tools approach" to government action (see John de Monchaux and J. Mark Schuster, "Five Things to Do," in Schuster, *Preserving the Built Heritage,* 3), but it describes four tools whereas Schuster de-scribes five. I develop the understanding of the approach in the appendix to this book.

7. See generally *Smoking Policy: Law, Politics, and Culture,* edited by Robert L. Rabin and Stephen D. Sugarman (New York: Oxford University Press, 1993); Lawrence Lessig, "The Reg-ulation of Social Meaning," *University of Chicago Law Review* 62 (1995): 943, 1025–34; Cass R. Sunstein, "Social Norms and Social Roles," *Columbia Law Review* 96 (1996): 903.

8. These technologies are themselves affected, no doubt, by the market. Obviously, these constraints could not exist independently of each other but affect each other in significant ways.

9. The ACLU lists twelve states that passed Internet regulations between 1995 and 1997; see http://www.aclu.org/issues/cyber/censor/stbills.html#bills (visited May 31, 1999).

10. See, for example, the policy of the Minnesota attorney general on the jurisdiction of Minnesota over people transmitting gambling information into the state; available at http://www.ag.state.mn.us/home/consumer/consumernews/OnlineScams/memo.html (vis-ited May 31, 1999).

11. See, for example, *Playboy Enterprises v Chuckleberry Publishing, Inc.,* 939 FSupp 1032 (SDNY 1996); *United States v Thomas,* 74 F3d 1153 (6th Cir 1996); *United States v Miller,* 166 F3d 1153 (11th Cir 1999); *United States v Lorge,* 166 F3d 516 (2d Cir 1999); *United States v Whiting,* 165 F3d 631 (8th Cir 1999); *United States v Hibbler,* 159 F3d 233 (6th Cir 1998); *United States v Fellows,* 157 F3d 1197 (9th Cir 1998); *United States v Simpson,* 152 F3d 1241 (10th Cir 1998); *United States v Hall,* 142 F3d 988 (7th Cir 1998); *United States v Hockings,* 129 F3d 1069 (9th Cir 1997); *United States v Lacy,* 119 F3d 742 (9th Cir 1997); *United States v Smith,* 47 MJ 588 (CrimApp 1997); *United States v Ownby,* 926 FSupp 558 (WDVa 1996).

12. See Julian Dibbell, "A Rape in Cyberspace," *Village Voice,* December 23, 1993, 36.

13. See, for example, "AOL Still Suffering but Stock Price Rises," *Network Briefing,* January 31, 1997; David S. Hilzenrath, "'Free' Enterprise, Online Style; AOL, CompuServe, and Prodigy Settle FTC Complaints," *Washington Post,* May 2, 1997, G1; "America Online Plans Better Information About Price Changes," *Wall Street Journal,* May 29, 1998, B2; see also Swisher, *Aol.com,* 206–8.

14. USENET postings can be anonymous; see Henry Spencer and David Lawrence, *Man-aging USENET* (Sebastopol, Calif.: O'Reilly & Associates, 1998), 366–67.

15. Web browsers make this information available, both in real time and archived in a cookie file; see http://www.cookiecentral.com/faq.htm (visited May 31, 1999). They also per-mit users to turn this tracking feature off.

16. PGP is a program to encrypt messages offered both commercially and free.

17. Encryption, for example, is illegal in some international contexts; see Baker and Hurst, *The Limits of Trust,* 130–36.

18. Mitchell, *City of Bits,* 159.

19. See Katsh, "Software Worlds and the First Amendment," 335, 340. "If a comparison to the physical world is necessary, one might say that the software designer is the architect, the builder, and the contractor, as well as the interior decorator."

20. See *Rummel v Estelle,* 445 US 263, 274 n.11 (1980).

21. Interestingly—and again, a reason to see the future of regulation talk located else-where—this is not true of architects. An example is the work of John de Monchaux and J. Mark Schuster. In their essay "Five Things to Do" and in the collection that essay introduces, *Preserving the Built Heritage,* they describe the "five and only five things that governments can do—five distinct tools that they can use—to implement their" policies (4–5): ownership and operation (the state may own the resource); regulation (of either individuals or institutions); incentives; property rights; information. Monchaux and Schuster's five tools map in a complex way on the structure I have described, but significantly, we share a view of regulation as a constant trade-off between tools.

22. See, for example, James C. Carter, *The Provinces of the Written and the Unwritten Law* (New York: Banks & Brothers, 1889), who argues that the common law cannot be changed (38–41).

23. See, for example, the discussion of wage fund theory in Hovenkamp, *Enterprise and American Law,* 193–96.

24. For a fascinating account of the coming of age of the idea that the natural environment might be tamed to a productive and engineered end, see John M. Barry, *Rising Tide: The Great Mississippi Flood of 1927 and How It Changed America* (New York: Simon & Schuster, 1997).

25. As Roberto Unger puts it, "Modern social thought was born proclaiming that society is made and imagined, that it is a human artifact rather than the expression of an underlying natural order"; *Social Theory,* 1.

26. The idea of a free market was the obsession of the realists, especially Robert Hale; see Barbara Fried, *The Progressive Assault on Laissez-Faire: Robert Hale and the First Law and Economics Movement* (Cambridge, Mass.: Harvard University Press, 1998): "Economic life, like Clark's moral market, was constituted by a regime of property and contract rights that were neither spontaneously occurring nor self-defining, but were rather the positive creation of the state" (2–3). For a modern retelling, see Cass R. Sunstein, *The Partial Constitution* (Cambridge, Mass.: Harvard University Press, 1993), 51–53.

27. Americans with Disabilities Act (ADA) of 1990, 42 USC §§ 12101 et seq. (1994).

28. See Alain Plessis, *The Rise and Fall of the Second Empire, 1852–1871,* (1979) translated by Jonathan Mandelbaum (English-language edition, New York: Cambridge University Press, 1985), 121; "Haussmann, Georges-Eugene Baron," in *Encyclopedia Britannica,* 5th ed., vol. 5 (1992). Steven Johnson criticizes other aspects of the change in *Interface Culture,* 63–64.

29. See Robert A. Caro, *The Power Broker: Robert Moses and the Fall of New York* (New York: Alfred A. Knopf, 1974), 318.

30. Brin, *The Transparent Society,* 293.

31. Consider civil rights in the American South. During the legislative hearings on the Civil Rights Act of 1964, supporters of the bill called before the committee white, southern employers and business owners whose discrimination against blacks was the prime target of the legislation. Some of these employers and businessmen supported the bill because business would improve: the labor pool would increase, causing wages to decrease, and the demand for services would increase—so long, that is, as whites did not shift their custom. This last point is what set the stage for business support for the Civil Rights Act. What business leaders feared was the retaliation of whites against their voluntary efforts to integrate. The Civil Rights Act changed the context to make discrimination against blacks illegal. The businessman could then—without fear of the retaliation of whites—hire or serve a black because of either his concern for the status of blacks or his concern to obey the law. By creating this ambiguity, the law reduced the symbolic costs of hiring blacks. This example demonstrates how law can change norms without government having control over the norms. In this case, the norm of accommodating blacks was changed by giving it a second meaning—the norm of simply obeying the law; see Lessig, "The Regulation of Social Meaning," 965–67.

32. Thurgood Marshall, Esq., oral argument on behalf of respondents, *Cooper v Aaron*, 358 US 1 (1958) (no. 1), in *Fifty-four Landmark Briefs and Arguments of the Supreme Court of the United States: Constitutional Law,* edited by Philip B. Kurland and Gerhard Casper (Washington, D.C.: University Publications of America, 1975), 533, 713.

33. See, for example, Dyson, *Release 2.0:* "Government can play a divisive role vis-à-vis communities. Often, the more government provides, the less community members themselves contribute" (43); in "The Regulation of Groups: The Influence of Legal and Nonlegal Sanctions on Collective Action" (*University of Chicago Law Review* 63 [1996]: 133), Eric A. Posner argues that government help to a community can undermine the community.

34. Cass Sunstein points to seatbelt law as a hypothetical of "government regulation permit[ing] people to express preferences by using the shield of the law to lessen the risk that private actors will interfere with the expression [through normative censure]"; "Legal Interference with Private Preferences," *University of Chicago Law Review* 53 (1986): 1129, 1145. Alternatively, seatbelt laws have been used as the factual basis for critiques of norm sponsorship as ineffective and no substitute for direct regulation; see Robert S. Alder and R. David Pittle, "Cajolery or Command: Are Education Campaigns an Adequate Substitute for Regulation?" *Yale Journal on Regulation* 1 (1984): 159, 171–78. However, the observations may have been premature. John C. Wright, commenting on television's normative content, claims that "we have won the battle on seatbelts, just by a bunch of people getting together and saying, 'It is indeed macho to put on a seatbelt. It is macho and it is smart and it is manly and it is also feminine and smart and savvy and charming to put on a seatbelt'"; Charles W. Gusewelle et al., "Round Table Discussion: Violence in the Media," *Kansas Journal of Law and Public Policy* 4 (1995): 39, 47.

35. The analysis here was in part suggested by Minow, *Making All the Difference: Inclusion, Exclusion and American Law* (1990).

36. See Tracey L. Meares, "Social Organization and Drug Law Enforcement," *American Criminal Law Review* 35 (1998): 191.

37. Eric Posner ("The Regulation of Groups") points to contexts within which government action may have had this effect.

38. See Tracey L. Meares, "Charting Race and Class Differences in Attitudes Toward Drug Legalization and Law Enforcement: Lessons for Federal Criminal Law," *Buffalo Criminal Law Review* 1 (1997): 137.

39. In the mid-1970s the U.S. government sponsored a campaign to spray paraquat (a herbicide that causes lung damage to humans) on the Mexican marijuana crop. This sparked a public outcry that resulted in congressional suspension of funding in 1978. However, following a congressional amendment in 1981, paraquat spraying was used on the domestic marijuana crop during the 1980s. The publicity surrounding the use of paraquat in Mexico is generally believed to have created a boom in the domestic marijuana industry and also an increase in the popularity of cocaine during the 1980s. See generally Michael Isikoff, "DEA Finds Herbicides in Marijuana Samples," *Washington Post,* July 26, 1989, 17. In "Drug Diplomacy and the Supply-Side Strategy: A Survey of United States Practice" (*Vanderbilt Law Review* 43 [1990]: 1259, 1275 n.99), Sandi R. Murphy gives a full history of the laws passed relevant to paraquat; see also "A Cure Worse Than the Disease?," *Time,* August 29, 1983, 20.

40. *Roe v Wade,* 410 US 113 (1973).

41. *Rust v Sullivan,* 500 US 173 (1991).

42. *Maher v Roe,* 432 US 464 (1977).

43. *Hodgson v Minnesota,* 497 US 417 (1990).

44. This distinction between "direct" and "indirect" regulation, of course, has a long and troubled history in philosophy as well as in law. Judith J. Thomson describes this difference in her distinction between the trolley driver who must run over one person to save five and the surgeon who may not harvest the organs from one healthy person to save five dying people; see "The Trolley Problem," *Yale Law Journal* 94 (1985): 1395, 1395–96. This difference is also

known as the "double effect doctrine," discussed in Philippa Foot, "The Problem of Abortion and the Doctrine of the Double Effect," in *Virtues and Vices and Other Essays in Moral Philosophy* (Berkeley: University of California Press, 1978), 19. See also Thomas J. Bole III, "The Doctrine of Double Effect: Its Philosophical Viability," *Southwest Philosophical Review* 7 (1991): 91; Frances M. Kamm, "The Doctrine of Double Effect: Reflections on Theoretical and Practical Issues," *Journal of Medicine and Philosophy* 16 (1991): 571; Warren Quinn, "Actions, Intentions, and Consequences: The Doctrine of Double Effect," *Philosophy and Public Affairs* 18 (1989): 334. The trouble in these cases comes when a line between them must be drawn; here I do not need to draw any such line.

45. Richard Craswell suggests other examples making the same point: the government could (a) regulate product quality or safety directly or (b) disclose information about different products' quality or safety ratings, in the hope that manufacturers would then have an incentive to compete to improve those ratings; the government could (a) allow an industry to remain monopolized and attempt directly to regulate the price the monopolist charged or (b) break up the monopolist into several competing firms, in the hope that competition would then force each to a more competitive price; the government could (a) pass regulations directly requiring corporations to do various things that would benefit the public interest or (b) pass regulations requiring that corporate boards of directors include a certain number of "independent" representatives, in the hope that the boards would then decide for themselves to act more consistently with the public interest.

46. See *New York v United States*, 505 US 144 (1992).

47. Aida Torres, "The Effects of Federal Funding Cuts on Family Planning Services, 1980–1983," *Family Planning Perspectives* 16 (1984): 134, 135, 136.

48. *Rust v Sullivan*, USNY (1990) WL 505726, reply brief, *7: "The doctor cannot explain the medical safety of the procedure, its legal availability, or its pressing importance to the patient's health."

49. See *Madsen v Women's Health Center, Inc.*, 512 US 753, 785 (1994) (Justice Antonin Scalia concurring in the judgment in part and dissenting in part: "Today's decision . . . makes it painfully clear that no legal rule or doctrine is safe from ad hoc nullification by this Court when an occasion for its application arises in a case involving state regulation of abortion" [quoting *Thornburgh v American College of Obstetricians and Gynecologists*, 476 US 747, 814 (1986) (Justice Sandra Day O'Connor dissenting)]).

50. *Shelley v Kraemer*, 334 US 1 (1948).

51. See Herman H. Long and Charles S. Johnson, *People Versus Property: Race-Restrictive Covenants in Housing* (Nashville, Fisk University Press, 1947), 32–33. Douglas S. Massey and Nancy A. Denton point out that the National Association of Real Estate Brokers adopted an article in its 1924 code of ethics stating that "a Realtor should never be instrumental in introducing into a neighborhood . . . members of any race or nationality . . . whose presence will clearly be detrimental to property values in that neighborhood" (citing Rose Helper, *Racial Policies and Practices of Real Estate Brokers* [1969], 201); they also note that the Fair Housing Authority advocated the use of race-restrictive covenants until 1950 (citing Kenneth T. Jackson, *Crabgrass Frontier: the Suburbanization of the United States* [1985], 208); *American Apartheid: Segregation and the Making of the Under Class* (Cambridge, Mass.: Harvard University Press, 1993), 37, 54.

52. See Massey and Denton, *American Apartheid*.

53. Michael Froomkin points to the Clipper chip regulations as another example. By using the standards-setting process for government purchases, the federal government could try to achieve a standard for encryption without adhering to the Administrative Procedure Act. "A stroke of bureaucratic genius lay at the heart of the Clipper strategy. Congress had not, and to this date has not, given the executive branch the power to control the private use of encryption. Congress has not even given the executive the power to set up an escrow system for

keys. In the absence of any formal authority to prevent the adoption of unescrowed cryptography, Clipper's proponents hit upon the idea of using the government's power as a major consumer of cryptographic products to rig the market. If the government could not prevent the public from using nonconforming products, perhaps it could set the standard by purchasing and deploying large numbers of escrowed products"; "It Came from Planet Clipper," 15, 24, 1–33.

54. See http://thestandard.com/articles/display/0,1449,4165,00.html.

55. See "Legal Eagle" (letter to the editor), *The Industry Standard,* April 26, 1999 (emphasis added), available at http://www.thestandard.com/articles/article_print/0,1454,4306,00. html (visited May 30, 1999).

CHAPTER EIGHT

1. I want to sidestep the raging debate about whether to call this movement the free software movement, the open source software movement, or something altogether different. The reality is more important than the label. Activists will work out how best to claim the tradition. My aim is simply to understand the consequences of the struggle.

2. By "closed code" I don't mean anything conspiratorial. I mean simply code that does not reveal its source. A code writer might have many reasons for hiding the source—including economic survival, security, or embarrassment. The crux of my argument is that, regardless of the reason, closed code is not as easily modified as open code.

3. Hunt, *TCP/IP: Network Administration,* 1–22, 6, 8; Loshin, *TCP/IP: Clearly Explained,* 13–17.

4. There is no standard reference model for the TCP/IP layers. Hunt refers to the four layers as the "network access," "internet," "host-to-host transport," and "application" layers; *TCP/IP: Network Administration,* 9. Loshin uses the terminology I follow in the text; *TCP/IP: Clearly Explained,* 13–17. Despite the different moniker, the functions performed in each of these layers are consistent. As with any protocol stack model, data are "passed down the stack when it is being sent to the network, and up the stack when it is being received from the network." Each layer "has its own independent data structures," with one layer "unaware of the data structures used by" other layers; Hunt, *TCP/IP: Network Administration,* 9.

5. Loshin, *TCP/IP: Clearly Explained,* 18.

6. As Hafner and Lyon explain: "The general view was that any protocol was a potential building block, and so the best approach was to define simple protocols, each limited in scope, with the expectation that any of them might someday be joined or modified in various unanticipated ways. The protocol design philosophy adopted by the NWG [network working group] broke ground for what came to be widely accepted as the 'layered' approach to protocols"; *Where Wizards Stay Up Late,* 147.

7. The fights over encryption at the link level, for example, are fights over the TCP/IP protocols. Some within the network industry have proposed that encryption be done at the gateways, with a method for dumping plain text at the gateways if there were proper legal authority—a kind of "private doorbell" for resolving the encryption controversy; see Elizabeth Kaufman and Roszel Thomsen II, "The Export of Certain Networking Encryption Products Under ELAs," available at http://www.cisco.com/warp/public/779/govtaff/policy/paper/ paper_index.html (visited May 30, 1999). This has been opposed by the Internet Architectural Board (IAB) as inconsistent with the "end-to-end" architecture of the Internet; see IAB statement on "private doorbell" encryption, available at http://www.ietf.org/mail-archive/ietf-announce/msg01937.html (visited May 30, 1999).

8. See John C. Morley and Stan S. Gelber, *The Emerging Digital Future: An Overview of Broadband and Multimedia Networks* (Danvers, Mass.: Boyd & Fraser Publishing Co., 1996);

Jerome H. Saltzer et al., "End-to-End Arguments in System Design," in *Integrated Broadband Networks*, edited by Amit Bhargava (New York: Elsevier Science Publishing Co., 1991), 30.

9. See Timothy Wu, "*Internet v Application:* An Introduction to Application-Centered Internet Analysis," *Virginia Law Review* 86 (1999).

10. See Hafner and Lyon, *Where Wizards Stay up Late,* 174.

11. A 1994 HTML manual lists twenty-nine different browsers; see Larry Aronson, *HTML Manual of Style* (Emeryville, Calif.: Ziff-Davis Press, 1994), 124–26.

12. See Ibid., 4.

13. Of course, not always. When commercial production of computers began, software was often a free addition to the computer. Its commercial development as proprietary came only later; see Ira V. Heffan, "Copyleft: Licensing Collaborative Works in the Digital Age," *Stanford Law Review* 49 (1997): 1487, 1492–93.

14. Netscape's Communicator is an exception. As I explained, in 1998, the company gave the source code for the product (minus some encryption modules) to Mozilla, which would continue the development of Mozilla as part of the open source movement; see "Mozilla Public License," available at http://www.mozilla.org/NPL/NPL-1_1Final.html (visited May 31, 1999). See the discussion in Robert W. Gomulkiewicz, "The License Is the Product: Comments on the Promise of Article 2B for Software and Information Licensing," *Berkeley Technology Law Journal* 13 (1998): 891, 924.

15. See Amy Harmon, "The Rebel Code," *New York Times Magazine,* February 21, 1999, 34.

16. At the time Linux was developed, the dominant thinking among computer scientists was against a monolithic operating system operating out of a single kernel and in favor of a "microkernel"-based system. MINIX, a microkernel system, was the primary competitor at the time. Torvalds consciously rejected this "modern" thinking and adopted the "traditional" model for Linux; see "The Tanenbaum-Torvalds Debate," in *Open Sources: Voices from the Open Source Revolution,* edited by Chris DiBona et al. (Sebastopol, Calif.: O'Reilly & Associates, 1999), 221–52.

17. Technically, it does not sit in the public domain. Code from these open source projects is licensed. GNU/Linux is licensed under the GNU GPL, which limits the possible use you can make of Linux; essentially, you cannot take the public part and close it, and you cannot integrate the open part with the closed; see Bruce Perens, "The Open Source Definition," in DiBona et al., *Open Sources,* 181–82. But for purposes of future open source development, the code sits in the commons. On the idea and values of the commons, see, for example, Michael A. Heller, "The Tragedy of the Anticommons: Property in the Transition from Marx to Markets," *Harvard Law Review* 111 (1998): 621; Stephen M. McJohn, "Fair Use and Privatization in Copyright," *San Diego Law Review* 35 (1998): 61; Mark A. Lemley, "The Economics of Improvement in Intellectual Property Law," *Texas Law Review* 75 (1997): 989; Mark A. Lemley, "Romantic Authorship and the Rhetoric of Property," *Texas Law Review* 75 (1997): 873; Jessica Litman, "The Public Domain," *Emory Law Journal* 39 (1990): 965; Carol M. Rose, "The Several Futures of Property: Of Cyberspace and Folk Tales, Emission Trades and Ecosystems," *Minnesota Law Review* 83 (1998): 129.

18. See, for example, Stephen Shankland, "Big Blue Gives Green Light to Linux," *CNET News.com,* February 16, 1999, available at http://www.news.com/News/Item/0,4,32476,00.html (visited May 30, 1999); Stephen Shankland, "Big Blue Latches onto Linux," *CNET News.com,* February 18, 1999, available at http://www.news.com/News/Item/0,4,32563,00.html (visited May 30, 1999).

19. Peter Harter, "The Legal and Policy Framework for Global Electronic Commerce," comments at the Berkeley Center for Law and Technology Conference, March 5–6, 1999.

20. As I explain in more detail in chapter 16, transparent modular code would do the same thing as open code. Thus, the code could be closed yet achieve these same objectives.

CHAPTER NINE

1. Justice Holmes himself called the wiretapping a "dirty business"; *Olmstead v United States,* 277 US 438, 470 (1928) (Justice Oliver Wendell Holmes Jr. dissenting).

2. Ibid., 457 (Chief Justice William H. Taft: the obtaining of evidence by wiretaps inserted along telephone wires was done without trespass and thus did not violate the Fourth Amendment).

3. Ibid., 471 (Justice Louis D. Brandeis dissenting; Justices Holmes, Stone, and Butler also filed dissents).

4. There is an extensive debate about the original meaning of the Fourth Amendment and how it should be applied today. For the two camps, see Akhil Reed Amar, "Fourth Amendment First Principles," *Harvard Law Review* 107 (1994): 757; Tracey Maclin, "The Complexity of the Fourth Amendment: A Historical Review," *Boston University Law Review* 77 (1997): 925 (critiquing Amar's argument).

5. See *California v Acevedo,* 500 US 565, 582 (1991) (Justice Antonin Scalia concurring: describing warrant requirement as "riddled with exceptions").

6. See Bradford P. Wilson, "The Fourth Amendment as More Than a Form of Words: The View from the Founding," in *The Bill of Rights: Original Meaning and Current Understanding,* edited by Eugene W. Hickok Jr. (Charlottesville: University Press of Virginia, 1991), 151, 156–57. As many have pointed out, there were not really any "police" at that time in the sense that we understand the term today. The modern police force is a creation of the nineteenth century; see Carol S. Steiker, "Second Thoughts About First Principles," *Harvard Law Review* 107 (1994): 820, 830–34; Stuntz, "The Substantive Origins of Criminal Procedure."

7. See Amar, "Fourth Amendment First Principles," 767; Stuntz, "The Substantive Origins of Criminal Procedure," 400.

8. Indeed, as Professor William Stuntz argues quite effectively, one danger with warrants in general is that judges become lax and yet the product of their work (the warrant) receives great deference in subsequent proceedings; "Warrants and Fourth Amendment Remedies," *Virginia Law Review* 77 (1991): 881, 893.

9. See Stuntz, "The Substantive Origins of Criminal Procedure," 396–406.

10. See *United States v Virginia,* 518 US 515, 566–67 (1996) (Justice Antonin Scalia dissenting: "Closed-minded they were—as every age is . . . with regard to matters it cannot guess, because it simply does not consider them debatable").

11. See Lawrence Lessig, "Fidelity in Translation," *Texas Law Review* 71 (1993): 1165, 1230.

12. *Olmstead v United States,* 277 US 438, 470 (1928), 464–65.

13. Ibid., brief for the Pacific Telephone & Telegraph Company (nos. 493, 532, 533).

14. Ibid., 473 (Justice Louis Brandeis dissenting).

15. "Translation" is not Brandeis's term, though it is a term of the courts. The idea is best captured by Justice Robert H. Jackson in *West Virginia State Board of Education v Barnette,* 319 US 624, 639–40 (1943): Nor does our duty to apply the Bill of Rights to assertions of official authority depend upon our possession of marked competence in the field where the invasion of rights occurs. True, the task of translating the majestic generalities of the Bill of Rights, conceived as part of the pattern of liberal government in the eighteenth century, into concrete restraints on officials dealing with the problems of the twentieth century, is one to disturb self-confidence. These principles grew in soil which also produced a philosophy that the individual was the center of society, that his liberty was attainable through mere absence of governmental restraints, and that government should be entrusted with few controls and only the mildest supervision over men's affairs. We must transplant these rights to a soil in which the laissez-faire concept or principle of non-interference has withered at least as to economic affairs, and social advancements are increasingly sought through closer integration of

society and through expanded and strengthened governmental controls. These changed conditions often deprive precedents of reliability and cast us more than we would choose upon our own judgment. But we act in these matters not by authority of our competence but by force of our commissions. We cannot, because of modest estimates of our competence in such specialties as public education, withhold the judgment that history authenticates as the function of this Court when liberty is infringed."

16. See Robert Post, *Constitutional Domains: Democracy, Community, Management* (Cambridge, Mass.: Harvard University Press, 1995), 60–64.

17. See Lessig, "Fidelity in Translation," 1214–68; Lawrence Lessig, "Translating Federalism: *United States v Lopez,*" *Supreme Court Review* 1995 (1995): 125, 146. For a more sophisticated analysis of how changing technologies in the context of telecommunications is affecting legislation and judicial doctrine, see Monroe E. Price and John F. Duffy, "Technological Change and Doctrinal Persistence: Telecommunications Reform in Congress and the Court," *Columbia Law Review* 97 (1997): 976.

18. So, for example, the translations to support federalism are translations on the right, while the translations to support criminal rights are translations on the left.

19. *Katz v United States,* 389 US 347, 353 (1967).

20. Laurence H. Tribe, "The Constitution in Cyberspace: Law and Liberty Beyond the Electronic Frontier," address at the First Conference on Computers, Freedom, and Privacy, March 26, 1991, reprinted in *The Humanist* (September-October 1991): 15, 20–21.

21. *Katz v United States,* 389 US 347, 351 (1967).

22. As the history of the Fourth Amendment's protection of privacy since *Katz* will attest, the technique used by Stewart was in the end quite ineffectual. When tied to property notions, no doubt the reach of the Fourth Amendment was narrow. But at least its reach went as far as the reach of property. Because "property" is a body of law independent of privacy questions, it was resilient to the pressures that privacy placed on it. But once the Court adopted the "reasonable expectation of privacy" test, the Court could later restrict these "reasonable expectations" in the Fourth Amendment context, with little consequence outside that context. The result has been an ever-decreasing scope for privacy's protection.

23. See Lessig, "Translating Federalism," 206–11.

24. Tribe, "The Constitution in Cyberspace," 15.

25. See Lawrence Lessig, "Reading the Constitution in Cyberspace," *Emory Law Journal* 45 (1996): 869, 872.

26. This example is drawn from *Maryland v Craig,* 497 US 836 (1990).

27. See Tribe, "The Constitution in Cyberspace," 15.

28. "A latent ambiguity arises from extraneous or collateral facts which make the meaning of a written instrument uncertain although the language thereof be clear and unambiguous. The usual instance of a latent ambiguity is one in which a writing refers to a particular person or thing and is thus apparently clear on its face, but upon application to external objects is found to fit two or more of them equally"; *Williston on Contracts,* 3d ed., edited by Walter H. E. Jaeger (Mount Kisco, N.Y.: Baker, Voorhis, 1957), § 627, 898.

29. See *United States v Virginia,* 518 US 515, 566–67 (1996) (Justice Antonin Scalia dissenting).

30. See Bernard Williams, "The Relations of Philosophy to the Professions and Public Life," unpublished manuscript.

CHAPTER TEN

1. Harold Smith Reeves, "Property in Cyberspace," *University of Chicago Law Review* 63 (1996): 761.

2. This in the end was not his conclusion. He concluded instead, not that boundaries should not be protected in cyberspace, but rather that the unconventional nature of cyberspace requires that boundaries be set along nontraditional context-specific lines. This conclusion, Reeves asserts, requires the law to understand both the environment of cyberspace and the interests of those who transact in that space; see ibid., 799.

3. Cf. Yochai Benkler, "Free as the Air to Common Use: First Amendment Constraints on Enclosure of the Public Domain," *New York University Law Review* 74 (1999): 354.

4. Maureen O'Rourke has extended the idea of the technological fences that cyberspace might provide, describing techniques that web sites, for example, might use to control, or block, links from one site to another; see "Fencing Cyberspace: Drawing Borders in a Virtual World," *Minnesota Law Review* 82 (1998): 610, 645–47.

5. See, for example, Stephen Breyer, "The Uneasy Case for Copyright: A Study of Copyright in Books, Photocopies, and Computer Programs," *Harvard Law Review* 84 (1970): 281.

6. Copyright gives other rights as well—such as the right to reclaim an assigned copyright or the right of first sale. For a lucid introduction, see William F. Patry, *Latman's The Copyright Law*, 6th ed. (Washington, D.C.: Bureau of National Affairs, 1986). For something more than lucid, see James Boyle, "Intellectual Property Policy Online: A Young Person's Guide," *Harvard Journal of Law and Technology* 10 (1996): 47.

7. See Richard A. Posner, *Law and Literature*, 2d ed. (Cambridge, Mass.: Harvard University Press, 1998), 389–92 (discussing incentives to write even without copyright).

8. For the real constraint on publication initially was paper, not presses. Before the invention of wood-based paper, paper was produced from cloth. Cloth, however, was extremely expensive. While a persistent myth is that one source for this cloth was Egyptian mummies (Scott D. N. Cook, "Technological Revolutions and the Gutenberg Myth," in *Internet Dreams: Archetypes, Myths, and Metaphors*, edited by Mark Stefik [1996], 75), there is no support for this claim. See Joseph A. Dane, "The Curse of the Mummy Paper," *Printing History* 17 (1996): 18. Nonetheless, the shortage of paper is well established (ibid., 18–19). I am grateful to Consuele Dutschke for help with this history.

9. For a complete and readable account of the transformation in technology, and law's response, see Paul Goldstein, *Copyright's Highway: The Law and Lore of Copyright from Gutenberg to the Celestial Jukebox* (New York: Hill and Wang, 1994).

10. See *Sony Corporation of America v Universal City Studios, Inc.*, 464 US 417, 421 (1984), which, in defining "time-shifting" as using a VTR principally to record a program one cannot view as it is being televised and then to watch it once at a later time, classifies this practice as a fair use of a copyrighted work that does not entitle the copyright holder to any remedy.

11. See Jonathan Evan Goldberg, "Now That the Future Has Arrived, Maybe the Law Should Take a Look: Multimedia Technology and Its Interaction with the Fair Use Doctrine," *American University Law Review* 44 (1995): 919; Mary L. Mills, "New Technology and the Limitations of Copyright Law: An Argument for Finding Alternatives to Copyright Legislation in an Era of Rapid Technological Change," *Chicago-Kent Law Review* 65 (1989): 307; Kenneth P. Weinberg, "Cryptography: 'Key Recovery' Shaping Cyberspace (Pragmatism and Theory)," *Journal of Intellectual Property Law* 5 (1998): 667.

12. Judge Posner usefully distinguishes between changes that might help an individual author and changes that help authors as a class. Some decreased copyright protection for authors as a whole would benefit authors as a whole, since copyright imposes costs on authors (the writing of others is an input to their own future writing); see *Law and Literature*, 389–405.

13. See Michelle Skatoff-Gee, "Changing Technologies and the Expectation of Privacy: A Modern Dilemma," *Loyola University of Chicago Law Journal* 28 (1996): 189, 201–4, who discusses Congress's enactment of the Electronic Communications Privacy Act of 1986 in an effort to update existing law and keep pace with changing technology. But see Sandra Byrd

Petersen, "Your Life as an Open Book: Has Technology Rendered Personal Privacy Virtually Obsolete?," *Federal Communications Law Journal* 48 (1995): 163, who argues that privacy laws in the United States have not kept pace with technological developments.

14. See Esther Dyson, "Intellectual Value," *Wired* (July 1995): 137, who discusses the effect of the new economic environment of the Net on intellectual property. John Perry Barlow ("The Economy of Ideas," *Wired* [March 1994]: 85) asserts that "copyright and patent law was developed to convey forms and methods of expression entirely different from the vaporous cargo it is now being asked to carry."

15. As Nicholas Negroponte puts it, "Most people worry about copyright in terms of the ease of making copies. In the digital world, not only the ease is at issue, but also the fact that the digital copy is as perfect as the original and, with some fancy computing, even better. In the same way that bit strings can be error-corrected, a copy can be cleaned up, enhanced, and have noise removed. The copy is perfect"; *Being Digital* (1995), 58.

16. U.S. Department of Commerce, Task Force—Working Group on Intellectual Property Rights, "Intellectual Property and the National Information Infrastructure: The Report of the Working Group on Intellectual Property Rights," available at http://www.uspto.gov/web/of-fices/com/doc/ipnii/ (visited May 30, 1999, and hereinafter referred to as the White Paper). See also Boyle, "Intellectual Property Policy Online," 66.

17. George Smirnoff III ("Copyright on the Internet: A Critique of the White Paper's Rec-ommendation for Updating the Copyright Act and How the Courts Are Already Filling in Its Most Important Shortcoming, Online Service Provider Liability," *Cleveland State Law Review* 44 [1996]: 197) criticizes the White Paper's lack of completeness, inconsistencies, and appar-ent lack of adequate consideration; see also Pamela Samuelson, "The Copyright Grab," *Wired* (January 1996): 134, 136. By contrast, Gary W. Glisson ("A Practitioner's Defense of the White Paper," *Oregon Law Review* 75 [1996]: 277) argues that the White Paper is neither a mislead-ing summary of the state of intellectual property law nor a proposal for dramatic changes. For an extensive analysis of the copyright issues raised by cyberspace, see Trotter Hardy, "Project Looking Forward: Sketching the Future of Copyright in a Networked World," U.S. Copyright Office final report (1998), available at http://lcweb.loc.gov/copyright/reports (visited May 30, 1999).

18. For a summary of the changes called for by the White Paper, see Bruce Lehman, ad-dress before the Inaugural Engelberg Conference on Culture and Economics of Participation in an International Intellectual Property Regime, reprinted in *New York University Journal of International Law and Politics* 29 (1996–97): 211, 213–15; White Paper, 17.

19. The latest such threat is the anticircumvention provision of the Digital Millennium Copyright Act, which makes it a crime (subject to complex exceptions) to manufacture code to circumvent a copyright protection mechanism, even if the use of the underlying material itself would be a fair use; see Pub.L. 105–304, 112 Stat 2877 (1998) (prohibiting the manufac-ture, importation, or distribution of "devices, products, components" that "defeat technolog-ical methods of preventing unauthorized use").

20. See Barlow, "The Economy of Ideas," 129; see also John Perry Barlow, "Papers and Comments of a Symposium on Fundamental Rights on the Information Superhighway," *An-nual Survey of American Law* 1994 (1994): 355, 358. Barlow argues that "it is not so easy to own that which has never had any physical dimension whatsoever," unlike traditional forms of property. "We have tended to think," he adds, "that copyright worked well because it was physically difficult to transport intellectual properties without first manifesting them in some physical form. And it is no longer necessary to do that."

21. See Mark Stefik, "Shifting the Possible: How Trusted Systems and Digital Property Rights Challenge Us to Rethink Digital Publishing," *Berkeley Technology Law Journal* 12 (1997): 137; Mark Stefik, "Trusted Systems," *Scientific American* (March 1997): 78; Mark Ste-

fik, "Letting Loose the Light: Igniting Commerce in Electronic Publication," in Stefik, *Internet Dreams,* 220–22, 226–28.

22. See Joel R. Reidenberg, "Governing Networks and Rule-Making in Cyberspace," *Emory Law Journal* 45 (1996): 911.

23. In *Shifting the Possible* (142–44), Stefik discusses how trusted printers combine four elements—print rights, encrypted online distribution, automatic billing for copies, and digital watermarks—in order to monitor and control the copies they make.

24. Ibid.

25. David Hackett Fischer, *Albion's Seed: Four British Folkways in America* (New York: Oxford University Press, 1989), 765.

26. See *American Legal Realism,* edited by William W. Fisher III et al. (New York: Oxford University Press, 1993), 98–129; John Henry Schlegel, *American Legal Realism and Empirical Social Science* (Chapel Hill: University of North Carolina Press, 1995). For a nice modern example of the same analysis, see Keith Aoki, "(Intellectual) Property and Sovereignty: Notes Toward a Cultural Geography of Authorship," *Stanford Law Review* 48 (1996): 1293.

27. See Fried, *The Progressive Assault on Laissez-Faire,* 1–28; see also Joel P. Trachtman ("The International Economic Law Revolution," *University of Pennsylvania Journal of International Economic Law* 17 [1996]: 33, 34), who notes that many realists and critical legal theorists have asserted that "private law" is an oxymoron.

28. Judges have also made this argument; see *Lochner v New York,* 198 US 45, 74 (1905) (Justice Oliver Wendell Holmes Jr. dissenting).

29. This is the epistemological limitation discussed in much of Friedrich A. von Hayek's work; see, for example, *Law, Legislation, and Liberty,* vol. 2 (Chicago: University of Chicago Press, 1978).

30. Boyle, *Shamans, Software, and Spleens,* 174.

31. I am hiding a great deal of philosophy in this simplified utilitarian account, but for a powerful economic grounding of the point, see Harold Demsetz, "Toward a Theory of Property Rights," *American Economics Review* 57 (1967): 347.

32. For a wonderfully clear introduction to this point, as well as a complete analysis of the law, see Robert P. Merges et al., *Intellectual Property in the New Technological Age* (New York: Aspen Law and Business, 1997), ch. 1.

33. Thomas Jefferson, letter to Isaac Mcpherson, August 13, 1813, reprinted in *Writings of Thomas Jefferson, 1790–1826,* vol. 6, edited by H. A. Washington (1854), 180–81, quoted in *Graham v John Deere Company,* 383 US 1, 8–9 n.2 (1966).

34. For the classic discussion, see Kenneth J. Arrow, "Economic Welfare and the Allocation of Resources for Invention," in *The Rate and Direction of Inventive Activity: Economic and Social Factors* (Princeton, N.J.: Princeton University Press, 1962), 609, 616–17.

35. For a powerfully compelling problematization of the economic perspective in this context, see Boyle, "Intellectual Property Policy Online," 35–46. Boyle's work evinces the indeterminacy that economics ought to profess about whether increasing property rights over information will also increase the production of information.

36. Some will insist on calling this "property"; see Frank H. Easterbrook, "Intellectual Property Is Still Property," *Harvard Journal of Law and Public Policy* 13 (1990): 108.

37. This is the message of Justice Stephen Breyer's work on copyright, for example, "The Uneasy Case for Copyright."

38. For an extensive and balanced analysis, see William M. Landes and Richard A. Posner, "An Economic Analysis of Copyright Law," *Journal of Legal Studies* 18 (1989): 325, 325–27, 344–46. These authors note that because ideas are a public good—that is, an infinite number of people can use an idea without using it up—ideas are readily appropriated from the creator by other people. Hence, copyright protection attempts to balance efficiently the benefits

of creating new works with the losses from limiting access and the costs of administering copyright protection; copyright protection seeks to promote the public benefit of advancing knowledge and learning by means of an incentive system. The economic rewards of the marketplace are offered to authors in order to stimulate them to produce and disseminate new works (326). See also Posner, *Law and Literature*, 389–405.

39. These limits come from both the limits in the copyright clause, which sets its purposes out quite clearly, and the First Amendment; see, for example, *Feist Publications, Inc. v Rural Telephone Service Co.*, 499 US 340, 346 (1991).

40. The "first sale" doctrine was developed under § 27 of the former Copyright Act (17 USC [1970]) and has since been adopted under § 109(a) of the present Copyright Act; see *United States v Goss*, 803 F2d 638 (11th Cir 1989) (discussing both versions of the Copyright Act).

41. Europeans like to say that "moral rights" have been part of their system since the beginning of time, but as Professor Jane C. Ginsburg has shown with respect to France, they are actually a nineteenth-century creation; see "A Tale of Two Copyrights: Literary Property in Revolutionary France and America," *Tulane Law Review* 64 (1990): 991.

42. Or so it is argued in *Eldred v Reno* (DDC filed January 4, 1999).

43. It is useful to compare the protection that copyright gives to the protection of trade secret law. All of the protection of trade secret law comes, in a sense, from the architectural constraints I have described. One is always permitted, that is, to reverse-engineer to discover a trade secret; see *Kewanee Oil Company v Bicron Corporation*, 416 US 470, 476 (1974): "A trade secret law . . . does not offer protection against discovery by fair and honest means, such as by independent invention, accidental disclosure, or . . . reverse engineering."

44. 86 F3d 1447 (7th Cir 1996); see also Easterbrook, "Intellectual Property Is Still Property," 113–14. For an excellent account of the debate, see Charles R. McManis, "The Privatization (or 'Shrink-Wrapping') of American Copyright Law," *California Law Review* 87 (1999): 173, 183.

45. This is a reference to the recent battle to draft what was originally called the Uniform Commercial Code 2B, and more recently the Uniform Computer Information Transactions Act (UCITA). By essentially ratifying the click-wrap agreement, this code would facilitate online mass consumer contracts governing the sale of "online information." This move has been widely criticized; see "Symposium: Intellectual Property and Contract Law for the Information Age: The Impact of Article 2B of the Uniform Commercial Code on the Future of Information and Commerce," *California Law Review* 87 (1999): 1; Lawrence Lessig, "Pain in the OS," *The Industry Standard*, February 5, 1999, available at http://www.thestandard. com/articles/display/0,1449,3423,00.html (visited May 30, 1999). My criticism is that while the rhetoric of this move is grounded in the "freedom of contract," the code actually does nothing to ensure that the contracting process produces understanding of the terms of the contract by both parties to the contract. The incentives created by provisions like the "Restatement (Second) of Contracts" (§ 211) are not present in the UCITA. UCITA presupposes that if the consumer had a chance to understand, he understands. But from an efficiency perspective, let alone a justice perspective, the consumer is not the cheapest understanding producer. The code simply ratifies the contract that the seller proposes. This is not "freedom of contract," but contract according to whatever the seller says. For a useful analysis, see Walter A. Effross, "The Legal Architecture of Virtual Stores: World Wide Web Sites and the Uniform Commercial Code," *San Diego Law Review* 34 (1997): 1263, 1328–59.

46. See William W. Fisher III, "Compulsory Terms in Internet-Related Contracts," *Chicago-Kent Law Review* 73 (1998). Fisher catalogs public policy restrictions on freedom of contract, which he characterizes as "ubiquitous."

47. An argument is raging about whether, even through law, this modification of the default copyright law should be permitted. Mark A. Lemley has catalogued the provisions of the Copyright Act that are arguably put at risk by contracting behavior; see "Beyond Preemption:

The Law and Policy of Intellectual Property Licensing," *California Law Review* 87 (1999): 111; see also A. Michael Froomkin, "Article 2B as Legal Software for Electronic Contracting—Operating System or Trojan Horse?," *Berkeley Technology Law Journal* 13 (1998): 1023; Michael J. Madison, "Legal-War: Contract and Copyright in the Digital Age," *Fordham Law Review* 67 (1998): 1025; David Nimmer et al., "The Metamorphosis of Contract into Expand," *California Law Review* 87 (1999): 17; Pamela Samuelson, "Intellectual Property and Contract Law for the Information Age: Foreword," *California Law Review* 87 (1999): 1. The questions Lemley raises, however, cannot be easily raised when it is the code that protects the intellectual property interest; Maureen A. O'Rourke, "Copyright Preemption After the ProCD Case: A Market-Based Approach," *Berkeley Technology Law Journal* 12 (1997): 53.

48. See Tom W. Bell, "Fair Use vs. Fared Use: The Impact of Automated Rights Management on Copyright's Fair Use Doctrine," *North Carolina Law Review* 76 (1998): 557, 581–84. Bell argues that technology will prove more effective than fair use in curing the market failure that results when transaction costs discourage otherwise value-maximizing uses of copyrighted work; see also the White Paper observation that "it may be that technological means of tracking transactions and licensing will lead to reduced application and scope of the fair use doctrine" (74).

49. See Bell, "Fair Use vs. Fared Use," 582–84; U.S. Department of Commerce, Task Force—Working Group on Intellectual Property Rights, "Intellectual Property and the National Information Infrastructure," 66 n.228, notes the difficulty of defining the bounds of the fair use doctrine.

50. For a foundational modern work on the nature of fair use, see Wendy J. Gordon, "Fair Use as Market Failure: A Structural and Economic Analysis of the Betamax Case and Its Predecessors," *Columbia Law Review* 82 (1982): 1600. A more recent work by William Fisher ("Reconstructing the Fair Use Doctrine," *Harvard Law Review* 101 [1988]: 1659, 1661–95) considers both the efficiency and utopian goals of copyright law.

51. See *Gibbons v Ogden*, 22 US 1 (1824) (striking down New York's grant of a monopoly of steamboat navigation on the Hudson River as inconsistent with the federal Coasting Act of 1793); *McCulloch v Maryland*, 17 US 316 (1819) (pronouncing that Congress has the power to do what is "necessary and proper" to achieve a legitimate end, like the regulation of interstate commerce).

52. See Bernard C. Gavit, *The Commerce Clause of the United States Constitution* (Bloomington, Ind.: Principia Press, 1932), 84.

53. See *Pensacola Telegraph Company v Western Union Telegraph Company*, 96 US 1, 9 (1877).

54. As one commentator put it near the turn of the century: "If the power of Congress has a wider incidence in 1918 than it could have had in 1789, this is merely because production is more dependent now than then on extra-state markets. No state liveth to itself alone to any such extent as was true a century ago. What is changing is not our system of government, but our economic organization"; Thomas Reed Powell, "The Child Labor Law, the Tenth Amendment, and the Commerce Clause," *Southern Law Quarterly* 3 (1918): 175, 200–201.

55. See Alexis de Tocqueville, *Democracy in America*, vol. 1 (New York: Vintage, 1990), 158–70, on the idea that the framers' design pushed states to legislate in a broad domain and keep the local government active.

56. See *Maryland v Wirtz*, 392 US 183, 201 (1968) (Justice William O. Douglas dissenting: the majority's bringing of employees of state-owned enterprises within the reach of the commerce clause was "such a serious invasion of state sovereignty protected by the Tenth Amendment that it . . . [was] not consistent with our constitutional federalism"); *State Board of Insurance v Todd Shipyards Corporation*, 370 US 451, 456 (1962) (holding that "the power of Congress to grant protection to interstate commerce against state regulation or taxation or to withhold it is so complete that its ideas of policy should prevail") (citations omitted).

57. See Michael G. Frey, "Unfairly Applying the Fair Use Doctrine: *Princeton University Press v Michigan Document Services*, 99 F3d 1381 (6th Cir 1996)," *University of Cincinnati Law Review* 66 (1998): 959, 1001; Frey asserts that "copyright protection exists primarily for the benefit of the public, not the benefit of individual authors. Copyright law does give authors a considerable benefit in terms of the monopolistic right to control their creations, but that right exists only to ensure the creation of new works. The fair use doctrine is an important safety valve that ensures that the benefit to individual authors does not outweigh the benefit to the public"; Marlin H. Smith ("The Limits of Copyright: Property, Parody, and the Public Domain," *Duke Law Journal* 42 [1993]: 1233, 1272) asserts that "copyright law is better understood as that of a gatekeeper, controlling access to copyrighted works but guaranteeing, via fair use, some measure of availability to the public."

58. See Mark Gimbel ("Some Thoughts on the Implications of Trusted Systems for Intellectual Property Law," *Stanford Law Review* 50 [1998]: 1671, 1686), who notes that fair use can be "explained as a method of curing the market failure that results when high transaction costs discourage otherwise economically efficient uses of copyrighted material," and that "because technologies like trusted systems promise to reduce the costs of licensing copyrighted works—thereby curing this market failure—some argue that the doctrine of fair use will for the most part be rendered unnecessary, obviating the need to regulate technologies that undermine it"; Lydia Pallas Loren ("Redefining the Market Failure Approach to Fair Use in an Era of Copyright Permission Systems," *Journal of Intellectual Property Law* 5 [1997]: 1, 7) asserts that under a "narrowed market failure view of fair use, if a copyright owner can establish an efficient 'permission system' to collect fees for a certain kind of use, then the copyright owner will be able to defeat a claim of fair use."

59. Stefik, "Letting Loose the Light," 244.

60. Efficient here both in the sense of cheap to track and in the sense of cheap to then discriminate in pricing; William W. Fisher III, "Property and Contract on the Internet," *Chicago-Kent Law Review* 74 (1998).

61. Julie E. Cohen, "A Right to Read Anonymously: A Closer Look at 'Copyright Management' in Cyberspace," *Connecticut Law Review* 28 (1996): Reading anonymously is "so intimately connected with speech and freedom of thought that the First Amendment should be understood to guarantee such a right" (981, 982).

62. "The freedom to read anonymously is just as much a part of our tradition, and the choice of reading materials just as expressive of identity, as the decision to use or withhold one's name" (ibid., 1012).

63. See Lessig, "Translating Federalism," 125.

64. See *Olmstead v United States* 277 US 438, 474 (1928) (Justice Louis Brandeis dissenting: "Can it be that the Constitution affords no protection against such invasions of individual security?").

65. Peter Huber relies explicitly on the high costs of control in his rebuttal to Orwell's *1984*; see *Orwell's Revenge: The 1984 Palimpset* (New York: Maxwell Macmillan International, 1994). But this is a weak basis on which to build liberty, especially as the cost of networked control drops. Frances Cairncross (*The Death of Distance: How the Communications Revolution Will Change Our Lives* [Boston: Harvard Business School Press, 1997], 194–95) effectively challenges the idea as well.

66. Washington, *Writings of Thomas Jefferson*, 6:180–81.

67. A founding work is David Lange, "Recognizing the Public Domain," *Law and Contemporary Problems* 44 (1981): 147. There are many important foundations, however, to this argument. See, for example, Benjamin Kaplan, *An Unhurried View of Copyright* (New York: Columbia University Press, 1967). Gordon ("Fair Use as Market Failure") argues that the courts should employ fair use to permit uncompensated transfers that the market is incapable of effectuating; see also Wendy J. Gordon, "On Owning Information: Intellectual Property and Restitutionary Impulse," *Virginia Law Review* 78 (1992): 149. In "Reality as Artifact: From

Feist to Fair Use" (*Law and Contemporary Problems* 55 5PG [1992]: 93, 96), Gordon observes that, while imaginative works are creative, they may also comprise facts, which need to be widely available for public dissemination. Gordon's "Toward a Jurisprudence of Benefits: The Norms of Copyright and the Problem of Private Censorship" (*University of Chicago Law Review* 57 [1990]: 1009) is a discussion of the ability of copyright holders to deny access to critics and others; see also Wendy Gordon, "An Inquiry into the Merits of Copyright: The Challenges of Consistency, Consent, and Encouragement Theory," *Stanford Law Review* 41 (1989): 1343.

68. In addition to Boyle, I have learned most from Keith Aoki, Yochai Benkler, Julie Cohen, Niva Elkin-Koren, Peter Jaszi, Mark Lemley, Jessica Litman, Neil Netanel, Margaret Radin, and Pam Samuelson, but no doubt I have not read widely enough. See, for example, Keith Aoki, "Foreword to Innovation and the Information Environment: Interrogating the Entrepreneur," *Oregon Law Review* 75 (1996): 1; in "(Intellectual) Property and Sovereignty," Aoki discusses the challenges to the traditional concept of property that arise from the growth of digital information technology; in "Authors, Inventors, and Trademark Owners: Private Intellectual Property and the Public Domain" (*Columbia-VLA Journal of Law and the Arts* 18 [1993]: 1), he observes the shifting boundaries in intellectual property law between "public" and "private" realms of information and argues that trends to increase the number of exclusive rights for authors are converting the public domain into private intellectual property and constraining other types of socially valuable uses of expressive works that do not fit the "authorship" model underlying American copyright traditions; he also argues that recent expansion of trademark law has allowed trademark owners to obtain property rights in their trademarks that do not further the Lanham Act's goal of preventing consumer confusion. Benkler, "Free as Air to Common Use"; Yochai Benkler, "Overcoming Agoraphobia: Building the Commons of the Digitally Networked Environment," *Harvard Journal of Law and Technology* 11 (1998): 287; Julie E. Cohen, "Copyright and the Jurisprudence of Self-Help," *Berkeley Technology Law Journal* 13 (1998): 1089; Julie E. Cohen, "Lochner in Cyberspace: The New Economic Orthodoxy of 'Rights Management,'" *Michigan Law Review* 97 (1998): 462; Julie E. Cohen, "Some Reflections on Copyright Management Systems and Laws Designed to Protect Them," *Berkeley Technology Law Journal* 12 (1997): 161, 181–82; Julie E. Cohen, "Reverse-Engineering and the Rise of Electronic Vigilantism: Intellectual Property Implications of 'Lock-Out' Programs," *Southern California Law Review* 68 (1995): 1091. Niva Elkin-Koren, "Contracts in Cyberspace: Rights Without Laws," *Chicago-Kent Law Review* 73 (1998); Niva Elkin-Koren, "Copyright Policy and the Limits of Freedom of Contract," *Berkeley Technology Law Journal* 12 (1997): 93, 107–10 (criticizing the ProCD decision); Niva Elkin-Koren, "Cyberlaw and Social Change: A Democratic Approach to Copyright Law in Cyberspace," *Cardozo Arts and Entertainment Law Journal* 14 (1996): 215; in "Copyright Law and Social Dialogue on the Information Superhighway: The Case Against Copyright Liability of Bulletin Board Operators" (*Cardozo Arts and Entertainment Law Journal* 13 [1995]: 345, 390–99), Elkin-Koren analyzes the problems created by applying copyright law in a digitized environment. In "Goodbye to All That–A Reluctant (and Perhaps Premature) Adieu to a Constitutionally Grounded Discourse of Public Interest in Copyright Law" (*Vanderbilt Journal of Transnational Law* 29 [1996]: 595), Peter A. Jaszi advocates the development of new, policy-grounded arguments and constitutionally based reasoning to battle expansionist legislative and judicial tendencies in copyright to diminish public access to the "intellectual commons"; see also Peter A. Jaszi, "On the Author Effect: Contemporary Copyright and Collective Creativity," *Cardozo Arts and Entertainment Law Journal* 10 (1992): 293, 319–20; Peter A. Jaszi, "Toward a Theory of Copyright: The Metamorphoses of 'Authorship,'" *Duke Law Journal* 1991 (1991): 455. On the misuse of copyright, see Lemley, "Beyond Preemption"; Mark A. Lemley, "The Economics of Improvement in Intellectual Property Law," *Texas Law Review* 75 (1997): 989, 1048–68; in "Intellectual Property and Shrink-wrap Licenses" (*Southern California Law Review* 68 [1995]: 1239, 1239), Lemley notes that "software ven-

dors are attempting en masse to 'opt out' of intellectual property law by drafting license provisions that compel their customers to adhere to more restrictive provisions than copyright
. . . law would require." Jessica Litman ("The Tales That Article 2B Tells," *Berkeley Technology
Law Journal* 13 [1998]: 931, 938) characterizes as "dubious" the notion that current law enables publishers to make a transaction into a license by so designating it. In her view, article
2B is "confusing and confused" about copyright and its relationship with that law, and would
make new law. She believes that "whatever the outcome" of the debate over whether copyright makes sense in the digital environment (see "Reforming Information Law in Copyright's Image," *Dayton Law Review* 22 [1997]: 587, 590), "copyright doctrine is ill-adapted to
accommodate many of the important interests that inform our information policy. First
Amendment, privacy, and distributional issues that copyright has treated only glancingly are
central to any information policy." See also Jessica Litman, "Revising Copyright Law for the
Information Age," *Oregon Law Review* 75 (1996): 19; and "The Exclusive Right to Read"
(*Cardozo Arts and Entertainment Law Journal* 13 [1994]: 29, 48), in which Litman states that
"much of the activity on the net takes place on the mistaken assumption that any material
on the Internet is free from copyright unless expressly declared to be otherwise." In "Copyright as Myth" (*University of Pittsburgh Law Review* 53 [1991]: 235, 235–37), Litman provides a general overview of the issues of authorship and infringement in copyright law,
indicating that debate continues regarding the definition of "authorship" (she defines "author" "in the copyright sense of anyone who creates copyrightable works, whether they be
books, songs, sculptures, buildings, computer programs, paintings or films" [236, n.5]); she
also discusses why copyright law is counterintuitive to the authorship process. See also "The
Public Domain" (*Emory Law Journal* 39 [1990]: 965, 969), in which Litman recommends a
broad definition of the public domain ("originality is a keystone of copyright law" [974]).
Neil Weinstock Netanel, "Asserting Copyright's Democratic Principles in the Global Arena,"
Vanderbilt Law Review 51 (1998): 217, 232 n.48, 299 n.322; Neil Netanel, "Alienability Restrictions and the Enhancement of Author Autonomy in United States and Continental
Copyright Law," *Cardozo Arts and Entertainment Law Journal* 12 (1994): 1, 42–43; in
"[C]opyright and a Democratic Civil Society" (*Yale Law Journal* 106 [1996]: 283, 288,
324–36), Netanel analyzes copyright law and policy in terms of its democracy-enhancing
function: "Copyright is in essence a state measure that uses market institutions to enhance
the democratic character of society."Margaret Jane Radin and Polk Wagner, "The Myth of
Private Ordering: Rediscovering Legal Realism in Cyberspace," *Chicago-Kent Law Review* 73
(1998); Margaret Jane Radin, *Reinterpreting Property* (Chicago: University of Chicago Press,
1993), 56–63. Pam Samuelson, "Encoding the Law into Digital Libraries," *Communications of
the ACM* 41 (1999): 13, 13–14; Pamela Samuelson, foreword to "Symposium: Intellectual
Property and Contract Law for the Information Age," *California Law Review* 87 (1998): 1;
Pamela Samuelson observes in "Embedding Technical Self-Help in Licensed Software"
(*Communications of the ACM* 40 [1997]: 13, 16) that "licensors of software or other infor-
mation . . . will generally invoke self-help"; see also the criticism of the European database
directive in J. H. Reichman and Pamela Samuelson, "Intellectual Property Rights in Data?,"
Vanderbilt Law Review 50 (1997): 51, 84–95; Samuelson, "The Copyright Grab," 134; Pamela
Samuelson, "Fair Use for Computer Programs and Other Copyrightable Works in Digital
Form: The Implications of Sony, Galoob and Sega," *Journal of Intellectual Property Law* 1
(1993): 49.

    69. For a recent and compelling account of the general movement to propertize informa-
tion, see Debora J. Halbert, *Intellectual Property in the Information Age: The Politics of Expanding Ownership Rights* (Westport, Conn.: Quorum, 1999). Seth Shulman's *Owning the
Future* (Boston: Houghton Mifflin, 1999) gives the story its appropriate drama.

    70. "We favor a move away from the author vision in two directions; first towards recog-
nition of a limited number of new protections for cultural heritage, folkloric productions,
and biological 'know-how.' Second, and in general, we favor an increased recognition and

protection of the public domain by means of expansive 'fair use protections,' compulsory licensing, and narrower initial coverage of property rights in the first place"; Boyle, *Shamans, Software, and Spleens,* 169.

71. James Boyle, "A Politics of Intellectual Property: Environmentalism for the Net?," *Duke Law Journal* 47 (1997): 87.

CHAPTER ELEVEN

1. For a comprehensive account of the American protections for privacy, as well as a comparison with European protections, see Peter P. Swire and Robert E. Litan, *None of Your Business: World Data Flows, Electronic Commerce, and the European Privacy Directive* (Washington, D.C.: Brookings Institution Press, 1998). I have drawn from Phil Agre's historical framing of the question in "Beyond the Mirror World: Privacy and the Representational Practices of Computing" (in *Technology and Privacy: The New Landscape,* edited by Philip E. Agre and Marc Rotenberg [Cambridge, Mass.: MIT Press, 1997], 29) in building the argument of this chapter.

2. MIT Professor Hal Abelson, interview with the author, Newton, Mass., May 29, 1999.

3. Swisher cites an estimate that AOL earned $7 million per month in the spring of 1996 from sex chat; *Aol.com,* 226.

4. See M. Ethan Katsh, *Law in a Digital World* (New York: Oxford University Press, 1995), 228.

5. Obviously, this concern is not new. Alan Westin's work in the early 1970s was foundational in raising awareness about the relationship between computers and privacy; see Alan F. Westin and Michael A. Baker, *Databanks in a Free Society* (New York: Quadrangle Books, 1972).

6. See *Olmstead v United States,* 277 US 438 (1928).

7. For a comprehensive treatment of the legal issues raised by cases of surveillance, see Christopher Slobogin, "Technologically Assisted Physical Surveillance: The American Bar Association's Tentative Draft Standards," *Harvard Journal of Law and Technology* 10 (1997): 383.

8. Communication attributes can be defined as "encompass[ing] all of the other information that can be learned about a communication, such as when and where it occurred, to whom and from whom it was sent and how long it lasted"; Susan Freiwald, "Uncertain Privacy: Communication Attributes After the Digital Telephony Act," *Southern California Law Review* 69 (1996): 949, 951. Freiwald argues that new technology has increased the amount of communication attributes that can be stored and retrieved, thus rendering this data highly informative and extremely intrusive (951–52).

9. For instance, *USA Today* reported in "The Hunt for bin Laden" (August 21, 1998, A1) that "the supersecret National Agency in Fort Meade, Md., uses computers to scan tapped international phone calls"; see also "Cash-and-Carry Diplomacy" (*Time,* February 24, 1997, 22ff.), which mentions that the National Security Agency monitors communications like international phone calls and electronic messages.

10. Lew Platt, keynote address at Spring Internet World '98, March 11, 1998, available at http://www.hp.com/financials/textonly/personnel/ceo/keynote98.html (visited May 30, 1999). David Brin reports that Kodak can do the same in fifty bytes; *The Transparent Society,* 241.

11. Michael Kemp, "Centurion to Fight Crooks; 'Thinking' Spy Camera Could Put an End to Car Crimes," *Daily Mail* (London), May 20, 1995, 49; "Centurion" is a "real-time recognition and identification of number plates system" that "allows comparison of license plates with user databases."

12. See, for example, the reports in George Cole, "Smart Building Looks Sharp" (*Financial Times* [London], November 2, 1995, 14), on a Japanese company that uses a video camera license plate scanner to control access to a garage and image-processing technology in the staff cafeteria in conjunction with an automatic till operator; in Bill Dawson, "Polluters Beware:

Laser to Pick Out Foulest Tailpipes; Thousands of Commuters' Cars Will Be Checked As They
Pass By" (*Houston Chronicle,* October 6, 1998, A1), on a new Houston program to catch "gross
polluters" using a combination of laser technology and video cameras; in Tom Godfrey,
"Canada Customs to Border on Hi-Tech" (*Toronto Sun,* July 20, 1997, 16), on an experimen-
tal system being tested by Canadian customs to automate border crossings by using voice
recognition, fingerprint and eye scanners, and real-time video cameras and license plate readers; and in Alex Salkever, "Too Many Unseen Cameras?" (*Christian Science Monitor,* June 5,
1998, 1), on Honolulu's installation of "video cameras at key points along a main thorough-
fare to help catch petty thieves and prevent prostitution."

13. See Center for Democracy and Technology, "Filing Before the FCC in the Matter of
the Communications Assistance for Law Enforcement Act, CC docket no. 97–213," December
14, 1998, http://www.cdt.org//digi_tele/filing121498.html.

14. See *Minnesota v Dickerson,* 508 US 366, 381 (1993) (Justice Antonin Scalia concurring).

15. See, for example, William J. Stuntz, "Privacy's Problem and the Law of Criminal Procedure," *Michigan Law Review* 93 (1995): 1016, 1026; in "The Substantive Origins of Criminal
Procedure," Stuntz discusses the origins of the Fourth Amendment.

16. Stuntz, "Privacy's Problem and the Law of Criminal Procedure," 1026.

17. Alien and Sedition Acts of 1798, Act of June 18, 1798, ch. 59, 1 Stat. 566 (repealed 1802),
Act of June 25, 1798, ch. 63, 1 Stat. 570 (expired); Act of July 6, 1798, ch. 70, 1 Stat. 577 (expired),
Act of July 14, 1798, ch. 77, 1 Stat. 596 (empowering the president to deport anyone he deems
dangerous to the country's peace and safety) (expired). The Alien and Sedition Acts were declared unconstitutional in *New York Times Co. v Sullivan,* 376 US 254, 276 (1964), though, of
course, by then their terms they had expired. See Neal Devins, *Constitutional Values* (Baltimore:
Johns Hopkins University Press, 1996), on overruling (13); and James Morton Smith, *Freedom's
Fetters: The Alien and Sedition Laws and American Civil Liberties* (Ithaca, N.Y.: Cornell University Press, 1956), on the history, enforcement, and impact of the Alien and Sedition Acts.

18. Stuntz, "Substantive Origins,"395.

19. See Cass R. Sunstein, "Incompletely Theorized Agreements," *Harvard Law Review* 108
(1995): 1733, 1735–36. "Participants in legal controversies," Sunstein observes, ". . . need not
agree on fundamental principle. . . . When they disagree on an abstraction, they move to a
level of greater particularity. The distinctive feature of this account is that it emphasizes
agreement on (relative) particulars rather than on (relative) abstractions."

20. There is a growing literature that is rethinking the implications of that choice. David
Brin's *The Transparent Society* is among the most arresting; he argues for a fundamental shift
in our conception of privacy (see my discussion of Brin in chapter 10). Amitai Etzioni's *The
Limits of Privacy* (New York: Basic Books, 1999) is closer to the ground, working through the
balance that privacy choices demand. Although I have problems with some of the specifics in
Etzioni's account, his method is right, and some of his conclusions (in particular about the
use of data by commercial entities) are extremely strong. The great strength of the book, however, is that it engages these questions of value from a contemporary perspective. I do not
have much of a taste for the communitarianism in his account, but the value in such a work
is its power to generate argument.

21. The law thinks about it as a question of "information privacy." The Constitution has
very little time for the idea; see Albert W. Alschuler, "Interpersonal Privacy and the Fourth
Amendment," *Northern Illinois University Law Review* 4 (1983): 1; see also Priscilla M. Regan,
Legislating Privacy: Technology, Social Values, and Public Policy (Chapel Hill: University of North
Carolina Press, 1995): 69–108; Paul M. Schwartz, "Privacy and Participation: Personal Informa-
tion and Public Sector Regulation in the United States," *Iowa Law Review* 80 (1995): 553.

22. And they do not come from Janna Malamud Smith's "fallacy of perspective," discussed
by David Brin (*The Transparent Society,* 68–70). My argument is not that privacy thrived in
the past; it is that privacy was different in the past, and that the construction of searchable

databases constitutes a different sort of threat. We might approach the community of the past if we adopted a policy of forgetfulness, as Brin explores (247–48). Purging records might well be a key to a certain kind of liberation.

23. See Gandy, *The Panoptic Sort,* 66–68. In support of the theory that collectors of voluntarily given data can do whatever they like with that data, some have argued that the primary constitutional issue is free speech rather than privacy; once information is freely released, any restrictions on corporate speech, such as customer lists, should be disfavored (107).

24. Ibid., 87–90. For example, a targeting system that classified neighborhoods according to thirty-four different descriptors that accounted for 87 percent of the variance in socio-economic levels across neighborhoods was hugely successful with clients such as *Newsweek* and Colgate-Palmolive (88).

25. Peter H. Lewis, "Forget Big Brother," *New York Times,* March 19, 1998, G1.

26. Brin, *The Transparent Society,* 8–15.

27. For a good story that effectively summarizes the state of Web advertising, and for a discussion of how DoubleClick operates and the case study of 3M's sale of projectors through the advertising placement company, see Zina Moukheiber, "DoubleClick Is Watching You," *Forbes* (November 4, 1996): 342; see also http://www.alexa.com (visited May 30, 1999); and http://www.spinner.com (visited May 30, 1999). Spinner asks you to rate music as you listen to it (à la Firefly), and Alexa is like DoubleClick but has not caused any of the similar uproar over privacy. When a user downloads Alexa, it monitors every site (not just ones that display a certain type of ad) that the user visits.

28. See Federal Trade Commission, "Privacy Online: A Report to Congress," June 1998, n.107, available at http://www.ftc.gov/reports/privacy3/toc.htm (visited May 30, 1999).

29. See Gandy, *The Panoptic Sort,* 1–3.

30. Johnson, *Interface Culture,* 192–205. Andrew Shapiro calls this the "feedback effect" but argues that it narrows the range of choices; see *The Control Revolution,* 113.

31. See, for example, *McIntyre v Ohio Elections Commission,* 514 US 334, 341–43 (1995).

32. See Janai S. Nelson, "Residential Zoning Regulations and the Perpetuation of Apartheid," *UCLA Law Review* 43 (1996): 1689, 1693–1704.

33. Examples of laws that aim at segregation based on social or economic criteria include: regulations requiring a minimum lot size for housing; single-family ordinances prohibiting "nontraditional" families from living in certain areas; and residential classifications that exclude apartment housing. All such restrictions significantly increase the cost of housing for lower-income individuals; see ibid., 1699–1700.

34. In 1926 the Supreme Court held zoning to be a valid exercise of local governmental power. See *Village of Euclid v Ambler Realty Company,* 272 US 365 (1926) (holding that a state has the right to separate incompatible uses). Not until the twentieth century were municipalities given much power to regulate areas of law such as zoning decisions; see Richard Briffault, "Our Localism: Part I—The Structure of Local Government Law," *Columbia Law Review* 90 (1990): 1, 8–11, 19.

35. In 1917 the Supreme Court outlawed racial zoning as a violation of the Fourteenth Amendment; see *Buchanan v Warley,* 245 US 60 (1917). However, "nonexclusionary" zoning regulation was used to preserve residential segregation; even though facially neutral and based on economic factors (ostensibly to prevent property devaluation), various laws and regulations have resulted in *de facto* segregation; see Briffault, "Our Localism," 103–4; Meredith Lee Bryant, "Combating School Resegregation Through Housing: A Need for a Reconceptualization of American Democracy and the Rights It Protects," *Harvard BlackLetter Journal* 13 (1997): 127, 131–32.

36. See Joel Kosman, "Toward an Inclusionary Jurisprudence: A Reconceptualization of Zoning," *Catholic University Law Review* 43 (1993): 59, 77–86, 101–3.

37. See Gordon S. Wood, *The Radicalism of the American Revolution* (New York: Alfred A. Knopf, 1992), 5–8, 271–86.

38. See Lynne G. Zucker, "Production of Trust: Institutional Sources of Economic Structure, 1840–1920," *Research in Organizational Behavior* 8 (1986): 53.

39. Price discrimination is the ability to charge different prices for the same good. Airplane tickets are the best example—the same seat can cost hundreds of dollars more for a traveler who cannot stay over Saturday night. See, for example, Joseph Gregory Sidak, "Debunking Predatory Innovation," *Columbia Law Review* 83 (1983): 1121, 1132–35; see also Easterbrook, "Intellectual Property Is Still Property"; Fisher, "Reconstructing the Fair Use Doctrine," 1659; but see Janusz A. Ordover et al., "Predatory Systems Rivalry: A Reply," *Columbia Law Review* 83 (1983): 1150, 1158–64.

40. Viviana A. Zelizer, *The Social Meaning of Money,* 2d ed. (Princeton, N.J.: Princeton University Press, 1994), 94–95 (footnote omitted).

41. It is quite clear that the government's data encryption standard (DES) is unreliable. The Electronic Frontier Foundation (EFF), to its great credit, has made it that way. In *Cracking DES: Secrets of Encryption Research, Wiretap Politics, and Chip Design,* EFF provides the code and plans to build a machine that can crack a DES key. As Whitfield Diffie, one of the inventors of public key encryption, writes, "With the appearance of this book and the machine it represents, the game changes forever. It is not a question of whether DES keys can be extracted by exhaustive search; it is a question of how cheaply they can be extracted and for what purposes" (xi). Other standards are increasingly available, and if the move to liberalize the regulation of encryption succeeds, powerful encryption technologies will be generally available (both in the United States and abroad) soon; see *Cryptography's Role in Securing the Information Society,* edited by Kenneth W. Dam and Herbert S. Lin (Washington, D.C.: National Academy Press, 1996). For a discussion of computing technologies that might well make these "safer" key systems unsafe (including DNA and quantum computing), see Brin, *The Transparent Society,* 280–82.

42. For a discussion of the law governing compelled disclosure of keys and plaintext, see Phillip R. Reitinger, "Compelled Production of Plaintext and Keys," *University of Chicago Legal Forum* 1996 (1996): 171.

43. See Michael Adler, "Cyberspace, General Searches, and Digital Contraband: The Fourth Amendment and the Net-Wide Search," *Yale Law Journal* 105 (1996): 1093, 1109–10, 1113.

44. Cf. ibid., 1100; see also Brin, *The Transparent Society,* 158–61 (discussing mutual monitoring).

45. Cf. Froomkin, "The Metaphor Is the Key."

46. See Joel R. Reidenberg, "Privacy in the Information Economy: A Fortress or Frontier for Individual Rights?," *Federal Communications Law Journal* 44 (1992): 195, 237–38. The principles account for concern that "the privacy concerns of data collection (including notice, consent, necessity, and accuracy), uses (including associated uses), and the duration of storage require careful consideration" (238, footnotes omitted).

47. For example, the Video Privacy Protection Act (18 USC, § 2701 [1988]) was adopted in response to outrage over the media's acquisition of a list of films rented by Judge Robert Bork at the time of his ill-fated nomination to the Supreme Court.

48. One highly touted system has been TRUSTe. When a web site becomes licensed by TRUSTe, it has agreed to disclose its information-gathering and dissemination practices (which can be brought up by clicking on the "trustmark") and pledged that the disclosure is backed by third-party assurance; see TRUSTe, "Building a Site You Can Believe In," available at http://www.etrust.org (visited May 30, 1999).

49. See Joseph M. Reagle and Lorrie Faith Cranor, "The Platform for Privacy Preferences," *Communications of the ACM* (February 1999): 48.

50. See ibid.

51. Joseph M. Reagle Jr., "P3P and Privacy on the Web FAQ, Version 2.0.1," available at http://www.w3.org/P3P/P3FAQ.html (visited May 30, 1999).

52. In its current design, the protocol is fairly unwieldy. It also lacks encryption, leaving user data open to interception; see Kenneth Lee and Gabriel Speyer, "Platform for Privacy Preferences Project and Citibank" (1998), available at Citibank Advanced Development Group, "White Paper: Platform for Privacy Preferences Project (P3P) and Citibank" (October 22, 1998), http://www13.w3.org/P3P/Lee_Speyer.html (visited May 30, 1999). The most significant challenge, however, will simply be in implementation. If applications implement P3P in a way that facilitates simple user control, it could be successful. For a balanced and powerful account of the value of standardized data models, see Agre and Rotenberg, *Technology and Privacy.*

53. See Guido Calabresi and A. Douglas Melamed, "Property Rules, Liability Rules, and Inalienability: One View of the Cathedral," *Harvard Law Review* 85 (1972): 1089, 1105–6. "Property rules involve a collective decision as to who is to be given an initial entitlement but not as to the value of the entitlement. . . . Liability rules involve an additional stage of state intervention: not only are entitlements protected, but their transfer or destruction is allowed on the basis of a value determined by some organ of the state rather than by the parties themselves" (1092). Andrew Shapiro discusses a similar idea in *The Control Revolution,* 158–65.

54. Cf. Margaret Jane Radin, *Contested Commodities* (Cambridge, Mass.: Harvard University Press, 1996); Martha Nussbaum, "Aristotelian Social Democracy," in *Liberalism and the Good,* edited by R. Bruce Douglass et al. (New York: Routledge, 1990), 232.

55. Cf. Margaret Jane Radin, "Property Evolving in Cyberspace," *Journal of Law and Communications* 15 (1996): 509, 524–26.

56. See "Privacy Now Campaign," available at http://www.simson.net/pn.html53

57. See Marc Rotenberg, "Data Protection in the United States: A Rising Tide?," speech given at the Nineteenth International Conference of Privacy Data Protection Commissioners, Brussels, September 17–19, 1997, available at http://www.privacy.fgov.be/conference/pt1_3.html (visited May 30, 1999).

58. Cf. Breyer, "The Uneasy Case for Copyright."

59. John Perry Barlow, "The Economy of Ideas," *Wired* (March 1994), available online at http://www.wired.com/wired/archive/2.03/economy.ideas.html.

CHAPTER TWELVE

1. Two excellent examples include Owen M. Fiss, *The Irony of Free Speech* (Cambridge, Mass.: Harvard University Press, 1996); and Cass R. Sunstein, *Democracy and the Problem of Free Speech* (New York: Free Press, 1993).

2. See 47 CFR § 73.658(e) (1998); see also Herbert J. Rotfeld et al., "Television Station Standards for Acceptable Advertising," *Journal of Consumer Affairs* 24 (1990): 392.

3. See Strafgesetzbuch (penal code) (StGB) §§ 130–31, reprinted in *German Criminal Law,* vol. 1, edited by Gerold Harfst, translated by Otto A. Schmidt (Würzburg: Harfst Verlag, 1989), 75–76.

4. Built by industry but also especially by Cypherpunks—coders dedicated to building the tools for privacy for the Internet. As Eric Hughes writes in "A Cypherpunk's Manifesto" (in *Applied Cryptography,* 2d ed., by Bruce Schneier [New York: Wiley, 1996], 609): We the Cypherpunks are dedicated to building anonymous systems. We are defending our privacy with cryptography, with anonymous mail forwarding systems, with digital signatures, and with electronic money. Cypherpunks write code. We know that someone has to write software to defend privacy, and since we can't get privacy unless we all do, we're going to write it. We publish our code so that our fellow Cypherpunks may practice and play with it. Our code is free for all to use, worldwide.

5. John Perry Barlow has put into circulation the meme that, "in cyberspace, the First Amendment is a local ordinance"; "Leaving the Physical World," available at http://www.eff.org/pub/Publications/John_Perry_Barlow/leaving_the_physical_world.article (visited May 30, 1999).

6. See David Rudenstine, *The Day the Presses Stopped: A History of the Pentagon Papers Case* (Berkeley: University of California Press, 1996), 101, 139.

7. Ibid., 100.

8. See ibid., 2.

9. See ibid., 2, 42.

10. Ibid., 47–63.

11. Sanford J. Ungar, *The Papers and the Papers: An Account of the Legal and Political Battle over the Pentagon Papers* (New York: Columbia University Press, 1989), 120; cited in Rudenstine, *The Day the Presses Stopped*, 92.

12. See ibid., 105.

13. *Near v Minnesota*, 283 US 697, 716 (1931); cf. *United States v Noriega*, 917 F2d 1543 (11th Cir 1990) (affirming the prior restraint of audiotapes of the defendant's conversations with his attorney on the grounds that they might impede his right to a fair trial), cert. denied, 498 US 976 (1990) (Justice Thurgood Marshall dissenting).

14. See, for example, *Organization for a Better Austin v Keefe*, 402 US 415, 418–19 (1971); *Bantam Books, Inc., v Sullivan*, 372 US 58, 70 (1963); *Near v Minnesota*, 283 US 697, 713–14.

15. The standard arguments are summarized well by Kathleen M. Sullivan and Gerald Gunther: "(1) It is easier for an official to restrict speech 'by a simple stroke of the pen' than by the more cumbersome apparatus of subsequent punishment. . . . (2) Censors will have a professional bias in favor of censorship, and thus will systematically overvalue government interests and undervalue speech. (3) Censors operate more informally than judges and so afford less procedural safeguards to speakers. (4) Speech suppressed in advance never reaches the marketplace of ideas at all. (5) When speech is suppressed in advance, there is no empirical evidence from which to measure its alleged likely harms"; *First Amendment Law* (New York: Foundation Press, 1999), 339–40, citing Thomas Emerson, "The Doctrine of Prior Restraint," *Law and Contemporary Problems* 20 (1955): 648. Frederick Schauer offers a nice balance to this commonplace theory; see "Fear, Risk, and the First Amendment: Unraveling the 'Chilling Effect,'" *Boston University Law Review* 58 (1978): 685, 725–30.

16. In a particularly telling exchange, Justice Stewart asked Professor Bickel about a case in which disclosure "would result in the sentencing to death of a hundred young men whose only offense had been that they were nineteen years old and had low draft numbers. What should we do?" Bickel replied that his "inclinations of humanity overcome the somewhat more abstract devotion to the First Amendment in a case of that sort"; *May It Please the Court: The Most Significant Oral Arguments Made Before the Supreme Court Since 1955*, edited by Peter Irons and Stephanie Guitton (New York: Free Press, 1993), 173.

17. In a concurring opinion, Justice Potter Stewart wrote that the prior restraint at issue was invalid since he could not "say that disclosure of [the Pentagon Papers] will surely result in direct, immediate, and irreparable damage to our Nation or its people"; *New York Times Company v United States*, 403 US 713, 730 (1971) (per curiam). This standard has frequently been thought to reflect the position of the Court; see Laurence H. Tribe, *American Constitutional Law* (Meneola, N.Y.: Foundation Press, 1978), 731; Morton H. Halperin and Daniel N. Hoffman, *Top Secret: National Security and the Right to Know* (Washington, D.C.: New Republic Books, 1977), 147 n.22; see also *Alderman v Philadelphia Housing Authority*, 496 F2d 164, 170 (3d Cir 1974), cert. denied, 419 US 844 (1974) (prior restraint must be supported by "compelling proof" that it is "essential to a vital government interest").

18. See *United States v Progressive, Inc.*, 467 FSupp 990 (WDWis 1979); see also L. A. Powe Jr., "The H-Bomb Injunction," *University of Colorado Law Review* 61 (1990): 55, 56.

19. The *Milwaukee Sentinel* and *Fusion* magazine had published articles dealing with similar concepts; see A. DeVolpi et al., *Born Secret: The H-Bomb, The Progressive Case, and National Security* (New York: Pergamon Press, 1981), 102, 106; see also Howard Morland, *The Secret That Exploded* (New York: Random House, 1981), 223, 225–26.

20. See Floyd Abrams, "First Amendment Postcards from the Edge of Cyberspace," *St. John's Journal of Legal Commentary* 11 (1996): 693, 699.

21. NTSB Chairman Jim Hall announced later that investigations confirmed that a fuel tank explosion caused the crash; see "Statement of Jim Hall, Chairman, National Transportation Safety Board," July 16, 1998, available at http://www.ntsb.gov/pressrel/980716.htm (visited May 30, 1999).

22. See Robert E. Kessler, "TWA Probe: Submarines off Long Island/Sources: But No Link to Crash of Jetliner," *Newsday,* March 22, 1997, A8.

23. See, for example, James Sanders, *The Downing of TWA Flight 800* (New York: Kensington Publishing, 1997), 131–37; Accuracy in Media et al., "TWA 800—Missile Website Roadmap," available at http://www.angelfire.com/hi/TWA800/ (visited May 30, 1999); Mark K. Anderson, "Friendly Ire," available at http://www.valleyadvocate.com/articles /twa3.html (visited May 30, 1999); Ian W. Goddard, "TWA Flight 800 and Facts Pertaining to U.S. Navy Culpability," available at http://www.erols.com/igoddard/twa-fact.htm (visited May 30, 1999).

24. See Sanders, *The Downing of TWA Flight 800,* 29–30, 75, 70–79, 171–73.

25. We can tell that it is false, of course, as in, "The cat was alive and not alive."

26. Andrew Shapiro has a powerful analysis of a particularly smart loon; see *The Control Revolution,* 133–41.

27. As Shapiro puts it, "What we need are trusted intermediaries: people to whom we entrust certain tasks because we recognize the value of their perspective, their expertise, their time, and their independence"; ibid., 188.

28. See Zucker, "Production of Trust," 63–65.

29. Obscenity is not constitutionally protected speech, and federal laws prohibit the transportation of obscene materials; see 18 USCA § 1462 (1984), amended by 18 USCA §1462 (Supp 1999). In *Miller v California,* the Supreme Court described the test for obscenity as: "(a) whether 'the average person, applying contemporary community standards' would find that the work, taken as a whole, appeals to the prurient interest; (b) whether the work depicts or describes, in a patently offensive way, sexual conduct specifically defined by the applicable state law; and (c) whether the work, taken as a whole, lacks serious literary, artistic, political, or scientific value;" *Miller v California,* 413 US 15, 24 (1973) (5–4 decision), rehearing denied, 414 US 881 (1973). Porn, on the other hand, is protected by the First Amendment but may be regulated to promote the state's interest in protecting children from harmful materials so long as the regulation is the least restrictive means to further the articulated interest; see *Ginsberg v New York,* 390 US 629, 637–40 (1968). Child porn may be prohibited as obscene material even if it is not obscene under the *Miller* test, owing to the strong state interest in preventing the sexual exploitation of children; see *New York v Ferber,* 458 US 747, 764 (1982). Child porn is not constitutionally protected, and federal law prohibits the transportation of child porn; see 18 USCA § 2252 (1984), amended by 18 USCA §2252 (Supp 1999).

30. Justice Sandra Day O'Connor listed more than forty states with such law in her concurrence in *Reno v ACLU,* 521 US 844, 887 n.2.

31. *Ginsberg v New York,* 390 US 629 (1968).

32. See Godwin, *CyberRights,* 206–59.

33. See Blake T. Bilstad, "Obscenity and Indecency in a Digital Age: The Legal and Political Implications of Cybersmut, Virtual Pornography, and the Communications Decency Act of 1996," *Santa Clara Computer and High Technology Law Journal* 13 (1997): 321, 336–37.

34. Marty Rimm, "Marketing Pornography on the Information Superhighway: A Survey of 917,410 Images, Descriptions, Short Stories, and Animations Downloaded 8.5 Million Times by Consumers in over 2,000 Cities in Forty Countries, Provinces, and Territories," *Georgetown University Law Journal* 83 (1995): 1849. Godwin provides the whole history of the Rimm article, describing the most significant problems and consequences of the "misleading" and "false" statements, and its eventual demise; *CyberRights,* 206–59; see also Jonathan Wallace and Mark Mangan, *Sex, Laws, and Cyberspace* (New York: M&T Books, 1996), ch. 6.

35. See Philip Elmer-DeWitt, "On a Screen Near You: Cyberporn—It's Popular, Pervasive, and Surprisingly Perverse, According to the First Survey of Online Erotica—And There's No Easy Way to Stamp It Out," *Time,* July 3, 1995.

36. 47 USCA § 223(e)(5)(A) (Supp 1999).

37. The law was extinguished (at least in part) at 521 US 844 (1997); see Eugene Volokh, "Freedom of Speech, Shielding Children, and Transcending Balancing," *Supreme Court Review* 1997 (1997): 141.

38. See *Federal Communications Commission v Pacifica Foundation,* 438 US 726, 748–50 (1978) (plurality). Though *Pacifica* has been criticized strongly, see Steven H. Shiffrin, *The First Amendment, Democracy, and Romance* (Cambridge, Mass.: Harvard University Press, 1990), 80, as Jonathan Weinberg convincingly argues, *Pacifica* continues to have influence in the broadcasting context; "Cable TV, Indecency, and the Court," *Columbia-VLA Journal of Law and the Arts* 21 (1997): 95.

39. See *Gentile v State Bar of Nevada,* 501 US 1030, 1048–51 (1991) (vague regulations of speech are void owing to the impermissible risk of chilling speech); *Dombrowski v Pfister,* 380 US 479, 494 (1965) (chilling speech).

40. For a more extensive discussion of this system, see Lawrence Lessig and Paul Resnick, "The Architectures of Mandated Access Controls," *Michigan Law Review* (forthcoming, 1999).

41. 47 USC § 230 (Supp 1999). Charles Nesson and David Marglin suggest that the constitutionality of the CDA—and by extension of COPA—will change over time: even if it was not constitutional initially, technological change may render it constitutional later; see Charles Nesson and David Marglin, "The Day the Internet Met the First Amendment: Time and the Communications Decency Act," *Harvard Journal of Law and Technology* 10 (1996): 113.

42. See World Wide Web Consortium, "Platform for Internet Content Selection (PICS)," available at http://www.w3.org/PICS/ (visited October 25, 1998).

43. See Diane Roberts, "On the Plurality of Ratings," *Cardozo Arts and Entertainment Law Journal* 15 (1997): 105, 113–15.

44. Paul Resnick, "PICS-Interest@w3.org, Moving On," January 20 1999, available at http://lists.w3.org/Archives/Public/pics-interest/1999Jan/0000.html (visited May 30, 1999); Paul Resnick, "Filtering Information on the Internet," *Scientific American* 106 (March 1997), also available at http://www.sciam.com/0397issue/0397resnick.html (visited May 30, 1999); Paul Resnick, "PICS and Intellectual Freedom FAQ," available at http://www.w3.org /PICS/PICS-FAQ-980126.html (visited May 30, 1999); Paul Resnick and Jim Miller, "PICS: Internet Access Controls Without Censorship," *Communications of the ACM* 39 (1996): 87, also available at http://www.w3.org/PICS/iacwcv2.htm (visited May 30, 1999); Jim Miller, Paul Resnick, et al., "PICS 1.1 Rating Services and Rating Systems—and Their Machine-Readable Descriptions," October 31, 1996, available at http://www.w3.org/TR/REC-PICS-services) (visited May 30, 1999); Tim Krauskopf, Paul Resnick, et al., "PICS 1.1 Label Distribution—Label Syntax and Communication Protocols," October 31, 1996, available at http://www.w3.org/TR/REC-PICS-labels (visited May 30, 1999); Christopher Evans, Paul

Resnick, et al., "W3C Recommendation: PICS Rules 1.1, REC-PICS, Rules–971229," December 29, 1997, available at http://www.w3.org/TR/REC-PICSRules (visited May 30, 1999).

45. See Jonathan Weinberg, "Rating the Net," *Hastings Communications and Entertainment Law Journal* 19 (1997): 453, 478 n.108.

46. See, for example, the Center for Democracy and Technology's endorsement of parental empowerment through rating systems and blocking software rather than government regulation in "Internet Family Empowerment White Paper," July 16, 1997, available at http://www.cdt.org/speech/empower.html (visited May 30, 1999); a similar point of view is found in Esther Dyson, "Release 1.0: Labels and Disclosure," December 1996, available at http://www.edventure.com/release1/1296body.html (visited May 30, 1999).

47. This claim, of course, is too strong. The site could block deceptively, making it seem as if the user were gaining access but actually not giving her access to what she believes she is gaining access to.

48. See Richard Thompson Ford ("The Boundaries of Race: Political Geography in Legal Analysis," *Harvard Law Review* 107 [1994]: 1841, 1844), who asserts that jurisdictional boundaries perpetuate racial segregation and inequality; Gerald E. Frug ("Universities and Cities," *Connecticut Law Review* 30 [1998]: 1199, 1200), explains how universities erect borders to divorce themselves from surrounding poverty and argues that universities should critique these borders; Lani Guinier ("More Democracy," *University of Chicago Legal Forum* 1995 [1995]: 1, 3) advocates a cross-racial participatory democracy that demands a concern for, and a familiarity with, the views of others.

49. See *Regents of the University of California v Bakke*, 438 US 265, 312 (1978) (Justice Lewis F. Powell, quoting *Keyishian v Board of Regents*, 385 US 589, 603 [1967]: "The Nation's future depends upon leaders trained through wide exposure to that robust exchange of ideas which discovers truth 'out of a multitude of tongues, [rather] than through any kind of authoritative selection'").

50. See Fiss, *The Irony of Free Speech*, 3, 37–38; Sunstein, *Democracy and the Problem of Free Speech*, xvi–xx. Andrew Shapiro's powerful analysis of Sunstein's point is better tuned to the realities of the Net; see *The Control Revolution*, 107–12.

51. Ithiel de Sola Pool, *Technologies Without Boundaries: On Telecommunications in a Global Age*, edited by Eli M. Noam (Cambridge, Mass.: Harvard University Press, 1990), 15.

52. See Geoffrey R. Stone, "Imagining a Free Press," *Michigan Law Review* 90 (1992): 1246, 1264.

53. But see Thomas G. Krattenmaker and L. A. Powe Jr. ("Converging First Amendment Principles for Converging Communications Media," *Yale Law Journal* 104 [1995]: 1719, 1735), who argue that First Amendment principles urge that consumers, not the government, control the content they consume in the area of emerging media technologies; Sunstein ("The First Amendment in Cyberspace," *Yale Law Journal* 104 [1995]: 1757, 1765) contends that emerging media technologies produce new areas for applying old Madisonian First Amendment principles.

54. For an early and extraordinary work that struggles with the complexity of the question about which information you should be able to own, see Anne Wells Branscomb, *Who Owns Information?: From Privacy to Public Access* (New York: Basic Books, 1994). My conclusions are different from hers, but I agree with her insight that "ownership" cuts across different kinds of information in different ways. James Boyle advances a similar theme in *Shamans, Software, and Spleens*.

55. See 47 CFR § 73.277 (1998).

56. 47 USCA §§ 81–119 (1927) (repealed by the Communications Act of 1934).

57. See *Red Lion Broadcasting Company v Federal Communications Commission*, 395 US 367, 375–77 (1969); *National Broadcasting Company v United States*, 319 US 190, 212–13

(1943). Thomas Hazlett makes a powerful critique of Frankfurter's history of the emergence of any necessity for FCC regulation; see *Physical Scarcity*.

58. See *Turner Broadcasting System, Inc. v Federal Communications Commission*, 512 US 622, 637–38 (1997); see also Huber, *Law and Disorder in Cyberspace*.

59. See *National Broadcasting Company, Inc. v Columbia Broadcasting System*, 213.

60. See Huber, *Law and Disorder in Cyberspace*, 28–34. The dominant voice in this debate is Thomas W. Hazlett, who has argued strongly against the licensing regime for spectrum and in favor of a property auction. His work on the history of the Radio Act is particularly good; see, for example, "Assigning Property Rights to Radio Spectrum Users: Why Did FCC License Auctions Take Sixty-seven Years?," *Journal of Law and Economics* 41 (1998): 529; "Oak Leaves and the Origins of the 1927 Radio Act: Comment," *Public Choice* 95 (1998): 277; "Physical Scarcity, Rent Seeking, and the First Amendment," *Columbia Law Review* 97 (1997): 905; "The Rationality of U.S. Regulation of the Broadcast Spectrum," *Journal of Law and Economics* 33 (1990): 133; Thomas W. Hazlett and David Sosa, "Was the Fairness Doctrine a 'Chilling Effect'?: Evidence from the Postderegulation Radio Market," *Journal of Legal Studies* 26 (1997): 279. For another historical account, see Morton I. Hamburg and Stuart N. Brotman, *Communications Law and Practice*, vol. 1 (New York: Law Journal Seminars–Press, 1995), 5–8. Ithiel de Sola Pool was an early advocate of a position close to Hazlett's; see *Technologies Without Boundaries*, 108–88.

61. See Ronald H. Coase, "The Federal Communications Commission," *Journal of Law and Economics* 2 (1959): 1.

62. See Patrick M. Garry, *Scrambling for Protection: The New Media and the First Amendment* (Pittsburgh: University of Pittsburgh, 1994), 97–106.

63. There is an important argument supporting a different treatment for the "press" under the First Amendment, though the Supreme Court has not yet developed this distinctive jurisprudence. Justice Potter Stewart sketched some of the potential in "Or of the Press" (*Hastings Law Journal* 26 [1975]: 631), and his argument takes on a new significance in the context of the Internet. For a persuasive account, see Garry, *Scrambling for Protection*, 107–21.

64. See Hazlett, *Physical Scarcity*, 911–12; Anna Couey, "The Birth of Spread Spectrum," available at http://www.sirius.be/lamarr.htm (visited May 30, 1999); Jack Glas, "The Principles of Spread Spectrum Communication," available at http://cas.et.tudelft.nl/~glas /ssc/techn/techniques.html (visited May 30, 1999). One important reason for the shortage of spectrum is its inefficient use; see de Sola Pool, "Technologies Without Boundaries," 42–45.

65. Yochai Benkler's article provides (for lawyers) the most extensive discussion of the technology; see "Overcoming Agoraphobia," 287. He describes the change in technology: "The technological shift derives from various techniques—such as spread spectrum and code division multiple access, time division multiple access, frequency hopping, and packet switching—for allowing multiple users to communicate at the same time using the same frequency range. Some of these technologies complement each other; some conflict with each other. What is crucial to understand about these technologies is that they challenge the underlying assumption of both licensing and privatization: that the only way to assure high quality wireless communications is to assign one person the right to transmit in a given frequency band"(324, footnote omitted). The appendix to his article then describes the related technologies, including spread spectrum (395), time division multiple access (TDMA) (397), and frequency hopping (399). For a discussion of code division multiple access and frequency division multiple access, see Ted Stevens, "Regulation and Licensing of Low-Earth-Orbit Satellites," *Santa Clara Computer and High Technology Law Journal* 10 (1994): 401.

66. Ethernet literally functions like this. Data on an Ethernet network are streamed into each machine on that network. Each machine sniffs the data and then pays attention to the data intended for it. This process creates an obvious security hole: "sniffers" can be put on

"promiscuous mode" and read packets intended for other machines; see Loshin, *TCP/IP Clearly Explained*, 44–46.

67. See Yochai Benkler and Lawrence Lessig, "Net Gains," *New Republic*, December 14, 1998.

68. The founder of this argument must be Eli Noam; see "Spectrum Auctions: Yesterday's Heresy, Today's Orthodoxy, Tomorrow's Anachronism—Taking the Next Step to Open Spectrum Access," *Journal of Law and Economics* 41 (1998): 765. Benkler has spiced it up a bit (in my view, in critical ways) by adding to it the value of the commons. For an extraordinarily powerful push to a similar political (if not technological) end, see Eben Moglen, "The Invisible Barbecue," *Columbia Law Review* 97 (1997): 945. Moglen notes the lack of debate regarding the sociopolitical consequences of carving up telecommunication rights at the "Great Barbecue" and draws a parallel with the Gilded Age's allocation of benefits and privileges associated with the railroad industry.

CHAPTER FOURTEEN

1. See Stephen Holmes, "What Russia Teaches Us Now; How Weak States Threaten Freedom," *American Prospect* (July-August 1997): 30.

2. See *Restatement (Third) Of Foreign Relations Law* (1986), § 402(2) and comment (e).

3. Child Sexual Abuse Prevention Act, 18 USC § 2423(b) (1994). See Margaret A. Healy, "Prosecuting Child Sex Tourists at Home: Do Laws in Sweden, Australia, and the United States Safeguard the Rights of Children as Mandated by International Law?," *Fordham International Law Journal* 18 (1995): 1852, 1902–12.

4. See Bill Grantham, "America the Menace: France's Feud With Hollywood," *World Policy Journal* 15, no. 2 (Summer 1998): 58; Chip Walker, "Can TV Save the Planet?," *American Demographics* (May 1996): 42.

5. These are among the most watched television shows in the world; see Henry Goldblatt, "The Universal Appeal of Schlock," *Fortune*, May 12, 1997, 32.

6. Akhil Reed Amar, "Of Sovereignty and Federalism," *Yale Law Journal* 96 (1987): 1425, 1430–31.

7. U.S. Constitution, art. VI, cl. 2.

8. See, for example, David R. Johnson and David Post, "Law and Borders: The Rise of Law in Cyberspace," *Stanford Law Review* 48 (1996): 1367, 1369–76.

9. Ibid., 1379–80.

10. See Jack L. Goldsmith, "Against Cyberanarchy," *University of Chicago Law Review* 65 (1998): 1199; Jack L. Goldsmith, "The Internet and the Abiding Significance of Territorial Sovereignty," *Indiana Journal of Global Legal Studies* 5 (1998): 475; see also David Johnston, Sunny Handa, and Charles Morgan, *Cyberlaw: What You Need to Know About Doing Business Online* (Toronto: Stoddart, 1997), ch. 10. Allan R. Stein ("The Unexceptional Problem of Jurisdiction in Cyberspace," *The International Lawyer* 32 [1998]: 1167) argues that the jurisdictional problems in cyberspace are like those found in real-space international law.

11. See Litman, "Revising Copyright Law for the Information Age," 38–39.

12. Ibid.

13. As Katie Hafner and Matthew Lyon put it: "The best hackers were professionals. Meddlesome and malicious network users, of which there were virtually none at the outset, were first referred to as 'network randoms' or 'net randoms' or just plain 'randoms.' It would be another decade before hacking was given a bad name"; *Where Wizards Stay Up Late*, 190.

14. Cf. Bruce Sterling, *The Hacker Crackdown: Law and Disorder on the Electronic Frontier* (New York: Bantam Books, 1992), 55–57.

15. See Kaare Christian and Susan Richter, *The UNIX Operating System*, 3d ed. (New York: Wiley, 1994), 5–8.

16. See, for example, Allen H. Lipis et al., *Electronic Banking* (New York: Wiley, 1985),159–87.

17. Examples include the hacking of the Defense Department computers by the German Peter Carl, and then an authorized break-in to demonstrate the vulnerability; see Katie Hafner and John Markoff, *Cyberpunk: Outlaws and Hackers on the Computer Frontier* (New York: Simon & Schuster 1991), 173–79, 266.

18. Morris's father, Robert Morris Sr., was the NSA's expert on data security at the time; see ibid., 253–341.

19. A commercial version of the software is not free, and of course, that version includes updates to correct for "bugs."

20. See Computer Fraud and Abuse Act, 18 USC § 1030(a)(5)(A) (1988) (current version at 18 USC § 1030[a][5][A] [1994], amended by 18 USC 1030[a][5][A] [Supp II 1996]).

21. *United States v Morris*, 928 F2d 504, 506 (2d Cir 1991).

22. Julian Dibbell, "The Prisoner: Phiber Optik Goes Directly to Jail," *Village Voice*, January 12, 1994, available at http://www.levity.com/julian/phiber.html (visited May 30, 1999).

23. See *United States v LaMaccia*, 871 FSupp 535 (DMass 1994); see also Mitchell Zuckoff, "Software Piracy Charges Dismissed Against Student," *Boston Globe*, December 30, 1994, 1; *United States v LaMaccia*, memorandum of decision and order on defendant's motion to dismiss, December 28, 1994, http://photo.net/dldf/dismiss-order.html (visited May 30, 1999).

24. See *Steve Jackson Games, Inc. v U.S. Secret Service*, 36 F3d 457 (5th Cir 1994); see also Joe Abernathy, "Trial Set This Week in Computer Case; Publisher Sues Secret Service," *Houston Chronicle* (January 18, 1993), 13; *Steve Jackson Games v U.S. Secret Service*, complaint, May 1, 1991, available at http://www.eff.org/pub/Legal/Cases/Inc./SJG/complaint.sjg (visited May 30, 1999).

25. Nevertheless, there is arguably something of a revival among hackers—as distinct from "crackers"—at least among new hackers who emphasize political or social ends; see, for example, Jim Kerstetter, "A Reprieve for 'Ethical Hacking,'" *PC Week Online*, July 20, 1998, available at http://www.zdnet.com/zdnn/stories/zdnn_display/0,3440,337644,00.html (visited May 30, 1999); Alex Wellen, "'Cracker' Term Gains Acceptance by Media," ZDTV, May 19, 1998, available at http://www.zdnet.com/zdnn/content/zdtv/0519/317307.html (visited May 30, 1999).

26. See Alan Schwartz, "The Default Rule Paradigm and the Limits of Contract Law," *Southern California Interdisciplinary Law Journal* 3 (1993): 389.

27. See Goldsmith, "Against Cyberanarchy," 1205–12.

28. *ProCD, Inc. v Zeidenberg*, 86 F3d 1447, 1453–55 (7th Cir 1996).

29. "The landowner's right to exclude [is] 'one of the most essential sticks in the bundle of rights that are commonly characterized as property'"; *Loretto v Teleprompter Manhattan CATV Corporation*, 458 US 419, 433 (1982) (quoting *Kaiser Aetna v United States*, 444 US 164, 176 [1979]); see also *Cape Cod Nursing Home Council v Rambling Rose Rest Home*, 667 F2d 238 (1st Cir 1981) (organizations seeking access to rest home to inform residents of services they provided could be excluded); *Asociacion Trabajadores Agricolas de Puerto Rico v Green Giant Company*, 518 F2d 130 (3d Cir 1975), (company-owned camp for migrant workers could exclude union officials); cf. *Kaiser Aetna v United States*, 444 US 164 (1979) (requiring public access to a private marina was a taking).

30. See, for example, *Laguna Publishing Company v Golden Rain Foundation*, 131 CAL App3d 816, 845, 182 Calif Rptr 813 839 (1982) (noting that the only means for competitors of a community newspaper to distribute samples was through the mail); *Guttenberg Taxpayers and Rentpayers Association v Galaxy Towers Condominium Association*, 297 NJSuper 404, 410–11, 688 A2d 156, 159 (NJSupCtChDiv) aff'd 297 NJSuper 309, 688 A2d 108 (NJ-

SupCtAppDiv 1996) (noting that the plaintiffs, who were seeking to distribute political materials to condominium residents, had only the inadequate alternative of distributing their materials through the mail).

31. The reader may wonder whether this kind of cyberspace relationship is more than "phone sex." Yes. The intensity of this form of exchange is wildly beyond the panting of a telephone lover; see Julian Dibbell,"Keys to the Kingdom: Cryptography, the Black Art of Spies and Diplomats, Moves Center Stage on the Net," *Time,* November 11, 1996, TD38ff. "But it is also incontrovertible proof that some kinds of arithmetic can reach meaningfully into our lives at every point on the spectrum of human experience—in our political contests, in our economic dealings and, as anyone who has used the office computer to E-mail a lover can attest, in the most intimate recesses of our emotional affairs."

32. Timothy S. Wu has a more careful and balanced picture of the conditions under which sovereignty might exist; see "Cyberspace Sovereignty?: The Internet," *Harvard Journal of Law and Technology* 10 (1997): 647.

33. David R. Johnson and David G. Post both favor, not no government, but decentralized emergent norms that resist top-down control; see, for example, "And How Shall the Net Be Governed?: A Meditation on the Relative Virtues of Decentralized, Emergent Law," in *Coordinating the Internet,* edited by Brian Kahin and James H. Keller (Cambridge, Mass.: MIT Press, 1997), 62. I have not addressed the means for governing in cyberspace, except to the extent that the means are implied by an architecture of open code. My primary focus is on the set of values.

34. See Judith N. Shklar, *American Citizenship: The Quest for Inclusion* (Cambridge, Mass.: Harvard University Press, 1991), 25–62; James A. Gardner, "Liberty, Community, and the Constitutional Structure of Political Influence: A Reconsideration of the Right to Vote," *University of Pennsylvania Law Review* 145 (1997): 893; *Quiet Revolution in the South,* edited by Chandler Davidson and Bernard Grofman (Princeton, N.J.: Princeton University Press, 1994): 21–36.

35. See Lani Guinier, *The Tyranny of the Majority: Fundamental Fairness in Representative Democracy* (New York: Free Press, 1994); Richard Thompson Ford, "Beyond Borders: A Partial Response to Richard Briffault," *Stanford Law Review* 48 (1996): 1173; Richard Thompson Ford, "Geography and Sovereignty: Jurisdictional Formation and Racial Segregation," *Stanford Law Review* 49 (1997): 1365; Jerry Frug, "Decentering Decentralization," *University of Chicago Law Review* 60 (1993): 253; Jerry Frug, "The Geography of Community," *Stanford Law Review* 48 (1996): 1047.

36. See Michael Walzer, *Spheres of Justice: A Defense of Pluralism and Equality* (New York: Basic Books, 1983).

37. See Charles M. Tiebout, "A Pure Theory of Local Expenditures," *Journal of Political Economy* 64 (1956): 416; see also Clayton P. Gillette, *Local Government Law: Cases and Materials* (Boston: Little, Brown, 1994), 382; Vicki Been, "'Exit' as a Constraint on Land Use Exactions: Rethinking the Unconstitutional Conditions Doctrine," *Columbia Law Review* 91 (1991): 473, 514–28.

38. See David G. Post, "Governing Cyberspace," *Wayne Law Review* 43 (1996): 155; David Post, "The New Electronic Federalism," *American Lawyer* (October 1996): 93; David G. Post, "The 'Unsettled Paradox': The Internet, the State, and the Consent of the Governed," *Indiana Journal of Global Legal Studies* 5 (1998): 521, 539; David R. Johnson and Kevin A. Marks, "Mapping Electronic Data Communications onto Existing Legal Metaphors: Should We Let Our Conscience (and Our Contracts) Be Our Guide?," *Villanova Law Review* 38 (1993): 487; Johnson and Post, "Law and Borders"; David G. Post, "Anarchy, State, and the Internet: An Essay on Law-Making in Cyberspace," *Journal of Online Law* (1995): article 3, available at http://www.law.cornell.edu/jol/post.html (visited May 30, 1999).

39. See Phillip E. Areeda et al., *Antitrust Law,* vol. 2A (Boston: Little, Brown, 1995), 85–87.

40. See Post, "Anarchy, State, and the Internet," 29–30.

41. This was not quite true of MUDing in the past. When the communities were smaller, there were portals that allowed characters to move from one MUD to another. Famous MUD characters became well known in many different communities, and it was unethical to take the name of a well-known MUDer, even from a different MUD. But as the world of MUDing has grown, the ability to port yourself elsewhere is less meaningful. The communities here are simply associations, and the associations do not transfer.

42. I am not saying that this situation could not be different. We might imagine regions of communities in cyberspace that facilitate moving between communities. I am speaking only about the space as it is now.

43. See Post, "Anarchy, State, and the Internet," 82–83, 100.

44. Ibid., 100.

45. See, for example, George A. Bermann, "Taking Subsidiarity Seriously: Federalism in the European Community and the United States," *Columbia Law Review* 94 (1994): 331; Albert Breton et al., "Decentralization and Subsidiarity: Toward a Theoretical Reconciliation," *University of Pennsylvania Journal of International Economic Law* 19 (1998): 21; Clayton P. Gillette, "The Exercise of Trumps by Decentralized Governments," *Virginia Law Review* 83 (1997): 1347.

46. See, for example, George A. Bermann, "Subsidiarity and the European Community," *Hastings International and Comparative Law Review* 17 (1993): 97, 103, 105; Bermann, "Taking Subsidiarity Seriously," 452–53.

47. Or at least three of the four regions in the early United States shared this history; see Fischer, *Albion's Seed,* 827–28.

48. Article V of the Constitution states (obscurely no doubt) that "provided that no Amendment which may be made prior to the Year One thousand eight hundred and eight shall in any Manner affect the first and fourth Clauses in the Ninth Section of the first Article." These clauses state: "(1) The Migration or Importation of such Persons as any of the States now existing shall think proper to admit, shall not be prohibited by the Congress prior to the Year one thousand eight hundred and eight, but a Tax or duty may be imposed on such Importation, not exceeding ten Dollars for each Person"; and "(4) No Capitation, or other direct, Tax shall be laid, unless in Proportion to the Census or Enumeration herein before directed to be taken."

49. See John F. Kennedy, *Profiles in Courage* (New York: Harper, 1956), ch. 3.

50. For example, in its development of PICS, the World Wide Web consortium made a commitment to both value and vendor neutrality; see "Platform for Internet Content Selection (PICS)," available at http://www.w3.org/PICS (last modified June 4, 1998).

51. See World Intellectual Property Organization, "Final Report of the WIPO Internet Domain Name Process," April 30, 1999, forthcoming in hardcover as WIPO Publication No. 92–805–0779–6, available at http://wipo2.wipo.int/process/eng/final_report.html (visited May 30, 1999).

52. Quoted in Brin, *The Transparent Society,* 218. For an excellent account of the more general question, see A. Michael Froomkin, "The Internet as a Source of Regulatory Arbitrage," in *Borders in Cyberspace: Information Policy and the Global Information Infrastructure,* edited by Brian Kahin and Charles Nesson (Cambridge, Mass.: MIT Press, 1997), 129. Froomkin considers both the technological features of the Net that enable arbitrage and the limits on arbitrage that we might expect.

53. Ethan Katsh makes a similar point in "Software Worlds and the First Amendment," where he argues that legislators will come to understand the plasticity and regulation in code. Tim Wu makes the same point in "Cyberspace and the International System." For a thoughtful account of how a federalist structure in cyberspace might look, see Dan L. Burk, "Federalism in Cyberspace," *Connecticut Law Review* 28 (1996): 1095. Burk's analysis, made from the perspective of American federalism, is a template for the same questions raised internationally.

54. Some conceive of constitutional values, for example, as constraints on efficiency; see Brin, *The Transparent Society*, 223, quoting Godwin: "Governments have to sacrifice some efficiency to preserve those rights."

CHAPTER FIFTEEN

1. *Missouri v Holland*, 252 US 416, 433 (1920).

2. See, for example, Jack N. Rakove, *Original Meanings: Politics and Ideas in the Making of the Constitution* (New York: Alfred A. Knopf, 1996), 289–90; see also Akhil Reed Amar, "The Bill of Rights as a Constitution" (*Yale Law Journal* 100 [1991]: 1131), for another such understanding of the Bill of Rights.

3. This is not to deny that some aspects of the equality delineated in the Civil War amendments echoed in our constitutional past. The abolitionists, of course, made great weight of the Declaration of Independence's claims to equality; see, for example, Trisha Olson, "The Natural Law Foundation of the Privileges or Immunities Clause of the Fourteenth Amendment," *Arkansas Law Review* 48 (1995): 347, 364. An amendment can be transformative, however, even if it is simply recalling a part of the past and reestablishing it—as Germany did, for example, after World War II.

4. See *Plessy v Ferguson*, 163 US 537 (1896).

5. See A. Leon Higginbotham Jr., "Racism in American and South African Courts: Similarities and Differences," *New York University Law Review* 65 (1990): 479, 495–96.

6. These laws permitted compelled labor to pay a debt; see *Bailey v Alabama*, 219 US 219 (1911) (striking peonage laws under the Thirteenth Amendment).

7. *Brown v Board of Education*, 347 US 483 (1954).

8. See, for example, *Dennis v United States*, 341 US 494 (1951) (upholding convictions under the Smith Act, which banned certain activities of the Communist Party).

9. See *Korematsu v United States*, 323 US 214 (1944).

10. See, for example, John Hart Ely, *Democracy and Distrust: A Theory of Judicial Review* (Cambridge, Mass.: Harvard University Press, 1980).

11. I've overstated the security of the American judiciary. A recent incident with District Court Judge Harold Baer suggests continued insecurity, especially in the context of the war on drugs. Baer released a criminal defendant after suppressing a search that had discovered eighty pounds of narcotics; Don Van Natta Jr., "Judge's Drug Ruling Likely to Stand," *New York Times*, January 28, 1996, 27. The decision was then attacked by presidential candidate Robert Dole, who called for Baer's impeachment; Katharine Q. Seelye, "A Get Tough Message at California's Death Row," *New York Times*, March 24, 1996, 29. President Clinton then joined the bandwagon, suggesting that he might ask for Baer's resignation if Baer did not reverse his decision; Alison Mitchell, "Clinton Pressing Judge to Relent," *New York Times*, March 22, 1996, 1. Baer then did reverse his decision; Don Van Natta Jr., "Under Pressure, Federal Judge Reverses Decision in Drug Case," *New York Times*, April 2, 1996, 1. Chief Judge Jon Newman, of the Second Circuit Court of Appeals, along with other judges, then criticized Dole's criticism of Baer, arguing that he went "too far"; Don Van Natta Jr., "Judges Defend a Colleague from Attacks," *New York Times*, March 29, 1996, B1. Soviet citizens would recognize the pattern.

12. I describe the Court's conception of its role in more detail in Lessig, "Translating Federalism."

13. Robert H. Bork, *The Antitrust Paradox: A Policy at War with Itself* (New York: Basic Books, 1978), 83.

14. See, for example, Felix Frankfurter, *The Commerce Clause Under Marshall, Taney, and Waite* (Chapel Hill: University of North Carolina Press, 1937): 82.

15. The relationship between a contested ground and a political judgment is more complex than this suggests. I discuss it more extensively in Lawrence Lessig, "Fidelity and Constraint," *Fordham Law Review* 65 (1997): 1365.

16. *ACLU v Reno,* 929 FSupp 824 (EDPa 1996); *Shea v Reno,* 930 FSupp 916 (SDNY 1996).

17. I discuss this in Lessig, "Fidelity and Constraint."

18. One could well argue that during the crisis of the Depression deference by the Court to the Congress would have been well advised; see, for example, Sunstein, *Democracy and the Problem of Free Speech,* 39.

19. Fischer (*Albion's Seed*) shows how town planning in the United States followed habits in Europe.

20. David P. Currie, *The Constitution of the Federal Republic of Germany* (Chicago: University of Chicago Press, 1994), 182–87.

21. This is the system that associates a name on the Internet (for example, "cyber.law.harvard.edu") with an Internet protocol address (for example, 128.12.12.01). People register domain names, now primarily through a company called Network Solutions. Their name, if it is available, is then associated with a particular server.

22. *Payne v Tennessee,* 501 US 808, 844 (1991) (Justice Thurgood Marshall dissenting).

23. In 1999 it was revealed that with some versions of Microsoft Word a unique identifier was embedded in Word documents. Microsoft subsequently provided an upgrade to remove the identifier data.

CHAPTER SIXTEEN

1. Deborah Hellman, in "The Importance of Appearing Principled" (*Arizona Law Review* 37 [1995]: 1107), describes the illegitimacy costs that courts incur when they overrule precedents for apparently political reasons.

2. Guido Calabresi, *A Common Law for the Age of Statutes* (Cambridge, Mass.: Harvard University Press, 1982), 16–32; Guido Calabresi, "The Supreme Court, 1990 Term—Foreword: Antidiscrimination and Constitutional Accountability (What the Bork-Brennan Debate Ignores)," *Harvard Law Review* 105 (1991): 80, 83, 103–7, 119–20.

3. Or come close to doing so; see Richard A. Posner, *The Problems of Jurisprudence* (Cambridge, Mass.: Harvard University Press, 1990), 300–301.

4. I am grateful to Viktor Mayer-Schönberger for demonstrating this point to me. Hal Abelson points out that the components would have to be verifiable if they were not themselves open. Otherwise, components could function as Trojan Horses—pretending to be one thing while in reality being something else.

5. Mark A. Lemley and David W. O'Brien, "Encouraging Software Reuse," *Stanford Law Review* 49 (1997): 255.

6. For an extraordinary account of the damage done by copyright law to software development, see Mark Haynes, "Black Holes of Innovation in the Software Arts," *Berkeley Technology Law Journal* 14 (1999): 503.

7. Kennedy, *Profiles in Courage,* 71.

8. Negroponte, *Being Digital,* 238.

9. See *Buckley v Valeo,* 424 US 1 (1976) (striking campaign finance reform under the First Amendment).

10. See, for example, James S. Fishkin, *The Voice of the People* (New Haven, Conn.: Yale University Press, 1995).

11. Dean Henry H. Perritt Jr. provides a well-developed picture of what "self-regulation" in the Internet context might be, drawing on important ideals of democracy; see "Cyberspace Self-government: Town Hall Democracy or Rediscovered Royalism?," *Berkeley Technology Law Journal* 12 (1997): 413. As he describes it, the possibility of self-governance depends impor-

tantly on architectural features of the Net—not all of which are developing in ways that will support democracy; see also Shapiro (*The Control Revolution*, 150–57, 217–30), who discusses "push-button politics" and tools of democracy.

12. Alexis de Tocqueville, *Democracy in America*, vol. 1 (New York: Vintage, 1990), 284–85.

CHAPTER SEVENTEEN

1. In "Accountability in a Computerized Society" (*Science and Engineering Ethics* 2 [1996]: 25), Helen Nissenbaum discusses the erosion in accountability within computerized societies, including accountability about code itself.

2. Andrew L. Shapiro, "The Disappearance of Cyberspace and the Rise of Code," *Seton Hall Constitutional Law Journal* 8 (1998): 703, 721.

APPENDIX

1. Lessig, "The New Chicago School," 661.

2. See H. L. A. Hart, *The Concept of Law*, 2d ed. (New York: Oxford University Press, 1994), 6–13, 27–33.

3. For example, Illinois law states: "The third Monday in January of each year is a holiday to be observed throughout the State and to be known as the birthday of Dr. Martin Luther King, Jr. Within 10 days before the birthday of Dr. Martin Luther King, Jr., in each year the Governor shall issue a proclamation announcing the holiday and designating the official events that shall be held in honor of the memory of Dr. Martin Luther King, Jr., and his contributions to this nation"; 5 *Illinois Comprehensive Statutes Annotated* 490/65 (West 1998).

4. See Robert Cooter, "Expressive Law and Economics," *Journal of Legal Studies* 27 (1998): 585.

5. Cf. Paul N. Bracken, *The Command and Control of Nuclear Forces* (New Haven, Conn.: Yale University Press, 1983), 179–237; Christopher Chant and Ian Hogg, *The Nuclear War File* (London: Ebury Press, 1983), 68–115.

6. On the other side, the military built into the system technological brakes on the ability to launch, to ensure that no decision to launch was ever too easy; see also Daniel Ford, *The Button: The Nuclear Trigger—Does It Work?* (London: Allen & Unwin, 1985), 118–21.

7. "The phenomena of social meaning and incommensurability constrain rational choice (individual and collective). Generalizing, it is irrational to treat goods as commensurable where the use of a quantitative metric effaces some dimension of meaning essential to one's purposes or goals. It would be irrational, for example, for a person who wanted to be a good colleague within an academic community to offer another scholar cash instead of comments on her manuscript. Against the background of social norms, the comment's signification of respect cannot be reproduced by any amount of money; even to attempt the substitution conveys that the person does not value his colleague in the way appropriate to their relationship"; Dan M. Kahan, "Punishment Incommensurability," *Buffalo Criminal Law Review* 1 (1998): 691, 695.

8. Many scholars, Robert Cooter most prominently among them, argue that norms are special because they are "internalized" in a sense that other constraints are not; see Robert D. Cooter, "Decentralized Law for a Complex Economy: The Structural Approach to Adjudicating the New Law Merchant," *University of Pennsylvania Law Review* 144 (1996): 1643, 1662; Robert D. Cooter, "The Theory of Market Modernization of Law," *International Review of Law and Economics* 16 (1996): 141, 153. By internalization, Cooter is just describing the same sort of subjectivity that happens with the child and fire: the constraint moves from being an ob-

jectively ex post constraint to a subjectively ex ante constraint. The norm becomes a part of the person, such that the person feels its resistance before he acts, and hence its resistance controls his action before he acts. Once internalized, norms no longer need to be enforced to have force; their force has moved inside, as it were, and continues within this subjective perspective. In my view, we should see each constraint functioning in the same way: we subjectively come to account for the constraint through a process of internalization. Some internalization incentives may be stronger than others, of course. But that is just a difference.

9. Cf. Dan M. Kahan, "Ignorance of Law Is an Excuse—But Only for the Virtuous," *Michigan Law Review* 96 (1997): 127.

10. See, for example, Schuster et al., *Preserving the Built Heritage;* Peter Katz, *The New Urbanism: Toward an Architecture of Community* (New York: McGraw-Hill, 1994); Duany and Plater-Zyberk, *Towns and Town-Making Principles.*

11. Michael Sorkin, *Local Code: The Constitution of a City at 42°N Latitude* (New York: Princeton Architectural Press, 1993), 11, 127.

INDEX